Pit-folk and Peers
The Remarkable History of the People of Fryston

Volume I – Echoes of Fryston Hall (1809-1908)

David P. Waddington

route

First published by Route in 2020
Pontefract, UK
info@route-online.com
www.route-online.com

ISBN: 978-1901927-82-5

First Edition

David P. Waddington asserts his moral
right to be identified as the author of this book

Cover Design:
John Sellards

Typeset in Bembo by Route

Printed & bound in Great Britain by TJ Books Limited

Dedicated to 'Our Dor' and in loving memory of
Mary, Peter and Joanna Waddington

Chapter One
Back to the Future

One Road In, One Road Out

The defeat of the year-long national miners' strike of 6 March 1984 to 3 March 1985 opened the floodgates on a pit closure programme which culminated in the total disappearance of the UK's 170 remaining deep coal mines. Among the 23 pits to be closed by the end of 1985 was Fryston Colliery in West Yorkshire, whose miners worked their final production shift on 6 December, thereby terminating a 112-year tradition of coal mining in this tiny Castleford village. Other Castleford collieries, and those in nearby Pontefract, eventually shared the same fate: Glasshoughton and Wheldale closed in the 1980s; Ledston Luck and Allerton Bywater in the 1990s; Pontefract Prince of Wales in 2002; and finally, the 'super-pit' at Kellingley in 2015. Of all these pit closures, the loss of Fryston spoke most forcibly and poignantly of the possible extinction of a working-class community and a once-fabled way of life.

The isolated, outlying nature of Fryston village had imbued in its residents a unique sense of togetherness and self-sufficiency which saw it described by one newspaper reporter as 'a mining Shangri-la'.[1] Nestling between the River Aire on one side and the colliery rail track on the other, the village could only be entered or departed from via the solitary 'one road in and one road out'[2] that traversed a narrow railway bridge: 'They used to say that in winter when heavy snow fell they were completely isolated, for there is a river running right round the back and snow blocked the only entrance and exit.'[3]

Fryston's twelve terraced rows of houses accommodated a population of around 1,500 people. The colliery employed 1,300 men and a handful of canteen women. The village had its own public house, school, general-store-cum-post-office, two chapels, a church, and a civic hall, complete with games and reading rooms. There were annual flower and vegetable shows, each run by a dedicated committee, while a thriving informal economy provided everything from home-made pickled onions to bicycle repairs: 'For the people of Fryston, virtually their whole world revolved within the village boundaries, many of them rarely crossing the bridge to visit Castleford. There was really no need to leave it. It had everything. It had real life.'[4]

Within five years of the strike, only four of the village's longstanding terraces remained intact. Writing in 1990, one observer remarked:

> Today the site of the pit is a desolate brick-strewn prairie. The bus service to Castleford has been withdrawn and the village has no reason for being there anymore. To walk round Fryston is to walk round a ghost village. Carthorses graze in the fields, miners walk their whippets and neighbours gossip on their doorsteps, as they did half a century ago [...] Coal pickers sift handfuls of muck and drop slivers of coal into sacks slung over their bicycle handlebars [...] A strange silence haunts the place, with time curiously suspended. Lupins bloom among the twisted wires poking from the ground; children's voices echo from estates two miles away; chirping birds can be heard for the first time in 110 years.[5]

My father and his brother both worked at Fryston pit, though neither was born in the village. *Their* father spent all his working life at the nearby Wheldale Colliery, while my paternal grandma came up from the Staffordshire coalfield and originally settled in Normanton, on the outskirts of Castleford. My maternal grandfather, Samuel Holmes, came to Fryston from Shropshire in 1902, aged nine, and worked in the local mine until he retired, aged seventy. He married my Grandma Holmes – a Castleford-born glass bottle blower – when he returned home from World War I. My mother, her two brothers and five sisters were born in Fryston village. I, too, was born in my grandparents' house (the 'family home', number 23, Brook Street) in 1957.

Originally, I had been inspired to write a history of the village when watching Ken Loach's *cinéma vérité* television drama, *Days of*

Hope,[6] which tracked the fate of mining families from the 1910s, via World War I and up to the General Strike of 1926; but it was not until 1986, when a local newspaper portrayed Fryston as a 'ghost village' close to its demise,[7] that I was galvanised into compiling the interviews with 60 residents and former residents of Fryston, which constituted a small, locally published oral history, *One Road In, One Road Out: A People's History of Fryston*.[8]

An important road map for my own investigation was provided by Jim Bullock's memoir, *Them and Us*, which encompassed the years he went from 'pony lad' to manager of Fryston colliery.[9] During this period (approximately 1920 to 1955), the pit and/or its allied community were forever in the headlines – as and when local miners built their own social club and athletics stadium from scratch. My objective in *One Road In, One Road Out* was to expand on Bullock's extremely colourful but highly personalised account by incorporating the corresponding recollections of a much wider spectrum of people who had lived and worked there. The book was never intended as a precise, 'factual' documentation of Fryston's social history but rather as an impressionistic account of village life and as a lasting testament to the special ethos and community spirit that prevailed from its formation in the late nineteenth century to the day the mine ceased working.

Relatively under-emphasised in Bullock's and my own discussions (both of which were entirely preoccupied with the local mining community) was a former era in Fryston's history, marked by the existence of Fryston Hall and the exploits of the first Lord Houghton (the former Richard Monckton Milnes) and of his successor to that title, Robert Offley Ashburton Milnes (the eventual Marquess of Crewe). This omission most probably reflected the class affinities of Bullock and myself, and our corresponding indifference towards the local aristocracy. Even though the state secondary school I attended was located on Crewe Road, and notwithstanding the fact that other street names (e.g. Milnes Grove and Monckton Drive) were coined in deference to this heritage, few local people were conscious of (or, to be perfectly frank, remotely interested in) the history of Fryston Hall. The only exceptions were the handful of older residents and religious worshippers who were possibly aware that parts of the long-demolished mansion had been redeployed in the construction of the Holy Cross Church in nearby Airedale.

It therefore stands to reason that the vast majority of local residents, and the population as a whole, remains ignorant of the incredible scale and significance of the contribution made by Lord Houghton and other occupants of Fryston Hall to the cultural and political history of the nation.

The present volume seeks to redress this longstanding (and somewhat scandalous) lack of awareness and appreciation. It is ironic that one of the strongest existing testaments to the importance of Fryston Hall and its celebrated Victorian occupants resides within the contemporary 'fantasy-time-travel' genre, otherwise known as 'alternative history'. It is onto this unlikely but resounding back-handed endorsement of the significance and reputation of the most central character of our historical account that we therefore focus our preliminary attention.

An 'Alternative History' of Fryston

The first chapter of Mark Hodder's remarkably intriguing alternative history novel *The Expedition to the Mountains of the Moon* focuses, bizarrely, on a 'Murder at Fryston'.[10] The occasion is a fancy dress party staged on New Year's Day 1863 at the Yorkshire manor house of the Victorian poet, politician and socialite, Richard Monckton Milnes. We are told that:

> Fryston [Hall], which dated from the Elizabethan Age, lacked a ballroom but behind its stone mullioned windows there were many spacious oak panelled chambers, warmed by inglenook fireplaces, and these were filled with costumed guests. They included the Pre-Raphaelite artists, leading Technologists, authors and poets and actors, government ministers, Scotland Yard officials, and members of the Royal Geographical Society […] and among the female notables [was] the famous Eugenicist – now Geneticist – Nurse Florence Nightingale, making for a very well attended soiree, such as Monckton Milnes was famous for.[11]

The hapless victim of the piece was the well-known barrister, magazine proprietor and academic Thomas Bendyshe, who, posing ironically as the 'Grim Reaper', had gulped down a poisoned glass of brandy, which it later transpired was intended for the explorer, adventurer, ex-soldier and anthropologist Sir Richard Francis Burton. This novel is actually the third in a series of six that focus collectively on the exploits of Burton and an improbable accomplice, the eccentrically controversial poet, Algernon Charles Swinburne.[12]

In the first of these novels, *The Strange Affair of Spring Heeled Jack* (2010), Burton is sent out, as the title suggests, on a mission to investigate successive sexual assaults perpetrated by a mythical demon of that name.[13] Hodder explains in the acknowledgements of *The Strange Affair* that the 'famous names' he refers to 'are national heroes who loom large in the British consciousness'. He states, with tongue-in-cheek, how he has 'mercilessly trampled on their reputations and turned them into something they most definitely were not'.[14] Richard Monckton Milnes is introduced in the novel as an 'enigmatic and rather saturnine' member of a group of 'hell-raisers', known as the 'Cannibal Club', which met in rooms located above Bartolini's restaurant in London's Leicester Square.[15] Milnes is characterised as a 'prime example' of a Libertine – i.e. harbouring an essential commitment to 'art, beauty, and nobility of spirit'.[16] It is only in the succeeding novel, *The Curious Case of the Clockwork Man* (2011), that Hodder provides a fuller profile of his subject:

> Tall, handsome, enigmatic, and saturnine in aspect, Milnes was one of Richard Burton's best friends and staunchest supporters. Rich and influential, he'd interceded many times in the past when lesser men had tried to undermine the famous explorer. He also owned the largest collection of erotica ever gathered. It included everything ever written by the Marquis de Sade – plus thousands of banned volumes concerning witchcraft and the occult. He was, of course, a Libertine. However, he was also a man who, at an emotional level, separated himself from others, preferring to conduct all his relationships on a purely intellectual basis. Others, Burton among them, realised that he was simply one of life's onlookers, a man who studied everything but who never fully engaged with anything. This included the Libertine movement, which suited his temperament but failed to draw him in too deeply. He rarely became involved with its politics or various causes.[17]

The next novel in the sequence, *The Secret of Abdu El Yezdi* (2013), embellishes this physical description, characterising Milnes as a lanky individual 'with the brow of an intellectual, long hair, and a preference for high collars and bright cravats'.[18] We also learn that, professionally, Milnes was 'a wielder of influence in High Society; a writer; a poet; and a dabbler in politics'.[19] The reader is also reminded that Fryston contained the largest collection of erotica and occult literature of anywhere in Europe.[20]

Milnes cuts a prominent figure in this novel. He is cast in the role of the romantic suitor of Florence Nightingale, who is dramatically and mysteriously abducted while they are attending the London theatre together. Elsewhere in the novel, Burton is informed by no less an authority than Benjamin Disraeli that Milnes has been secretly playing 'a major role in history' by operating since 1840 as an intermediary between Disraeli and a sinister spirit, Abdu El Yezdi, who was engineering the downfall of Prime Minister Lord Palmerston.[21] We also learn that Milnes is the mysterious anonymous author of the notorious pornographic poem, 'The Betuliad' (otherwise known as 'The Rodiad'), which dwells on the subject of homoerotic flagellation.[22]

In the final novel of the series, *The Rise of the Automated Aristocrats* (2015), we are given an insight into Milnes's political credo, learning that it was he who coined the name 'Young England' for the radical new political movement led by Benjamin Disraeli. Milnes had since grown disillusioned with Young England, feeling it had departed from an initial commitment to a sense of *noblesse oblige* which had been predicated on the notion that 'the landed gentry has a duty to fulfil social responsibilities, that it must earn its privileges by working to improve the lot of the lower classes, rather than seeking ever more influence, as Palmerston had done'.[23] Under Disraeli's leadership, the aristocracy were becoming increasingly detached from the masses, while the common people were now 'subjects of a cold-hearted plutocracy', which was stifling popular opposition and dissent by militarising the police.[24]

The 'Real' Richard Monckton Milnes

So much for this fictionalised account of Milnes and his associates. In this section, we briefly examine academic insight – however contradictory and disputed that might be – into the nature of the man. It was my namesake, Patrick Waddington, who once described this politician, poet, critic and 'collector of erotica' as one of the 'most curious' and 'kaleidoscopic' figures of Victorian society.[25] Another commentator refers to Milnes as 'one of the most interesting figures of his generation'.[26] He was certainly one of the most conspicuous:

> It is a commonplace that you can hardly take up a volume of English nineteenth-century reminiscences without coming across his name [...] Like one of the more ubiquitous characters of [the French novelist] Balzac, Milnes glides in and out of the studies and dining-rooms of his great contemporaries. He is usually remembered to-day in certain specific roles: the man of whom Carlyle could speak no evil; the man Disraeli ridiculed and despised; the man who wanted to marry Florence Nightingale; who liberated the mind of young Swinburne and saved innumerable lesser poets from starvation; and wrote the first published biography of Keats. You could compile a yet more indiscriminate list of Milnes' activities, and it was for his variety that he was mocked by some of his own countrymen.[27]

Milnes was born in Mayfair, London, in 1809. His father, Robert Pemberton Milnes, was a 'brilliant and somewhat erratic country gentleman', Member of Parliament for Pontefract, and descendant of a wealthy family of Wakefield woollen manufacturers. His mother, Henrietta Maria Monckton, (a 'vivacious, talented, and most kindly lady') was the second daughter of the Viscount of Galway.[28] Milnes was bright (and wealthy) enough to enter Trinity College, Cambridge University, as a 'Fellow Commoner' in 1827 (a term denoting an affluent, usually aristocratic, student who had the privilege of sharing with the College Fellows the amenities of the 'high table'). At Trinity, he was elected into the elite group of Cambridge 'Apostles' alongside such literary giants as the poets Arthur Hallam and Alfred Lord Tennyson. Following extensive travel in Europe and a short period of study in Germany, he began writing poetry. In 1837, he followed family tradition by becoming MP for Pontefract.

Boucher describes Milnes as a 'poet of small reputation',[29] while nevertheless acknowledging that, 'His own prose writings, including his life of Keats (the first one ever written), exhibit a flawless diction and a smooth, graceful style, as well as a fine understanding of human relations.'[30] Milnes's political career was driven by a rare reformist appetite, but he was twice overlooked for promotion to much-coveted cabinet posts. His elevation to the peerage (as Lord Houghton) in 1863 was a distinction he himself dubbed a 'Second Class in the School of Life'.[31]

During his lifetime, Milnes earned the reputation of being the foremost socialite, raconteur and party host of the Victorian era, someone who was 'much sought in society for his witty table-talk and his seemingly inexhaustible supply of anecdotes'.[32] Everyone who was anyone appeared to know him: 'There never lived so perfect a host,' claimed Russell.[33] When in London, Milnes entertained his guests at his bachelor dwelling in Pall Mall. Back in Fryston, his parents meted out invitations on his behalf to the most eminent political and cultural figures of the era. In the 1840s, while completing his biography of Keats, he did, indeed, enter into a long courtship with Florence Nightingale. Following the termination of this relationship, Milnes became engaged to and eventually married the Hon. Annabella (Annabel) Crewe, whose brother was the owner of the Crewe Hall estate. The death of Milnes's father in 1858 resulted in Fryston Hall (which he, of course, inherited) becoming an even greater Mecca for the most outstanding personalities of Victorian society, including the aforementioned Richard Burton and Algernon Charles Swinburne.

It was typical of Milnes's indefatigable spirit of adventure, curiosity and mischief that most of these invitees 'had either done something or were somebodies, and occasionally their fame was not of the kind that commends itself to everybody'.[34] Milnes's particular forte was to bring together guests (including the greatest writers, actors, painters, politicians, royal figures and dignitaries of their day) of seemingly opposing and incompatible points of view. His motives have sometimes been interpreted as Machiavellian – nowhere more emphatically than in the 'piece of calculated corruption' by which he is alleged to have not only initiated the improbable relationship between the naïve Swinburne and the hell-raising Burton, but also exercised considerable 'Mephistophelean malice' in steering Swinburne towards the evil writings of the Marquis de Sade.[35] Also making up the 'unedifying' whole of Milnes's character were his alleged appetite for visiting flagellation brothels, having pornographic material illicitly imported from the continent, and, if the rumours are true, actually being the author of 'The Rodiad'.

By contrast, his humanitarian deeds were legendary. Walker touchingly maintains that, 'To the memory of Milnes there clings the fragrance of a thousand generous deeds. It was to him that everybody turned when in need.'[36] The financial and practical assistance freely volunteered to aspiring or struggling poets and writers was given, it has been said, 'for their sakes and not for his own aggrandisement'.[37] Ultimately, the portrait of Milnes that emerges is extremely enigmatic: 'Perhaps Carlyle put it best when he said that Richard Monckton Milnes would make the ideal president of a Heaven and Hell Amalgamation Society.'[38]

Like Father?

Monckton Milnes and his wife were the parents of two daughters, Amicia and Florence (born in 1852 and 1855, respectively), and a son, Robert (1858). These children were blessed with social advantages that even their father had not enjoyed:

> From the nursery state onwards they were accustomed to see everyone of interest amongst their parents' contemporaries: poets, politicians, men of letters, actors, painters, languid members of the fashionable world, foreign visitors of every nationality, explorers like Sir Richard Burton or clever clergymen like Frederick Maurice.[39]

While Amicia ('Amy') became immersed in the supportive role of wife and mother in an aristocratic marriage, Florence and Robert perpetuated the conspicuous family traditions in literature and politics, and maintained their father's reputation for hosting gatherings of the Victorian artistic and political elite. They share with their father the distinction of having featured in 'fictionalised' accounts of important aspects of their lives.

In the case of Robert Offley Ashburton Milnes (who succeeded his father as the 2nd Lord Houghton and eventually became Lord – and later, Marquess – of Crewe), this concerns a brief appearance in Colm Tóibín's *The Master*, a fact-based though imaginary account of the experience of the acclaimed American novelist Henry James in England and Ireland in the 1890s. The episode in question centres on James's visit to Dublin Castle at the invitation of Lord Crewe, who was occupying the position of Viceroy (or 'Lord Lieutenant') of Ireland – i.e. Queen Victoria's senior representative in relation to her Irish subjects. James had accepted the invitation to travel from London in an attempt to escape from the ignominy and disappointment arising from the poor critical reception of his most recent play.

According to Tóibín, the 'vehemence' of Crewe's invitation was a reflection of the fact that the elite social classes ('the landlords') were boycotting the social season at Dublin Castle due to their displeasure concerning the Liberal government's attitude to Home Rule. James had been a friend of the first Lord Houghton, and Tóibín draws an unfavourable comparison between the Viceroy and his father:

> While old Lord Houghton had been informal in both his manners and his personal habits, and given especially in his later years to delighting himself and amusing others, his son was stern and self-important...He strutted about the place, being the only one it seemed not to realize that while he meant well, he did not matter.[40]

In the preface to Pope-Hennessy's biography of Lord Crewe, the latter's widow concedes that, whilst her husband was prone to a hesitancy of expression, and carried a formal demeanour that made him seem somewhat arrogant and over-reserved, this was more than compensated for by an abundance of moral courage, soundness of judgement, inherent trustworthiness, charming manners and a steady diplomatic air which saw him rise to political prominence, initially as private secretary, then Viceroy of Ireland, Colonial Secretary and Liberal Leader of the House of Lords.[41] Crewe's public profile was undoubtedly magnified by his second marriage to Peggy Primrose (daughter of the former Liberal Prime Minister Lord Rosebery and Hannah Primrose, a member of the supremely affluent Rothschild dynasty) in 1899. Without reaching his father's stature, he was also a published poet, and (like his father) a host of distinction. It is as a politician, though, that he is principally remembered.

Similar artistic liberty is exercised by Jacobson in his 'fictitious' reporting of the case of unrequited passion felt by the famous British novelist Thomas Hardy towards the second of Monckton Milnes's two daughters, Florence Henniker.[42] Drawing a comparison between the events surrounding an unsatisfactory romantic encounter in a railway carriage (a 'queer elopement') involving Jude, the eponymous main character of Hardy's *Jude the Obscure*, and his female counterpart, Sue Bridehead, Jacobson recalls in an imaginative and rather flippant manner the occasion – 'an abortive train trip of the heart' – on which Hardy was rejected in his attempt to woo his co-passenger, Ms Henniker (a married woman and early-career novelist in her own right), during a two-day outing to Winchester.

Employing lavish speculation, Jacobson asserts that the disappointment and resentment resulting from Hardy's rejection by this 'apparently emancipated and promising society woman' was subsequently reflected in his literary creation of the corresponding encounter in *Jude the Obscure*, which Hardy was writing at the time. More specifically, Hardy's determination to have Jude 'made to look an oaf is a reproach to Mrs Henniker, a prick, if ever there was one, to her Christian conscience, just as the sepulchral humour of the scene is a go at putting a brave face on mortification'.[43]

Even as a child, Florence displayed a precocious talent for literature that resulted in the publication of six novels, three collections of short stories and a play.[44] Being naturally high-spirited and vivacious, she followed in her father's footsteps by becoming a hostess of distinction. Her marriage in 1882 to the professional soldier Arthur Henry Henniker-Major did not prevent her from acting as hostess on her brother's behalf. She was accordingly on hand for the receptions given, firstly, to Henry James (as described above) and thereafter to Thomas Hardy. Henniker's place in literary history has since been enshrined due to the unrequited love Hardy allegedly felt for her (as described in Jacobson's passage), for their collaboration on a short story, and for the fact that she allegedly became his muse for the central female character in *Jude* and some of his other works, as we shall see.

These brief portraits of Lord Houghton and his two children allude to, but scarcely begin to convey, the true scale and significance of their contributions to British history. The lack of class affinity that made Jim Bullock and myself relatively indifferent to the nature and achievements of the local aristocracy helps to explain our ignorance of the great reformist, humanitarian and philanthropic interventions they consistently carried out, and which current generations would undoubtedly consider admirable. Such interventions not only helped shape the nature and outcome of the major events of the nineteenth century, but determined the direction of significant political and cultural developments. One principal objective of this, the first of two volumes, is, therefore, to ensure that this legacy is adequately documented and duly recognised. The second volume will take up the story thereafter, placing particular emphasis on the development of Fryston village and the corresponding contribution of the local proletariat (the 'pit-folk' of the title). This 200-year, two-part history is the result of a rigorous, evidence-based approach, the methods, objectives and scope of which are now described in detail.

Bailey's 'Black Diamonds'

An important prototype for the present study is *Black Diamonds: The Rise and Fall of an English Dynasty,* a book written by the award-winning documentary film-maker, Catherine Bailey.[45] *Black Diamonds* tells the story of the monumental Wentworth House, lying nine miles north-east of Sheffield. This mansion was the architectural jewel in the crown of the 20,000-acre estates belonging to the Fitzwilliam family. It also straddled the most prosperous seam in the entire South Yorkshire coalfield. Said to be the largest privately-owned house in England, 'Wentworth' could boast one room for every day of the year, and its East Front alone was twice the width of Buckingham Palace. One esteemed guest was reputedly so afraid of getting lost within its five miles of corridors that he took to crumbling wafers along the journey from his bedroom to the dining rooms, as in a game of 'fox and hounds'. Subsequently, guests were presented with caskets of coloured confetti precisely for this purpose.

The book contains an important industrial subplot, tracing the instigation and development of a small number of bitter, protracted strikes (most notably the two-year Cadeby-Denaby 'Bag Muck' strike of 1902-1904 and the General Strike of 1926), and the visit of King George V and Queen Mary in July 1912, which coincided with a massive and disastrous underground explosion at Cadeby Colliery. Bailey's background research was hampered by the fact that some sixteen tons of family archives had been destroyed in 1972 by order of the tenth (and final) Earl Fitzwilliam. She manages to enhance the authenticity of the account by drawing on relevant newspaper articles and the testimonies of eyewitnesses or the descendants of those involved. Bailey also employs a degree of 'artistic license' to enliven her description of events, as in her account of the arrival by train of strike-breakers brought in to replace the Cadeby/Denaby miners.[46]

Black Diamonds constitutes a fascinating account of this particular epoch in the history of Wentworth and the Fitzwilliam family. It is my ambition to present in this study an even more comprehensive history of Fryston Hall and the people who worked in the local mine over two volumes. This history will commence with the birth of the first Lord Houghton (Richard Monckton Milnes) in 1809 and culminate in the present day. In so doing, the study will demonstrate that Fryston Hall and its occupants wielded an influence on British cultural and political life far in excess of that exerted by the Fitzwilliams or, indeed, any other known Victorian dynasty. What distinguishes this work from Bailey's remarkable volume is its emphasis on verifiable evidence in the form of biographical accounts, literary artefacts, newspaper archives, census and other statistical data.

The 'Sum of Biographies'

A second important source of inspiration for the present study is Bill Williamson's sociological analysis of the Northumbrian mining village of Throckley.[47] Williamson set out to compile an historical and biographical account of his grandfather's life as a miner, with the intention of demonstrating in the process 'that biography is a form of writing and analysis appropriate to the study of social change and representing a way of reconciling the work of historians and sociologists'.[48] Williamson draws on personal reminiscence and the experience of other family members to 'reconstruct', in as rich a manner as possible, 'some of the major, complex moments of social change' occurring in British society from the 1870s to the mid-

1950s – a period encompassing two World Wars, major industrial confrontations of the 1920s, and the Great Depression of the 1930s.[49]

Williamson triangulates information arising from conversations he held with family members with more conventional documentary sources in an attempt to 'personalise social change' by reproducing the experience of it from the perspective of one individual and his family.[50] He bemoans the developing preoccupation in social science with 'large numbers' and argues that the generalisations emerging from empirical research has negated the potentially more interpretive understanding made possible by focusing empathically on the experience of the individual. He points to the activities of such founding fathers of interpretive sociology as the German philosopher Wilhelm Dilthey, who used the biographies of influential men as the cornerstones of historical research. The intelligent reflections of such 'thinking individuals' are what make historical insight and empathy available to those of us from subsequent generations.[51]

This would doubtless have resonated with the view of the first Lord Houghton, who famously proclaimed that 'History is the summary of biographies'.[52] It is a testament to Houghton's own pre-eminence that he is the subject of a pair of two-volume biographies, one written by a close friend and confidant, Thomas Wemyss Reid,[53] the second commissioned over sixty years after he died by his son, the Marquess of Crewe, written by James Pope-Hennessy.[54] Each biographer had unlimited access to Houghton's letters and other personal documents. Just as Reid's narrative may possibly have been affected by his close personal ties to Lord Houghton, there is a danger that Pope-Hennessy's indebtedness to the Marquess may also have had some bearing on the way his subject was characterised.

Thankfully Milnes's ubiquity within nineteenth-century cultural and political society has guaranteed that he is mentioned extensively in the corresponding biographies of most elite individuals of his own era. The task of the present study has been to decode and evaluate all of these impressionistic accounts of Houghton's character (including those of Wemyss Reid and Pope-Hennessy) in terms of the objectives and agendas being pursued by the biographers of the individuals concerned. The aim here is to consider the merits of sometimes discrepant or contradictory accounts and mediate between them wherever necessary.

This approach to compiling a local history applies, albeit on smaller scale, to the descendants of Lord Houghton, especially his son, Robert, and daughter, Florence, each of whom had been subject to particular biographical scrutiny.[55] These and other biographical and autobiographical accounts (e.g. of Jim Bullock[56] and relevant trade unionists, such as Herbert Smith[57]) will be used as staple sources of inquiry for the two volumes constituting the history of Fryston.

As in Williamson's analysis, there will be a complementary emphasis on the life histories of 'ordinary' individuals. These will include the 60 interviews with Fryston residents conducted in 1986–87.[58] Like Williamson, I shall also draw on my personal recollections as an 'insider' of Fryston village, and son, grandson, and nephew of former residents, and on such relevant family artefacts as my grandfather's letters from World War I. This will be supplemented by other documentary material, ranging from commemorative programmes and brochures (e.g. for the openings of Fryston sports centre and pit-head baths) to television documentaries (e.g. *Jim Bullock, Miner Extraordinary*[59] and *The Boy From Bowers Row*[60]). Last but not least, is data resulting from an extensive trawl of the *Pontefract and Castleford Express* microfiche archive from 1873 to the present and articles from other regional and national newspaper archives (notably *Leeds Mercury*, *Sheffield Telegraph*, *Wakefield Express*, *The Times*, and *Yorkshire Evening Post*).

Objectives and Scope

The principal objective of this study is not simply to provide updated and more comprehensive biographies of Lord Houghton and his descendants. Rather, it is intended to show how the great changes of the past two centuries impacted on the personal lives of the lay and land-owning people of Fryston, and to reveal how such people helped shape in turn – often in remarkable ways – the major cultural, industrial and political developments occurring locally, nationally, and on the wider world stage. As such, it is consciously intended as a piece of *cultural reclamation, rejuvenation and celebration* – what some students of mining communities have referred to as 'emotional regeneration'[61] – re-focusing on the unique heritage of a village whose identity and *raison d'être* have otherwise been erased. This history is presented sequentially in two volumes, each bearing the main title of *Pit-folk and Peers*.

The first of these volumes, subtitled *Echoes of Fryston Hall (1809-1908)*, retells the story from the birth of the first Lord Houghton to the sale of Fryston Hall in the wake of the cataclysmic two-year miners' strike of 1902-4. Chapters 2-4 describe the formative effects on the character of Milnes of his family background, relationship with his parents, experience of life at Cambridge University, and his extensive stays in Europe. The subsequent fifteen chapters are chiefly concerned with the many and varied ways in which Milnes contributed so significantly and conspicuously (in the roles of politician, literary figure, patron of the arts, philanthropist and bon viveur) to major developments occurring in nineteenth-century British cultural, social and political life.

The remaining chapters of Volume One dwell principally on the corresponding achievements of his children, Robert and Florence. In Robert's case, the discussion focuses on the preliminary stages in the formation of a political legacy primarily to be achieved in the course of the twentieth century. Such a legacy is therefore dealt with more comprehensively in the second volume. Chapters 23-24 and 28 explore, not only the direct contributions made by Florence Henniker to English literature and animal welfare, but also the impact (emotional, artistic and humanitarian) of her relationship with Thomas Hardy. Integral to this narrative are the exploits of Henniker's husband, Arthur, a central figure in the British Anglo-Boer campaign (1899-1902), whose military role is subject to close analysis in the brief digression constituting Chapter 27.

The 'cataclysmic' strike referred to in the penultimate chapter (Chapter 29) of Volume One occurred in the immediate wake of the South African war. Three of the preceding chapters in the volume (17, 21 and 26) outline the evolution of industrial relations leading up to the stoppage, and establish biographical profiles of trade unionists who were either prominent in the strike per se, or central to forthcoming episodes in Fryston's history. Crucially, we shall see from Chapter 29 how the 1902-04 dispute greatly affected the demography and culture of Fryston village.

The days of Fryston Hall were now numbered. For almost three decades afterwards, it lay derelict and disused. A new community had been forming in its shadow, whose social evolution and own distinctive, far-reaching contribution to British history will be highlighted in our second volume, *Diamonds and Rust (1909-2023).* A bridging point between the volumes is provided by Chapter 30 of this book, which previews the crucial twentieth- and twenty-first century developments in the lives of the local pit-folk and landed gentry, which comprise the second phase of Fryston's remarkable and, arguably, unrivalled heritage.

Chapter Two
Antecedents

The Milnes Dynasty of Wakefield

It has been claimed that Richard Monckton Milnes (Milnes) was born at one of the most auspicious junctures of the nineteenth century:

> For the birth of great men 1809 is the *annus mirabilis* of English history. Alfred Tennyson and William Ewart Gladstone and Charles Darwin all first saw the light then. If we look across the Atlantic we have to add Abraham Lincoln, the saviour of the Union, and, among men of letters, O. W. Holmes and E. A. Poe. In England, to the names of the giants we have to add those of A. W. Kinglake, R. Monckton Milnes and Edward FitzGerald.[62]

Milnes's only son, the eventual Marquess of Crewe, observed that his father's first name represented a continuation of the family tradition of calling the eldest son Richard or Robert. His middle name was the surname of his mother, who was the daughter of the fourth Viscount Galway.[63]

The ancestral origins of the Milnes family trace back to the Derbyshire landed gentry. It was only when two of the five sons of the Chesterfield-based Richard Milnes (i.e. Richard junior and his younger brother John) resettled in Wakefield around 1670 that the family became established as one of the West Riding's most prominent and affluent cloth merchants.[64] By the mid-1700s, the family had accumulated a fantastic wealth, partly by virtue of exporting cloth to Russia, but also in consequence of the marriage of the younger Richard Milnes to Bridget Pemberton (daughter of the immensely rich John Pemberton of Liverpool), which further consolidated its fortune.

The family's unrivalled wealth and social standing was reflected in the size and grandeur of their impressive mansions, which dominated the Westgate district of Wakefield's city centre. These magnificent townhouses were designed by John Carr, the country's foremost architect, who also acted as consultant to the celebrated Fitzwilliam family of Wentworth Woodhouse. In keeping with the family's commercial activity, the three buildings in question were made up (in 1751-1752) of bricks manufactured in their own kilns and timber imported from Russia.[65]

Easily the most impressive of the three was the property belonging to John Milnes:

> His house in Westgate, the largest and most luxurious in Wakefield, contained a suite of ballrooms and concert rooms. Tate Wilkinson described it as 'one of the most elegantly furnished houses of any private gentleman in the kingdom'. Milnes brought over Italian artists to paint the ceiling. A fine collection of books lined the shelves of his library and a fine collection of paintings was displayed on the walls. The grounds at the rear of the house were wholly ornamental. A garden with an arbour and an Italian summer-house stretched down to the Ings, the meadowland of the River Calder. A sunken fence at its foot hid a public footpath, and from the summer-house Milnes enjoyed 'an unbroken view of pleasant fields up to Lawe Hill'.[66]

This property sat alongside a smaller mansion, belonging to John Milnes's cousin James, and across the road from a third mansion belonging to Pemberton Milnes and his nephew, Richard Slater Milnes.[67]

By 1770, the family business was being run by three brothers, Pemberton, Robert and James (the sons of Richard and Bridget Milnes). The family's vast wealth enabled them to 'open up social and political horizons far beyond the narrow confines of a market town'.[68] They were now content both to slacken their virtual monopoly of the Wakefield woollen trade and acquire properties well outside of the city boundaries:

> Partly the relaxation was a question of family circumstances, largely it was a matter of choice [...] Pemberton Milnes's only daughter married the second son of Archbishop Drummond of York in 1775. Four years later he spent a further £30,000 on an

estate at Bawtry, near Doncaster, where he devoted more time to the politics of the Yorkshire Association, horse racing and drinking port which he bottled himself and reputedly drank more of 'than any other gentleman in Yorkshire'.[69]

This Milnes dynasty had cultivated correspondingly lavish lifestyles. Within his Westgate mansion, John Milnes accumulated an unrivalled collection of landscape paintings, including those of the celebrated Joseph Wright of Derby, and by 1780 was waited on by six male servants.[70]

By the end of the 1770s, the Milnes family formed part of a self-selecting oligarchy of trustees – alongside other affluent woollen merchants like the Naylors and a host of small-scale manufacturers and other figures of authority, such as schoolmasters – who not only financed the running of the Westgate chapel and its minister, but also shaped and maintained a prevailing culture of *rational dissent.* The internal 'opulence' and 'elegance' of such chapels symbolised a rejection of 'the strictness of earlier puritan generations' and was 'counterposed to the gloomy religiosity of evangelicalism and calvinism'.[71] This rational dissent was predicated on insights related to secular authority – ranging from lived experience to scientific progress, and classical literature and philosophy – rather than the traditional external authority of the Bible.[72] Supplanting an accent on 'material austerity', there emerged a 'moral ethos of laxity':

> Accounts of the secular world as a vale of tears – a wretched place of exile to be endured only in the expectation of a better life after death – could hardly reflect the real experience of the prosperous merchant, lawyer or shopkeeper. Rational dissent legitimized not just the accumulation of capital but also the enjoyment of its fruits: good food and wine, the theatre and the assembly room, good pictures and books, the ball and the race meeting.[73]

Seed observes that this Yorkshire brand of rational dissent was 'neither politically chaste nor impotent'.[74] The mercantile elite of the Westgate chapel were closely aligned to the Whigs, with a prominent influence being exercised by Richard Milnes, who was a close advisor to the first Marquess of Rockingham. Such influence was underscored by the subsequent relationship between their two sons, the second Marquess and Pemberton Milnes, who was prominent in the political affairs of the West Riding. In return for keeping the Marquess (and his successor, the Earl of Fitzwilliam) well informed of political feeling in the Wakefield area, and for mobilising political support on their behalf, Pemberton Milnes was granted insights into national political machinations and could lobby for policy developments consistent with his own commercial interests.[75]

Being 'particularly attentive to the pleas of Pemberton Milnes', Earl Fitzwilliam was apt to make political interventions that 'often reflected Milnes's point of view which was not necessarily that of the entire trade'.[76] A prime example of this occurred in 1787-88, when the woollen manufacturers of the West Riding generally fell into line with the leaders of the Wiltshire and Somerset woollen industry in supporting legislation designed to tighten existing prohibition on the export of raw wool. Pemberton Milnes strongly suspected that the West Country manufacturers were striving to block the coastal shipment of raw wool in order to undermine the prosperity of their Yorkshire rivals.

> Thus he urged Fitzwilliam and his friends to maintain a watch on the parliamentary machinations of the conniving west country men and to ensure that all those friendly to the needs of Yorkshire attended the House of Commons to oppose the bill. A meeting of merchants and manufacturers, held at Bradford in January, 1787, reiterated this plea, and through Fitzwilliam's intervention the Whig party committed its forces against the measure which failed to pass that session. Undaunted, the west country presented a new bill in the following session. Milnes again demanded resistance; in spite of modifications introduced to mollify the West Riding, in spite of Yorkshire's general support, Fitzwilliam therefore pressed for another postponement. Three years later the Earl again served as Milnes's spokesman, this time to oppose the Government's Russian policy and to repudiate its claims that the value of the woollen trade between the two countries was small.[77]

It was Pemberton Milnes's only child, Mary Bridget (more commonly known as 'Bridget'), who inherited the family's Bawtry estate. She was already married to Viscount Galway, an alliance that brought together the Milnes and Monckton dynasties. The family fortune was further expanded when Pemberton Milnes's nephew, Richard Slater Milnes, married Rachel Busk, the daughter and co-heiress of Mr Hans Busk, a wealthy woollen manufacturer in Leeds.[78] On marrying Rachel, Slater Milnes received a 'handsome dowry' of £100,000 and acquired the Great Houghton estate, near Barnsley.[79] At the tender age of 25, Slater Milnes was elected (in 1784) as the Member of Parliament for York. Two years later, he purchased the 1,373-acre Fryston estate, thus establishing the family's first connection with the Hall and its surrounding lands. He remained there until his death in 1804, which occurred only two years after he retired from politics.[80]

The Fryston Hall Estate

Padgett records that the manor of Fryston was owned in the Middle Ages by the De Rotherfields, and in the Stuart era by the Hollings family.[81] Of greater relevance for us is the fact that, in 1726, Fryston Hall was purchased by George Crowle (1696-1754), a member of a prominent Hull family of merchants, councillors, benefactors and ship owners. Crowle was Member of Parliament for Hull from 1724-1747. In 1752, he became Consul in Lisbon. The 800-acre estate was then passed on to William Crowle (who held the important post of Clerk of the Peace for the West Riding from 1765-1772); and following William's death (in 1772) to his brother 'Captain' Roger Crowle.

According to an unpublished document contained in Castleford Lending Library, it was Captain Crowle who first endeavoured to develop the coal seams underlying the magnesium limestone strata on the Fryston estate.[82] Crowle went so far as to install a steam-pumping engine for that purpose in 1774. A wooden rail-track was laid down with the intention of transporting the newly-won coal to the riverside. Coal was briefly produced, but the associated costs proved financially crippling for Crowle, who was forced to put the estate and its mineral wealth up for sale. Having failed to attract a buyer, the captain continued to live at Fryston Hall until his death in 1784. The estate then passed into the hands of a relative, John Charles Crowle – a friend of Horace Walpole, who visited Fryston Hall in

1755, while staying at Kippax with John Bland, 'the fashionable gambler who shot himself'.[83]

Fryston Hall was advantageously located on the banks of the 'silvery' River Aire, of which, according to Wemyss Reid, 'poets once sang, and which the angler loved to wander'.[84] The significance of this river was underlined by Forrest:

> The River Aire [...] is the most important stream of West Yorkshire, whether we regard the population located on its banks, or the great benefit it confers on commerce and industry. Starting at once with a full current from Malham Cove, it wanders for awhile a pure and bright stream among the hills and valleys of Craven, as if loath to leave them, until it falls into the deep valley which bears its name where its purity and brightness are lost, and its banks covered with towns and manufactories. Passing the large and important town of Leeds, it continues its course to Castleford where it receives the Calder from Halifax and Wakefield, and the united streams continue their course downward to the Humber and North Sea.[85]

The Hall had the additional advantage of close proximity to Ferrybridge, which, before the advent of railway travel, was a major coaching station, replete with stables, a large staff of coachmen, guards, postillions, post-boys, grooms and porters, and several popular inns.[86] In consequence, the Great North Road, connecting the West Riding to the North Riding and onwards, crossed the Aire at Ferrybridge and skirted the semi-rural village of Brotherton.

> Indeed, it was probably because of this proximity to the Great North Road that [Slater Milnes], who liked London life, had bought it [in 1786] from Walpole's friend Charles Crowle. At the time of this purchase, effected just before the French Revolution, Fryston was a rambling and irregular block of a house standing high above the river bank. Slater Milnes imposed a superficial unity upon the conglomerate architectural features of the old house by erecting a new front, with four grand Ionic pillars carrying an Ionic pediment, refacing the whole building with slabs of white stone, and adding a pillared porch over the steps to the front door. The Ionic columns on the front of the house rose to the height of the two main stories, and had long windows in between them;

> a glass door between the centre pair of pillars gave egress from the first-floor drawing-room to a little balcony or terrace, from which two flights of steps curved down to a gravel drive. All along the top of the house a balustrade was constructed. The effect of these additions was to increase the dignified appearance of the house, to make it look noble, expensive and clean. Here and there above the new pediment and the balustrade peeped out the chimney-stacks and the angular irrelevant roofs of the old hall.[87]

In one fell swoop, Slater Milnes had become owner of 'one of the most important country seats of Yorkshire'.[88] He clearly took his new-found responsibilities seriously. In 1791, he was awarded a gold medal by the Society for the Encouragement of Arts, Manufacture and Commerce for having planted 384,300 trees on the Fryston estate.[89]

Slater Milnes continued to run the family business until his death in 1804. At this point, ownership of the family estates at Fryston and Bawtry, and the responsibility for maintaining the business, transferred to his widow, who continued to conduct the relevant commercial affairs in partnership with 'a fellow Unitarian', Benjamin Heywood. The younger of Milnes's two sons, Rodes, initially played an active management role, travelling two or three times a week from Fryston to Wakefield in execution of his duties. All too soon, Rodes tired of his business commitments and became part of the 'Prince Regent Set'. This involved a recklessly expensive lifestyle, characterised by excessive drinking, gambling and ill-considered investments in horse-racing stock, which all but depleted the family fortune.[90] 'There is no need to dwell on the story of Rodes Milnes,' states Wemyss Reid:

> He was a typical representative of fashionable society in the days in which he had the misfortune to live – those of the Regency. Witty, hospitable, good-tempered, a keen sportsman, and a devoted patron of the turf, he was extremely popular in all the circles in which he moved. The friend of the Prince Regent and of Beau Brummell, he had long moved in circles in which a reckless extravagance was regarded as something like virtue. He was addicted to gambling, betted freely on his own horses, and played a prominent part in the

> gaieties alike of York and of London [...] Nobody could have been more careless in money matters than Rodes Milnes.[91]

It was left to his mother and older brother, Robert Pemberton Milnes (the father of Richard Monckton Milnes), to pick up the pieces by paying off Rodes's debts and restoring the family's reputation.

The Father-Child Relationship

The early scholastic and political careers of Robert Pemberton Milnes were marked by his individual brilliance, suggesting a fantastic potential that was not ultimately realised. Following a private education at school in Liverpool, he entered Trinity College, Cambridge, from which he emerged in 1804 both with a Bachelor of Arts degree and an unrivalled academic reputation. His father's death that year resulted, as we have seen, in the family property staying, in the short term at least, in the hands of his mother. Two years later, at 22-years-old, he was elected as MP for Pontefract.[92]

The downfall of Pitt's government, which was dismissed by the King due to its pro-Catholic sympathies, resulted in the formation of the Portland administration and the ascension of George Canning as Secretary of State. It was only when members of the opposition set about vilifying Canning in the course of 1807 that Pemberton Milnes stepped forward to deliver a speech of such power and dexterity in Canning's defence that it 'aroused more enthusiasm than has probably ever before or since been created by the oratorical effort of a young man of three-and-twenty'.[93]

Pemberton Milnes also showed himself to be in favour of the abolition of the slave trade; he had significant social and personal assets at his disposal; and, in addition to already being a particular favourite of London society, his considerable good looks encouraged one member of the House of Lords to rate him 'the handsomest man he had ever seen; his small head and the expression of his countenance being quite unequalled, and bearing such a stamp of genius and high breeding'.[94]

On 22 September 1808, Robert Pemberton Milnes married the Honourable Henrietta Maria Monckton, the second daughter of Viscount Galway:

> This lady [...] was, like her husband, of something more than merely agreeable appearance, and like him, she was endowed with exceptional talents. According to the reminiscences of those who knew her in her early days, she was a woman of remarkably beautiful features, and the possessor of a singularly fine voice, which had been carefully trained by *émigrés*, to whom Lord Galway was very hospitable.[95]

The birth of their first child, Richard Monckton Milnes (Milnes), occurred soon afterwards on 19 June 1809 at the home of Pemberton Milnes's parents in London's Mayfair. A mere two months later, the young couple took their infant son on holiday to Scarborough. It was during this visit that:

> While Mrs Milnes and her husband were at breakfast [...] a King's Messenger drove up in a post-chaise with a dispatch from the Prime Minister, Perceval, offering Milnes the choice of a seat in the Cabinet either as Chancellor of the Exchequer or Secretary of War. Milnes was only twenty-six, and the offer was made on the strength of his able speaking in the House. The compliment was a great one. He immediately replied: 'Oh no. I will not accept either. With my temperament I should be dead in a year.' His wife knelt and begged him to take office, if only for his child's sake; he remained adamant, went up to London to refuse the offer, and shortly afterwards gave up his interest in politics and his Pontefract seat.[96]

One theory posits that it was Pemberton Milnes's susceptibility to illness since leaving college that deterred him from entering a ministerial career heaving with 'political toil and excitement'.[97] It is more probable that his decision was governed by an overriding commitment to the lifestyle and myriad social responsibilities of the role of 'country gentleman', which he regarded as his foremost priority.[98]

Despite his disinterest in political office, Pemberton Milnes was re-elected as MP for Pontefract in 1812 and continued to participate in politics until his retirement in 1818. Nonetheless, he maintained an increasingly lower profile, only intervening on issues of particular personal concern (e.g. when he voted against Catholic relief in May 1813 and opposed an inquiry into the Regent's expenditure in May 1815).[99]

In 1815, Milnes's mother gave birth to a little girl, Harriette, whom he doted upon for the remainder of his life. Though initially residing at Fryston, the family was still reeling from the indebtedness created by Rodes when they were forced in 1817 to temporarily shut down the estate and move into the smaller residence at Thorne, near Doncaster, which stood in relatively modest 25-acre grounds. Pemberton Milnes was happy in this pleasant small market town on the Yorkshire/Lincolnshire border, where he used the latest scientific methods to reclaim the wasteland and wetlands around the nearby Fishlake and Sykehouse estates. Though yearning for the type of 'metropolitan' existence to be found on the continent, Henrietta consoled herself by playing music and gardening. In the meantime, Milnes and his sister overcame their boredom by playing in the woods, climbing trees and observing the local deer. Pope-Hennessy speculates that it was at this time that Milnes 'contracted the pronounced distaste for all country pursuits which never after left him'.[100]

Milnes's early education was administered by a private tutor who travelled to Thorne from Wakefield. Prevented from entering Harrow by persistent illness, he continued to receive private tuition in English, Latin, Greek, mathematics and French.[101] Latterly, he spent a brief spell at a private school near Doncaster, only to return home for further personal tuition in preparation for university. There are those who (like Milnes's son, Robert) contend that the absence of a public school career imbued in him a lifelong lack of self-discipline.[102] Others are apt to regard this as a blessing: 'When we call to mind what the great schools were like in his boyhood,' says Peacock, 'we cannot but believe that it would have been an unmixed evil had a mind so sensitive and gentle been subjected to a regime so heartless.'[103]

Russell is more inclined to attribute Milnes's highly idiosyncratic nature (his 'unlikeliness to his fellow-Englishmen') to the fact that this 'only son of a gifted, eccentric, and indulgent father, was brought up at home'.[104] Milnes was literally overshadowed by his father, who was a tall and exceedingly handsome man. By comparison, Milnes was plain-looking and 'did not come much above the shoulders of a man of average height'.[105] It is generally agreed that this father-son relationship was crucial to the formation of Milnes's adult personality and outlook on life:

> It was in reaction against [the father's] prejudices and interests that his son's character developed. Where the father was strict, the son became tolerant; where the father was sternly logical, the son cultivated paradox and hyperbole, became sentimental and seemed frivolous.[106]

While greatly fond of Shakespeare and an occasional poet himself, Pemberton Milnes harboured an enduring contempt for the arts. This 'prim philistinism' underpinned the father's distaste of his son's predilections towards poetry, literature and art.[107] In his ambition to see his son achieve the position of political power and influence that he had formerly spurned, Pemberton Milnes saw the boy's fascination with poetry as a potentially 'dangerous drawback'.

> In his day the House of Commons had been composed of hard-bitten country gentlemen, not poets or novelists, and he could not foresee that the House of the eighteen-forties would contain men such as Bulwer-Lytton and Disraeli. Upon the romantic youths of Trinity, living in the shadow of the Byronic tradition, he turned the cold, clear eye of the eighteenth century.[108]

It was in this sure knowledge of his father's antipathy towards the arts that Milnes embarked on another formative episode shaping his outlook on life – his undergraduate days at Trinity College, Cambridge.

Chapter Three
Milnes the Apostle

Cambridge Undergraduate

Richard Monckton Milnes followed in his father's footsteps by entering Trinity College, Cambridge, in 1827. Like his father, he entered Trinity as a Fellow Commoner. Like his father, he found certain aspects of the undergraduate experience quite wearing.[109] Cambridge life had a sober, restrictive tone, exemplified by the 'detested chapel system' which required every student to attend the 7am religious service.[110] Standing amidst the daunting magnificence of its buildings, the elaborate furnishings and portraits of famous alumni, Milnes experienced a stifling of his natural exuberance. Cambridge was undoubtedly impressive:

> But for the daily life performed against this splendid architectural background, Milnes had little use. One day, he complained, seemed very like another. Even the air was insipid. It was only in retrospect that he romanticised his undergraduate career.[111]

Whether in response to this chronically repressive environment or, as Allen suggests, as a calculated attempt to take the fast track to an intended career as politician and orator,[112] Milnes threw himself into the debating cauldron of the Cambridge Union, and joined a number of other private debating clubs. On one particular day towards the end of his first term, he participated in three debates, already embracing the somewhat 'Whiggish spirit of the Union' despite his Tory background.[113]

Allen speaks rather disparagingly of the undergraduate Milnes, describing him as 'an attractive if apparently insubstantial person – a vain, charming, lightheaded dilettante, somewhat eccentric and disarmingly unaware that anyone might find him ridiculous'.[114] In physical terms, 'a somewhat effeminate, playful, rather pretty youth [...] Milnes at once set out to explore the undergraduate world, with the aim of moving in all the best circles as soon as possible'.[115] He allegedly looked upon the Union merely 'as a curiosity and as another place to make his mark'.[116]

Milnes's status as a Fellow Commoner entitled him to dine alongside the Cambridge Fellows. On observing him from the gallery on the night of his arrival, his mother was moved to remark that Milnes 'seemed as much at home among all the dons as if he had been there for years'.[117] Around this time Milnes struck up one of his closest undergraduate friendships with the poet Arthur Hallam, the son of the famous historian Henry Hallam.

Soon after their first meeting, Milnes helped induct the charismatic and intellectually gifted Hallam into the Union and private debating circles. In May 1829, the pair spoke alongside three colleagues in providing the 'right' answer to the question, 'Has the spirit of Shelley's poetry been beneficial to mankind?' In the same month, Hallam accepted a much-prized invitation to become a member of the highly secretive and selective Cambridge 'Apostles', a group 'chosen for their outstanding minds and personalities', and devoted from its outset 'to the discussion of serious philosophical subjects that did not fit easily into the prescribed studies of the University'.[118] Milnes clearly coveted the possibility of also becoming an Apostle, an ambition he realised the following October.

The Cambridge Apostles

Founded in 1820, the Apostles actually originated from St John's College; but by the late 1820s most of its members were drawn from Trinity. Election to the Apostles was dependent on the person in question being known to, and earning the approval of, all existing members.[119] Though respectful of authority, the Apostles' credo reflected an anti-authoritarianism that challenged the underlying tenets of established religion and nationalism. Its ethical compass was provided by the ubiquitous Victorian concept of 'manliness':

> In contrast to aristocratic arrogance or intellectual prissiness, manliness was not so much masculine as it was courageous,

> frank, upright, mature, undogmatic, and earnest. It was the opposite of childishness, innocence and naïvety. Just as one became free by entering into a self-conscious awareness through discipline, so one became manly by performing one's duty. Status had to be earned and worth and respectability had to be achieved by courage and action and self-confidence.[120]

Among the more famous Apostles of Milnes's day were the poets Arthur Hallam and Alfred Tennyson; Francis Bacon's biographer, James Spedding; the future barrister and lead writer for *The Times* and *Saturday Review* George Stovin Venables; and Edmund Lushington, a future Professor of Greek at Glasgow University (who, like Venables, occasionally published poetry). The particular ethos that pervaded this 'set' was marked by a 'spirit of insurrection', involving 'a desire to help the downtrodden and oppressed wherever they might be found'.[121]

If an imaginative mind, combined with rhetorical skill and eloquence, was a prerequisite membership criterion, so too was a commitment to the in-group norms of candour combined with secrecy and confidentiality.[122] A well-worn ritual was observed, according to which the dozen or so members gathered on Saturday evening in the rooms of the man whose turn it was to present the paper. With everyone inside, the door was locked from within, and no minutes were kept, save for a record of the eventual vote:

> In turn, each of the brethren, in an order chosen by lot, took to the hearth-rug and commented on the paper. The discussion was spirited and they expected verbal virtuosity, but they were expected to take the paper seriously. They rivalled each other in flights of fancy and wit, but the truth, not display, was their object. Truth mattered; nothing else.[123]

Milnes was elected on the same day (in October 1829) as Alfred Tennyson. This was the start of a lifelong friendship with the future Poet Laureate. As we shall see below, Milnes was to exert a significant influence on Tennyson's literary career. The fact that the two new Apostles were Fellow Commoners is taken by Lubenow as an indication that 'the Aristocratic Apostles were not a parasitical lot, chosen for social snobbery'.[124] Allen attaches significance to the fact that Milnes was nominated for membership by Arthur Buller, 'with whom he may have had a more than friendly relationship': 'A note from Buller to Milnes survives from their undergraduate days: beginning "My Dearest Richard" and ending "Yours lovingly", it consists of homosexual ribaldry and contains a pretty explicit invitation.'[125]

Blocksidge goes further still in depicting Milnes as the exemplar of a homosexual predilection common to most of the Apostles:

> Milnes had crushes on people, and at the time of Hallam's arrival had been much taken up with another man in his own year, Augustus Fitzroy, though the friendship does not seem to have survived for long. Later he took up with Stafford O'Brien, who responded to Milnes's warmth of manner, by telling him that 'I have never seen anyone at all like you, and I am quite provoked when I hear anyone compared to you'. Although he eventually married, Milnes had, in modern parlance, a camp manner [...] He was affectionate, gregarious, and quick to throw his arms round his friends, of whom there was always a large number.[126]

It was towards Hallam that Milnes allegedly made his greatest attempts to form a lasting friendship. They continued to enter with gusto into the Union debates: in November 1829, they spoke in favour of Wordsworth in debating the question 'Is Wordsworth or Lord Byron the greater poet?' but were 'rebuffed' according to a vote of 50 to 23.[127] Then, on 26 November 1829, the pair joined Thomas Sunderland as speakers at the Oxford Union, where they advocated the merits of Shelley relative to those of Lord Byron. The Cambridge trio were subsequently lauded by no less an authority than Henry Manning, the Archbishop of Westminster, who recollected several years later how:

> Both Monckton Milnes and Arthur Hallam took us aback by the boldness and their manner. But I remember the effect of Sunderland's declamation and action to this day. It had never been seen or heard before among us: we cowered like birds and ran like sheep.[128]

This could not prevent a negative outcome. The final vote of 90 to 33 was cast resoundingly in favour of Lord Byron.

Milnes and Arthur Hallam

It certainly seems fair to say that no other Apostle had such an immediate or long-lasting impression on Milnes than the enigmatic Arthur Hallam. It was not only their common interest in politics and literature that encouraged such a friendship. An element of hero-worship was also in evidence. Milnes was profoundly impressed to discover that Hallam 'really seems to know everything, from metaphysics to cookery',[129] and was, in essence, 'the only man here of my own standing before whom I bow in conscious inferiority'.[130]

Hallam's feelings for Milnes were decidedly more ambivalent. There is no doubt that they enjoyed each other's company; and throughout their undergraduate careers, the two men corresponded regularly with an openness befitting the closest of confidants. Hallam often employed the warmest descriptions of Milnes: 'the witty, frank, light-humored Milnes, whose temper was never ruffled, nor his sauciness abashed, but in whose uniform kindness of feeling one forgets the extravaganzas of his always random conversation'.[131] Yet, Hallam was also wont to speak disparagingly or condescendingly of his friend – describing him to Gladstone, for example, as one 'of our aristocracy of intellect here; [a good] & kind-hearted fellow, as well as a very clever one, but vain and paradoxical'.[132] It is easy to conclude that the friendship between the two men was largely one-sided, especially as Hallam appeared to show no qualms about eventually breaking it off.[133]

An extended version of this narrative has been offered in evidence of Milnes's homosexual attraction to Hallam, and of Hallam's ultimate rejection of his advances.[134] In its extremist form, this version has been used to exemplify a 'homosexual dimension' to the membership of the Apostles as a whole:

> Although the Apostles existed in an environment in which male friendship could often be intense and was taken very seriously [...] it was also an environment in which there was no generally defined pattern of homosexual behaviour or identity [...] In the early nineteenth century, whist homoeroticism certainly existed, it did so with few explicit terms of reference. Richard Monckton Milnes has already been portrayed as someone whose behaviour conformed in many respects to that of a more modern homosexual (though he eventually

> married), and there seems little doubt that he found Hallam immediately attractive when he met him.[135]

It is nonetheless apparent that the evidential and inferential foundations of this narrative are both flimsy and transparently contrived.

It was Milnes, of course, who had instigated his relationship with Hallam in the process of introducing him to the debating clubs of which Milnes was already a member. Between May and December 1829, their friendship flourished as they engaged, sometimes as co-advocates or, less frequently, as adversaries, in public debate. It was during the summer of 1829 in particular, when Hallam briefly returned home due to illness, that an apparently deeper friendship was formed. At this point, Hallam confided to Milnes that he was experiencing 'fits of gloom' and looking 'death and insanity in the face'.[136] On returning home from a brief, recuperative tour of Scotland, Hallam returned to this theme: 'I really am afraid of insanity [...] for God's sake, send me letters, many letters, amusing letters. Mountains, or metaphysics; jokes or arguments [...] any thing to distract me, anything to give me hope, sympathy, comfort!'[137]

Milnes responded in the desired manner, writing among other things an account of the occasion when, accompanied by 'a well-known aeronaut and a fellow undergraduate', he took off in an air-balloon, which rose to the dizzying height of 2,000 feet. Hallam gleefully referred in replying from his sickbed to the 'increased reverence' he would henceforward be devoting to his friend, the 'Prince of all Aeronauts'.[138] It is therefore fair to say that:

> Whatever the nature of Hallam's previous and subsequent misgivings about Milnes, the correspondence of this period shows that Milnes was Hallam's closest confidant in the late summer of 1829 [...] This is evident not only in the confessional nature of so much that Hallam wrote to him, but also in the way he viewed Milnes as a fellow-poet. His letters to Milnes include samples of work-in-progress (or recently completed) as well as poems specifically addressed to him [...] and also a sonnet addressed to him on his return from Italy of which Milnes thought sufficiently highly to include it in a letter to his father.[139]

Thus, by the time that Hallam embarked on his second year of study, on 22 October 1829, he and Milnes were 'on close personal terms',[140] which were cemented when Milnes gained membership of the Apostles that term and accompanied Hallam and Sunderland to the debate at the Oxford Union.

Milnes's period of study reached an inglorious climax when, in March 1830, he joined Hallam in a production of *Much Ado About Nothing* by the Cambridge Amateur Dramatic Club. Milnes had made several pivotal contributions to a production that was scheduled to appear one month before his final departure from Cambridge. He not only occupied the role of stage manager but also wrote a stirring epilogue and played 'a somewhat portly Beatrice', who hilariously fell through a couch onto the floor of the stage while delivering an unscripted expletive.[141]

The case for a possible homosexual attraction between Hallam and Milnes (whether one-sided or reciprocal) is put forward by Dellamora[142] as part of a wider academic agenda to demonstrate that some of the Apostles were 'readily categorizable as Victorian "bachelors" or even, if somewhat anachronistically, as "closeted homosexuals"'.[143] Dellamora employs the somewhat questionable logic that, since Milnes was friendly with Arthur Buller (an active homosexual), and Hallam was friends with Milnes, it therefore follows that Hallam was also a homosexual and was potentially attracted to Milnes. Dellamora reinforces this supposition by referring to the confessional nature of one of Hallam's letters to Milnes, written during his period of illness in 1829:

> In a letter written to Milnes during the brief period of their close friendship in 1829, Hallam avers: 'Though I have been the creature of impulse, though the basest passions have roused themselves in the deep caverns of my nature, and swept like storm-winds over me [...] I will struggle yet, and have faith in God, that when I ask for bread, I shall not receive a stone.' The statement may be taken as a veiled confession of genital attraction to other men.[144]

Kolb objects to Dellamora's conclusion and argues that, by taking into account 'the larger context of Hallam's correspondence', it becomes evident that, far from referring to a 'genital attraction', Hallam is alluding to a *spiritual*, rather than sexual personal crisis.[145] 'I thought more severely among the Scottish hills, than anywhere ever,' he confides in his letter to Milnes, 'and am now employed in committing to paper the result of my strivings in mind. I had many grapples with Atheism, but beat the monster back, taking my stand on strongholds of Reason.'[146]

Kolb takes similar issue with Dellamora's assertion that Hallam's letters to Milnes in July 1831 'represent a withdrawal of (homosexual) affections, or at least enticements, earlier promised'.[147] On 31 July, for example, Hallam was supposedly the author of a 'Dear John' letter to Milnes, which insisted that any possible attraction between them was not mutual:

> You seem to labor under an illusion which I think it due to myself to endeavor to dispel, especially as your tone seems intended to convey reproach. I am not aware, my dear Milnes, that, in that lofty sense in which you are accustomed to attach to the name of Friendship, we ever were, or ever could be friends. What is more to the purpose, I never fancied that we could, nor intended to make you fancy it. That exalted sentiment I do not ridicule – God forbid – nor consider it as merely ideal: I have experienced it, and it thrills within me now – but not – pardon me, my dear Milnes, for speaking frankly – not for you.[148]

For Kolb, the letter constitutes nothing more than an indication that Hallam no longer considered it wise or expedient to continue to confide in Milnes on matters of such religious and spiritual significance: 'As Hallam's subsequent letters make clear, the flighty Milnes was scarcely the person in whom to confide this fundamental transformation of character, and Hallam quickly distanced himself from his friend.'[149]

Kolb further maintains that Dellamora is guilty of understating the extent to which the Hallam-Milnes relationship was just 'one among many such close mutual affections' characterising the wider 'Trinity set'. He uses extracts from Milnes's letters quoted by Pope-Hennessy[150] (e.g. 'Sir Jacob and I are inseparable, he is one of the dearest creatures I have ever seen. You would I am sure approve of our friendship, it is so unlike the routine of Cambridge arms-in-arms.') to show how male intimacy was a common feature of Trinity life.[151]

Finally, Kolb takes exception to Dellamora's assertion that he had received a private communication from a fellow-academic, Peter Allen, that confirmed that Hallam was aware of Milnes's sexual involvement with males. Having been somewhat taken aback by this disclosure, Kolb sought clarification from Allen and duly received the following reply:

> So Milnes was bisexual (not hard to guess, from other hints that we have) and this may be one reason that he lost Hallam's friendship, but we certainly can't say what you quote Dellamora as saying [above]. Much less attribute the idea to me, as he did.[152]

Milnes and Alfred Tennyson

The relationship between Milnes and Alfred Tennyson was as unlikely as it was undoubtedly fascinating. The future Poet Laureate's first impression on meeting Milnes was that he 'looked the best-tempered creature he had ever seen' – so much so that Tennyson immediately asked to meet him.[153] The fact that the pair were 'poles apart temperamentally' was in no way detrimental to the lifelong friendship that followed.[154] While Milnes was gregarious and full of gaiety, Tennyson was outwardly silent and taciturn; and while Milnes pitched himself wholeheartedly – and, according to some tastes, over-enthusiastically – into the role of Apostle, Tennyson was, by contrast, 'a most unApolistic member', who hardly said anything during the mere five meetings he attended.[155]

Imposingly tall, dark-featured, handsome but unkempt, Tennyson allegedly sat through such meetings, feet up on the hob, amidst a cloud of his ever-present pipe smoke:

> Shy, moody, often withdrawn, he was far from being easy to know and something of a mystery even to his friends. Like Maurice, he had experienced a painful, disturbing upbringing that had left him the victim of acutely sensitive feelings and bouts of depression. While he had remarkable powers of imaginative sympathy, verging on the mystical, his insights found their natural medium in poetry. Writing prose was

> unpleasant to him, and he spoke for the most part in succinct, isolated, rather awkwardly phrased sentences. In refreshing contrast to the smoothly proficient rhetoric and easy wit achieved by so many of the Apostles, Tennyson's conversation was almost childlike in its directness, unpretentiousness, and simple delight in humour.[156]

Tennyson had actually been fined five shillings for not attending the first two scheduled meetings; and when the occasion inevitably arrived (in February 1830) for him to present a paper of his own (on the subject of 'Ghosts'), he was so consumed by 'stage fright' that he tore up his notes and threw them into the fire before resigning on the spot. Neither his behaviour nor his physical appearance detracted from the admiration of his fellow Apostles, least of all Milnes, whose friendship proved unwavering.

When, in a spirit of adventure epitomising the Apostles' eagerness to stretch social and experiential boundaries, Milnes went up in the air balloon as described above, Tennyson commemorated the escapade in his poem, 'A Dream of Fair Women'.[157] Also in October of that year, Arthur Hallam had written to Milnes to say that his father, Henry Hallam, had forbidden the publication of a proposed joint volume of poetry with Tennyson:

> Milnes had obviously been trying to get in on this publishing venture as well, though Hallam's tactful absence of enthusiasm for it was made clear when he wrote to Milnes in October: 'You have my free vote for publishing along with Tennyson, and myself; but mine alone is not enough, and, as he refused his brother on the score of not wishing a third, some difficulty may lie in your way.' No more was heard about Milnes's involvement in the project.[158]

Far more will be made in subsequent chapters of the relationship between Tennyson and Milnes. We shall see how theirs was destined to become a longstanding friendship, on the strength of which Tennyson prospered both financially and artistically from the influence and benevolence of his fellow Apostle.

The Cambridge Legacy

We learned in the introduction to this chapter of one prevailing view that Milnes had used his experience as a Cambridge undergraduate in nakedly opportunistic manner – as a vehicle on which to realise his political ambitions. The accompanying notion that he was fundamentally a 'misfit' or 'dilettante' has been reinforced (as we shall see in subsequent chapters) by the fact that, in the course of sitting his final examinations, Milnes experienced a sudden panic attack and, in his words, 'became excessively faint and giddy, and could hardly see before me [...] I lost all self-possession and rushed out of the hall in a most miserable state, and cried myself to sleep on my sofa.'[159]

These unflattering characterisations of Milnes not only obscure the fact that he passed his degree overall, but also underemphasise the earnest passion and devotion with which he committed himself to undergraduate life and thus formed an enduring network of important cultural and political friendships. Milnes's undergraduate experience also had a crucial shaping effect on his core political outlook. The political and philosophical credo of the Apostles was fundamental to the abiding sense of *noblesse oblige* and benevolent paternalism that became staunch features of Milnes's political career. In particular:

> The Apostles' reaction against the party politics, factionalism and flamboyant speechifying of the Union had its effect on Milnes. In a letter written to his parents on the day Sunderland went down he protested against being asked to identify his politics and claimed that he had arrived at certain political principles that were too general to be classified in party terms or even 'to be applied with any accuracy to business of the day'.[160]

Allen maintains that it was precisely this 'inability to follow a party line' that would eventually prove to be a major obstacle to Milnes's attainment of the 'political eminence' he had firmly set his sights on.[161] It nonetheless provided the cornerstone of the singular political independence and conviction for which he would ultimately be renowned.

Chapter Four
A 'Quite UnEnglish' Socialite

European Sojourns

In May 1828, during Milnes's first year at Cambridge, his parents and sister, Harriette, left Thorne and sailed from Dover to Calais, where they dined with Beau Brummell, a fashion icon, associate of the Prince Regent, and close friend of Milnes's father. The family spent a year in the French northern coastal city of Boulogne before moving via Chantilly to Paris. They spent only ten days in the capital before uprooting themselves for the Italian city of Milan, where they settled for the next four years. The fact that Milan was then under Austrian rule, with Northern Italy occupied by some 100,000 troops, rankled with Milnes, although an agreement with his father, permitting him to divide his time between the host country and England, made the situation tolerable.[162]

In the wake of his examination debacle at Cambridge, the 21-year-old Milnes spent the remaining summer and early autumn of 1830 at London University, followed by the University of Bonn. When not attending lectures, he mixed with German students who were, in the main:

> such fine, free fellows with moustaches and big blue eyes, who wore their hair long, fought duels, drank Moselle wine, and sang divinely as they swaggered about the quiet streets of the old town on the Rhine bank [...] and behaved with the general display of emotion which always attracted Richard Milnes.[163]

Milnes left Bonn in September 1830 to join his family in Milan, where they had rented a large apartment in Palazzo Arconati. Milnes was not quite as enamoured of Milan as his mother and sister, preferring the 'splendour and decay', and 'overall melancholy' of Venice, to which he travelled alone in March 1831.

> Mrs. Milnes, with her great love of music and her uncommon powers as an executant, thoroughly enjoyed the society of the many artists of distinction, both amateur and professional, who were at that time to be found in Milan, whilst her daughter steadily pursued her education under the best masters the city could afford. Richard Milnes [...] from the first, seems to have formed a warm attachment, not only for Italian life, but for the Italian character. His sympathetic temperament quickly enabled him to enter into the feelings of those around him, and the development of that cosmopolitanism of mind and temperament, which to the last was so striking a feature in his character, made rapid advances during these years of his early sojourn in Italy.[164]

During the next four years, Milnes spent extended periods in Venice and Rome, interspersed with visits to relatives in London, and to Ireland (notably, Dublin and Belfast), where he was reunited with old friends, such as Eliot Warburton, Richard Trench and Stafford O'Brien. He was not overly impressed with Ireland's crumbling streets but developed a lasting friendship with the poet Aubrey de Vere. The 'enticements of antiquity' encountered in Rome provided the spur to a six-month tour of Greece, starting in July 1832, and the inspiration for what would become the first of his published volumes of verse. Among other things, Milnes's extended stays in Germany and Italy had brought him into contact with numerous artists, art historians, critics and writers (such as Alexis-François Rio, the author of *De la poésie chrétienne*), who awakened in him a fresh appreciation of early Italian and German painting and of its religious symbolic significance.[165]

It was around about this time that Milnes resumed contact with his fellow Apostle Alfred Tennyson, whom he informed of the imminent publication of *Memorials of a Tour in Some Parts of Greece: Chiefly Poetical* (a volume dealt with in more detail in Chapter 5).[166] Tennyson's reply (of 3 December 1833) highlights the extent to which the pair had been estranged for the past three years, and of how each placed the responsibility for this on the other. 'My Dear Milnes,' Tennyson began:

> A letter from you was like a message from the land of shadows. It is so long since I have looked upon and conversed with you,

that I will not deny but that you had withdrawn a little into the twilight. Yet you do me a wrong in supposing that I have forgotten you. I shall not easily forget you, for you have that about you which one remembers with pleasure. I am rejoiced to hear that you intend to present us with your Grecian impressions. Your gay and airy mind must have caught as many colours from the landskip you moved through as a flying soap-bubble a comparison truly somewhat irreverent, yet I meant it not as such; though I care not if you take it in an evil sense, for is it not owed to you for your three years' silence to me whom you professed to love and care for?[167]

Tennyson signed off in the hope that Milnes had provided in his book of poems 'much glowing description and little mysticism'.[168]

In June 1833, Henrietta Milnes and her daughter set off to join her husband in Berne. Milnes was now in Florence, where he contracted malaria, but was moved to Fiesole, where he stayed with the English poet and writer Walter Savage Landor in his beautiful villa. Milnes was much taken by Landor's power of conversation but also enjoyed meeting Charles Brown, a retired fur-trader and close friend of Keats.

Once recovered, Milnes joined his family in Switzerland then, in September 1833, travelled with his father to London to arrange for the printing and publication of *Memorials.* Part way through the journey, he learned of the death of Arthur Hallam and immediately wrote a letter of condolence to Henry Hallam and asked if he might be allowed to attend the funeral. He also produced a short verse, called 'On the Death of –', as a tribute to his friend:

I thought, how should I see him first,
How should our hands first meet,
Within his room, upon the stair,
At the corner of the street?
I thought, where should I hear him first,
How catch his greeting tone, –
And thus I went up to his door,
And they told me he was gone![169]

Blocksidge has since asserted that 'On the Death of –' constitutes a 'clear prefigurement' of a central part of Tennyson's best-known and most cherished poem – namely, 'In Memoriam A. H. H.' – Section VII, ('Dark house by which once more I stand').[170] As Blocksidge points out, 'Milnes's poem was published in 1838 and the section of "In Memoriam A. H. H." in question was not composed until ten years later, so it is more than likely that Tennyson had read it.'[171]

Return to Fryston Hall

Milnes subsequently spent periods back in Rome (where he met the Irish poet and mathematician, George Darley) and then Munich. By this time, the family had taken a house on the Brenta, but plans were made in autumn of 1835 for them to permanently return to England, where their fortunes were taking a turn for the better.

In November 1835, Henrietta and Harriette arrived back in London, where Milnes was waiting to greet them. Whilst there, Henrietta received a letter informing her of the death of her stepmother, the Dowager Lady Galway, who was also a second cousin of Pemberton Milnes.[172] This meant that Milnes's father was now owner of the Bawtry estate (on the borders of Lincolnshire and the West Riding), which had first been acquired by his great uncle. The death of Milnes's grandmother later that year would also place the Fryston estate in Milnes's father's possession, while leaving him with the moral responsibility of looking after his three 'maiden' sisters – the Misses Louisa, Jane and Caroline Milnes – all of whom were considerably younger than him.[173]

Following a further two weeks in London, Milnes travelled north to Fryston with his mother and sister, thus bringing a ten-year absence to an end.

> Here they received a body of persons described by Mrs. Milnes as 'twenty-five of our most intimate friends,' gave an impromptu dinner and tenants' ball and then returned to pass the rest of the winter at Bawtry. The Milnes parents were, on the whole, enchanted to be back where they belonged. Harriette settled easily down into the role of a country belle, though her acquirements were now vastly superior to those of other Yorkshire girls. She was taller than her brother, and unlike Richard she was beautiful. She wore her hair in braids and had large blue eyes described by one admirer as 'mooney.' From her father she had inherited a sharp wit and a satirical turn of speech.[174]

It is known that Tennyson had been a visitor to Fryston in 1835. There are no details of the occasion, other than that he found the place cold enough to refer to it as 'Freezetown'.[175] Other visitors included Milnes's old college friends, such as Stafford O'Brien, and his tutor Connop Thirlwall, who pitched themselves into a game of charades:

> One which illustrated the principal scenes in 'Nicholas Nickleby,' which had just appeared, gained special popularity. In the performance Stafford O'Brien played Nicholas, whilst Connop Thirlwall made an inimitable Squeers, whose antics were the delight not only of the residents of the house, but of the village children whom O'Brien swept into the drawing-room with an entire disregard of the fitness of their attire for the scene into which they were unceremoniously ushered.[176]

Pope-Hennessy maintains that any influence imposed on Richard's character by his strict, methodical father, was moderated by the softening and 'civilising' effect of the warmer relations he enjoyed with his mother and sister, Harriette.[177] Henrietta Monckton 'had retained throughout the long years at Thorne a zest for living which she afterwards deliciously indulged in Milan, in Venice and Florence and Rome in the early eighteen-thirties'. Insofar as Pope-Hennessy is concerned, 'The chief explanation of Richard Monckton Milnes's complicated psychology lies in these family relationships.'[178] This is not to downplay, of course, the experiential influence of the novel and diverse cultures (such as those, as we have seen, of Germany and Italy) to which the young Milnes had been exposed during his continental travel.

This immediate post-Cambridge period had imbued in Milnes 'a gayety [sic] of spirit, a frankness of bearing, a lightness of touch', which, according to Russell, 'were quite un-English'.[179] There was, in Russell's estimation, none of the 'morbid self-repression and proud humility', the 'frigid dignity and arrogant reserve' of the typical English gentleman. This had altogether been replaced, 'strikingly – even amusingly', by the 'un-English' qualities of empathy and tolerance, and by a 'frank openness of speech and bearing'.[180] 'I never saw him kiss a guest on both cheeks,' Russell concluded, 'but if I had I should not have felt the least surprised.'[181]

The quality of life now enjoyed by the Milnes family represented a far cry from the 'penurious existence' they had been forced to make the best of at Thorne Hall. The possibility briefly existed of Milnes's father selling off one or the other of his sprawling estates, though he ultimately relinquished neither.

> Richard, who lacked the childhood memories his father had of Fryston and had not Mr. Milnes' acute comprehension of the standards of life and hospitality which the world still demanded of an English country gentleman, was not deeply concerned whether Fryston went or not. When its sale seemed inevitable in 1831, he had been more disturbed over the fate of his grandfather's small library – fat, calf-bound volumes of speeches and trials, tracts, English poets, letter-writers such as Horace Walpole – than at the prospect of losing his patrimony. Fryston gave him a kind of right to stand for the borough of Pontefract, but apart from this it was then of no importance to him.[182]

In no time at all, Fryston Hall would play host (initially under the ownership of Milnes's father, and thereafter of Milnes himself) to a steady stream of illustrious guests, making it 'one of the most famous country-houses in Victorian England'. But the plain truth remained that Milnes 'never loved it'.[183]

A Capital Existence

Pope-Hennessy makes the point that there was nothing especially remarkable about Fryston to set it apart from other Northern country houses. What eventually made it unique was the fact that its occupant of fifty years was not only 'an intellectual and a cosmopolitan', but also in due course 'a Yorkshire landowner who hated the land and country pursuits, preferred London to the West Riding, and Paris and Italy to both of these'.[184]

Milnes's career prospects received a tremendous boost in the spring of 1836 when his father, now freed of the financial constraints that had driven the family abroad, rented a property at the junction of London's South Street and Park Lane, a fashionable location overlooking Hyde Park. A new world of opportunity thus opened up before him.

> But he had now to face up to making a career. His father's wishes and his own darting interest in public affairs, as well as a harmless youthful vanity, made him want to strike out at once into political life. So far as a seat in the House went, little could be done until the ageing king should die. Since political reputation was still partly made in certain drawing-rooms and club-rooms in London, the most Richard could hope for during 1836 was to leave his mark in these circles and to foster a vague reputation for 'promise'.[185]

The English 'society' of this era was a 'heavily ramified fortress' that few were entitled or able to penetrate. The fact that Milnes *was* able to make such headway was due to a combination of his family standing on his mother's side, the influential friendships he had forged as an undergraduate, his membership of literary circles, and the widespread curiosity aroused by his reputation as a young poet.[186] Also relevant, of course, was Milnes's highly vivacious, self-confident and gregarious manner. He was not everyone's cup of tea, however, inviting such unflattering nicknames as 'The Cool of the Evening', 'London Assurance' and 'In-I-go Jones'.[187]

Milnes not only frequented the most fashionable salons and breakfast parties of the day (notably those given by the great Victorian wit Samuel Rogers), but also prospered from the similar occasions hosted by his mother at which as many as forty guests were present:

> Mrs Milnes records in her journal that the dinner-parties which they gave in the house in South Street, during this season of 1836, were chiefly to the friends of her son, 'some of them being very agreeable and literary' – amongst others, Wordsworth and Samuel Rogers.[188]

Crossing Swords with Tennyson

Milnes had last seen Tennyson when the latter paid a brief, but highly convivial, visit to Bawtry in April 1836.[189] They resumed contact in December 1836, when Milnes wrote in characteristically breezy fashion to ask Tennyson if he might contribute a poem to an anthology for the *Tribune* being compiled by Milnes's associate, Lord Northampton. He also suggested that Tennyson might use this as an opportunity to re-visit Fryston:

> Your brief was infallibly pleasant. I shall wait for you in December. If you like, we will have 'Freezetown' (Fryston) all to ourselves and you may smoke while I play the organ. Now be a good boy and do as you're told. Lord Northampton is getting up a charity book of poetry for the destitute family of a man of letters, born in the dead letter office, and he earnestly prays you to contribute not your mite but your might to it. I have half promised you will give him something pretty considerable, for the fault of the book will be that the contributions are not as great in dimension as in name. He has got original things of Wordsworth, Southey, Miss Bailey, R. M. M. etc. I will love you more and more therefore if you will send some jewels directed to the Marquis of Northampton, Castle Ashby, Northampton, as soon as convenient.[190]

The light-hearted though somewhat tactless tone of the letter unfortunately misfired. Tennyson not only objected to having been so taken for granted, but also confessed to finding publications of this nature extremely distasteful:

> That you had promised the Marquis I would write for him something exceeding the average length of 'Annual compositions'; that you had promised him I would write at all: I took this for one of those elegant fictions with which you amuse your aunts of evenings, before you get into the small hours when dreams are true. Three summers back, provoked by the incivility of editors, I swore an oath that I would never again have to do with their vapid books, and I brake it in the sweet face of Heaven when I wrote for Lady What's-hername Wortley [...] To write for people with prefixes to their names is to milk he-goats; there is neither honour nor profit. Up to this moment I have not even seen *The Keepsake*: not that I care to see it, for the want of civility decided me not to break mine oath again for man nor woman, and how should such a modest man as I see my small name in collocation with the great ones of Southey, Wordsworth, R. M. M., etc., and not feel myself a barndoor fowl among peacocks?[191]

Milnes felt angered in turn by the 'insulting irony' employed by Tennyson and took particular objection to the characterisation of the planned volume as 'vapid'. Tennyson replied with more contrition, acknowledging that he had been wrong to use the word 'vapid', and excused himself by explaining how he was applying it in reference to annuals of this nature and not in direct relation to Milnes and the other contributors. 'I thought you knew me better than even to insinuate these things,' Tennyson went on. The problem, as Tennyson saw it, lay in the fact that their conversation had been conducted in writing: 'Had I spoken the same things to you laughingly in my chair, and with my own emphasis, you would have seen what they really meant.'[192] Tennyson concluded by doubting whether arrangements would allow him to make a visit to Fryston but promised to get the poem to Milnes in one way or another.[193]

Tennyson was so sluggish in fulfilling his promise that Milnes was forced to issue a reminder, and Tennyson took one of his partly-written poems and hurriedly completed it. The upshot of this was that 'Stanzas' was published in *The Tribute* for 1837, alongside contributions by the likes of Wordsworth, William Whewell (the Master of Trinity), John Frere (also of Trinity), Aubrey de Vere, Chenevix Trench, and, of course, Milnes himself. 'Stanzas' was actually an updated version of a lyric first written in 1834 to commemorate the death of Arthur Hallam. Tennyson was unhappy with the poem,[194] which he revisited in 1854, transforming it into one of his most famous works, the melodramatic 'Maud', published in 1856.[195]

Throughout the spring and early summer of 1837, Milnes was obliged, due to a serious illness of Harriette, to spend most of his time at Fryston Hall, where he read his way voraciously through countless books, including Carlyle's *French Revolution* and Browning's play *Strafford*. This hiatus also gave him the opportunity to contemplate the furnishing of the rooms he was in the process of acquiring at 26 Pall Mall. These premises were situated above a tailor's shop, within easy reach of several gentlemen's clubs of which he was already a member. Among the 'bachelor comforts' he enjoyed were a manservant and his own carriage and horses.[196] Milnes had quickly emerged as one of the foremost socialites of Victorian England. The time had now arrived for him to advance his corresponding literary and political careers.

Chapter Five
Good Citizen Milnes

The Multifaceted Monckton Milnes

In this chapter and in Chapter 6 we redirect our attention onto the diverse and multifaceted *political, literary* and *philanthropic* activities occurring in Milnes's early career. The present chapter focuses in chronological order on Milnes's somewhat controversial election as Member of Parliament for Pontefract; the earliest examples of his poetic work; his patronage and support of the emergent great writers of the era (notably Thomas Carlyle and Ralph Waldo Emerson); and an indicative example of his lifelong preoccupation with great humanitarian issues – involving, in this case, a visit to Newgate prison with William Makepeace Thackeray in order to 'taste' the experience of a public execution.

Chapter 6 highlights the growing significance of Fryston as arguably the major social, artistic and political hub of Victorian society outside of London. We focus in particular on visits by Carlyle and Thackeray. The chapter lends much credence to the view that Milnes was one of the greatest philanthropists of the era. It documents the ready beneficence he extended to the poets Tennyson and Patmore, and to the journalist and editor Thomas Hood. Further emphasis is placed on Milnes's distinctive political independence of thought and action, illustrated by his use of poetry to challenge western stereotypes of Muslim society (most notably its womenfolk), the opposition to conventional criticism of Catholicism he displayed in his essay writing, and his ultimately successful campaigning against the application of the death penalty.

MP for Pontefract

In June 1837, following the death after long illness of William IV, the long reign of Queen Victoria began. Parliament was dissolved and, in the general election that followed, Milnes stood successfully as the member for Pontefract. According to one version of the campaign, Milnes canvassed assiduously and effectively:

> The fight was undoubtedly a hot one while it lasted, but Milnes threw himself into it with spirit, speaking frequently, and evidently gaining courage in doing so, delighting his father by his ease and self-possession, and fulfilling the high hopes of his friends.[197]

This view is contradicted by Richardson, who contends that Milnes 'displayed a certain arrogance' in addressing the electorate.[198] She uses local newspaper reports (drawn from the *Leeds Mercury*) to show that he preferred to dwell 'romantically' on his recent tour of the continent than to mention anything of true political substance.

The campaign was undoubtedly marred by an unresolved controversy. The once-traditional, though now frowned-upon practice of paying 'head money' as an inducement to potential voters was alleged to have resurfaced to Milnes's advantage – much to the chagrin of the former MP, Sir Culling Eardley-Smith, a Radical who had polled 529 votes seven years earlier when standing as a Tory. But when the poll was declared on 25 July 1837, Milnes achieved 507 of the votes and Eardley-Smith 123 (some way behind the third candidate, W.M. Stanley, who accounted for 403).[199]

The most remarkable feature of Milnes's success was that, 'until he actually came forward as a Conservative candidate, even those who knew him best had been in some doubt as to the precise character of his political opinions'.[200] While congratulating Milnes, the liberal-minded scholar, theologian, and future Bishop of St David's, Connop Thirlwall said, 'I can hardly bring myself now to consider you as a Tory, or as belonging to a party at all [...] still my first hope as well as expectation as to your political career is that it may be distinguished by some degree of originality.'[201]

Milnes dutifully took up his place in the House on 20 November and was seated alongside another new Tory member, Benjamin

Disraeli, on 7 December when Disraeli delivered his maiden speech, in which he provocatively questioned the validity of certain Irish elections. Disraeli's speech was a humiliating debacle. It was universally greeted with 'hisses, hoots, laughter and catcalls' and its final sentence completely drowned out amidst the uproar.[202] Afterwards, Milnes gleefully reported that 'Disraeli nearly killed the House' and 'Peel quite screamed with laughter'.[203] On 8 December, the spotlight shifted onto Milnes, whose maiden speech focused on the subject of 'Pensions on the Civil List'.[204] Though initially nervous, Milnes had good reason to feel satisfied with his performance, which was subsequently endorsed by Stafford O'Brien, who verified that Milnes spoke 'confidently' and with an attitude 'devoid of anything like mannerism or Milnesism, which I feared'.[205]

On 13 February 1838, Milnes suffered the ignominy of having to sit and look on while Sir Henry Ward (MP for Sheffield) presented a petition from Sir Culling Smith that called for a Select Committee to investigate the possible payment of head money in Pontefract. Milnes responded by assuring the House that, since he had nothing to hide, he would have no objection to such an inquiry. He then turned to a skilful, condemnatory explanation of what he regarded as the 'real reason' for Culling Smith's failure to regain his seat:

> Sir Culling Smith first went down to Pontefract under Conservative banners and professing Conservative principles, and he was then elected. In [1837] he attempted the same thing under Radical banners and professing Radical principles, and, therefore, as was very natural, was not elected. Whatever course might be taken, whether head-money were given or not, it was impossible that any two persons, professing Radical principles could ever become the representatives of the borough of Pontefract.[206]

Milnes had expertly fended off this issue. It soon became apparent, though, that his subsequent speeches fell short of igniting the enthusiasm of his fellow parliamentarians. It was widely held that Milnes's style of delivery was over-earnest and verbose. Reflecting what became a lifelong rivalry and animosity between the two men, Benjamin Disraeli harboured an even less charitable view of Milnes's shortcomings:

> Disraeli, who was not an unprejudiced witness and who dismissed 'Dicky' as 'one of the most insignificant members of the House of Commons,' attributed Milnes' failure to his physical appearance as weak as to his nervousness and pomposity. Describing Milnes' face 'like an Herculaneum mask or a countenance cut out of an orange' and as 'irresistibly comic,' he says that when speaking Milnes produced 'the effect of some celebrated droll [...] and before he had proceeded five minutes, though he might be descanting on the wrongs of Poland or the rights of Italy, there was sure to be a laugh.'[207]

Disraeli maintained that, for all Milnes's undoubted intelligence and good nature, he was ultimately undone by his own 'insane vanity' and envy of those in office.[208]

This did not deter Disraeli from striving to enlist Milnes's support in the creation of a political movement that would eventually go by the name of 'New England' (see Chapter 7). Refusing to be tied to any party line, Milnes focused principally on the great humanitarian issues of the day.[209] In any case, his mind was more occupied in early 1838 by the marriage of his sister, Harriette, to their cousin Lord Galway. This came as a devastating blow to Milnes. Though greatly attached to his cousin, the fact remained that:

> The one to whom throughout his life his own heart had been most closely bound was now to enter upon a new life, with new ties and new sympathies, and it seemed to him for the moment that with her marriage must end that perfectly frank and affectionate intercourse which had hitherto subsisted between them.[210]

Poet and Patron of the Arts

There were other distractions for Milnes to have to contend with. He was also preoccupied at this time with the virtually simultaneous publication of two volumes of poetry, *Memorials of a Residence on the Continent, and Historical Poems*,[211] and *Poems of Many Years*.[212] Horne has stated with simple but telling clarity that 'The poetry of Richard Monckton Milnes has met with considerable praise in many quarters, yet hardly as much as it deserves; and it has met with peculiar dispraise, more than it deserves, either in kind or degree.'[213]

Peacock similarly declared that one would have to look in vain for 'some precious gems' in these early volumes, while adding that Walter Savage Landor referred to Milnes in 1838 as 'the greatest poet then living in England'.[214]

The first of these volumes, *Memorials of a Residence*, was dedicated to Harriette in celebration of her marriage. This publication was a reissue of the poems that first appeared in *Memorials of a Tour in Some Parts of Greece: Chiefly Poetical*,[215] supplemented by sonnets and poems relating to Milnes's years spent in Italy and in Bonn. Milnes's son, Lord Crewe, ventures to suggest that his father's 'memorials' of Greece and Italy have since lost their 'freshness',[216] a view seemingly not subscribed to by Peacock, who comments on the 'high order of beauty' characterising the verses collected as 'The Immortality of Rome'.[217]

A second volume, *Poems of Many Years*, was initially self-published for private circulation only. Its contents were organised under the separate themes of 'Youth', 'Friendship', 'Love', 'Reflection' and 'Sorrow'. Pope-Hennessy singles out four poems from this volume which 'were especially admired':[218] 'The Flight of Youth', in particular, 'The Lay of the Humble', 'Shadows', 'The Long-Ago'. Horne also singles out two of these poems, 'The Lay of the Humble' and 'The Long-Ago', for special mention,[219] while Lord Crewe has commented that the latter sits alongside 'The Flight of Youth' as his father's own particular favourite.

Youthful Hope's religious fire,
When it burns no longer, leaves
Ashes of impure Desire
On the altars it bereaves;
But the light that fills the Past
Sheds a still diviner glow,
Ever farther it is cast
O'er the scenes of Long-ago.

Many a growth of pain and care,
Cumbering all the present hour,
Yields, when once transplanted there,
Healthy fruit or pleasant flower;
Thoughts that hardly flourish here,
Feelings long have ceased to blow,

Breathe a native atmosphere
In the world of Long-ago.[220]

The *Flight of Youth* is the title given to the second volume of Milnes's biography by Pope-Hennessy.[221] It is therefore ironic that the merits of the above two volumes of poetry were only grudgingly conceded by this author. 'Scattered throughout the two volumes there are passages showing real sensibility,' Pope-Hennessy grudgingly maintains, while adding that, 'These lie embedded in much that is stilted, conventional and commonplace.'[222]

Milnes was already forging a considerable reputation as philanthropist and patron of the arts. It was during the summer of 1838 that he befriended the distinguished American politician, academic lawyer and anti-slavery campaigner Charles Sumner. The American wrote warmly of his new English friend, describing him as 'a member of Parliament, a poet, and a man of fashion, a Tory who does not forget the people and a man of fashion with sensibilities, love of virtue and merit among the simple, the poor and the lowly'.[223]

Sumner referred to the fact that Milnes had already become a staunch admirer and advocate of the work of the Scottish philosopher Thomas Carlyle. In the remainder of this chapter, we examine the benevolence, encouragement and influence brought to bear by Milnes, not only in relation to Carlyle, but also to the American writer Ralph Waldo Emerson, and to his old friend and fellow Apostle William Makepeace Thackeray.

Rallying Behind Carlyle

Much uncertainty surrounds the precise date on which Carlyle and Milnes were first introduced. All we know for definite is that, in April 1837, James Spedding wrote to Milnes asking him to use all his influence to encourage as many people as possible to attend the six London lectures Carlyle was due to present later that month. Not yet enjoying the economic fruits of published authorship, Carlyle was dependent on subscriptions to his lectures; but as Spedding explained:

> The list of subscribers is at present not large, and you are just the man to make it grow. As it is Carlyle's first essay in

> this kind, it is important that there should be a respectable muster of hearers [...] We want your name to represent the great body of Tories, Roman Catholics, High Churchmen, metaphysicians, poets and Savage Landor.[224]

Kaplan reports that, prior to the lecture series, Jane Carlyle (the author's wife) had organised a soirée of between 20 and 30 'brilliant bits of personages', which possibly included Milnes.[225] This publicity certainly proved effective. Though trembling with fear throughout, Carlyle duly completed a well-attended series, earning £135 in the process – enough to live on for a year.

Carlyle's rapid development as a writer and lecturer of great significance meant that, by the end of 1838, he had become 'eagerly pursued by the well-born, the wealthy, and the talented [...] [and] the word had gone round that he was company worth having'.[226] It was not long before Milnes began inviting Carlyle to dinner parties and, thereafter, to his famous breakfasts.

Milnes was already a great admirer of Carlyle's *The French Revolution*; and, as Pope-Hennessy points out, 'It seems peculiar that the world should have seemed something to Milnes that it also seemed to Carlyle, but in spite of apparently antipathetic characteristics and ways of living, they made fast friends.'[227] For one thing, Carlyle enjoyed the contrast between Milnes's optimistic gaiety and his own 'moroseness and irascibility'.[228] Kaplan maintains that, in the early stages of their friendship, Carlyle felt ambivalent towards Milnes:

> Carlyle rather liked Milnes, though like everyone else he did not take him seriously. Years later the story was told that Carlyle 'who when some ecclesiastic gloomily inquired in his presence "What would happen if Jesus Christ returned to earth *now*?" retorted – "*Happen*! why Dickie Milnes would ask him to dinner, to be sure, and would ask Pontius Pilate to meet him."'[229]

Nevertheless, it is said that the two men never quarrelled in the course of a lifelong friendship, even though Milnes 'took great delight in provoking [Carlyle] into abusive torrents, particularly about well-known people'.[230]

As 1838 was coming to its close, Carlyle approached Milnes with a view to solicit his practical support with a project close to his heart:

> Carlyle had been much troubled by the want of a really good subscription library in London. The national library in the British Museum was even then admirable in its way, but no one was allowed to remove a volume from the reading-room, and the treasures of which the library boasted were not therefore accessible to those who wished or who were compelled to study at home. Carlyle sought to enlist the sympathies of his friends in a movement for the formation of a new library, which should supply the want he had felt so sorely. He had little difficulty in rallying round him an enthusiastic band of supporters, amongst whom none was of better service than Milnes, though in the first instance he had been somewhat sceptical regarding the scheme.[231]

The time was also becoming ripe for Carlyle to ask Milnes to help further the career of a rising American literary star.

Milnes and Ralph Waldo Emerson

By the spring of 1839, the work of the American writer Ralph Waldo Emerson was starting to make a great impact on the British literary establishment. Carlyle lobbied incessantly with the intention of 'stirring up a few new friends' on his behalf. It was Milnes, however, who became the first English writer to publish a criticism of Emerson's essays – in the *London and Westminster Review*[232] – in what 'may have been the most important event for Emerson's future'.[233]

Two months prior to the publication of this piece, Carlyle had written to Emerson (on 6 January 1840), informing him that he had personally helped clear it with the editors of the *Review* for Milnes (or the 'courageous youth', as he called him) to submit a critique of the essays. 'We shall see whether it comes out or not,' cautioned Carlyle, 'keeping silence till then.' His accompanying description of Milnes was surprisingly uncomplimentary:

> Milnes is a *Tory* Member of Parliament; think of that! For the rest, he describes his religion in these terms: 'I profess to be a Crypto-Catholic.' Conceive the man! A most bland-smiling, semi-quizzical, affectionate, high-bred, Italianized little man,

> who has long olive-blond hair, a dimple, next to no chin, and flings his arm round your neck when he addresses you in public society! Let us hear now what he will say of the American *Vates*.[234]

It was possible to interpret Milnes's review of the work as 'an indictment of Emerson's lack of originality, evidence that his own contemporaries recognized his massive and largely unacknowledged debt to transatlantic sources'.[235]

Milnes had clearly observed that there was little to be found in Emerson's work that would be unfamiliar to students of Carlyle and several other European philosophers. It has been argued, however, that Milnes's actual intention was to praise Emerson by likening his work to that of Carlyle. This was why Milnes ventured that it was possible to witness in both their work 'the same tender complaint, the same indignant exhortation', albeit 'sufficiently modified by circumstances of personality and place'.[236] In other words, this was all part of a deliberate ploy to ensure Emerson's acceptance by an English audience that retained a lofty and somewhat sneering attitude towards its transatlantic counterparts:

> Milnes's strategy is one of establishing common ground, of reading Emerson's texts against the background of their cisatlantic origins. By presenting *Nature*, the 'Divinity School Address,' and the orations on the 'American Scholar' and 'Literary Ethics' as essentially Carlylean productions, Milnes renders Emerson's texts less exotic and more accessible to their contemporary British Readers.[237]

Afterwards, Carlyle thanked Milnes for having written 'a very beautiful article'.[238] He then wrote to Emerson (on 1 April 1840), underlining the importance of Milnes's critical intervention. It had succeeded, he stated, in laying 'the first plank of a kind of pulpit for you here and throughout all Saxondom: a thing rather to be thankful for'. By now, Carlyle had nothing but affection for Milnes, whom he described as 'a pretty little robin-redbreast of a man'.[239] Having received Milnes's copy and accompanying personal note, Emerson wrote back in great appreciation.[240] His gratitude was well-founded since, as Tilton explains, Milnes's review set the stage for the English publication of Emerson's *Essays*, which, with the practical help of (and preface by) Carlyle, appeared in August 1841.[241] The beneficial effect of this joint sponsorship was incalculable:

> For American authors, particularly in the first half of the nineteenth century, to receive the notice of an English critic was crucial. Carlyle and Milnes together helped to secure an English audience. English recognition was encouragement for American authors and their publishers. Emerson's mother was happy to write: 'they are talking about you in England'; a New York paper had noted Milnes's article.[242]

The first English edition sold well enough to warrant a reprint two years later, and it created what Carlyle gleefully referred to as 'an appropriate sensation' among readers and critics alike.[243]

Going to See a Man Hanged

Aside from his poetic and philanthropic activities, Milnes was beginning to engage in the type of humanitarian activities which were to become the hallmarks of his political career. In the summer of 1840, he travelled with his old friend and fellow Apostle William Makepeace Thackeray to witness first-hand the execution of Courvoisier, a valet who had been found guilty of murdering his elderly employer, Lord William Russell. The fact that the victim was the uncle of the well-known politician and statesman Lord John Russell was a key factor in attracting 40,000 people to the execution, which was staged on 4 July 1840 outside Newgate Prison.

> Both Thackeray and Milnes had more or less professional excuses for deciding to join the crowd and witness the event. As a member of Parliament, Milnes had recently voted in favor of an unsuccessful motion by the reformer William Ewart to abolish the death penalty, and Milnes wished to observe the effect of a public execution on its audience. As a not-yet-famous writer with a wife and two small children to support, Thackeray planned to use the execution as the basis for an article for which he hoped some periodical would pay.[244]

Thackeray had not previously witnessed a public hanging and showed no hesitation in accepting Milnes's invitation to join him.[245] Executions of that era were typically carried out at 5 or 6am, and it was customary for attendees to stay up all night following a very late preparatory supper. Thackeray chose in favour of a good night's sleep, leaving Milnes to spend the night at his club, being jovially treated to an incessant stream of gallows humour by 'one of the most eminent wits in London'.[246]

The two men rode together in Milnes's carriage 'through the sleeping streets' and among the 'leafy trees' of a seemingly typical London morning, only to experience 'a dumb electric shock' as they caught their first sight of the gallows on finally approaching the prison. They forced their way into an already sizeable, but 'gentle, good-humoured crowd',[247] where they settled in as observers for the next four hours. Their presence was observed by Charles Dickens who, along with his brother-in-law and the painter Maclise, had rented a room from which to view the proceedings.[248] Nothing, it transpired, could have prepared them for the horror of the spectacle that followed. As Thackeray subsequently reported to his mother:

> I have been to see Courvoisier hanged & am miserable ever since. I can't work and yet work must be done for the poor babbies' sake. It is most curious the effect his death has had on me, and I am trying to work it off in a paper on the subject. Meanwhile it weighs upon the mind, like cold plum pudding on the stomach, & as soon as I begin to write, I get melancholy.[249]

Thackeray nonetheless succeeded in writing a now-famous essay, 'Going to see a man hanged', which was published in the Jul-Dec 1840 edition of *Fraser's Magazine*.[250] Charles Dickens's own account of the execution emphasised (in the form of a letter to *The Daily News*) the ribaldry and debauchery of the crowd.[251] Thackeray placed a different spin on the event, representing an arguably more powerful case for the abolition of capital punishment:

> I fully confess that I came away down Snow Hill that morning with a disgust for murder, but it was for the murder I saw done. As we made our way through the immense crowd, we came

> upon two little girls of eleven and twelve years: one of them was crying bitterly, and begged, for Heaven's sake, that some one would lead her from that horrid place. This was done, and the children were carried into a place of safety. We asked the elder girl – and a very pretty one – what brought her into such a neighbourhood? The child grinned knowingly, and said, 'We've koom to see the mon hanged!' Tender law, that brings out babes upon such errands, and provides them with such gratifying moral spectacles![252]

Cooper maintains that the negative impact on Milnes was every bit as great as it had been on Thackeray, but that 'the impression remained longer with Milnes; his resolve to do something about public executions was firmer and deeper'.[253] The paradoxical nature of Milnes's character is evident in the contrast between his repugnance at the spectacle and the joviality he engaged in on the eve of the execution. Pope-Hennessy also remarks on the obvious contradiction between his distaste for capital punishment and his 'bizarre taste for hangmen's autographs', his obsessive interest in flogging, and collected volumes on school discipline:

> There was nothing secretive about Milnes' attitude to these matters. On Sunday mornings at Fryston he would sometimes amuse himself by watching his guests recoil before a piece of the dried skin of a notorious murderer, which he kept pressed between the pages of some appropriate book.[254]

In the late summer of 1840, Milnes spent time in the south-west of England, visiting Arthur Hallam's father and other friends in the area before returning briefly that September to Fryston. All the political auguries suggested that the Melbourne Government was living on borrowed time and that the election of a Tory Ministry under Peel might see the MP for Pontefract assigned to the post of Under-Secretary of State for Foreign Affairs. With much to ponder amidst a chilling Fryston winter, Milnes adjourned to France, where he spent some time with Thackeray 'who had passed a good deal of time in Paris [writing journalistic sketches] without getting either to like or understand the French'.[255]

Thackeray was staying close to the sanctuary in which his ailing wife, Isabella, was located. The two men witnessed the funeral of Napoleon, an event which Thackeray reported in one of his newspaper articles. Afterwards, Milnes met up with several friends, including the novelist and socialist Madame George Sand; the writer and politician Alphonse de Lamartine; and, more notably, the aristocratic historian and author of *Democracy in America*, Alexis de Tocqueville. It was a precarious political position in France with massive fortifications being erected in anticipation of an imminent attempt to overthrow an unpopular monarchy.

Chapter Six
Ready and Sympathetic Hands

Decorating the Palace

On returning home from France, Milnes spent the early spring of 1841 in London, where he was appointed to a Royal Commission charged with determining a decorative scheme for the Houses of Parliament. Seven years earlier, the Palace of Westminster had been destroyed by fire. A previous select committee had already decreed that the reconstructed buildings should follow a Gothic or Elizabethan architectural style. Attention now focussed on the most appropriate form of decoration.[256] Chaired by Sir Robert Peel, the select committee comprised a 'group of connoisseurs' that was 'fairly representative of the art historical knowledge of the time'. Of these, Milnes was 'at the height of his popularity in the more intellectual circles of London'.[257]

According to Bullen, Milnes played 'a prominent part in the discussion',[258] reflecting the fondness for religious-inspired German and Italian art-forms he had developed during his earlier tours of the continent. Other committee members followed suit: 'Though views on how the British might imitate the Germans differed there was almost complete unanimity for the idea that the German model was the most appropriate for the Palace of Westminster.'[259]

Beyond his committee work, Milnes appears to have had a specific influence on the 'Christian-oriented' poetry of Robert Browning, whom he had first met one year earlier. Bullen places Milnes alongside Anna Jameson as the two friends of Browning who 'stand out as being eminently well informed about both ancient and modern art'.[260] Bullen rates it likely that Browning was inspired by informal conversations with Milnes to develop a keen interest in religious art, to make related trips to Italy, and eventually publish such well-known religiously-focussed poems as 'Pictor Ignotus' and 'The Bishop Orders His Tomb'.

Carlyle's First Visit to Fryston

In April 1841, Milnes travelled up to Fryston for the Easter period in the company of Thomas Carlyle. Kaplan remarks that, although now well-established and secure in his chosen profession, Carlyle was nonetheless feeling 'the anxiety of a writer whose freedom to write whatever he wanted was as much a burden as an opportunity'.[261] Carlyle and his wife Jane's 'nerves and tempers clashed', and Carlyle's typical way of dealing with this was to occasionally leave London for another destination. Milnes's invitation provided Carlyle with a ready-made excuse to get out of the house by visiting Fryston en route to his family home in Annandale.[262]

The two men travelled to the West Riding on 5 April on the newly-constructed railway line. They shared a carriage with Sir Robert Peel's son, who was making his way to Tamworth. Carlyle informed Jane (by letter dated 5 April) that he and Milnes 'got on beautifully', Milnes having spent most of the journey reading the *Oxford Tracts* or arguing and talking 'in the smartest manner', while Carlyle quietly smoked cigars and appreciated the passing countryside.[263] They made their way from Pontefract station by carriage but, as Carlyle explained in another letter to Jane (dated 7 April):

> Richard made me dismount some two miles of our appointed goal, and walk homewards by a smarter way through woods, over knolls, &c. Walking was not my forte; however I persevered and did well enough. Over rough-looking places, some of them, we got at last to the Fryston mansion, a large irregular pile of various ages, rising up above ragged old woods in a rough large park, also all sprinkled with trees, grazed by sheep and horses, a park chiefly beautiful because it did not set up for beauty. Ancient-looking female figures were beautiful through the windows as we drew nigh. Mrs. Milnes, a tall ancient woman, apparently of weak health, of motherly kind heart, of old-fashioned stately politeness – a prepossessing woman – welcomed me at the door of the drawing-room 'in the silence of the stately hall.'[264]

The three maiden aunts who had gathered alongside Mrs Milnes 'all laid themselves out to be agreeable to their opinionated and insomniac guest'. Robert Pemberton Milnes impressed Carlyle with regular flashes of wit and intelligence, but spent long periods alone, smoking and reading in the library. Harriette Galway and her husband joined the party for a couple of days. The former impressed Carlyle with her obvious intelligence, physical beauty and sense of fun. She sang and played in Carlyle's honour and talked with him enthusiastically about German and Italian literature. Lord Galway, whom Carlyle described as 'a furious everlasting hunter of foxes, but good to all other things and men', undoubtedly elicited a more ambivalent reaction.[265]

Carlyle was clearly unimpressed by the trappings and lifestyle of the 'idle wealth' he had encountered. For the duration of his visit, a valet watched over him 'like a silent-assiduous minister', attending his every need. He was consigned to a massive bedroom with four enormous windows, and a bed of eight-feet wide requiring a ladder to climb into it, thus making it, as he said in a letter to Jane, 'the most absurd place I have lived in'.[266] He subsequently elaborated in yet another letter to his wife how:

> I never lived before in such an element of 'much ado about *almost* Nothing'; life occupied altogether in getting itself lived; troops of flunkeys bustling and becking at all times, the meat-jack creaking and playing all day, and I think all night, for I used to hear it very early under my room; and such champagning, claretting, and witty conversationing. *Ach Gott!* I would sooner be a ditcher than spend *all* my days so. However, we got rather tolerably through it for these ten days, and I really think I can report a favourable change in my inner man in spite of every drawback. I have not yet made out one good sleep.[267]

Carlyle clearly objected to the degree to which Milnes appeared intent on showing him off to local dignitaries and insisted on him attending church on Easter Sunday. Otherwise, they got on famously.[268] Carlyle confessed in yet another letter to Jane that, 'I like Richard better and better – a most good-humoured, kind and cheery-hearted fellow, with plenty of savoir-faire in him too.' Milnes's transparent sense of mischief was something the notoriously spikey philosopher clearly found endearing:

> Richard had to exert himself; but he is really dexterous the villain. He pricks into you with questions, with remarks, with all kinds of fly-tackle to make you bite; does generally try to get you into some sort of speech. And then his good humour is extreme; you look in his face and forgive him all his tricks.[269]

One month later, Carlyle wrote to Emerson (on 8 May 1841), explaining how the Fryston visit had enabled him to shake off a lingering bout of influenza and generally had a calming effect. The ten days he spent riding and 'sauntering' across the Yorkshire countryside, the solitude he enjoyed and the 'the great Silence of the Earth' proved 'balm to this weary, sick heart'. Milnes was now incapable of doing wrong. It was, according to Carlyle, the 'mild, cordial, though something dilettante nature of the man' that distinguished his host from all those lesser individuals.[270]

One Tract More

Carlyle's reference to Milnes's reading matter on the journey north to Fryston is worthy of further comment. In 1841, Milnes entered the controversy surrounding the publication of *Tract 90*, a pamphlet written by the theologian John Henry Newman, which maintained that the *Thirty-Nine Articles* underpinning the doctrines and principles of the Church of England were not contrary to the teachings of Catholicism.[271] Newman's was the latest and most contentious of a series *Tracts for the Times* written by members of the Anglo-Catholic Oxford Movement. The opprobrium heaped on Newman by his Bishop and the elders of the university Houses deterred him from any further writing. Milnes had been following the tracts with sympathetic eyes, and it was he who, somewhat audaciously, took it upon himself to add to the debate.[272] The title he chose for his own provocative pamphlet was *One Tract More, Or, the System.*[273]

In purporting to bring a detached and unbiased perspective to the table, Milnes produced a considered piece of work that was 'remarkable for its lucidity as well as for its entire lack of prejudice in any direction'.[274] It is likely that Milnes's character was more receptive than most to the ritualistic and aesthetic values of Catholicism. He wrote provocatively in support of Papal Infallibility and was critical of the 'No-Popery' sentiment now endemic in British society. Despite the fact that it was widely lauded as a work of remarkable insight and intellectual rigour, the political fallout of Milnes's pamphlet was considerable:

> *One Tract More* forms the best single instance of Monckton Milnes' real capacity for thought and extreme adroitness of mind. But it did him no good with his dour Dissenting constituents. Milnes was the least calculating of men. He had just written and published *One Tract More* as a protest against injustice and without thinking of the consequences to his political career.[275]

Thackeray Visits Fryston

The general election of 1841 was already in full sway when Milnes was called to York on grand jury service. He had arranged for Thackeray to visit him while the latter was briefly present in the north of England, having travelled over from Paris. Thackeray deliberately prolonged his stay to enable him to travel down, in mid-July, from York to Fryston, by which time Milnes had not only concluded his jury service but also been re-elected as MP for Pontefract.

Pope-Hennessy characterises the Thackeray of this era as 'still no more than a clever journalist with a small but distinct reputation, a tall round-faced personage with a ridiculous little nose'.[276] He arrived at Fryston Hall in the company of a friend – the young lawyer, Frederick Pollock:

> Getting out in the park they strolled up between the trees in the July afternoon, towards the square, white house. As they neared it, they saw two figures standing outside the front door in the sunshine – their friend Richard Milnes and his spare, elderly father, who was wearing a dressing-gown and smoking a cigar. Milnes welcomed his guests by handing a cigar to each of them. 'You may smoke anywhere in this house,' he said, 'in your bedrooms if you please; and Mrs. Milnes does not mind it in her drawing-room. Only you must not smoke in Richard's room, for he doesn't like it.' Here we can catch an echo of that simplicity and charming hospitality which

> made Mr. [Pemberton] Milnes' country neighbours love him. There had never been any nonsense about him, and his house reflected his practical temperament. 'Fryston,' said Thackeray, as he left a week later, 'combines the freedom of the tavern with the elegance of the château.'[277]

President of the Heaven and Hell Amalgamation Society

Milnes geared up with trepidation for the new parliament, which he fully expected to be 'full of stupid violence and blind party spirit'.[278] This sense of foreboding proved well justified. Contrary to personal expectations, Peel overlooked him for a place in the cabinet. 'He was destined thus early in his political career to learn the price, as he had already experienced the advantages, of that political independence of which he was proud.'[279] According to Wemyss Reid:

> Years afterwards Carlyle and Milnes were talking at the Grange, the home of Lord and Lady Ashburton, of the Administration just formed by Sir Robert Peel, and Milnes was evincing some disappointment at the fact that he had not been offered a post in it. 'No, no,' said Carlyle, 'Peel knows what he is about; there is only one post fit for you, and that is the office of perpetual president of the Heaven and Hell Amalgamation Society.'[280]

Palm Leaves

A lasting disillusionment with politics had firmly set in by now. Milnes campaigned in 1842 for the establishment of a copyright act for the protection of authors. In the late summer of 1842 and well into 1843, he travelled to Constantinople and Cairo. One lasting legacy of this journey was a book of verse, *Palm Leaves*, eventually published in 1844,[281] which used poetry in documentation of his travels in order to distinguish it from the existing travelogues of the East, which Milnes regarded as already far too numerous.[282] Inevitably, Milnes courted controversy by underscoring, not just the poetry itself, but also the keynoting preface with his boldly 'unconventional' views of the Muslim world:

> Westernisation had produced little but 'unmixed evil' in the East. We had taught the Moslems to drink and had ruined

> their natural taste in dress. Eastern women seemed to be in as good a position of those of the West (except for their lack of education), and the harem was a harmless convention confined to the richest class. Our ideas of 'Eastern domesticity,' he declared, were taken from the ballet and so coloured by ferocity and vice that 'what is really commonplace becomes paradoxical.' The 'Frankish' attitude to Mohammedanism he found deplorable. Just as years ago in Rome he had been sincerely receptive to Roman Catholicism, so he was now profoundly impressed by the teaching of Mahomet.[283]

Pope-Hennessy regards this as further evidence of Milnes's lack of prejudice or preconception, and of his readiness to try and sympathise with, or at least try to understand, every new experience or phenomenon that might have crossed his path.

Help comes in many forms, and Milnes was always prepared to show a willing pair of ready and sympathetic hands. Wemyss Reid points out that, at this point in time, 'Appeals of every kind were [...] constantly pouring in on Milnes, and his purse – which was not at this period of his life, if, indeed, it ever was, a heavy one.'[284] In the two-year period from 1844 to 1845, Milnes responded in ready fashion to three such petitions for assistance, all of which added lustre to his reputation.

Sending To Coventry

During 1844, Milnes had received letters from his close and trusted friend Anne Procter (wife of the poet, 'Barry Cornwall', and literary patron), in which references were made to a promising English poet by the name of Coventry Patmore. Milnes first cast eyes on the latter at a dinner thrown by Mrs Procter, and allegedly inquired: 'And who is your lean young friend with the frayed coat-cuffs?'[285] Procter is said to have admonished Milnes by insisting that he would never have spoken in such manner had he realised how 'clever' and 'unfortunate' the object of his condescension was.[286] Though raised in a comfortable and literary middle-class home, and already boasting a well-received first book of poetry,[287] Patmore was nonetheless struggling to make a living.

Milnes left Mrs Procter's with copies of Patmore's letters tucked inside his coat. A mere one day later he wrote to Mrs Procter, not only apologising for his 'heartless flippancy', but offering to nominate the young man to the post of supernumerary assistant in the Department of the Printed Books in the British Museum. 'His book is the work of a true poet,' Milnes enthused, 'and we must see that he never lacks butter for his bread.'[288] Patmore was duly employed in this post in November 1846, a position he maintained until 1865: 'The official salary thus secured was not wealth, and hardly comfort, but it was a competence, and on the strength of it Patmore proposed to Emily Andrews, and was accepted.'[289]

Milnes also lent him money and enlisted his help in the preparation and arrangement of *The Life and Letters of Keats*.[290] With his social position thus stabilised, Patmore set about working on *The Angel in the House*, the first of numerous critically lauded and best-selling volumes.[291] His second volume of poems, *Tamerton Church Tower* was dedicated to Milnes, who also became godfather to the poet's elder son, who was given the name Milnes Patmore.[292]

The Song of the Shirt

Born in London in 1798, the humourist and poet Thomas Hood was initially an apprentice engraver but turned because of ill-health to a life of writing.[293] For a six-year period from 1815 to 1821, he served as a journalist in Dundee. When, in 1821, the editor of the *London Magazine* was killed in a duel, ownership of the publication fell fortuitously into the hands of a group of Hood's friends, who duly installed him as sub-editor.[294] This proved a timely springboard into a literary society that allowed him to rub shoulders with such renowned essayists as Thomas De Quincey and Charles Lamb, and with poets of the calibre of Samuel Taylor Coleridge. With growing confidence, he became a regular contributor to the *Athenaeum* and edited such publications as *The Gem* (in which he included several of Tennyson's early poems) and *New Monthly Magazine*, while finding time to write a novel, *Tylney Hall*.[295]

By the early 1840s, however, Hood's physical health went into sharp decline. It is ironic that his best-known and most celebrated work (including 'The Song of the Shirt', a poem which he published anonymously in the Christmas 1843 edition of *Punch*) was published at the time. The poem constitutes a searing critique of the 'exploitation of the cheap labour of seamstresses'.[296] Its influence and renown spread rapidly when it was reprinted in *The Times* and subsequently appeared in newspapers as far afield as France, Germany, Italy and Russia. This and related poems, such as 'The Song of the Labourer', stimulated the Victorian Social Conscience.[297] As Milnes proclaimed:

> He started a magazine in his own name, for which he secured the assistance of many literary men of reputation and authority, but which was mainly sustained by his own intellectual activity. From a sick-bed, from which he never rose, he conducted this work with surprising energy, and there composed those poems, too few in number, but immortal in the English language, such as the 'Song of the Shirt,' the 'Bridge of Sighs,' and the 'Song of the Laborer', which seized the deep human interests of the time, and transported them from the ground of social philosophy into the loftier domain of the imagination. They are no clamorous expressions of anger at the discrepancies and contrasts of humanity, but plain, solemn pictures of conditions of life, which neither the politician nor the moralist can deny to exist, and which they are imperatively called upon to remedy.[298]

It was predictable that Milnes should not only have befriended this witty and talented 'champion of the people', but also to have rallied to his support as he became increasingly prone to illness and the related conditions of poverty. The assistance Milnes provided surpassed the mere pecuniary:

> Money was provided when required, but Hood's independence of spirit was carefully respected [...] and Milnes found that the distressed poet preferred to receive assistance in the shape of gratuitous literary work for his magazine rather than in money.[299]

In addition to canvassing widely among his friends and literary associates for them to donate contributions to *Hood's Magazine*, Milnes applied himself to sustaining Hood's personal morale and ensuring that his family were not short on creature comforts.[300] In the wake of Hood's eventual death, on 3 May 1845, Milnes not only instigated arrangements for the poet to be buried in the prestigious

Kensal-Green Cemetery, but also helped raise subscriptions to cover the funeral costs and 'place Mrs Hood in comfort for the rest of her days'.[301] Following a public campaign to raise funds for a commemorative plaque installed in Hood's honour, it was Milnes who, fittingly, did the unveiling.[302]

A Pension for Tennyson

It became apparent sometime in 1845 that Milnes's old friend Alfred Tennyson had incurred financial difficulties arising from the failure of a 'wood-carving speculation' in which he had ill-advisedly become involved.[303] Carlyle is said to have been most active in urging Milnes to ask the Prime Minister, Sir Robert Peel, to secure a pension of £200 to enable Tennyson to continue fulfilling his poetic vocation. Milnes was initially quite hesitant. 'What will my constituents say if I do get the pension for Tennyson?' he protested to Carlyle. 'They know nothing about him or his poetry, and they will probably think he is some poor relation of my own, and that the whole affair is a job.'[304] Carlyle's reply was emphatic: 'Richard Milnes,' he proclaimed, 'on the Day of Judgment, when the Lord asks you why you didn't get that pension for Alfred Tennyson, it will not do to lay the blame on your constituents; it is you that will be damned.'[305]

It appears that it was Henry Hallam who had first written to Peel to lobby in Tennyson's interests. Hallam also suggested, however, that the Prime Minister might turn to Milnes for an assessment of Tennyson's merits. Peel acted on Hallam's advice but the outcome was slightly complicated due to the fact that:

> At the same moment Peel was approached for a similar stipend for the old Irish dramatist and actor James Sheridan Knowles. Knowing nothing of the work of either writer, he turned for advice to Milnes, who sent him (or, in another version of the story, read him aloud) Ulysses and Locksley Hall, telling Peel that if the pension was to be awarded as a charitable gift and for services rendered, it should go to Sheridan Knowles; if 'in the interests of English literature and of the English nation' it should be given to Alfred Tennyson. Peel gave the pension to Tennyson, who was grateful but reluctant.[306]

By Punishment of Death

In this final section, we return to the political issue of primary contemporary concern to Monckton Milnes and Thackeray – that of capital punishment. In particular, we trace the evolution of Milnes's attitude to public executions, as reflected in his parliamentary interventions, and explore the intriguing likelihood that his views were profoundly influential on relevant themes and views explored in Thackeray's best-known works.

On 1 July 1845 (almost five years to the day since he witnessed the Newgate execution), Milnes rose in the House of Commons 'to call the attention of the House to the evils attendant on the present mode of conducting the public execution of criminals'. Though personally opposed to the need to publicise executions, Milnes advocated a compromise approach (a more civilised and humane basis) on which to achieve the minimum publicity required:

> The plan he was prepared to recommend was, that the Judge who passed sentence on the prisoner should also be authorized to name the place (within the walls of the prison) of his execution. He proposed that the execution should take place in the presence of the authorities, and also that the reporters of the public press should be admitted. The press afforded the true publicity, and it was right, therefore, that the reporters should be admitted. Public executions were defended on the ground that they improved the morals of the people. This could hardly be the case, when they reflected that those who attended executions were the dissolute and the desperate, and they were looked at as a sort of gladiatorial exhibition, and were visited as a kind of barbarous diversion.[307]

Milnes had not yet completed his speech when it became apparent that there were only thirty-two members present and the House was therefore adjourned. Milnes did not subsequently return to the topic; yet, as Thomas points out:

> [Milnes's] speech was certainly, as he later described it, a 'pioneer' attempt in the sense of being an early effort to break with long-established custom and to promote what eventually came to be seen by most Victorians as a preferable way of handling the punishment of death.[308]

It was not until 7 May 1868 (while in the process of lending his support for the 'Capital Punishment Within Prisons Bill') that Milnes (who accompanied Dickens to another public hanging on 13 November 1868) could express 'a personal satisfaction that private executions were likely to become law, because he had kept the subject of the evil consequences of public executions before the House of Commons on several occasions'.[309]

Thomas maintains that Milnes's parliamentary intervention of 1845 had a second major impact.[310] He notes that, during the 1840s, Thackeray's view on public hangings was gradually transformed from a position that they be totally abolished to a preference that they 'only' be conducted in private. Thus, whilst the sentiments expressed by Thackeray in such early 1840s publications as *Miss Tickletoby's Lectures on English History*,[311] and *The Irish Sketch Book*[312] are consistent with those expressed in 'Going to See a Man Hanged', his depiction of the demise of Joseph Sedley in the final chapter of the late-1840s novel, *Vanity Fair*, indicates a changed preference for simply removing executions from public view.

Thomas refutes the popular notion that Thackeray's change of heart was encouraged by the standpoint adopted by Charles Dickens in a series of letters to *The Times*. He maintains that, given the intense rivalry between Thackeray and Dickens, it is highly unlikely that the former would have been influenced in this way. According to Thomas, it is more likely that Thackeray's opinion was swayed by that of his 'friend and companion at that earlier event', Richard Monckton Milnes:

> [All] writers on the subject of Thackeray and capital punishment have overlooked an important shift in Milnes's position on this topic and the possible relevance of this shift to Thackeray's opinion [...] [L]ike Milnes, Thackeray did indeed come to favor removing capital punishment from public view and that his change of position in this regard can be discerned from the evidence of his own writings, including his treatment of the demise of Jos Sedley [...] published more than a year before Dickens's letters to the *Times*.[313]

Chapter Seven
'Dicky' and 'Dizzy'

Friends or Foes?

In referring to the famous occasion of 7 December 1837, when Benjamin Disraeli made his disastrous maiden speech in parliament, Milnes's son, Robert, maintained that, contrary to popular belief, his father had been extremely sympathetic towards Disraeli, in a manner befitting of the close friendship already existing between them:

> And the intimacy continued over years, with possibly a slight tinge of jealousy on each side – though Disraeli paid many visits to Fryston and Bawtry, the two Milnes houses in Yorkshire, and developed a special cult for his friend's father, whom he apparently regarded as the ideal country squire. Later on a breach occurred which has never been completely explained.[314]

In striving to explain this 'breach', Robert explored the possibility that 'Disraeli's attachment to George Smythe' (a controversially divisive character who, as we shall see, was appointed to the cabinet in preference to Milnes) 'might be taken to account for a quarrel'. He also dwelled on other possible reasons: that Disraeli's amusing, 'certainly not ill-natured, though a shade patronising' portrait of 'Vavasour', in his acclaimed *Tancred* novel, caused offence to Milnes, who is widely held to have been the prototype of this character; or that Milnes's critiques of *Tancred* and other novels by Disraeli were not always replete with 'unmixed admiration'.[315] Robert was left with the abiding memory that, 'When they met, as I once or twice remember their doing, their relations were apparently quite friendly, though in no way cordial.'[316]

This chapter explores in more detail the political and artistic differences separating the two men, and examines the source of friction between Milnes and his detested adversary (but friend of Disraeli) George Smythe, a theme continued in Chapter 8. The discussion begins with a preparatory explanation of the differing ideological perspectives subscribed to by Disraeli and Milnes, and of how Milnes played a small, though significant part in promoting the future Prime Minister's rise to historical prominence.

Milnes and Victorian Paternalism

It was a staunch commitment to so-called paternalistic ideals that underpinned Milnes's political and poetic orientations during the early 1840s.

> The phrase, 'property has its duties as well as its rights,' became in the 1840s the hallmark of the paternalist. No other phrase said so much about paternalism's main aims and principal methods. It is a phrase that emphasizes 'duties' rather than 'rights.' There is no doubt that paternalists believed in their own rights whether as titled nobility, holders of office, or landlords, but they based those rights on the usefulness of their station and rank and on the duties they performed.[317]

As Roberts points out, 'Paternalism as a literary and political force reached its apogee in the year 1844.'[318] At this time, Milnes stood shoulder to shoulder with fellow politicians and poets (and, generally speaking, Cambridge graduates) such as Alexander Baillie-Cochrane, Lord John Manners and, indeed, George Smythe, who – egged on by *The Spectator* magazine – were in favour of such benevolent public policies as reforming the poor laws, encouraging state education, and limiting the working day in factories and mines to a ten-hour maximum.

> Early in the decade that small but hopeful group spoke out spiritedly on behalf of the poor in workhouses and children and women in factories and mines. They vied with each other in support of measures to encourage allotments, provide more schools, and return poor-law management to the parishes. They also spoke in defence of that Corn Law that protected the landowners, themselves the protectors of the poor. Until 1846 [they all] voted to sustain the Corn Law.[319]

The crowning achievement of 'the paternalists' arrived with the passage of Lord Ashley's amendment to the Factory Bill in March 1844, which required a ten-hour working day. Monckton Milnes subsequently rejoiced that he 'saw banded together on that occasion a large body of men who were more regardful of the interests of the people than of any political consequences'.[320] Milnes had certainly been resolute in his stance, defending the Corn Laws, and urging the landowners to treat their labourers as fellow Christians and brothers; to not only provide them with employment but to minister to their needs 'in sickness and calamity'.[321] Indeed, it is fair to say that:

> In all public philanthropic activities Milnes was from now on prominent. By 1844 he was taking a leading place on the platform of London meetings for the amelioration of the working-class conditions; and at this epoch he introduced the first of his bills to establish juvenile reformatories and try to stem at its source the flood of vice and crime. His reformatory schemes, which later became law, were at this time discussed by most people as the vagaries of an idealist and a poet. There was little general support for the belief of Milnes and Lord Ashley that environment was in itself a cause of crime.[322]

Milnes's family origins and upbringing had alerted him to the poor conditions endured by factory and country labourers. The sympathy he demonstrated by voting in support of the Factory and Education Bills ran contrary to the hard-faced attitudes of his constituents. Not that this was any deterrent:

> Each view from the windows of Fryston Hall reminded him of his responsibilities: the plumes of factory smoke smudging the horizon, the dour mining villages a few miles from the gates of the park, the coal-barges passing slowly, slowly on the oily waters of the River Aire, the smutty cypresses in the garden and the rhododendron shrubberies dark with dust. His goodness of heart, hitherto confined within the wide circle of his friends, now ranged out in a genuine concern for the English poor.[323]

Roberts maintains that a similar 'chivalry and romanticism' pervaded Milnes's poetry of this period, citing the poem 'Alms-

Giving', from *Poetry for the People and Other Poems*,[324] 'which calls for the poor to be patient in their allotted place and chastises the rich for their indifference'.[325] Critics of Milnes's poetry (including his own son) have nonetheless applauded its highly lyrical and melodic quality, while bemoaning its lack of underlying 'fire' and passion.[326] In speaking of *Poems, Legendary and Historical*,[327] Walker acknowledges that Milnes is capable of writing extremely effective and memorable poetry, epitomised by the 'beautiful and pathetic *Strangers Yet*'.[328]

Doubt has been cast, however, on Milnes's capacity to engage with proletarian sensibilities:

> Notwithstanding that he has written 'Poetry for the People,' neither in the work in question nor in any other, has he given evidence of a genius calculated for popular appeals [...] For Mr. Milnes is an aristocrat in literature and modes of thought; though we are far from meaning to insinuate that he merely 'writes like a gentleman;' his mind and heart are too strong in the 'humanities.' [...] He thinks the truth out boldly, and feels generously the use of speaking it; but the medium of expression between him and the public, is somewhat conventionally philosophical in its character, and too fine and recondite in its peculiarities, to be appreciated by the people popularly so called.[329]

Peacock is altogether more complimentary on the subject of *Palm Leaves*,[330] Milnes's memorial of Eastern travel (first mentioned in Chapter 4),[331] which is said to contain 'some of the highest poetry Milnes ever wrote'.[332] Crewe goes further in doubting whether 'any English poet has obtained a closer perception of the Near East, or of the spirit by which the followers of the Prophet live and move'.[333] He may be correct in asserting that his father's interests were far too diverse and unfocussed to allow him to accomplish greatness in any one particular cultural or political sphere.[334]

'Young England'

An integral place in this grouping was occupied by a cohort referring to itself as 'Young England'. Its prime movers were the 'rather Byronic' George Smythe and Lord John Manners, although it was Benjamin Disraeli who quickly emerged as its parliamentary spokesman and figurehead. The resonance between the credo of Young England and of the wider paternalist doctrine is evident in the fact that:

> Young England looked to the past for solutions to current problems. Its adherents concerned themselves with the welfare of the common people, looking to the paternalism of landlord and church to restore the well-being of the rural population.[335]

Milnes is often credited with having coined the term 'Young England' – as a shorthand way of likening his politics to those of similarly titled European movements and idealists emerging from the French Revolution of 1830.[336] It is therefore ironic that Milnes was never actually inclined (or, indeed, allowed) to be anything more than peripheral to the movement. This marginalisation was due primarily to mutual feelings of animosity between himself and George Smythe. Milnes also differed substantially from prominent Young Englanders on specific issues – e.g. in his denunciation of Manners for maintaining that education should be the sole responsibility of the Church of England, and not the business of the state.[337]

According to Weeks Jr, the political credo of Young England is encapsulated in the three major political novels for which Benjamin Disraeli is most renowned.[338] More specifically:

> Disraeli considered that *Coningsby*, *Sybil* and *Tancred* formed a trilogy because they treated the same subject, 'The origin and character of our political parties, their influence on the condition of the people of this country, some picture of the moral and physical condition of that people, and some intimation of the means by which it might be elevated and improved, were the themes which had long engaged my mediation.' The charge proved too vast for one volume, so *Coningsby* addressed political parties, *Sybil*, the condition of the people, and *Tancred* the duties of the church.[339]

The first to appear was *Coningsby* – which Millar upholds as the 'manifesto' of Young England.[340] Milnes's review of this book was one of the articles he 'donated' to *Hood's Magazine* – in this case, the June 1844 edition. Milnes's review was noticeably lukewarm in comparison with the effusive praise bestowed by most fellow critics.

Coningsby was 'the sensation of the year', causing everyone from famous politicians to sophisticated society women to fight over the circulating copies.[341] Against this, 'The characters were not created but copied straight from life; they were essentially ephemeral, and the book seemed to him, as it seems to posterity, artificial, smart and lacking in real quality.'[342]

Milnes then endeavoured to speak to Disraeli directly, only to find him not at home. Disraeli responded by writing in diplomatic manner to Milnes (in a letter dated 2 June 1844), saying that, had he been at home, he would have thanked the latter for having produced:

> one of those criticisms which honour alike the critic and the criticised, and we could have discussed together the points of controversy, assisted by Mrs Disraeli, who has several puissant arguments for you in store, though she, as well as myself, appreciates comments that at the same time indicate the thoughtful mind, the cultivated taste, and the refined pen.[343]

It was against this background that Disraeli and his wife, Mary Anne, were invited to visit Fryston – not by Milnes, but by his father, for whom Disraeli shared a mutual admiration (and common desire to reap fun at Milnes's expense). Disraeli had just delivered a famous speech, alongside Young England cohorts Smythe and Manners, at a meeting of the young artisans of the Manchester Athenaeum. On leaving Manchester, he and Mary Anne visited Lord Francis Egerton at Worsley Hall and W.B. Ferrand MP at Bingley in the West Riding. He was in the process of writing *Sybil*, central to which were the conditions of the working class in manufacturing centres. It has been speculated that the visit to Fryston provided source material, not only for this novel, but also for Disraeli's use of Milnes's character of Vavasour, who featured in *Tancred* in 1847.[344]

Disraeli's Visit to Fryston

The Disraelis arrived at Fryston Hall on 18 October and stayed for several days. By this time, they had been married for five years. At 52 years old, Mary Anne was twelve years her husband's senior. According to Pope-Hennessy, this age discrepancy was quite marked, being emphasised above all by Mrs Disraeli's girlish manner and 'simpering behaviour'.[345] The outward appearances of their hosts were similarly contrasting:

> Mr Pemberton Milnes, at the age of sixty, still retained the good looks of his earlier years, but Mrs Milnes, the pretty Miss Monckton of former days, about whom the beaux of her youth had made verses and invented charades, was now much changed by failing health.[346]

Mrs Milnes's poor physical condition was the main reason she now depended on her son to help receive guests at Fryston 'with a charm and an efficiency which collected about him all the remarkable men of his day'.[347]

Some eighteen to twenty other guests came and went while the Disraelis were visiting Fryston. One of these was Lady Elizabeth Spencer-Stanhope, a daughter of Mr George Coke of Holkham, the first Earl of Leicester. Earlier generations of Lady Elizabeth's family had visited Fryston Hall as long ago as 1807, and the current Mrs Milnes was well-known to the current generation due to the fact that she 'good-naturedly regaled them' with songs in the schoolroom whenever she visited Cannon Hall.[348] Though unimpressed both by the fact that the guests were required to stay up until too late and that the bedrooms were far too hot, Lady Elizabeth referred to the lavish food as 'sumptuous', and was heartily amused by a game of charades in which Milnes 'distinguished himself' in the role of Mrs Gamp. The Disraelis also met with her approval, as she subsequently reported to her husband:

> I sat by him at dinner (at least between him and Mrs Milnes) and was really charmed, not with any brilliancy of conversation but with his singularity and good nature which he exerted in dressing truffles for me. His manner is half foreign. I had not been introduced to him when, in the middle of dinner, a very soft voice said 'Does Lady Elizabeth drink Champagne?' He asked if you were not Minister at some foreign Court, and won my heart by the real regret he expressed at not meeting you here [...] Mrs D'Izzy was in a lace dress, looped up on each side, over pink satin, and a wreath on her head, though I should think near fifty. However, she is very amusing and off-hand, saying everything that comes uppermost and unfeignedly devoted to her D'Izzy.[349]

The second eyewitness of the occasion was 'young Gathorne Hardy' (an unknown barrister at the time, who would later become Lord Cranbrook), who received a 'very kind welcome' from the Milnes family and derived 'much pleasure' from the evening's entertainment. He, too, was generally impressed by Disraeli, albeit (if the following extract from his diary is anything to go by) less so than Lady Elizabeth:

> Disraeli's conversation is far from striking, and there is too much striving to be epigrammatic, but he gives, or rather confirms, the idea I had from his writings that he is a clever man. He seems too vain and full of self-esteem to talk freely lest he should lose ground, but his remarks, on men especially, seem to me equally clever and just, though perhaps my agreement with them may lead me to think more highly of them than I should.[350]

'Disraeli's Disciple', Milnes's Nemesis

If Millar is to be believed, *Coningsby* might never have seen the light of day but for the insistence of Disraeli's close friend and political associate George Smythe,[351] who 'prevailed' on Disraeli to 'write a polemical work of fiction, specifically on the Swiftian model of *roman á clef* [and who also] served as heroic model and provided factual details from his own life for the hero's biography'.[352] The intensely charismatic and socially captivating Smythe was the oldest son of one of Disraeli's closest friends, Lord Strangford. He cut a dashingly romantic and frequently rebellious figure in the image of his hero, Lord Byron:

> George Smythe's life was as full of paradox as his death. His most serious mistake was to outlive his brilliant youth. He had the other credentials for a romantic hero: sensual good looks, impossibly high ideals, and an abundance of passion [...] He thrived on flouting convention. His love affairs were innumerable, turbulent, and scandalous. He fought duels, or at least issued challenges to them. He was an inspired speaker whose wit and passion drew applause from unsophisticated audiences and respect from his peers. He was a political writer, displaying deep feeling in his poems and political acumen in his prose. But he did not die young enough, or dramatically

enough, to keep the public sympathy of his times. Like Keats he died the most romantic death of all – of consumption – but it took most of his life, too long to be considered romantic.[353]

The secret of *Coningsby's* success was that it 'caustically described a moribund political establishment which had forgotten it ever had ideals, let alone how to put them into practice'.[354] The book's eponymous hero, Harry Coningsby, forsakes a comfortably predictable political career in which he need only toe the party line in favour of the more highly principled role of independent Member of Parliament who might breathe new life into the moribund Conservatives. The heroic Coningsby is nothing short of 'a political Galahad shining in the dust and heat of a very murky arena, a fictional incarnation widely identified with its original'.[355]

The philosophical and politically prescriptive tenets that *Coningsby* espoused, and which soon provided the bedrock of the Young England movement, were seen as implicitly critical of and embarrassing for the Tory establishment, epitomised by the Prime Minister, Robert Peel. In 1846, Peel offered Smythe the post of Under-Secretary for Foreign Affairs, conceiving that, once in the party fold, his oppositional attitude would be blunted. This came as a huge and unpleasant bombshell to Milnes, who not only coveted the post but felt entitled to it, and who also harboured an intense mutual antagonism towards George Smythe.[356] Whilst Milnes regarded his rival as a reckless, unprincipled and irresponsible cad, Smythe saw Milnes as a vain and somewhat ridiculous dilettante. According to Smythe's biographer:

> [Smythe's] dislike of Milnes [...] led to occasional spats, the antipathy of a quick, witty intelligence towards a slower, humourless mind. When Hope's speaking did not improve, Milnes, 'with his queer face of solemn deprecation & conceit,' abruptly asked GSS, 'Why don't you interfere to prevent his speaking Smythe?' GSS could not resist: 'Why! I don't interfere to prevent you speaking Milnes!' was the retort, & even Milnes impudence was floored.[357]

Smythe was incommunicado in Europe when Peel first submitted his written offer of the post to him. Peel was so frustrated by the absence of an immediate reply that he was on the point of approaching an alternative candidate. It was during this hiatus that Milnes asked Gladstone to put a word in on his behalf, but the intervention made no difference: 'Gladstone did approach Peel, but it resulted only in Milnes's complete mortification.'[358] Smythe duly accepted Peel's offer before it was too late, prompting Milnes to angrily sound off to Gladstone, in a letter dated 19 January 1846:

> MY DEAR GLADSTONE, – When I wrote to you, I was not aware that Mr. Smythe had obtained the Under-Secretaryship, though I heard it was probable he might do this. Under the circumstances, you have done all for me I could desire [...] I am not ashamed to confess myself thoroughly disappointed. I am forced to look to new objects of thought, to new subjects of observation. No ingenuity could have made the blow more provoking from the hands of the man to whom I have shown the most public respect, through those of the one for whom I entertain the most private dislike. But in morals, as in physics, if well used, the bitter braces. Your kindness and good-will I shall never forget.[359]

This was not the only blow delivered by Smythe to Milnes's prestige and reputation. Even worse was to come some three years later, but not before the ill-feeling already fomenting between Milnes and Disraeli had dramatically resurfaced.

'He was Everywhere, and at Everything'

As Blake points out, '*Tancred* [published in March 1847] contained *en passant* an amusing caricature of Milnes, who, according to Disraeli, had complained bitterly at not figuring in either *Coningsby* or *Sybil*. If this is true, he was ill advised for the portrait of Mr Vavasour in *Tancred* was not calculated to assuage his feelings.'[360]

Vavasour is depicted as someone habitually engaged in all the dinner parties and soirées to be held in central London. He makes his debut in *Tancred* at one such dinner party, hosted by Sidonia, the Jewish banker, at which Coningsby is also present. That Disraeli is clearly basing the character of Vavasour on Milnes is evident from the following description:

> Mr. Vavasour was a social favorite; a poet and a real poet, and a troubadour, as well as a Member of Parliament; travelled, sweet-tempered, and good-hearted; amusing and clever. With catholic sympathies and an eclectic turn of mind, Mr. Vavasour saw something good in everybody and everything, which is certainly amiable, and perhaps just, but disqualifies a man in some degree for the business of life, which requires for its conduct a certain degree of prejudice. Mr. Vavasour's breakfasts were renowned. Whatever your creed, class, or country – one might also add your character – you were a welcome guest at his matutinal meal, provided you were celebrated [...] Vavasour moved amid the strife, sympathizing with everyone; and perhaps, after all, the philanthropy which was his boast was not untinged by a dash of humor, of which rare and charming quality he possessed no inconsiderable portion. Vavasour liked to know everybody who was known, and to see everything which ought to be seen. His life was a gyration of energetic curiosity; an insatiable whirl of social celebrity [...] He was everywhere, and at everything; he had gone down in a diving-bell and gone up in a balloon. As for his acquaintances, he was welcomed in every land; his universal sympathies seemed omnipotent.[361]

Blake further explains that *Tancred* contains numerous other 'subtle and malicious' references of a comedic and unflattering nature to Milnes's character.[362] Milnes took immediate revenge by having a review of *Tancred* accepted for publication in the July 1847 edition of *The Edinburgh Review*.[363] Pope-Hennessy maintains that Milnes's analysis was 'so able and so ruthless' as to account for Disraeli's abiding dislike of his critic.[364] Blake likewise contends that:

> The review is worth pausing over. The fact that it was prompted by personal irritation does not necessarily invalidate its conclusions. In fact, the seventeen pages of Milnes' article remains to this day the best statement for the prosecution against Disraeli's novels.[365]

Milnes's principal criticism of the trilogy as a whole concerns Disraeli's propensity to base his characters on *living persons*, rather than freshly created individuals. This not only suggests an artistic shortcoming, but also makes unwarranted assumptions about the readers' prior knowledge.[366] Thus, as Milnes pointed out:

> the moment a character is known to represent Lord ---- or Mr ---- it loses all power as a work of art. The 'historical picture' becomes 'the portrait of a gentleman'; the fidelity of the likeness is the only object of attention, not the moral fitness, the entireness, the beauty or the grandeur of the character. The great poet or novelist should mould his men and women out of the large masses of humanity, out of the manifold variety of strivers and losers, and actors and sufferers; and surely he degrades his function when he condescends to draw miniatures of individuals composing the least distinctive and frequently most vapid of all classes of the community – namely that which is conveniently called the highest.[367]

Turning then to evaluate the political philosophy being advocated and propagated within Disraeli's trilogy, Milnes is extremely critical of the author's outright denunciation of the patterns of civilisation and governance which had been evolving for the last three centuries:

> All that we are accustomed most to admire and desiderate [...] all that has been done by the Reformation, by the English and French Revolutions, by American Independence – is here proclaimed an entire delusion and failure; and we are taught that we can now only hope to improve our future by utterly renouncing our past.[368]

Milnes is even more scornful of the 'political solution' offered by Disraeli, who prescribes the subjugation of parliamentary influence in favour of 'substituting for them a sort of benevolent clerical monarchism supported by a conscientious aristocracy'.[369] This represented, in Milnes's opinion, 'nothing less than an abandonment of all principles of individuality, responsibility, and self-government; and a return to the narrowest principles of loyal dependence and local patriotism'.[370]

Finally, Milnes was among those people who objected to the conclusions arrived at by Disraeli in regard to the religious content of his novels. *Tancred* in particular drew widespread indignation due to its implicit assumptions regarding the innate superiority of the Hebrew race:

Richard (Dicky) Monckton Milnes, for example, in rejecting the idea of 'the essential and inalienable prerogative of the Jewish race to be at once the moral ruler and the political master of humanity', considered that he must 'distrust the fitness of such a man [as the author] to take such a prominent part in the direction of the affairs of a nation which he so little esteems and understands.'[371]

Chapter Eight
Discord and a Duel

Departure and Return

In the autumn of 1846, Milnes's parents had been looking forward to another visit to Fryston by Mary Anne and Benjamin Disraeli. Mrs Henrietta Milnes's already delicate state of health had been further affected at this time by a recent attack of cholera, which she contracted while visiting Brighton and had never fully recovered from.[372] Reflecting his growing emotional distance from Disraeli, Milnes recommended in a letter to his father: 'Mrs Dizzy is so much more your invitee than mine that you had better write her a line, merely saying that my mother will not be up to a party.'[373]

Mrs Milnes's health had rallied sufficiently by December to enable her son to host a small party at Fryston, including three old friends: Charles MacCarthy, the theologian and future Governor of British Ceylon, and his fellow Apostles George Venables and Henry Lushington. She recorded in her diary that 'Richard read aloud "Mrs Perkins' Ball", by Thackeray'. This was to prove the penultimate entry in the journal. On 1 May 1847, she passed away while staying at her daughter's home at Serlby. Pope-Hennessy observes that:

> To Richard (who was himself ill with gout and suffering from low spirits) his mother's death was a hammer-blow. He had always had far more in common with her than with his father, and it was from her that he inherited his flamboyance and his power of enthusiasm, as well as his easy, level good-humour.[374]

A month later, Milnes was distracted from his grief by the need to campaign for a general election in which he found his back to the wall due to his pro-Catholic sensibilities. A 'No-Popery' cry was reverberating throughout the land, and Milnes later complained that 'a placard has been circulated in my borough, stating that I intend "to give the Pope a seat in the British Parliament!"'.[375] Milnes's father informed him that a Fryston woman had begged him not to ask her to vote in favour of his son.[376] When the vote took place on 30 July, Milnes was re-elected – albeit by a slender margin of just nineteen votes.[377]

Milnes and the 'Jew Bill'

The quixotic spirit of political independence that became Milnes's hallmark was never more in evidence than in the second half of 1847. In August of that year, he joined Jane and Thomas Carlyle at the Bradford home of the Quaker woollen manufacturer W.E. Forster. This gathering occurred in the early days of what eventually became a lifelong friendship between Milnes and Forster. Henceforward, Milnes:

> who had taken to [Forster] from the first, made it his business during many years to lose no opportunity of serving his friend as best he could, by bringing him into contact with those upon whom and through whom he could wield the greatest influence for good.[378]

Following the social gathering, Forster spoke gleefully in a letter to a friend of the encounter between Milnes and Carlyle:

> Monckton Milnes came yesterday, and left this morning – a pleasant, companionable little man, well fed and fattening, with some small remnant of poetry in his eyes and nowhere else; delighting in paradoxes, but good-humoured ones; defending all manner of people and principles, in order to provoke Carlyle to abuse them, in which laudable enterprise he must have succeeded to his heart's content, and for a time we had a most amusing evening, reminding me of a naughty boy rubbing a fierce cat's tail backwards, and getting in between furious growls and fiery sparks. He managed to avoid the threatened scratches.[379]

In September 1847, Milnes set off for Spain and Gibraltar via Portugal, in acceptance of an invitation by Sir Henry Bulwer, a government minister located in Madrid. While in Spain, Milnes corresponded regularly with his father, pointing out on one occasion, for example, that he had come across a large liquorice manufacturer in Seville, the like of which would soon be established in Pontefract.[380]

England was embroiled by now in fearsome debate over the 'Jew Bill', occasioned by the election earlier that year of the Jewish candidate Lionel de Rothschild as one of four Members of Parliament for the City of London. The Bill, which Milnes had personally sponsored, sought to admit Jewish MPs without requiring them to profess an oath of office. Bulwer had cynically referred to England as 'Jewsland' while Milnes was visiting Spain. A similar anti-Semitic sentiment was also evident in a letter (dated December 1847) to Milnes from Carlyle, who made no attempt to disguise strong feelings of antipathy. Park partly deflects this issue by explaining that such feelings were consistent with Carlyle's contempt for *all* categories of 'usurer' and 'money lenders', regardless of religion:[381]

> Carlyle, who in the 1820's had been quite favourable to Catholic emancipation, was now coldly uninterested in this measure for extending the civil and political rights of another religious minority. Unlike many English public figures, he did not publicly oppose the 'Jew Bill', but referred scornfully to it in letters. His chilly indifference, however, was less actively hostile than that of its numerous public opponents, and not so unusual in the context of conventional English attitudes of that time. In December, 1847, he sarcastically wrote [to Milnes] that 'by the very fact of their desiring admission' into Parliament the Jews had declared themselves 'to be hypocritical men'. A 'Jew is bad', but what was a 'sham-Jew, a quack-Jew?' Carlyle wondered how a 'real Jew' could want to be a 'Senator' or even a citizen of any country 'except his own wretched Palestine, whither all his thoughts and steps and efforts tend – where, in the Devil's name, let him arrive as soon as possible, and make us quit of him!'[382]

Pemberton Milnes wrote, around the same time, expressing relief that his son would be out of the country when the Bill was put to the vote. He was unaware, however, that Milnes was already making his way back to London in order to be sure of casting his vote. The interlocking linkages between Milnes, Carlyle, Emerson and Tennyson were brought together in a letter from Carlyle to Emerson, dated 30 December 1847:

> This morning Richard Milnes writes to me for your address, which I have sent. He is just returned out of Spain; home swiftly to 'vote for the Jew Bill'; is doing hospitalities at Woburn Abbey; and I suppose will be in Yorkshire (home, near Pontefract) before long. See him if you have opportunity: a man very easy to see and get into flowing talk with; a man of much sharpness of faculty, well tempered by several inches of 'Christian fat' he has upon his ribs for covering. One of the idlest, cheeriest, most gifted of fat little men. Tennyson has been here for three weeks; dining daily till he is near dead; setting out a Poem withal. He came in to us on Sunday evening last, and on the preceding Sunday: a truly interesting Son of Earth, and Son of Heaven, who has almost lost his way, among the will-o'-wisps, I doubt; and may flounder ever deeper, over neck and nose at last, among the quagmires that abound! I like him well; but can do next to nothing for him. Milnes, with general co-operation, got him a Pension; and he has bread and tobacco: but that is a poor outfit for such a soul.[383]

The Bill passed its third reading in May 1848, only to be rejected soon afterwards in the House of Lords. It endured a similar fate in 1849 and it was only after almost a further decade of political lobbying and agitation that both houses reached a compromise with the passage of the Jews Relief Act 1858, allowing Jewish politicians to omit the words 'on the true faith of a Christian' from their oaths of political allegiance.

'Made of Sugar'

The reference to Emerson was extremely timely. Milnes's benevolence towards him extended much further and was far more enduring than the fillip provided by his article in the *London and Westminster Review.* During the American's lecture tour of 1848, Milnes went to great lengths to gain Emerson a visiting membership of the prestigious Athenaeum Club, engaged him in a whirl of social gatherings of the London elite – including an invitation to Lord Palmerston's in London – and concluded with a speech 'full of praise' as the tour came to its climactic ending at the Exeter Hall in June.[384]

Emerson wrote in deep appreciation of Milnes's patronage that:

> he's the most good natured man in England, made of sugar: he is every where, & knows every thing; has the largest range

of acquaintance (of anybody,) from the Chartist to the Lord Chancellor; fat, easy, affable & obliging; a little careless and sloven in his dress.[385]

By now, Milnes was widely looked upon as the 'symbol of aristocratic sympathy with democratic reform'.[386] Thackeray had recently contributed a highly satirical feature for *Punch*,[387] outlining an imaginary English revolutionary scenario, *à la française*, in which his make-believe cabinet prominently featured the 'Minister of Foreign Affairs, President of the Council, and Poet Laureate, Citizen Monckton Milnes'. Emerson affectionately seized on this portrayal to emphasise the comical dimension of his patron's character:

> His [Milnes's] speeches [in the Houses of Parliament] are always unlucky, & a signal for emptying the House – a topic of great mirth to himself & all his friends, who frankly twit him with it. He is so entirely at home everywhere, & takes life so quietly, that Sidney Smith called him 'the cool of the evening,' – and I remember I was told some anecdotes of well-bred effrontery. – They address him now as *Citoyen* Milnes, since Punch's, that is, Thackeray's late list of the Ministry: but with some feeling between jest & earnest, they speak of him as one who might play, one day, Lamartine, in England.[388]

Milnes's close connection with French society was undoubtedly instrumental in securing Emerson a reception at the home of Alexis de Tocqueville, who was famous for his book on American democracy.[389] During his stay in Paris, Emerson saw how Milnes ('one of the most valuable companions in London too for the multitude of anecdotes he tells about good people') appeared to be 'equally acquainted with everybody & a privileged man with his pockets full of free cards, which admitted him everywhere'.[390]

An undoubted highlight of Emerson's tour, for which he was once again indebted to Milnes, was an invitation to attend a social gathering hosted by Lord and Lady Palmerston and involving (according to the letter dated 2 April 1848 which Emerson sent his wife) 'quite an illustrious collection, such as only London and Lord Palmerston could collect'.[391] This not only included 'princes and high foreigners' but such local political and literary celebrities as Disraeli, Macauley and

Rothschild. Emerson conversed at length with Lady Palmerston's son, Mr Cowper, and described Lord Palmerston as 'frank and affable, of a strong but cheerful and ringing speech'.[392]

It was at the second night of two consecutive public lectures at Exeter Hall that Emerson's tour, which had begun in Manchester eight months earlier, was brought to an end by a 'farewell' speech by Milnes:

> The audience did their part 'by rising en masse, hearty cheering, and waving of hats, &c.' Emerson did his by coming forward to testify to 'the unbroken kindness he had received from a large number of Englishmen and Englishwomen during his stay here he had not been aware there was so much kindness in the world.'[393]

Milnes the Republican

Following his sojourns to the revolutionary crucibles of Spain, France and Italy, Milnes had developed a 'progressive distrust of aristocratic government' and corresponding 'passion for democracy'.[394] In evidence of his growing commitment to Republicanism, Milnes's letters and commonplace entries were 'devoid of any sycophantic reverence' to the British royal family: 'Queen Victoria emerges from those crowded pages as absurd, prejudiced, spartan, unintelligent and inconsiderate; Prince Albert as able, pettish and quick to take offence.'[395]

Early in 1849, Milnes published a pamphlet which set him apart from virtually all the aristocratic and political classes:

> Few influential Englishmen were enthusing over those transient insurrections, but among these few was Richard Monckton Milnes. Exasperated by the timidity with which his compatriots had watched the surge and ebb of Continental Liberalism, Milnes settled down to write his last political pamphlet, a seventy-page production cast in the form of a letter: The Events of 1848 especially in their relation to Great Britain – A Letter to the Marquis of Landsdowne, by Richard Monckton Milnes, MP. This pamphlet, which was executed in Milnes's most grandiose and authoritative manner, surveyed the state of Europe in 1848, heavily criticised English apathy, pleaded for England's support for liberal movements everywhere.[396]

Milnes distributed his pamphlet among his friends and political acquaintances. Praise for his peroration was in notably short supply. At best, the likes of Lord Brougham and Lord Gladstone politely expressed an agreement to disagree with Milnes's views. One conspicuous exception was Carlyle, who applauded Milnes's pamphlet as 'the greatest thing he has yet done: earnest and grave, written in a large, tolerant, kind-hearted spirit, and as far as I can see, saying all that is to be said on that matter'.[397]

One negative review stood out above all others, to the extent that it 'went beyond the bounds of fair-play or of courtesy' and was:

> manifestly written – not for the purposes of discussing Milnes's opinions, which had at least been put forward in a grave and serious spirit not unworthy of the events to which they had reference – but in order that a series of personal wounds might be inflicted upon the author.[398]

It was an article which, in short, 'was one of a class now almost extinct: brutal in its invective, insolent in its sarcasm, and reckless in its disregard of the decencies of debate'.[399]

A Chronicle of Contempt

Such was the trigger for the concluding, and most dramatic episode in the acrimonious relationship between Milnes and George Smythe. By 1848, Smythe had been consigned to the periphery of polite London society, due to his growing reputation as a 'hothead' and 'provoker of duels'.[400] Already condemned to an early death by consumption, Smythe spent most of the year vacating his seat in parliament to observe the French Revolution or visit Parisian or Venetian brothels. Correspondingly, he now spent more time in the role of journalist than that of politician, a development widely condemned as unbefitting of a future viscount.[401] He was, however, granted free rein by the editors and proprietor of the *Morning Chronicle* to rouse whatever controversy took his fancy:

> By early 1849, in fact, his carte blanche was allowing him to assassinate personal enemies. The feud with Milnes had, if anything, intensified since Milnes crossed the floor to the Liberals, making him fair game for the Lincolnites.[402]

It was with unrestrained malice that Smythe set about 'reviewing' *The Events* in such a way as to provoke Milnes's profoundest displeasure.

> After the levity of Lord Palmerston's characteristic defence of his own peculiar foreign policy, there was wanting nothing more than a pamphlet in its eulogy from Mr. Monckton Milnes. The professional jester has a prescriptive claim to break his bulrush (after the danger has passed away) where the lance of the knight had been ruefully shivered. Or, to use a metaphor more germane to both performers, if the venerable Harlequin has escaped cleverly and nimbly through 'a plain and well noted trap' there remains a Pantaloon (as Mr. Rogers tells us in the words of his noble poem, *an Italian character*) [...] Immethodic, absurd and illogical as is this pamphlet of Mr. Milnes, it is occasionally, and by involuntary glimpses, so unwittingly true, that it is not without a purpose that we propose to gibbet him, in front of every country of which he has written with universal ignorance and omniscient pretensions.[403]

Smythe did not stop there. He mercilessly derided Milnes for having defected from the Tories, scoffed at the latter's tendency to record events in his commonplace book (in the manner of a 'boy-Boswell at Cambridge'), and made fun of his growing corpulence.[404]

Milnes's initial instinct was to dash off a letter of complaint to the *Morning Chronicle*, accusing his reviewer of having falsified no fewer than four quotations and badly garbling as many again. He followed this up by resorting to the 'quaint' and anachronistic step of challenging his tormentor to a duel. Pope-Hennessy speculates that this bizarre move was so out of character to lead one to suppose that Milnes was acting on the advice of 'some foreigner or member of an older generation' still subscribing to these outdated notions of chivalry.[405] A further two months elapsed before both men's seconds brokered a settlement of the dispute, thereby averting an almost inevitable calamity.[406]

Chapter Nine
Ode to a Nightingale

Poet and Worthy?

The two entries in British history for which Milnes is arguably best-known are, firstly, as the man Florence Nightingale turned down the chance to marry in favour of tending to the sick and wounded of the faraway Crimean War; and secondly, as the biographer and champion of the controversial Victorian poet John Keats. These historical developments not only occurred within close temporal proximity to one another but converged with some significance. They are, therefore, considered jointly in this chapter.

There is no doubt that historians and biographers have credited Milnes with a crucial part in sustaining the legend of the 'Lady with the Lamp' and the 'founder of modern nursing'.[407] As Gill explains, Nightingale's relationship with Milnes is pivotal to the shaping of this legend:

> He was the man Florence Nightingale loved but sacrificed to her vocation. Clearly, biography has a stake in Florence Nightingale remaining single, since if she had yielded to the temptation of Monckton Milnes, she would never have gone to the Crimea, and her picturesque name and striking myth would have been lost to the world. But at the same time, part of the lustre of that name depends on the public knowledge that Miss Nightingale had been sorely tempted at least once and had only with great pain given up the joys of love and marriage.[408]

Gill is actually one of several contemporary biographers of Nightingale to doubt whether she was as 'sorely tempted' as the legend would have us believe.[409] One objective of this chapter is therefore to test the relative credibility of these competing claims.

The other interrelated objective of the chapter is to analyse the nature and impact of Milnes's *Life, Letters and Literary Remains of John Keats.*[410] Marquess observes that, 'It is oddly fitting that this extravagant dilettante who was called "the Bird of Paradox" should be remembered above all for his most disinterested act, *The Life of Keats.*'[411] Aside from appraising the book's intrinsic merits and wider cultural influence, it is imperative that we also note its implications for Milnes's reputation and the extent to which he was considered 'suitable' by Nightingale and her family.

Nightingale's Early Life

Florence Nightingale was born on 12 May 1820, the younger daughter of prosperous parents, William Edward Nightingale and Frances Smith Nightingale, whose families formed part of the moneyed and propertied Whig gentry of the day. 'W.E.N.', as her father was popularly known, hailed from the firmly rooted Derbyshire family, the Shores of Tapton, whose fortune derived from their lead-mining operations. Having inherited property from his maternal uncle, Peter Nightingale of Lea, in 1815, William Edward Shore changed his name to Nightingale. Following university education at Edinburgh and Trinity College, Cambridge, he took time out to travel the continent then became both an advocate of parliamentary reform and supporter of Lord Palmerston, who happened to live close by.[412]

Frances (or 'Fanny') Smith likewise belonged to a rich, socially prominent and politically-active Unitarian family. Her father, William Smith, spent 46 years as a Member of Parliament, during which he championed the causes of slaves, factory workers, dissenters and Jewish immigrants. Aged 29 when she married (six years older than her husband), Fanny was intent on becoming a hostess of renown and harboured political ambitions for her husband:

> At his wife's urging he stood for a seat in the House of Commons in 1835, and lost. His idealism bruised, he then refused to take any further active role in politics, indulging instead his preference for country life, local affairs, long solitary rides in the New Forest, speculation along religious and philosophical lines, and the education of his daughters.[413]

Both daughters had been born during their parents' extended 'honeymoon' in Italy, their names reflecting their birthplaces. The elder sister, Frances Parthenope (the name of an ancient Greek settlement on the site of Naples), preceded her sister by a year. Following his marriage to Fanny, W.E.N. purchased a large property in Hampshire, enabling the family to spend their summers at Lea Hurst in the north, spring and autumn at Embley Park in the south, and the winter 'social season' in London. As part of this enviable lifestyle, both girls received the type of classical education (with an accent on literature, ancient and modern languages, mathematics, science and philosophy) usually reserved for male heirs. Florence quickly showed an aptitude for learning and thirst for knowledge that earmarked her as the intellectually brighter and more enquiring of the two sisters. Parthenope, by contrast, found her lessons 'tedious and difficult' to bear, and chose to conform to the more 'conventional' feminine lifestyle of the Victorian era also subscribed to by her mother. It was therefore fair to say that:

> In the family constellation Fanny became allied with her elder daughter against her husband and Florence; the lines were clearly discernible by the time of Florence's adolescence. Florence Nightingale's greatest agony concerned her inability to accept her mother's irreducible ideas of the kind of life which she should lead and the unhappiness and vexation this inability caused her mother.[414]

At the age of 17, Florence Nightingale received the first of her 'callings' from God, 'entreating her to His service', even though 'she was uncertain what this implied'.[415]

Milnes and Nightingale (I): Early Courtship

Milnes and Florence Nightingale had first met in 1842 when both were the guests (Nightingale along with the rest of her family) of Lord and Lady Palmerston. Nightingale's biographers agree that, as the relationship between Nightingale and Milnes grew warmer, Nightingale's mother was increasingly hopeful that it would develop into marriage:

> A wedding between her younger daughter and the eminent and eligible Mr Richard Monckton Milnes of Fryston Hall in Yorkshire was exactly the sort of match of which Fanny Nightingale had dreamed. He was a man of fortune, although of course she wanted more than money for her daughter. She had read Milnes's speeches to Parliament and his volumes of poetry, and was certain that he was a poet with a following and a politician with a future [...] So what if he outraged opinion from time to time? The Nightingales were sufficiently worldly to bear a little scandal, and Fanny Nightingale could see that marriage to Milnes would put her Florence right at the centre of British political and artistic life.[416]

Though their attraction was clearly mutual, Nightingale and Milnes each harboured reservations about the prospect of getting married. Nightingale, for her part, had unreserved admiration for Milnes's consistently humanitarian attitude: 'He treated all his fellow mortals as if they were his brothers and sisters,' she once remarked.[417] She delighted in the fact that Milnes was such a staunch proponent of education for factory workers, penny savings banks for the working-class, and the abolition of capital punishment. She took great satisfaction from his sympathy for the famine-stricken Irish (whom he had controversially taken time to visit in order to help organise relief measures), for the pressure he was exerting for factory reform, and for his introduction of a Bill for establishing juvenile reformatories. All of these issues were extremely close to her heart.[418] Thus, as Sattin explains:

> Her issue was not with the man. She admired his mind, enjoyed his company, and later would refer to him as 'the man I adored'. Her objection, as ever, was to the role of women in the institution of marriage. Being married would give her no more freedom than she had at the present time, for she would merely swap one set of constraints and obligations for another. If she married, the legal and financial responsibility for her care would pass from her parents to her husband.[419]

Nightingale knew full well that a life spent hosting breakfast parties and gatherings at Fryston Hall would constitute a serious obstacle to her calling to work in the service of God. 'And yet, if there were to be a husband, Milnes would do very well indeed.'[420] Thus, 'She continued to play for time while she weighed up the possibilities.'[421]

Milnes, in turn, was slightly ambivalent about his possible liaison with Florence Nightingale. In a letter to his sister, Harriette, written in 1846, he was clearly wary of his father's preference for aristocratic 'breeding' rather than accumulated wealth. 'I fancy Papa looks on the Nightingales as rather vulgar people,' he wrote, and might therefore look upon their marriage 'as rather a descent in society'.[422] His portrayal of Nightingale was not unequivocally positive:

> F.N. is certainly a very remarkable person, with a gravity of deportment which I can conceive many people disliking and a clear observant critical way of looking at things, which many might dislike, but which I find analogous to my own. She is a companion worthy of any man of intellect.[423]

By this time, Nightingale had already rejected Henry Nicholson's proposal of marriage in 1845, which caused a permanent rift between their families.[424] This was something she revealed to Milnes, though it did nothing to deter him.[425] He accompanied the Nightingale family on various public outings, such as meetings of the British Association for the Advancement of Science in Southampton in 1846, and in Oxford one year later. During the latter visit, Milnes joined Nightingale and her father at a luncheon engagement with a famous naturalist who kept a three-month-old tame bear in his rooms. Nightingale subsequently recalled that the bear had 'climbed like a squirrel for the butter on the table'. Eventually, however, the animal 'became obstreperous' and had to be shoo-d out into the garden, where it continued to rear up and bellow. 'Let alone, I'm going to mesmerise it,' Nightingale protested in defiance of her father's attempt to restrain her. But it was Milnes who stepped forward and, in Nightingale's words, 'followed [my] suggestion and in ½ minute the little bear began to yawn, in less than 3 min. was stretched fast asleep on the gravel'.[426]

Sattin speculates that it was during this visit that Milnes made the first of a series of marriage proposals to Nightingale,[427] who was, therefore, forced to consider whether or not to go down the conventional path of marriage or fulfil her calling to care for others.

Sensing the anguish Nightingale was experiencing, some family friends, the Bracebridges, obtained her parents' permission to have their daughter join them on a three-month tour of Italy in the autumn of 1847.[428] While in Rome she visited the Vatican and Sistine Chapel; even more lasting in its impact was the time Nightingale spent visiting local orphanages and convents. On one such occasion, just as she was leaving, 'her *madre* warned her that God "calls you to a very high degree of perfection. Take care, if you resist you will be very guilty."'[429]

'Life, Letters and Literary Remains of John Keats'

The familiar archetype of the 'stricken romantic' has repeatedly been applied in discussions of the life and work of the nineteenth-century English poet John Keats.[430] In the words of Wolfson, 'Keats really suffered two deaths: one from consumption in Rome in February 1821 and another, later in the year, in Shelley's elegy, *Adonais*.'[431]

Shelley had responded out of sympathy and indignation to a pair of hostile reviews to Keats's work (in *Blackwood's Magazine* and the *Quarterly Review*), which, according to popular myth, had 'so wounded the vulnerable poet that he died of the anguish'.[432]

While Shelley's intention had been to celebrate the genius of his contemporary, his tribute unwittingly provided a gilt-edged opportunity for Keats's detractors. The focus – not exclusively by Shelley, but also by the influential left-wing poet Leigh Hunt – on Keats's failing health was appropriated by those who had a vested interest in deriding him as weak, pathetic and effeminate. Political sensitivities were also clearly important:

> The poet's 'lower-class' background, his febrile eroticism and his liberal politics would have been enough to prompt vitriol from his contemporary Tory reviews, but his association with the so-called 'Cockney School' of Hunt exacerbated matters and the journalistic *contretemps* over Keats's work was as much a political quarrel as a poetical one. From the right Keats was condemned as a politically subversive upstart whilst the liberal camp, with which the poet explicitly identified himself, eulogised his power and promise and condemned the malignity of attacks by government sycophants.[433]

No less a figure than Lord Byron referred to Keats in *Don Juan Canto XI* (1821), with thinly-disguised derision: 'Tis strange the mind, that very fiery particle,' he wrote, 'should let itself be snuffed out by an article.'[434] Amidst a 'riot of iterations that relentlessly across the nineteenth century recalled the poor fellow to snuff him out again'.[435] It befell Milnes to attempt to restore and, at best, elevate Keats's diminished reputation by attempting to 'uproot Shelley's frail flower and blunt Byron's barb'.[436]

Starting in 1841, Milnes began the seven-year process of writing Keats's biography. He was entrusted with the task by Keats's close friend and ardent admirer Charles Brown, who provided Milnes with a vast reservoir of source material, including letters and Brown's own lovingly compiled personal memoir. Brown's transference of source material was conditional on two important stipulations: that the biographer would do his utmost to redress the 'critically abusive' reviews of Keats appearing in the *Quarterly Review* and *Blackwood's Magazine*; and that he would offer an antidote for Leigh Hunt's emphasis on the poet's pathetic illness. As Marquess explains:

> The requests are understandable, coming from an associate who wished to set right what he considered a mistaken image. But the result was not entirely happy. Whereas Milnes's distance from the controversies of Keats's life promised an ideal biographical position of objectivity, Brown's stipulation threatened to compromise that stance.[437]

Milnes gladly accepted this remit. His primary concern in writing *Life, Letters and Literary Remains of John Keats* was that of, as he put it, 'vindicating the character and advancing the fame' of the poet.[438] It was, therefore, an 'exercise in rehabilitation'.[439]

In addition to introducing his readers to a raft of novels or previously obscure works by Keats, Milnes undoubtedly succeeded in transforming the poet's public image:

> Milnes's mid-century Keats was not only a poet of substantially under achievement than had been known but also a freshly presented, most appealing epistolary personality: ironic, sentimental, thoughtful, funny, passionate, and issuing brilliant, compelling formulations about poetic style and poetic method.

> This Keats was a craftsman and a philosopher, an aesthete and a reflective reader, an acute social observer and a practicing poet. With Milnes's production reviewed everywhere, Keats was reborn to a new generation. Whatever story was told about the historical John Keats (battered boy, effeminate gusher, avatar of beauty, martyr to art), appreciation for Keats's verbal craft and vibrant pictorial imaging was emerging and growing, shaping not only his fame but also the reading of poetry in a Keatsian vein, an artistry of an intense conception and verbal skill.[440]

An undue emphasis and possible misinterpretation has been placed on Milnes's continual use of the word 'manly' in relation to Keats's essential character and way of life. For Najarian this represents a deliberate 'attempt to unravel the connection between Keats and effeminacy [...] He self-consciously aims to present an active, energetic, pugnacious and masculine version of the poet.'[441] This criticism is developed in greater detail by Marquess, who says of Milnes:

> He describes Keats reciting the 'Ode to a Nightingale' to Haydon in 'his deep grave voice' [...] whereas Haydon mentions only a 'tremulous undertone,' and Bailey remembers a 'sweet-toned voice, "an excellent thing" in man, as well as in woman.' Again, Milnes suggests that Keats's protruding lower lip gave his face a pugnacious look, but all other accounts (and most pictures) agree that the upper lip was actually more prominent. These are small details, and they may represent mistakes rather than wilful distortions. Still, it appears likely that Milnes, in an attempt to portray the most masculine Keats possible, was too ready to misinterpret the evidence in favor of his own design.[442]

It is probable, though, that Milnes's heavy application of this adjective assumes an underlying definition akin to that outlined in Chapter 3. This view is implicitly endorsed by Saunders Boos, who explains how, 'Milnes emphasizes his subject's morality, high aspirations, love of friends and brothers, meditativeness, and increasing concern with philosophy [...] The book's chief concern is to impress its reader with Keats' nobility of spirit.'[443]

Either way, the immediate effect of Milnes's *Life* was to ignite a renewed appreciation of beauty and significance of Keats's work, not least in the estimation of the Pre-Raphaelite Brotherhood whose future works, poetic and visual, reflected Keatsian sensibilities.[444]

Modern criticism of Milnes's *Life* has focussed on the fact that it was essentially a 'public relations exercise' and on the various techniques of omission, distortion and interpretation by which it was achieved.[445] It is generally accepted that, in his desire to portray his subject in a manner 'more acceptable' to a mid-nineteenth century public – as someone of great decency, morality and high nobility – Milnes consciously downplayed the bawdier aspects of Keats's personality and even overlooked his tempestuous and (according to some) controversial relationship to Fanny Brawne. The contents of Keats's letters were sanitised to eradicate disparaging references to associates living or dead. Sentences were rephrased (their sloppy spelling and syntax corrected) and words de-selected or replaced in order to make the poet appear more learned and erudite, and his parentage and social background (especially his 'Cockney' origins) subtly upgraded to heighten his social standing.[446] The obvious political dimension and radical inclinations suffusing Keats's poetry were systematically downplayed,[447] along with those explicitly irreligious or sceptical remarks that revealed the poet's 'questioning spirit [that] doubted the worth of institutionalized faith'.[448]

Milnes and Nightingale (II): Nursing Ambitions

The evidence suggests that any implications that Milnes's *Life* may have had for his relationship with Florence Nightingale lay in its impact on the attitudes of her friends, rather than on her or her family. In the summer of 1848, Nightingale was permitted by her parents to do some teaching at a local school. Milnes had recently returned from Paris, where he had witnessed first-hand the emergence of the free republic. His visit to see Nightingale at Lea Hurst in the hilly Derbyshire countryside coincided with the publication of the Keats biography.[449]

Bostridge observes that, 'Although Milnes's book would in the long term rescue Keats's reputation from obscurity, in the short term it added fuel to the controversy about his character, especially concerning his supposed paganism.'[450]

The publication prompted Nightingale's childhood friend, Fanny

Allen, to warn her against marrying Milnes. She objected to his support of the 'pagan poet': no one could previously have been sure of Milnes's religious beliefs, but now one could expect 'to find an altar to Jupiter somewhere in his house'.[451] Allen also considered Milnes 'plain and common-looking', with thinning long brown hair and a paunch.[452] If, as Cromwell reports, Nightingale 'listened gravely' to Milnes's latest proposal of marriage on that summer day in Derbyshire, there is no evidence that her mood was affected by the latter's affinity with Keats.[453]

In June 1849, just as Milnes was turning forty, 'anxious to get married, and unwilling to be kept dangling any longer',[454] he attended a party thrown by the Nightingales at Embley, which was their customary way of announcing their intention to move back temporarily to Derbyshire. It provided just the opportunity he needed to press Nightingale into a final decision: 'There is no record of what passed between them, but it seems that she prevaricated. In his eagerness to have the matter settled, and to be married, Milnes took this as outright rejection.'[455]

There is evidence to suggest that Milnes's interpretation was mistaken:

> A letter, written several years afterwards to Fanny Nightingale by [her] Aunt Mai, suggests that, on Florence's part at any rate, the situation regarding Milnes's final proposal was by no means so clear cut, and that he misunderstood her intentions. According to Aunt Mai, Florence was slowly coming round to the idea of marriage to Milnes as 'the life next most valuable' to one of service, but Milnes 'seems not to have understood her, to have supposed her still to refuse him, & married another'. His immediate reaction to her response to his proposal, in whatever confused terms she framed it, may have been anger, or distress, or simply irritation.[456]

Bostridge maintains that this theory of a misunderstanding between them would help to account for 'the intense period of self-examination, weighing up the advantages and disadvantages of marriage to him', that Nightingale endured in the course of the next two years.[457] In the autumn of 1849, for example, she conceded in her diary:

> I do not understand it – I am ashamed to understand it, [...] I know that if I were to see him again, the very thought of doing so quite overcomes me. I know that since I refused him not one day has passed without my thinking of him, that life is desolate without his sympathy. And yet, do I want to marry him? I know that I could not bear his life – that to be nailed to a continuation or an exaggeration of my present life without hope of another would be intolerable to me – that voluntarily to put it out of my power ever to be able to seize the chance of forming for myself a true and rich life would seem to me like suicide.[458]

Her anguish was exacerbated by the attitudes of her parents and sister who were outraged that she had rejected such an eligible man. The Bracebridges stepped in again, taking Nightingale on a trip to Egypt (via Italy and Greece) in order to 'let time and distance heal the pain caused by the end of her relationship with Richard Monckton Milnes'.[459] Ironically, during the course of a brief stay in Hamburg, she and Milnes accidentally crossed paths while she was visiting a home for destitute boys: 'He was on his way to take the waters at Marienbad. They spent a happy day together and, when they parted, Nightingale declared herself "well satisfied with our lark".'[460]

She was not to know it at the time, but Milnes was on the point of announcing his engagement to someone else.

This meeting actually did little in the long term to relieve Nightingale's sense of despair. By Christmas 1850, she had reached her lowest ebb:

> It was now more than a year since she had told Monckton Milnes she could not marry him [...] but not a day went by without her thinking of him. Though the very thought of meeting him overcame her, she missed him all the time. It would not be so, she knew, if only she could get to the work she longed to do, and which she could not have done as his wife; but the dark, chilling fact seemed to be that no chance of leading what she thought of as the real life was going to arise – that she was doomed to go on as she was.[461]

Her mood was almost suicidal: 'I have no desire now but to die,' she wrote from her bedroom in Embley. She tended to stay in bed all day because she saw no reason to get up anymore. She once dreamt that Milnes had come to inform her 'that he had made the way clear for her to go to the life of nursing for which she longed'.[462] The pair actually resumed contact on 15 March 1851, when Milnes pushed his way through the other guests at a reception thrown by Lady Palmerston to address her directly. His tone of voice was uncharacteristically brusque as he complained that. 'The noise of this room [was] like a cotton-mill.'[463] On the following day, Nightingale recorded in her journal:

> Last night I saw him again for the second time for the last eighteen months. He would hardly speak. I was miserable [...] I wanted to find him longing to talk to me, willing to give me another opportunity to keep open another decision; or perhaps I only wanted his sympathy without looking any further. He was not ready with it. He did not show indifference, but avoidance. No familiar friendship. No confidence such as I felt towards him.[464]

On 20 March, Nightingale wrote formally to Milnes: 'Ostensibly she did so to ask him a favour for her cousin [Blanche], whose parents did not approve of their daughter's courtship by the poet A.H. Clough; but, clearly, she was also seeking a channel back to their old familiarity.'[465]

Clough and Milnes had first befriended each other in revolutionary Paris in 1849. It was during a social gathering at Fryston Hall, two years later, that Clough was introduced to, and captivated by, young Blanche, who was the daughter of Nightingale's Aunt Mai. 'Will you forgive me for asking a favour from you?' Nightingale tentatively asked of Milnes: 'I believe you are acquainted with Mr A.H. Clough. If you like him enough to speak a good word for him, that good word spoken at Embley might save a good deal of suffering.'[466]

Aside from disparities of wealth and social standing, there were other aspects of Clough's character, such as his intrinsic shyness, which might lessen his appeal to his prospective parents-in-law. Nightingale therefore asked Milnes if he could possibly introduce Clough to her parents, while coyly adding: 'I would not have asked it in this formal way if I had thought it likely that I should see you.'[467]

Bostridge rates it likely that Nightingale was now aware of Milnes's rumoured engagement, which quickly resulted in his marriage on 31 July,[468] and regards this union, and Nightingale's growing fondness for Milnes's bride, as a key factor in their reconciliation.

By now, Nightingale had, with her parents' blessing, begun observing nursing practices and witnessing operations in Kaiserwerth. Having 'lost the one man she could seriously have considered marrying', she could now press on in fulfilment of her destiny.[469]

Chapter Ten
Family Man, Philanthropist

Marriage and Madeley

James Pope-Hennessy insists that Florence Nightingale's refusal of Milnes's proposal was to have far more impact on her life than on his. Indeed:

> Looking back from the happy security of his own marriage, Milnes found nothing in Miss Nightingale's refusal that could cause him to repine. For in less than one year after her departure for Italy he realised that he had found someone whom he once described to Tennyson as 'a perfect woman.' She was as idealistic and as elegant as Florence Nightingale. She was gayer, gentler, prettier and more quiet. She was less public-minded and incidentally less rich. Above all else, she had a capacity for a purely personal affection, for concentrating love upon an individual in a way for which Florence Nightingale – with her sweeping anxiety for the reform of the War Office or of the Army in India – had neither the talent or the time. This young lady, whom Milnes married [on 31 July 1851] was Annabel Hungerford Crewe, who lived at Madeley in Staffordshire.[470]

Milnes had been linked to several other women who might have fulfilled his social ambition to 'marry well',[471] but it was the quietly modest and unprepossessing Annabel Crewe who captured his attention. She was six years his junior, the same age as his sister, Harriette Galway. It was of great advantage to him that her closest friend also happened to be his cousin, Charlotte Williams-Wynn.[472]

During the London season, Annabel stayed at her aunt's home in Upper Brook Street. Her preference was to reside in the more tranquil, 'unchanging and civilised' confines of the family seat in Madeley, near Crewe, on the Cheshire-Staffordshire border. Surrounded by smoky factories and mines, the 'modest, untidy, black and white-manor-house' was comparable in many ways to Fryston, 'but the scenery at Madeley was far more picturesque and far more rural. Fryston and its gaunt park were by contrast impersonal and bleak.'[473] Following her aunt's death in February 1850, Annabel retreated, grief-stricken, to Madeley. That spring, she established a monument to her aunt, consisting of a piece of land on which local villagers could raise their allotments, and spent the following autumn and winter having the manor repainted.

Milnes had written to Annabel in the meantime, expressing his warmest condolences. Life went on in her absence. In June 1850, for example, Milnes's old friend, Alfred Tennyson, was married, and, with typical generosity, Milnes proposed that the newlyweds spend their honeymoon at Fryston. Then, when they were in the process of house-hunting, he offered them temporary occupancy of a wing of Fryston Hall. Tennyson tactfully declined each of these offers.[474]

It was not until Annabel re-opened the house in London in the spring of 1851 that she and Milnes began seeing each other regularly.[475] At the end of April, the pair briefly went their separate ways – Annabel returning to Madeley and Milnes to stay with friends in Capesthorpe, though asking if he might visit her for Whitsun. He duly arrived on Whit-Sunday evening, looking by all accounts 'very ill and nervous'. When Annabel entered the library the following morning, he chose his moment to propose: 'When she accepted him, he told her that he had been wanting to ask this question for the last two years, but had not known what she felt.'[476]

For a short while afterwards, news of the couple's engagement was conveyed only to Annabel's sister Henrietta (an invalid based in a Catholic convent) and Milnes's father. Such secrecy was designed to give the newly betrothed couple time to decide how to break the news to Miss Crewe's brother, the rather eccentric Hungerford, Lord Crewe. As the third Baron Crewe, the Eton and Oxford educated Hungerford had inherited the massive and opulent Jacobean mansion of Crewe Hall in Cheshire following his father's death in 1835. In so doing, he also acquired the family's large estates in Cheshire, Staffordshire and Leicestershire. Milnes's perceived social standing was a matter of significance here:

> Lord Crewe's approval of the match was deemed essential. It seemed unlikely that this moody and unstable nobleman would ever marry, and it was obvious that Henriett, a religious invalid, would not do so either. In consequence, their considerable fortunes and, in Lord Crewe's case, estates, might be expected to devolve in time upon the children of their sister's marriage. The Crewes of Crewe could trace their ancestry back into the twelfth century, whereas the Milneses, who a couple of generations ago had been Methodist mill-owners at Wakefield, were not of ancient stock. They were not noble. They were not rich. These were important considerations in the English society of that epoch.[477]

For all the couple's trepidation, Hungerford showed no objection to the union. The couple decided to get married on the last day of July and Lord Crewe even gave away the bride. The village bells pealed throughout the morning. Following the wedding service, the newly-weds were cheered all the way from Madeley to Crewe. One hundred and twenty tenants of the village dined at the Crewe Arms before reuniting with wives and daughters for tea and dancing. In the meantime the principals sat down to dine in the more lavish surroundings of Crewe Hall, where the bridegroom and his brother-in-law were the pick of the speakers.[478]

Later that afternoon, the Milneses departed to spend three days at Teddesley Park with the Lord-Lieutenant of Staffordshire, before visiting the groom's aunts in Torquay. They briefly returned in mid-August to London (where they dined with Lord and Lady Palmerston) and then set off for their honeymoon in Austria and Germany.[479] Neither of them was too impressed by Vienna, but Munich was made all the sweeter by the company of Mr Thompson, an English tutor, who later became the Archbishop of York and who was a regular visitor to Fryston.[480]

Back in the Thick of It

Earlier in the year (on 27 June to be precise), Milnes had taken Annabel on an inspection tour of Fryston, where she 'did not care for what she saw'.[481] Annabel was already reconciled to the fact that her husband's responsibilities to his Pontefract constituents required them to live with his parents at Fryston Hall. The barren local landscape and its smoky environment were undoubtedly off-putting, but it was not long before she was won over by the old Hall itself: 'I am growing quite fond of Fryston!' she wrote in January 1852. 'I see it is a house & place full of capabilities & in doors [sic] & out might furnish plenty of interesting employment to render all pretty and enjoyable.'[482] They were not, in any case, tied down.

> Monckton Milnes' engagement and marriage did not modify his habit of scampering hither and thither. He still trotted from party to party, from house to house. His wife's health, as well as her distinct preference for domesticity, rendered her unwilling to take part in all of these activities, though she cordially entertained her husband's guests in London and at Fryston and, in the first years of her marriage, went the round of country houses with him too.[483]

The presence of a new daughter-in-law at Fryston Hall constituted a refreshing and stimulating change for Robert Pemberton Milnes, whose major preoccupation now was to heap praise on his political idol, Benjamin Disraeli, while bluntly decrying the views of his own son. It was evident that Milnes's 'recurring anxiety for office or a peerage seemed of a certain comic interest' to his father,[484] which was having an effect on his political appetite. Following the dissolution of parliament in July 1852:

> A number of members, Gladstone among them, experienced difficulty in retaining their seats. Monckton Milnes kept his at Pontefract, but he found it annoying work. Monckton Milnes had never stomached criticism. The personalities and the monetary intrigues of a contested election had always been hateful to him. He now minded these more than ever before, nor was Fryston, where across the dinner-table, his father maintained a quizzical interest in his speeches and prospects, a place in which to gather new daily confidence before setting off to face the tough self-interested burghers, the querulous Dissenters and the surly coal-operatives of his constituency.[485]

On 3 August, Annabel gave birth to the couple's first child, a daughter, Amicia ('Amy'), who was named after a forebear on the Crewe side of the family. Evidently, 'Mrs Milnes settled happily to the novel and exciting interests of motherhood, sewing sprigged muslin dresses and sending accounts of each new gesture of "the sweet Amice" to [her sister] Henriett Crewe at Torquay.'[486]

In truth, Milnes's social trajectory was already turning in a markedly different direction. The house in Upper Brook Street – let out since their wedding – was taken back into the Milneses' possession in the spring of 1852. Throughout the previous years in which he had kept his bachelor house at 26 Pall Mall:

> Milnes' breakfast parties had usually been male, though he would of course ask on occasion Mrs. Carlyle and Miss. Jewsbury, the ambitious Mrs. Nightingale and her elegant daughters Florence and Parthenope, or some visiting foreign novelist like the German Jewess Fanny Lewald. Now that he had a wife, a house of his own in a Mayfair street, and a considerably increased income, Milnes could embark on more frequent and more ambitious parties that had ever been possible for him before.[487]

In the political sphere, Milnes continued to be associated with reformist issues relating to the improved livelihoods of the working class. On 2 September 1852, for example, he sat alongside 'a glittering galaxy of the literary celebrities of that date' (such as Dickens, Thackeray and Bulwer-Lytton) as a guest speaker at the opening of the Manchester Free Library, the first to be instigated following the passage of William Ewart's Public Libraries Act of 1850.[488] Milnes had sat on the House of Commons select committee on the Establishment of Free Public Libraries in 1849. The purpose of the resulting Act was not only to promote the emergence of public libraries, but also to establish and extend the presence of scientific and artistic museums for the education and recreation of the general public. In rising to speak at Manchester, Milnes 'did not mention politics, except to applaud the ideas of community, reconciliation between different classes, and social amelioration'.[489]

Some of the greatest figures from Victorian literary, cultural and political life proved elusive to Milnes's attempts to draw them to Fryston, but this did not deter him from extending acts of patronage and benevolence to virtually anyone whose needs for financial, practical or emotional support were brought to his attention. This is exemplified by kindness and support he displayed towards two of Victorian England's greatest heroines: the writer Charlotte Brontë and the woman he almost married, Nurse Florence Nightingale.

Keeping a Secret from Charlotte Brontë

Milnes was already aware of the work of Charlotte Brontë by the time he was courting Florence Nightingale. He had taken some examples of Brontë's earliest poetry down to Lea Hurst in the autumn of 1846 and read them out loud to Nightingale. It would be a further five years before he would finally have the pleasure of meeting the writer of *Jane Eyre*.

In actual fact, Milnes had been unable to attend a dinner held in Brontë's honour at Thackeray's house near Kensington Square in 1849.[490] But he made a point of introducing himself at one of Thackeray's lectures on 'The English Humorists of the Eighteenth Century' two years later.[491] The young Yorkshirewoman was already 'drained and exhausted' by her visit to London and the attention foisted upon her. She therefore declined Milnes's invitation to join him at his house in Pall Mall, on the grounds that she had 'laid down myself the rule of not going out anywhere during my stay in "Town" and could not infringe that rule'.[492] This proved a source of considerable embarrassment when both parties subsequently bumped into one other after Brontë had 'been bullied' into attending a dinner thrown by a mutual acquaintance.[493]

Undeterred by this setback, Milnes set about inviting Brontë to Fryston Hall and asked for Brontë's address from W.E. Forster, who, along with his wife, Jane, had paid Brontë and her family a visit at her home in Haworth in January 1851. Forster warned Milnes that, since Brontë was always reluctant to leave her aged father unattended, it was unlikely that she would accept his invitation.[494] Milnes tried to get round this possibility by inviting Brontë's father to accompany her to Fryston; but, as Barker explains, 'Fortunately for Charlotte, this invitation arrived when she was at her weakest and she was able to hand over the task of replying to her father with a clear conscience.'[495]

In the process of declining Milnes's invitation (in a letter dated 16 January 1852), the Reverend Patrick Brontë explained how:

My Daughter, I regret to say, is not well enough to be a visitor anywhere, just now – She has been out of health, for some time, and though now better, requires care, and for the present, I should wish for her to stay at home. She begs me to express the pleasure she felt, at meeting you in London, – as well as her gratitude for the present attention.[496]

While no one could possibly have predicted it then, Milnes was still to play a crucial part in helping to secure Brontë's future happiness. This occurred when Milnes was approached in the autumn of 1851 by Elizabeth Gaskell, who would later become the acclaimed writer of *North and South* (1854), and who was a close friend and confidant of Charlotte Brontë's. Gaskell approached Milnes to see whether he might help break down Reverend Patrick's opposition to his daughter's possible marriage to the Reverend Arthur Nicholls. She explained that the romance was floundering because Reverend Patrick rated his daughter's suitor too poor a financial prospect and considered her worthy of someone of much higher social standing. Gaskell secretly enlisted Milnes's support in the hope that he might render Nicholls more appealing as a prospective son-in-law by doing something to augment his income.[497]

Unbeknown to Charlotte Brontë, Milnes visited Arthur Nicholls in his parish of Kirk Smeaton, where, with the blessing of the Vicar of Leeds, he offered Nicholls the choice of two well-paid positions. Afterwards, he wrote to Gaskell (in a letter dated 30 January 1852) as follows:

I must tell you that I made Mr Nicholl's acquaintance in Yorkshire. He is a strong-built, somewhat hard-featured man, with a good deal of Celtic sentiment about his manner & voice – quite of the type of the Northern Irishmen. He seemed sadly broken in health & spirits & declined two cures, which Dr. Hook enabled me to offer him – one in Lancashire of considerable interest, but requiring much energy; – another in Scotland, requiring none at all. He gave me the impression of a man whose ardour was burnt out. I was amused at his surprise over the interest I took in him & I carefully avoided any mention of you. He spoke with great respect of Mr. Brontë's abilities & character & of her simply and unreservedly.[498]

Milnes's somewhat sober mood was compounded by the fact that, as he also disclosed in his letter, Annabel had recently miscarried. He maintained that, while her 'cheerful temper' had done much to raise their morale, the disappointment they felt was nonetheless 'severe'.[499]

It is clear with hindsight that Milnes was underestimating the impact that his intervention eventually would have. Charlotte Brontë was soon writing to inform Elisabeth Gaskell of Arthur Nicholls's renewed determination to marry her.

> Nicholls was privately puzzled by the visit, as he had no idea who Milnes was, or that strings were being pulled on his behalf. But, putting two and two together, he must have been encouraged by the idea that his situation had been noted, and that Charlotte was somehow involved. He lost no time in pressing to be allowed to visit her again.[500]

Enclosing a recent letter from Brontë, Gaskell wrote in euphoric fashion to Milnes (on 20 April 1854), stating: 'I can't help fancying your kind words may have made him feel that he was not as friendless as he represented [himself and] believed himself to be at first; and might rouse his despondency up to a fresh effort. I like her letter; don't you?'[501] One month later, Gaskell wrote an equally buoyant letter to W.E. Forster, confidentially enclosing a 'quaint' correspondence from Charlotte Brontë, in which she announced her engagement to Arthur Nicholls.[502]

The Lady with the Lamp

The outbreak of the Crimean War occurred in March 1854, but it was not until several months later that reports of the terrible conditions and neglect being experienced by army personnel filtered through to British newspapers. Alongside this came urgent appeals for 'devoted women' to go out and help relieve their pain and suffering.[503] It was in response to such appeals that Florence Nightingale arranged with her friend Sidney Herbert (the Secretary of State for War), for herself and 38 nurses to be sent out to the front.

Nightingale immediately discovered, much to her dismay, that the wounded soldiers not only lacked such basic essentials as water vessels, soap, towels and clothing, but were lying in mud and filth, and risked encountering vermin. It was obvious to her that the strong likelihood of soldiers dying from secondary diseases was due, not only to the shortage of medical supplies, inadequate diet and poor hygiene, but also to the inadequate organisation and training of their nurses.[504]

Nightingale quickly used her influence to help redress these shortcomings and set about establishing on-site kitchens and laundry facilities. Reports soon appeared in *The Times* applauding Nightingale's commitment to ensuring that, 'When all the medical officers have retired for the night and sickness and darkness have settled down upon the miles of prostrate sick, she may be observed alone, with a little lamp in her hand, making her solitary rounds.'[505]

Thus she became immortalised as the 'Lady with the Lamp'.

Back in Britain, in August 1855, plans for a national appeal in recognition of 'the noble exertions of Miss Nightingale in the hospitals of the East'[506] were set in motion. Among the many publicity events that followed was one organised by Mrs Gaskell in Manchester, at which 'The star turn was Monckton Milnes, who quite lost himself in nostalgic reverie about the young Florence Nightingale.'[507] Fittingly, it was Milnes who became the first President of the Nightingale Fund.

Another even more personal tribute to Nightingale was about to be conferred by her former suitor. Annabel Monckton Milnes was close to delivering the Milnes's second child. Their first daughter, Amicia, was now three years old and Milnes was apt to take her for walks and write her short letters in block capitals. He described her in one letter to a friend as 'a large, light-hearted, cherubic-looking child, excitable and intelligent, wilful and yet sensible'.[508] She had the fetching appearance of a 'pretty Pre-Raphaelite child', was doted on by her grandfather, who confessed to never having seen anything 'so hilarious & so graceful'.[509] Hers was clearly a happy infancy:

> Mrs. Monckton Milnes' letters are filled with descriptions of the little girl – learning to spell with an ivory alphabet on the drawing-room carpet in Upper Brook Street, riding about the Bawtry paddock on her pony, taking her favourite doll 'Roberty' to salute the Emperor and Empress as they passed in procession on their visit to London in 1855, or being held aloft on the stalwart shoulder of Tom the young footman above the swirling crowds of Euston Square railway station.[510]

It was no secret that Richard and Annabel were hoping that the second child would be a son. Nevertheless, in December 1855, 'when the orange fogs of Victorian London were shrouding the streets, and you needed candles to read by at mid-day', a second daughter arrived. It has been said that, had it been a son, Lady Ashburton would have stood as godparent. As it was, Nightingale was asked to be the child's godmother, and the girl was christened 'Florence' in her honour.[511]

In 1856, with the war now ended, Nightingale returned home an invalid, ironically having contracted brucellosis.[512] She and Milnes continued to be lifelong friends. Milnes was a regular visitor to Lea Hurst and, as we shall see, their lives would often continue to overlap. Shortly after Milnes's marriage, Nightingale referred to herself as 'the idol of the man I adored'. She professed to admiring him because his deeds (whether political, social or literary) 'were inspired chiefly by good will toward men'.[513] There is no doubt that she brought out and highlighted an aspect of his character not always fully appreciated by others:

> Although he was not passionately in love with her (he was not capable of passionate love) Florence Nightingale evoked the best part of Milnes' nature. Of all the little mirrors in which we catch sight of his refracted image, that which Miss Nightingale holds out to us is amongst the clearest. Of all the little beams of light which flicker for a moment on Milnes' elusive, trotting figure, one of the strongest and the purest is that cast by the Lady with the Lamp.[514]

It is evident with hindsight that it was what Milnes *failed* to achieve in his pursuit of Florence Nightingale (namely, her hand in marriage) that so monumentally affected the course of nineteenth-century history. An entry in Milnes's diary written during one of his occasional visits to Lea Hurst poignantly reflects how, 'Fourteen years ago I asked her to marry me: if she had done so there would have been a heroine the less in the world & certainly not a hero the more.'[515]

It is difficult to contest his implicit conclusion that his loss was to the ultimate benefit of humanity.

Chapter Eleven
Fathers and Sons

A Family Without Peer

Having declined Palmerston's offer of a minor post in the Treasury the year before, Milnes's mood turned to euphoria when, in February 1856, the Prime Minister took him aside in the House of Commons to confide that Robert Pemberton Milnes had recently been sent a letter informing him of Her Majesty's intention to elevate him to the House of Lords. Milnes is said to have returned 'in ecstasy' to his home in Upper Brook Street, blissfully unaware that his father had already written back from Fryston library, where, 'without a moment's hesitation', he courteously but firmly declined the accolade.[516]

Many of Milnes's political adversaries and detractors reacted gleefully to this outcome and laughed heartily behind his back: 'Disraeli, who could be spiteful as well as vulgar, attributed Mr Milnes's refusal to a wish to "mortify" his son.'[517] It was of no consolation to Milnes that his father was acting entirely in keeping with his character. In one letter of 'glacial fury', Milnes accused him of delivering 'a blow at confidence'; while in another he 'accused him of "checking" the social advancement of [his] family'.[518]

This development clearly blunted Milnes's political ambition during the remaining years of the 1850s. Henceforward, he would only involve himself in political issues that were closest to his heart. Otherwise, as we shall see, he redoubled his propensity to lend much-needed practical or moral support to, or enhance the reputations of literary figures from Britain or overseas.

Milnes and Women's Rights

Relations between Lord Palmerston and Richard Monckton Milnes were unaffected by Pemberton Milnes's decision regarding the House of Lords. Indeed, in February 1857, the Milneses spent four days with Lord and Lady Palmerston at Broadlands. Milnes and Annabel broke off temporarily to pay a visit to the Nightingales at nearby Embley, though, unlike her parents and sister, Florence was not at home.[519]

One month later, a general election was called. Milnes gave much thought to the suggestion that he stand as MP for Manchester instead of Pontefract, but was too uncertain of the outcome to risk it:

> It was a terrible March of sleet and snow; Milnes fought the election with a fever and a sore throat, while his wife canvassed the icy countryside in her carriage, the victim of piercing headaches from the cold. The voting at Pontefract was conducted along traditional lines, with huge drink bills at the local pubs and all that 'knocking-about' of the candidate by which old Mr. Milnes (who unexpectedly voted for his son) was 'excessively entertained,' and which the candidate himself would have given worlds to avoid.[520]

The opening weeks of the new parliament were marked by an extreme dullness and political stagnation.[521] One interesting exception to this was the intense parliamentary debate concerning the absence of women's property rights in marriage, in which Milnes reinforced his credentials as a supporter of female social advancement.

Three years earlier, in May 1854, the well-known British feminist activist, Barbara Leigh Smith Bodichon had published a highly influential pamphlet, *A Brief Summary, in plain language, of the most important Laws of England concerning Women, together with a few observations thereon.*[522] This comprised a concise and lucid objection to the fact that, under common law, a woman was deprived of any separate legal identity from her husband. This concept was known as the 'coverture' of the wife. Leigh Smith was adamant that this be overturned:

> She insisted that parliament give statutory recognition to married women's rights to hold property, to contract, to sue and be sued in their own names, and otherwise to enjoy an independent legal personality from that of their husbands. Richard Monckton Milnes submitted Leigh Smith's pamphlet to the Law Amendment Society's Personal Laws Committee, and in the spring of 1856 the society issued a report calling for the revision of the laws governing married women's property,

> and embarked on a campaign to enact a law giving every married woman the status of *feme sole* with respect to her property and contracts. On 31 May the society held an open meeting on the status of women under the law. Consistent with its earlier efforts to eliminate the conflict between law and equity, the assembly unanimously adopted a resolution condemning the common law rule of married women's property and endorsed the equitable concept of separate estates.[523]

Encouraged by this endorsement, Leigh Smith and six of her colleagues accumulated a petition of 25,000 signatures. The cause was eventually taken up when, following the reconvening of parliament in the spring of 1857, a Married Women's Property Bill was introduced to the House of Commons by Sir Erskine Perry and seconded by Milnes. The Bill, which incorporated all the provisions endorsed by the Law Amendment Society, passed its second reading by 120 votes to 65.

In May 1857, Milnes further reinforced his growing reputation as a champion of women's rights by sternly rebuking his parliamentary colleague, Beresford Hope, who had referred to the 25,000 signatories of a petition in favour of Married Women's Property Rights as a 'large and manly body of "strong-minded women"'.[524] Milnes criticised Hope for 'sneering' in such manner, adding that, 'The House ought to address itself to the Amendment of our matrimonial law in a serious, not a jesting spirit.'[525] In the event, the Bill was stymied by the passage of the Divorce Act 1857 (to which Queen Victoria gave her royal assent on 25 August 1857). Central to this legislation was a clause enabling magistrates to protect women from any claims made on their earnings or property by husbands who may have deserted them.[526]

Disillusionment with the political system had now set in, such that:

> During the Session Milnes drifted further away from the political life in which he had once been so anxious to play a conspicuous part. His chronic state of dissatisfaction with both parties and their leaders seemed to be intensified as time passed, and more and more he found himself subsiding into that position of social moderator and literary patron which the world had almost from his first appearance in society assigned to him.[527]

Based largely in London, the Milneses attended numerous social gatherings in celebration of the engagement of the Princess Royal to Prince William of Prussia. They also hosted a series of breakfasts and dinner parties, and took the opportunity to attend various art exhibitions, including the first ever dedicated Pre-Raphaelite exhibition on 23 June. Within days of this event, rumours began circulating of a gathering revolt (or 'mutiny') in India. Sensationalist newspaper reports of atrocities against women and children in places like Delhi and Calcutta provoked a 'frenzied and bloodthirsty reaction' in England,[528] though Milnes was kept more accurately informed by such correspondents as Sir James Colville (Chief Justice of Bengal) and Sir Charles MacCarthy (Colonial Secretary at Kandy), who were both old friends of his. The crisis soon passed and, 'Save for providing an exciting new topic for conversation for a few weeks, the Indian Mutiny had but a transitory effect on the daily life of the English upper classes.'[529]

It has been speculated, however, that events in India indirectly affected the outcome of a determined and ultimately successful attempt by Lord Chief Justice Campbell to push through an Obscene Publications Bill. Campbell had been galvanised into taking such action when presiding over the trial in May 1857 of two men charged with selling obscene publications.[530] The Bill provided, quite simply, for police officers to be given the right, on the authority of a magistrate, to enter and search any property suspected of harbouring obscene publications, to seize such materials and destroy them.[531] A moral panic was unleashed in which the corrupting potential of such literature on middle-class youth was highlighted in the popular press.[532]

Predictably, the Bill was vigorously opposed by Milnes, who, as Russell Searle cynically observes, 'just happened to own an extensive library of erotica'.[533] Speaking in the House on 12 August 1857, Milnes referred to the sense of dread conveyed to him by innocent booksellers who collectively:

> entertained a well-grounded fear that, in a trade where so much competition existed, the Bill, if passed, would enable any man, hostilely disposed towards them, to give information,

> and declare upon oath, that he knew they had some obscene books in their possession.[534]

Given the tendency within this trade for booksellers to buy entire libraries in one go, there was every possibility of the existence of at least one incriminating volume on the premises, albeit without the proprietor's knowledge. Milnes asserted that the 'evil being complained of' was actually limited to two or three streets of the capital and was, therefore, 'not to be told that they could not provide an adequate remedy without establishing a system of domiciliary visits most dangerous in principle and most injurious to private individuals'.[535]

He indignantly maintained that the conferment of enhanced police powers was bound to considered 'disgustful' to the wider English public and that 'the Bill would never have reached its present shape if hon. Members had had the manliness to state what were their real opinions on the subject'.[536]

It is possible that Milnes had in his sights a substantial core of religious-minded Liberal colleagues who might balk at publicly opposing the Bill. Either way, the Bill was passed into law on 25 August 1857. Roberts contends that the timing of the debate proved highly propitious for advocates of the Act.[537] Not only were its opponents and detractors more concerned with (and therefore distracted by) other 'major libertarian concerns', notably the Married Women's Property Bill, but oppositional attitudes were undermined by the moral influence of the Indian Mutiny, insofar as:

> It strengthened the resolve of Evangelical interventionists to purify the home society to make it worthy of its imperial mission. It also immensely hardened the general public mood against 'sentimentality' in matters of social control, including the sexual. In a process significant for the future development of 'liberal' attitudes toward social regulation, it helped to detach a section of the progressive elite from the libertarian ranks of domestic political tradition and to make it more receptive to a paternalist-imperial set of social priorities at home as well as abroad.[538]

Supporting Foreign Writers

During this period, Milnes was assiduous in his corresponding attempts to elevate the profiles of three non-British writers of great distinction: the German, Heinrich Heine; the American, Nathaniel Hawthorne; and the Russian, Ivan Turgenev.

The Resurrection of Heinrich Heine

In late 1856, Milnes did for the recently deceased German writer, Heinrich Heine, what he had earlier done for Keats. Heine had first achieved prominence with the appearance of his notorious *Travel Sketches* (in 1826), a work that earmarked him as a 'witty and irreverent writer' whose caustic views on religion and anti-government stance resulted in the proscription of his work in some German states, but saw him become 'in the eyes of many the brave warrior of the pen and the noble champion of liberalism'.[539]

In the 1830s and 40s, writers and personal friends of Milnes, notably Carlyle and Charles Kingsley, had been scathing in their criticism of Heine's work. Carlyle referred to the German as 'that blackguard Heine' (and much later as 'That slimy and greasy Jew – fit only to eat sausages made of toads'), while Kingsley is alleged to have described him to his children as a 'wicked man'. There is anecdotal evidence that Milnes was already an enthusiastic reader of Heine's work when he went to Bonn in the summer of 1830.[540] It was during his visit to Paris in the winter of 1839-40 that Milnes first met Heine, following a letter of introduction from Lady Lucie Duff Gordon, and instantly formed a warm and lasting mutual admiration.[541] These sentiments were reflected in Milnes's somewhat eulogistic article, 'Heinrich Heine', which was published in the *Edinburgh Review* for July 1856[542] following Heine's death the previous February.

Milnes's article sat alongside a number of other pieces written in praise of the deceased poet. Prominent among these were three articles by George Eliot (appearing in *The Leader, The Saturday Review* and *The Westminster Review*). What most distinguished Milnes's article from those of his contemporary was its sharper and more subjective focus on Heine's core beliefs with regard to such issues as religion (e.g. the relative merits of Judaism and Christianity), Communism, and the position of the aristocracy. Eliot's was, by contrast, a more detached account of Heine's life and works. The more personalised tone of Milnes's tribute was greatly augmented by the content of letters from Duff to Milnes, recalling her meetings with Heine in 1853 and 1855, which she allowed Milnes to use on condition that he did not refer to her directly in his article. The resulting description of Heine's last days comprised an extremely touching and disarming tribute which generated great sympathy towards him:

> All that time he lay upon a pile of mattresses, racked by pain and exhausted by sleeplessness, till his body was reduced below all natural dimensions, and his long beard fell over the coverlid like swan's down or a baby's hair. The muscular debility was such that he had to raise the eyelid with his hand when he wished to see the face of any one about him: and thus in darkness, he thought, and listened, and dictated, preserving to the very last his clearness of intellect, his precision of diction, and his invincible humour. He bore his anguish in a perfectly unaffected manner, with no pretence of stoicism, and evidently pleased by tokens of sorrowful sympathy. He called himself 'the living Shade of the Champs Elysées,' and in his conversation exhibited a heartiness and indulgence towards others, almost foreign to his sarcastic nature, the identity of which, however, is prominent in his compositions to the last.[543]

Lipzin sees the tributes conferred on Heine by Milnes and Eliot as pivotal to the promotion and re-evaluation of the German's work and personality. They succeeded, in his view, 'in effecting a complete reversal of English sentiment, so that a generation later Heine came to be revered as the continuator of Goethe and as the foremost poet and wit of nineteenth-century Germany'.[544]

Toasting Hawthorne and Turgenev

On 15 April 1857, Milnes renewed his friendship with Nathaniel Hawthorne, who he first met in 1853 but had seldom seen subsequently. Both were attending a celebration of the laying of a cornerstone of the Free Library for Liverpool, which was being built on the strength of funds donated by William Brown MP, who had family connections with W. and J. Brown of Baltimore, a cotton-importing company for whom the MP had established an English headquarters in

Liverpool. This historic occasion not only symbolised a strengthening of transatlantic relations, but consolidated Milnes's pro-American credentials.

After the ceremony, a banquet for 900 guests was held at 2pm in St George's Hall. Hawthorne was one of the principal speakers and was introduced in laudatory fashion by Milnes, whose comments were quoted as follows by *The Liverpool Mercury*:[545]

> That connection which Mr Brown has established between the material interests of England and America, Nathaniel Hawthorne has done much to establish between the moral interests of the two countries. (Hear, hear.) His 'Scarlet Letter' has struck to the heart of every man with whom it came in contact. He has built his house of 'Seven Gables' in every town in England; and as for his 'Twice-Told Tales,' we all wish they had been told ten times. (Applause.) Gentlemen, therefore, in giving you the health of that distinguished citizen of the United States and that distinguished citizen of the literature of the world, I believe that you will join with me, and that you will feel you are in no degree derogating from the special purposes for which we have met together. (Applause.) Thank God, these two great nations, speaking the same great speech, carrying out in the main the same great institutions, are the hope and blessing of mankind – the hope of the future world, and, under Providence, a blessing to the nations.[546]

A second such act of literary patronage occurred one month later, with the arrival in London of the great Russian novelist Ivan Turgenev. Turgenev came equipped with a letter of introduction from the English-born socialite Madame Mohl, who 'held a famous though not too influential salon in the rue du Bac, where she lived with her husband Julius, the orientalist'.[547] Turgenev had breakfasted with the Mohls on 28 April 1857, just before leaving for England, and Mohl's badly punctuated letter was sent to Milnes prior to his arrival:

> 'This is to introduce to you Ivan Tourguenieff [sic] who has written a book called *Avantures d'un Chasseur Russe* [sic],' it started. 'he is very full of curious information has a passion for the English the translation of the book is enormously popular here he is a man to suit you & your house you'll see that with half an eye.'[548]

Standing six-feet-three in height, big-boned, with a full 'tawny white' beard, Turgenev was certainly difficult to miss.[549] Following his arrival in London on 24 May 1857, he was introduced in no time at all to Thackeray, Carlyle, Macauley, Disraeli and the Nightingales. Waddington considers it likely that most of these meetings were set up by Milnes,[550] whom Turgenev first encountered in the first week of June at the Englishman's residence at 16, Upper Brook Street, Mayfair.

Following their initial meeting, Milnes offered to show Turgenev round the Houses of Parliament. The Russian listened attentively to the debates, particularly when references were made to his own country, and when Milnes rose to speak on the confused and destitute condition of members of the Italian Legion who had been sent to settle in the Argentine Republic. Evidently, 'Turgenev did not actually think all this very interesting, though he could not fail to be amused by his friend's contribution to the proceedings.'[551]

This was followed by a 'rather splendid dinner', hosted by Richard and Annabel Monckton Milnes on Thursday 11 June. Included among the twelve guests were Benjamin Disraeli and William Makepeace Thackeray. The occasion is perhaps best remembered for the tetchy nature of this introductory encounter between Thackeray and Turgenev. Though feeling 'down-hearted and ill', Thackeray was at the height of his literary powers and reputation.[552] He was, therefore, taken aback by the seemingly disrespectful and challenging nature of someone whose limited canon of literary work (consisting only by then of *Rudin* and 'some poor translations of the Sportsman's Sketches') was scarcely known to British audiences. Clearly peeved by Turgenev's forthright demeanour, Thackeray maintained that Russia could not boast a single author of note. At this:

> Turgenev now saw red. 'I must inform you', he expostulated, 'that we have a satirical writer greater than yourself in all respects; and I say this despite my own high opinion of your talents.' Who on earth could that be? was Thackeray's furious reply, 'Gogol', said Turgenev, and proceeded to elaborate; but Thackeray, like most of educated Europe, had never heard of Gogol and waited to learn no more. The conversation ended here, and with it all relations between the two novelists.[553]

The relationship between Turgenev and Milnes was rekindled in the spring of 1858, by which time Turgenev's artistic stock was continuing to rise. Having recently arrived from Paris by boat, his first major social engagement was an eight-person breakfast hosted on 3 May by Milnes. Two days later, the two men were enjoined again at the annual dinner of the Royal Literary Fund, held at Freemasons' Hall, an event considered 'the year's most impressive gathering of British writers and patrons of the arts'.[554]

Milnes's philanthropic orientation to life was reflected in his role on the management committee of this charitable institution dedicated to relieving hardship among impoverished writers and their families. It was Milnes who had not only extended the invitation for Turgenev to attend, but also arranged for the Russian to be seated between Reeve and Thackeray. Turgenev and Milnes were disappointed (and suspicious) to hear that Thackeray had cried off due to 'spasms', but Turgenev was cheered up by the welcome presence of Lord Palmerston, who was also there at Milnes's invitation.[555]

Milnes had the honour of proposing a toast to 'the Literature of Continental Europe'. He had also arranged for Turgenev to speak at the meeting, knowing that he was keen to highlight a comparable institution which was in the process of being established in Russia. Turgenev clearly had an extremely high regard for Milnes, whom he referred to as a 'good man of letters' and one of 'the most agreeable and obliging men in the world'.[556] Milnes had nothing to gain tangibly from this relationship. However:

> As his half-century approached, Milnes himself no longer cared: life was its own remuneration. To this extent, Turgenev was right to call him 'good'. Milnes was also useful to Turgenev in his own current mood of premature decay and isolation, and for his part was attracted to the novelist by that warm yet level-headed humanity which endeared him to a long line of admirers.[557]

A Robin's Arrival in Winter

A parallel transformation was occurring in Milnes's family life. In the course of 1857, Milnes had lost two of his most intimate friends: his former Cambridge peer, Augustus Stafford (formerly Stafford O'Brien); and Lady Ashburton, whom he had asked two years earlier to stand as a godmother to his first son. That opportunity had passed by the time that, on 9 January 1858, Annabel produced a brother for their two girls. The name of the newly-born Robert Offley Ashburton Milnes (known within the family as 'Robin') derived from those of his paternal grandfather and two medieval ancestors on the Crewe side (Robert), his mother's clergyman cousin (Offley), and his godfather (Lord Ashburton, who took the place of his deceased wife).

Sadness lay just around the corner, however. The christening and breakfast in honour of young Robin were conducted in the absence of Robert Pemberton Milnes, who was far too ill to travel down from Yorkshire.

> He declared that he was now so thin that a carrion crow could not have lived on him for a week, and as the months of 1858 went by his languor grew. He would be with his feet up on a sofa in the newly-painted drawing-room at Fryston, but by the end of the summer he was practically bedridden, and stayed mostly in his own room, cared for alternately by his daughter, his daughter-in-law and his sisters.[558]

The end came on 9 November, when Pemberton Milnes failed to rally from the last in a series of recurring 'crises'. He was buried shortly after in the family tomb in the churchyard at Ferry Fryston. Milnes installed a brass plaque next to the church pulpit in his father's memory. Pope-Hennessy is adamant that the personal differences between father and son obscured the genuine fondness and admiration each harboured for the other.[559] Nevertheless, the younger man's conviction 'that his father had failed him, and had duly interfered in his life, no doubt inspired the careful education and training which he successfully gave to his own son'.[560]

Chapter Twelve
I Spy? The Adventures of 'Ruffian Dick'

Liberty Hall

Following the death of his father, Richard Monckton Milnes wrote to his old friend Charles MacCarthy from Fryston on 23 November 1858 to inform him of the news:

> My dear father died on the 9th of this month, closing a long and weary illness with a peaceful and easy transit to the spirit world. I am left with a fair gentleman's fortune and a considerable amount of debt, which I hope gradually to pay off and put Master Robert in a comfortable position [...] This event will make little difference in my course of life; it will keep me more here, as I have a large farm on my hands, and the place left in not very good condition. My wife and children remain well and promise well, learning everything with a pleasure incomprehensible to the mature mind.[561]

Ever since the death of his wife in 1847, Pemberton Milnes had overseen the gradual renovation and redecoration of Fryston Hall. His daughter-in-law had striven, meanwhile, to add lustre and allure to the rather dull and functional appearance of the estate by introducing lavender beds, nasturtiums and sweet-peas, in such a way as to 'make this bleak Yorkshire house "pretty and enjoyable"', thereby offsetting its typically northern 'roughness and austerity'.[562] Any qualms Milnes may have felt on being 'thrust into the inconceivably unsuitable role of landowner and Yorkshire squire'[563] were compensated by the fact that the Hall itself was tailor-made for staging the type of large parties that had long been his forte.[564]

From the summer of 1859 onwards, the Milneses hosted regular gatherings of up to sixteen people. The rich and famous of London mingled contentedly with their north-country counterparts. One such visitor that autumn was the celebrated socialite, old friend, and mutual admirer of Milnes, Lady William Russell, 'whose beauty, wit, scholarship and powers of conversation made their mark first in London and then in Paris'.[565] Lady Russell kept one of the 'choicest' salons in all London. It was therefore with some trepidation that Annabel Milnes anticipated her arrival at Fryston. She need never have worried, for the visit was resoundingly successful: 'As Lady William, carrying a big posy of lavender, stepped into the carriage for Knottingley station, she assured her hostess that she had seen "nothing so pleasant", as Fryston, "since the best days of Holland House".'[566]

Such praise was undoubtedly deserved. The hospitality extended to Mr and Mrs Milnes's guests was unrivalled:

> Milnes was an early riser, and he had usually been up some hours before the guests assembled at small round tables in the breakfast-room for a meal which he and they regarded as his especial province. He would seat himself in some vacant chair at one of the tables, or wander from group to group with a book in his hand, talking and joking away as briskly as at his breakfast-parties in London. These breakfast-room discussions were one of the peculiar features of a stay at Fryston. Another was the lack of billiards, for Milnes stood out against this game in a period when almost every country house in England contained a billiard-table in a converted room or new annexe. A third peculiarity of Fryston was the absence of 'circulating library books'. This drove people staying in the house to the thorough investigation of Fryston library.[567]

The library itself was long, narrow, handsomely furnished and comfortable, with wall after wall of books. Aside from the poetry of the nineteenth century, the books embraced such diverse subjects as works of fiction, theology, magic and witchcraft, the French Revolution, the causes and punishment of crime, school discipline, and French and Italian erotica (including the works of the Marquis de Sade).[568]

The sheer wealth and notoriety of this library proved irresistible to Milnes's many guests – none more so than Sir Richard Burton, the immensely charismatic and mysterious soldier, geographer, explorer, translator, writer and (allegedly) spy, who began visiting Fryston around this time. The relationship between Milnes and Burton was to prove enduring. Together, they helped shape Victorian attitudes to identity and sexuality, and strongly influenced the artistic and social directions undertaken by the celebrated but controversial poet Algernon Charles Swinburne. It is therefore imperative that we retrace the origins and trajectory of this relationship, as well as relations between the two men and Burton's wife, Isabel Arundell, who also figured prominently in this fascinating period in Fryston's history.

The Rake of the Orient

The son of an Irish-born British Army Colonel and a co-heir to the fortune of a wealthy English squire, Richard Burton was born in Devon on 19 March 1821. His father's scattered military postings meant that he was educated primarily by personal tutors. During his first term at Trinity College, Oxford, in 1840, Burton challenged another student to a duel. Two years later he was expelled for attending a steeplechase event in contravention of university rules. His immediate reaction was to embark on a military career, starting with a commission in the Indian Army where he was engaged in the Sikh wars.[569]

According to Colligan, Burton was assigned, in 1845, to the task of investigating the activities of male brothels in Karachi.[570] Burton conducted this mission in such persuasive undercover disguise as to enable him to understand the practices of sodomy, pederasty, and transvestism: 'As critics wondered how he obtained this information, the report damaged his reputation and his advancement in the army.'[571] Activities of this nature, and Burton's accompanying reputation, were to become a major obstacle in his bid to overcome the resistance of his prospective in-laws and win the hand of their daughter in marriage, though this was not the initial reason for their opposition.

Isabel Arundell was born on 20 March 1831 at Great Cumberland Place, within short distance of London's Marble Arch. She was the oldest child in a very large and prominent Roman Catholic family containing fourteen children of which ten died young. Although her parents were wealthy members of the minor English aristocracy (with ancestral links to Henry VIII), they were subject to anti-Catholic persecution, which remained evident despite the recent passage of the Catholic Emancipation Act. Isabel was reputed to be 'as physically active as any boy'.[572] She was also extremely well-read, and once proclaimed that *Tancred* was both 'the book of her life' and her 'second bible'.[573] The notable revival of anti-Catholic sentiment in the late 1840s (most vividly manifested in the 'No Popery riots' of the era) prompted her family to temporarily re-locate to the French coastal city of Boulogne, where she and her sisters were placed in the convent of the Sacré-Coeur, and lived according to the strict disciplinary code insisted on by their mother.[574]

Isabel was 19 years old when, in the autumn of 1850, she first crossed paths with Burton. Already widely rated as 'amazingly beautiful', she was, by now, 'a tall, willowy, independent, honey-blond, blue-eyed young woman of much self-assurance'.[575] She and her sister, Blanche, were unaccompanied and still in school uniforms when, in the process of walking along the city ramparts, they became aware of a striking figure coming in the opposite direction:

> The vision of my awakening brain came toward us [said Isabel]. He was five feet eleven inches in height, very broad, thin, and muscular; he had very dark hair, black, clearly defined, sagacious eyebrows, a brown weather-beaten complexion, straight Arab features, a determined-looking mouth and chin, nearly covered by an enormous black moustache [...] But the most remarkable part of his appearance was two large, black flashing eyes with long lashes, that pierced you through and through. He had a fierce, proud melancholy expression, and when he smiled, he smiled as though it hurt him, and looked with impatient contempt at things in general. He was dressed in a black, short, shaggy coat, and shouldered a short thick stick as if he were on guard.[576]

Aware that Burton had fixed a penetrating, appreciative stare on her, Isabel confessed to feeling 'completely magnetised'. She whispered prophetically to her sister: 'That man will marry me.'[577] A day later, their paths crossed once again. Burton followed the young women in their tracks and eventually chalked 'May I speak to you?' on the rampart. Isabel responded in like manner: 'No, mother will be angry.' Her prediction proved well-founded: having recognised her daughter's handwriting, Mrs Arundell took steps to ensure that Isabel would have no further contact with Burton.[578]

This preventative strategy failed: the couple's paths would still occasionally cross while Isabel was out walking under chaperone. Sadly for them, however, Isabel was forced to return home with her family to England, making it four years before the couple would meet again. Once back home, Isabel's parents tried to marry her off to a succession of 'young gentleman' from old-established Catholic families. She resolutely rejected every suitor. Meanwhile, Burton's notoriety was further enhanced when, in 1853, he was given leave by the East India Company to travel as an undercover agent to the sacred city of Mecca, a location considered off limits to non-Muslims.

Burton made the perilous journey, completed by only a handful of Europeans before him, in various disguises (a Persian Shia, a Sunni 'Shakykh', a simple Muslim). His riveting account, published as *Personal Narrative of a Pilgrimage to El-Medinah and Meccah* in 1855, became an ethnographic classic, going rapidly into four editions and turning Burton into an adventure hero in England.[579]

After rejoining his regiment in April 1854, Burton was temporarily assigned to the political department of the East India Company. It was not long, though, before he embarked on another expedition – this time to explore the Somali regions of Africa. On the first leg of this expedition, he was based in Harar (the present-day Ethiopia) where he assumed the guise of an Arab merchant. He then set out to explore the Somalian interior, a journey undertaken in the company of Lieutenant John Hanning Speke. Soon afterwards, the expedition party was attacked by 200 Somali warriors. Burton managed to escape, but a spear lodged in his face left a permanent facial scar. Speke was initially captured and only managed to escape after incurring several stab wounds. Burton's fascination with the sexual practices and proclivities of other societies was reflected in his subsequent *First Footsteps in East Africa; or, An Exploration of Harar.*[580] This included in-depth discussions of the taboo areas of prostitution, lovemaking positions, and male and female circumcision.[581]

After a brief spell back in the army, Burton set off on another expedition in 1856, this time in exploration of an inland sea flowing inwards from Zanzibar. Burton was accompanied, once again, by Speke. Although their official brief required them only to investigate the presence of local tribes and determine the area's trade potential,

Burton and Speke harboured private ambitions to locate the source of the Nile. Before setting out, Burton resumed his relationship with Isabel (and they got secretly engaged prior to his departure). The expedition proved to be a torrid experience for Burton:

> From late 1856 to early 1859 he traveled to Africa and deep into the Lake Regions. He suffered from debilitating parasites, ferocious fevers and 'a sensation of wretchedness.' And now that he was back, his personal life was falling apart. His traveling companion on the Nile expedition, John Hanning Speke, betrayed him and claimed credit for a discovery – the source of the Nile itself – that Burton did not believe they had made or, more to the point, did not believe that Speke could prove. Isabel Arundell, Burton's admiring and obsessive fiancée, told him that her parents had forbidden her to marry him. Meanwhile he was buried in the avalanche of notes and sketches he'd gathered in the Lake Regions, trying desperately to write a book that would somehow set it all straight.[582]

Feting the Returning Adventurer

Burton returned from Africa in the spring of 1859. According to Rice, his first few months back home were marked by countless invitations from 'the elite, the powerful and the influential', especially among the literary and bohemian sections of society.[583] Not surprisingly, Milnes (who was reputed to have been instrumental in getting one or more of Burton's expeditions funded by the Royal Geographical Society) was foremost among those who sought out and feted the returning adventurer.[584]

In August 1859, Burton made the first of a series of visits to Fryston. Among those gathered in his honour were Spedding and Venables; the painter Samuel Laurence, who was working on a portrait of Mrs Milnes; Robert Curzon of the Monasteries; Petherick of Khartoum; Sir Charles MacCarthy (who, with the help of Milnes's influence, was soon to be appointed Governor of Ceylon); and W.E. Forster. As Lovell points out, 'Fryston enjoyed the same reputation in the nineteenth century as did Cliveden in its heyday under the Astors, a hundred years later,'[585] and there is no doubt that Burton 'revelled in the erudite discussions that were the mark of Fryston house-parties'. What he prized most about such visits, however, was the opportunity to lose himself in the vast library – especially on Sunday mornings when he invariably stayed back while the other guests went off to worship.[586]

Of particular interest to Burton was Milnes's vast collection of erotica, recently made illegal and therefore driven underground by the publication of the Obscene Publications Act of 1857, which promised harsh penalties for those caught distributing, or in possession of, such material. This meant that, for avid collectors like Milnes, supply had to be maintained via the guileful use of the postal system or channels set up by private dealers from places like Paris and Rotterdam.[587] In Milnes's case, books continued to be provided by a British expatriate in Paris called Frederick Hankey.

The son of a distinguished English General and beautiful Grecian mother, Hankey had no other job or position save that of provider of erotica, but his relatively high social standing shielded him from close scrutiny by the law. His French apartment was decorated with a variety of statues and sexual objects which betrayed an undisguised obsession with flagellation and other forms of sado-masochism. According to Rice, Hankey became 'the stock figure of the English sadist' portrayed in Victorian-era French and English novels.[588] He always travelled in the company of his French mistress. Due partly to this:

> he was not welcome at Fryston when bringing erotica – what a commentary that was on the double standards of the Victorians! – and so he sent books over either in diplomatic pouches or strapped to the back of a Mr Harris, the manager of Covent Garden, a frequent visitor to France on business.[589]

Pope-Hennessy maintains that Burton's visit to Fryston served to strengthen his social ties to Milnes – so much so that, during the subsequent winter months, they regularly met up in London to enjoy 'bachelor evenings' together, sometimes, in the company of Burton's acquaintance, Colonel Studholme Hodgson, 'an elderly libertine who enjoyed describing his conquests and seductions'.[590]

Anthropologist or Spy?

Despite the 'many interruptions and distractions' cluttering up his daily life, Burton engaged in a sustained and productive spell of writing which saw the completion of the massive two-volume *Lake Regions of Central Africa*, which was despatched to his publisher on 10 April 1860. Any resulting euphoria or relief that Burton may have felt was nullified by the frustration he was enduring, due to the fact that the Arundells remained steadfastly opposed to his marriage to their daughter. He also learned to his chagrin that Speke was about to return to Africa, though this time in the company of a different fellow-traveller.[591] Burton had resorted by now to drinking heavily; and when the Swiss physician (and co-translator of the *Thousand and One Nights*) John Steinhauser suggested that he 'come with me and drink through America', Burton impulsively accepted, seeing this as a temporary solution to his problems. He therefore posted a note to Isabel (who was stricken down with the flu at the time), announcing his sudden departure.[592]

Rice considers it possible that Milnes helped Burton obtain the necessary extension of his leave to enable his visit to the United States.[593] The decision to travel west remained extremely perplexing: 'The subject of America had not previously appeared in Burton's published thoughts; there was no foreshadowing of such a journey as there had been of those into Arabia or Africa, no Mecca or Nile to discover.'[594]

Eventually, Burton focused his attention on the so-called Indian Wars, and on exploring the tenets and lifestyle of the Mormons in Utah. His findings and conclusions were subsequently documented in *The City of the Saints, and Across the Rocky Mountains to California*, a book dedicated to Milnes, 'a linguist, traveller, poet, and, above all, a man of intelligent insight into the thoughts and feelings of his brother men'.[595]

Significant voids in Burton's account of his American sojourn have encouraged speculation that the visit was driven by a more secretive objective.[596] Such speculation relates to an observation that, during a brief stay in Washington, Burton paid a visit to the US Secretary of War, John B. Floyd, to secure authorised passes into US military bases associated with the Indian Wars. In January 1860, Floyd had authorised the despatch of 115,000 muskets and rifles into the Southern states, prompting the Union Commander in Chief, Ulysses S. Grant, to suspect that he was in the process of equipping the South for imminent civil war.[597]

It is known that Burton proceeded from Washington to the South, but there are no details of his progress. Rice speculates that this paucity of information suggests that Burton was actually embarked on an espionage mission, in which Milnes was quite possibly also implicated:

> There is another aspect to those lost days in the South. The year of 1860 was one of approaching crisis in the United States. The Union was on the verge of splintering: long-seething quarrels over states' rights, slavery, even agriculture and industry, were bringing the nation to the brink of civil war. Many Englishmen favored the South – cotton among other raw materials was basic to the British economy. It might be assumed that Burton was on a secret mission arranged by influential friends in London to certain Southern leaders. Milnes, who was to favor the North when war broke out, still might have played a role in backing the mission. That so many of Burton's trips had multiple purposes rarely became apparent until years later.[598]

Friends in High Places

Another notable visitor to Fryston around this time was the then prime minister (and other central figure in Mark Hodder's alternative history), Lord Palmerston, who travelled up from London in October 1860. The main objective of Palmerston's trip was to visit the industrial centre of Leeds, but he also called in on two 'ragged schools' for poorer children and officially opened the new Market Hall in Pontefract before settling at Fryston Hall as the guest of Milnes.[599]

During this visit, Milnes hosted a large party in Palmerston's honour with a guest-list primarily made up of local dignitaries. The following day, Palmerston was taken to the small church at Ferry Fryston (where people crowded outside with the intention of taking a peep at the Premier). He later witnessed the start of a local fox hunt before setting off to visit his estate at Fairburn for the first time in 27 years.

> The villagers, of course, were in a great state of excitement at an event of such unusual importance; and though they cannot in strictness be said to have crowded the streets, they maintained quite as much interest in their way, in his lordship's visit, and gave him as warm a welcome as any one of the larger and more important places which he has yet visited. There were a great many visitors, too, from the outlying hamlets, who helped materially to swell their numbers. The inspection was of a very minute character, and appeared to give general satisfaction on both sides [...] The village school was visited, and the burial ground of the chapel of ease ordered to be enlarged by additional land given by the Premier, who then lunched with his tenants.[600]

The Premier's planned tour of the wider West Riding was then curtailed, however, when Lady Palmerston was suddenly overcome by illness, forcing the party to cancel a scheduled visit to Wakefield.

Lord Palmerston was to play a pivotal role (at Milnes's instigation) in helping ease the Burtons into elite English society after the pair secretly married in January 1861. Burton's own family had been just as opposed to their union as the Arundells. Each side publicly disguised their private feelings of dismay but it was generally left to the couple's good friends to help the marriage prosper. Milnes, of course, was central to this campaign. As Isabel subsequently recalled:

> We had a glorious season, and took up our position in Society [...] [Milnes] was very much attached to Richard, and he settled the question of our position by asking his friend Lord Palmerston to give a party, and to let me be the bride of the evening; and when I arrived, Lord Palmerston gave me his arm, and he introduced Richard and me to all the people we had not previously known, and my relatives clustered around us as well. I was allowed to put my name down for a Drawing-room. And Lady Russell, now the Dowager, presented me at Court 'on my marriage.'[601]

It was owing to the influence of Lady Russell's husband, Lord John Russell, that Burton was appointed to the post of the Consulship of Fernando Po, leaving him with jurisdiction over 700 miles of West African coastline running along the Bight of Biafra. The only drawback was that the climate was considered too hot and inhospitable for white women to tolerate, making it impossible for Isabel to join him.

'His Blue Eyes Beaming'

Before leaving for Africa, Burton regularly escorted Isabel to Milnes's Brook Street residence and Lord Strangleford's townhouse in Great Cumberland Place. That summer, the Burtons also paid visits to a number of the country's grandest country houses, including Bulstrode (which belonged to the Duke of Somerset); Broadlands, the seat of Lord Palmerston; and Knowsley, which was home to Lord Derby, a good friend of one of Isabel's relatives, Lord Gerrard. As Isabel explained, in the course of this season, they 'met all that was worth meeting of rank and fashion, beauty and wit, and especially all the most talented people in the world'.[602] The last port of call, on 12 August, was the first of Isabel's many visits to Fryston Hall. She would later remark on the warmth of the reception typically awaiting them:

> The hospitalities of Lord Houghton have long since made Fryston famous. None of those who have had that pleasant experience will forget the hearty reception which awaited them after their drive to the Hall – the figure of the host just about the middle height, his brown hair flowing carelessly from his broad forehead, his blue eyes beaming with gladness at the arrival of his friends, as he stood on the top of the stone steps, in front of the house, with both hands extended. Then followed the cup of tea in the library [...] Guests would thus arrive at the rate of sixteen or twenty a day, staying the best part of the week; and when they dispersed, with an agreeable recollection of new friendships sown, disjointed ones re-cemented, much fresh knowledge mutually given.[603]

Included on the guest list were Thomas Carlyle and his biographer, James Anthony Froude; the poet Algernon Swinburne; the painter Holman Hunt; the Christian socialist and novelist Charles Kingsley; and the British writer and Parisian salon hostess Madame Mary Mohl. The Burtons arrived when the proceedings were already well underway. According to Madame Mohl, the couple became the immediate focal point:

> *se sint distribues les roles* he acts a ferocious musselman [Muslim] to her lovely oppressed and impassioned slave and I suspect they chuckle over our simplicity instead of fighting in their secret compartment and if she told you he had beat her I would believe it unhesitatingly.[604]

Another of the guests enticed to this gathering was Arminius Vámbéry, the acclaimed Hungarian linguist and adventurer. Tall, powerful and intimidating in appearance, Vámbéry was, allegedly, 'a man as brave and as inquisitive as Burton, a master of obscure languages and fearless in traveling in parts of the world where a white face could bring death'.[605]

Like Burton, Vámbéry possessed an expert knowledge of Sufi mysticism and, he too, had studied the Persian manuscripts of the *Rubáiyát of Omar Khayyám* years before its actual publication.[606] Rice maintains that Burton looked upon Vámbéry as 'not a fellow scholar but a rival in exotic fields, and the two men remained cool toward one another in all their meetings'.[607]

Vámbéry had already established himself as a regular fixture at Milnes's Brook Street residence, where, in the presence of such contrasting individuals as 'the fanatical admirer of Mohammedanism, Lord Stanley of Alderley, and the equally fanatical Protestant Bishop of Oxford, Dr. Wilberforce', he witnessed fierce debates on the teachings of Christ versus those of the Prophet Mohammed. Now, here at Fryston, he was to play a mischievous, prescribed role (described in his own words, below) requiring him to welcome Burton back from his honeymoon in the North-West of Africa:

> The company [...] had met here in honour of Burton, the great traveller, and as he was the last to arrive, [Milnes] planned the following joke: I was to leave the drawing-room before Burton appeared with his young wife, hide behind one of the doors, and at a given sign recite the first *Sura* of the Koran with correct Moslem modulation. I did as arranged. Burton went through every phase of surprise, and jumping up from his seat exclaimed, 'That is Vámbéry!' although he had never seen or heard me before. In after years I entertained the most friendly relations with this remarkable man [...] [I]n a word, this strangely gifted man, who was never fully appreciated in

> his own country, and through his peculiarities laid himself open to much misunderstanding, was from the very first an object of the greatest admiration for me.[608]

All present were greatly impressed by the combined brilliance of the two adventurers, who, sitting crossed-legged on cushions, traded stories of their exploits, after which Burton recited *Omar Khayyám* in two languages and chanted the Muslim call to prayer.[609] One person said to have been especially enthralled by this encounter was the on-looking Algernon Swinburne. As we are about to discover, this was not the first meeting between Burton and Swinburne, and was certainly not destined to be the last.

Chapter Thirteen
Two Poets, Two Protégés

Below lies one whose name was traced in sand.
He died, not knowing what it was to live:
Died, while the first sweet consciousness of manhood
And maiden thought electrified his soul,
Faint beatings in the calyx of the rose.
Bewildered reader! pass without a sigh,
In a proud sorrow! There is life with God,
In other kingdom of a sweeter air;
In Eden every flower is blown: AMEN.

– 'The Epitaph' by David Gray[610]

In Eden Every Flower is Blown

One of Richard Monckton Milnes's main virtues was an instinct to 'do everything he could to help young and unrecognised genius'.[611] This characteristic is evident in his well-documented patronage of two highly contrasting Victorian poets: the aristocratic and world-renowned Algernon Charles Swinburne, and the relatively obscure Scottish poet of humble origins David Gray. As Pope-Hennessy puts it, 'Concurrently with his discovery of Swinburne, [Milnes] had been trying to save the life of another young poet, condemned by consumption, and by his own febrile temperament, to an early and despairing death.'[612] The juxtaposition of these two instances of Milnes's patronage – one high-profile and controversial, the other scarcely publicised but arguably more moving – provides an insight into the nature of the man and the impact he could have on the artistic destinies and reputations of fellow poets.

The Poet of Merkland

It was David Gray with whom Milnes first became familiar. Here was a young man who had been born on 29 January 1838 in a small, one-storey cottage in Merkland near Kirkintilloch, Scotland. He was the eldest of a family of five boys and three girls, their father being a handloom weaver whose workshop was attached to their home. It had been the fervent wish of his parents that Gray might one day become a minister for the Free Church of Scotland.[613] Having spent an early career as a classroom teacher and private tutor, he began to attend classes in Theology, Greek and Latin at Glasgow University, returning home each Saturday night to spend the following day with his family. Legend has it that he spent part of these weekend visits wandering the banks of the nearby River Luggie, a custom which became the inspiration for his poetry and prose, some of which he contributed to the *Glasgow Citizen,* albeit pseudonymously.[614]

According to Gray's close friend and fellow Scottish poet and biographer, Robert Buchanan:

> David was a tall young man, slightly but firmly built, and with a stoop at the shoulders. His head was small, fringed with black curly hair. Want of candour was not his fault, though he seldom looked one in the face; his eyes, however, were large and dark, full of intelligence and humour, harmonizing well with the long thin nose and nervous lips. The great black eyes and woman's mouth betrayed the creature of impulse; one whose reasoning faculties were small, but whose temperament was like red-hot coal.[615]

Embedded in Gray's nature was 'a strange and exquisite femininity – a perfect feminine purity and sweetness'.[616]

It was towards the end of 1859 – just after he had completed his studies and his spell of teacher-training was reaching its conclusion – that Gray confessed to having lost his appetite for entering the Church and tried, without success, to gain a position on one of the Glasgow newspapers. He was also dispatching letters to eminent literary figures (including Benjamin Disraeli) in the hope that they might offer him some much-needed support and advice. But his approaches were generally received with indifference. It therefore occurred to Gray and his friend Buchanan that their only remaining option was that of 'going to London and taking the literary fortress by storm'.[617]

The two friends consequently decided to meet up on 5 May 1860 in Glasgow and take the 5 o'clock train to London; but, by an unfortunate quirk of fate (involving a failure to specify which of Glasgow's two stations they should meet at), they made their departure from Scotland and arrived separately in London. As Buchanan dolefully remarked, 'Had we left Glasgow in company, or had we met immediately after our arrival in London, the story of David's life might not have been so brief and sorrowful.'[618]

With no more than small change in his pocket, Gray decided to preserve his meagre resources by spending the night in Hyde Park. Some days later, he explained in a letter to his father that he had contracted 'the worst cold I ever had in my life'. It has been speculated that this was actually the source of a far more serious and unfortunate illness.[619]

Out of all those people Gray had written to for encouragement and advice, only Milnes had taken the trouble to respond. Gray had attached some manuscript poems to a letter soliciting the older man's advice about going to London and forging a literary career. As Milnes later recollected:

> I was struck with the superiority of the verses to almost all the productions of self-taught men that had been brought under my observation, and I therefore answered the letter at some length, recognising the remarkable faculty which Mr Gray seemed to me to possess; urging him to cultivate it not exclusively nor even especially but to make it part of his general culture and intellectual development; and above all desiring him not to make the perilous venture of a London literary life, but, at any rate for some time, to content himself with such opportunities as he had, and to strive to obtain some professional independence, however humble, in which his poetical powers might securely expand and become the solace of his existence instead of the precarious purveyor of his daily bread.[620]

Having arrived in London and endured an uncomfortable evening under its night sky, Gray settled in a lodging-house, from where he wrote to the one person who had seemed to take a genuine interest in his work. 'You promised to read my poem,' he reminded Milnes. 'Shall I *send* or *bring* it?' he asked, also imploring Milnes to act quickly as he was two days away from starvation.[621] Before Milnes had chance to reply, Gray turned up in desperation on his doorstep. As soon as he entered the room, Milnes knew that 'it could be no other than the Scotch poet'. He was immediately put in mind of a plaster cast he had once seen depicting Shelley in his youth.[622]

Milnes instantly set about disinvesting Gray of any remaining ambition to stay in London and pressed him to return home without delay. 'I painted as darkly as I could the chances and difficulties of a literary struggle in the crowded competition of this great city,' Milnes recalled, 'and how strong a swimmer it required to be not to sink in such a sea of tumultuous life.'[623] Gray was already firmly set, however, on a particular direction. The young man declined Milnes's unsolicited offer of money, but gratefully took on some 'light literary work' on behalf of Milnes and Laurence Oliphant. A subsequent visit was arranged, during which Milnes went over some poems with him, and stated afterwards how, 'I shall not forget the passionate gratification he showed when I told him that, in my judgment, he was an undeniable Poet.'[624] Gray experienced a setback, though, when, despite Milnes's 'hearty recommendation' to the editor (his good friend Thackeray), his poem, 'The Luggie', was rejected for possible inclusion in the *Cornhill* periodical.[625] Worse soon followed when the cough he had acquired developed into a fever, and then consumption.

Milnes was the first to spot the potential seriousness of this illness. He implored Gray to return home and had his own physician attend him.[626] For a short while, Gray moved in with Buchanan, to whom he remarked: 'If I die, I shall have one consolation – Milnes will write an introduction to the poems.'[627] Milnes could scarcely have done much more to help:

> Mr Milnes himself, full of the most delicate sympathy, trudged to and fro between his own house and the invalid's lodging; his pockets laden with jelly and beef-tea, and his tongue tipped with kindly comfort. Had circumstances permitted, he would have taken the invalid into his own house. Unfortunately, however, David was compelled to remain, in company with

me, in a chamber which seemed to have been constructed peculiarly for the purpose of making the occupants as uncomfortable as possible.[628]

Following Gray's brief stay in a Richmond nursing home, Milnes arranged through his aunts for the young poet's admission into a Torquay hospital, where the ailing poet was meant to stay at the older man's expense. Gray travelled to the hospital via the splendid-looking seafront, but his initial optimism was shattered when he discovered the property to be unclean, its staff slovenly and rude.[629] He immediately 'escaped' to the sanctuary of a nearby hotel before making his way back to Scotland, where he stayed until he died in December 1861. A posthumous collection of Gray's poetry included the verse quoted at the outset of this chapter, which was written three months before his demise.

Gray is reported to have once said to his own father that Milnes 'had said things to him that had been "worth coming to London for alone"'.[630] Against this, Milnes had reproached himself for not having bought Gray an overcoat when he first arrived, which might have spared him from consumption.[631] In keeping with Gray's wishes, Milnes contributed an 'introductory notice' to the latter's anthology of poetry, in which he reproached himself again:

> I much regret that imperative circumstances did not permit me to take him under my roof, that I at least might have the satisfaction of thinking that all human means of saving his life had been exhausted: for there was in him the making of a great man. His lyrical faculty, astonishing as it was, might not have outlived the ardour and susceptibilities of youth; but there was that simple persistence of character about him, which is so prominent in the best of his countrymen. I was much struck with seeing how he had hitherto made the best of all his scanty opportunities; how he had got all the good out of the homely virtues of his domestic life with no sign of reproach at the plain practical people about him for not making much of his poetry and sympathising with his visions of fame.[632]

This was not Milnes's final act of benevolence. As Pope-Hennessy explains, Milnes 'quietly sent money' to the poet's parents until as late as 1879.[633] This proved especially welcome since two of the Gray children had also contracted tuberculosis. Milnes also played a huge part in having a monument for the poet installed in the Auld Aisle Burying Ground on the hill overlooking Kirkintilloch. In addition to personally providing half the sum required, Milnes composed the following inscription:

> THIS MONUMENT OF
> AFFECTION, ADMIRATION, AND REGRET,
> IS ERECTED TO
> DAVID GRAY,
> THE POET OF MERKLAND,
> BY FRIENDS FROM FAR AND NEAR,
> DESIROUS THAT HIS GRAVE SHOULD BE REMEMBERED
> AMID THE SCENES OF HIS RARE GENIUS
> AND EARLY DEATH,
> AND BY THE LUGGIE, NOW NUMBERED WITH THE STREAMS
> ILLUSTRIOUS IN SCOTTISH SONG.
>
> *Born 29th January, 1838;*
> *Died 3rd December, 1861.*[634]

At the inauguration of the monument on 29 July 1865, the editor of Gray's posthumous anthology of poems spoke warmly of Milnes's role as donor and benefactor: 'I know it was a labour of love for him,' he stated, 'and I know he was anxious to write such an epitaph as would be thought suitable both here and elsewhere; and I venture to say, and I hope you will agree with me, that he has admirably succeeded in the simplicity and truth of that epitaph which has now been engraved on the monument.'[635]

An 'Inn of Strange Meeting'?

Milnes's relationship with Algernon Charles Swinburne has been cloaked in great controversy. It was on 4 May 1861 that Swinburne received a note at his home address (Grafton Street, Fitzroy Square, in London) from Milnes, inviting him to pay a visit the following day to the his townhouse in Upper Brook Street.

> The strange young gentleman whom the Milnes's butler ushered up the staircase of the Upper Brook Street house that spring evening of 1861 looked, at first go, preposterous. His head was crowned with frantic scarlet hair, his little face was white and pointed, his eyes were green and fringed with dark brown lashes. In stature he was even shorter than Monckton Milnes himself. He had a girlish figure, bottle shoulders and a dainty skipping walk: a wraith-like darting creature, comparable to the marshland *fourolle* of the Amiens folk-tales, and forming a definite contrast to his plump, red-faced, gouty host.[636]

The course of history undoubtedly turned significantly on the strength of this invitation. In the four-year period that followed, Milnes exerted 'the dominant influence in Swinburne's development and, even after their estrangement; left in the poet's mind sufficient of a presence to exercise a remote control for the rest of his life'.[637] Milnes became in Thomas's words, Swinburne's 'angel of darkness'.[638]

For better or worse, Swinburne was now entering a social circle in which 'wit was vigorous and uninhibited and Milnes reigned supreme'.[639] In London, and especially the 'Fryston Hall salon', this represented, as Lutz puts it, 'the ideal testing ground for Swinburne to develop and refine his art'.[640] She has no doubt that 'he learned a good deal from his fellow houseguests, progressive freethinkers all'.[641]

It was, more accurately, the 'dark and intimidating presence' of Richard Burton that had the most profound effect on Swinburne. Burton was present on the next occasion that Swinburne was invited over by Milnes – a breakfast party on 5 June, also attended by Coventry Patmore and Aubrey De Vere. It was perceptible from the outset that sparks of mutual attraction and fascination passed between the 'eccentric poet and the darkly exotic rakish adventurer'.[642] The two of them had taken off into a nearby room, where they privately engaged in 'roars and shrieks of laughter, followed by earnest rapid talk of a quieter description'.[643] Two months later, Milnes, Burton and Swinburne were reunited at Fryston on the occasion on which Vámbéry also made his appearance:

> Unfortunately, no account exists of what must have been an awkward assortment of breakfasts, country strolls, and controversial evenings. One project that all these characters

> shared, and that Swinburne brought to the poetry he was writing at the time, was a questioning of the Christian faith, a move toward either a radical refashioning of belief or a loss of it entirely.[644]

Henceforward, Burton and Swinburne were socially inseparable, enjoying wildly unrestrained drinking bouts, invariably ending with Swinburne engaging in acts of violence (and being carried out, kicking and screaming, by Burton to be placed in a hansom cab) or otherwise losing consciousness. Milnes was among those who believed that this was the start of Swinburne's addiction to brandy.[645] Though physically contrasting (one being puny and the other resembling an ultra-virile Elizabethan hero), Burton and Swinburne each admired the intellectual and unconventional; each loved and had a personal knack for outrageous storytelling; they were both sceptical of religion; they loved to shock and had a passion for 'the freakish and unusual'.[646] Swinburne is alleged to have confided in one associate that he and Burton had instantly felt 'a curious fancy, an absolute fascination, for one another'; and that he now knew what it was like to have an older brother.[647]

Swinburne's early biographers have imputed a sinister motivation to Milnes's bringing together of the poet and the adventurer. 'Swinburne and Burton!' cried Hare. 'Surely even for Lord Houghton this juxtaposition was a masterpiece!'[648] Lafourcade refers to Milnes's alleged engineering of this relationship as 'an inspiration, its realization a work of art'.[649] Leaving aside the plausibility of these assertions, this was a ruse which ultimately produced unintended consequences:

> With what a smile of sarcastic pride must Milnes have watched the Herculean explorer shaking hands with the frail Pre-Raphaelite model! What thoughts must have passed through the mind of the keeper of this 'inn of strange meeting'! But to his great surprise he found that he had overshot the mark; if he expected mutual disapproval, or at least bewilderment on the part of these two creatures, he was disappointed. Swinburne and Burton struck up at once a fast and enduring friendship.[650]

There are firm grounds for supposing that Milnes had subsequent cause to regret ever introducing Swinburne and Burton to each other.

According to Thomas, '[Milnes] remonstrated with his protégé over his conduct with Burton. [But] it was to take more than the diplomacy of Milnes to separate the tempter and his youthful prey.'[651]

An equally sinister and diabolical slant has been placed on Milnes's introduction of his young protégé to the works of the Marquis de Sade. The latter is viewed by many critics and biographers as the other-worldly and dark force to which the younger man's poetic destiny was regrettably diverted and enslaved. As Rooksby explains, 'Swinburne's life in the early 1860s has often been caricatured as a cross between a farce and a morality play, where Gifted Innocence is led astray by the malign influence of Corrupt Age.'[652] This characterisation is evident in the work of Praz, who dwells on Milnes's allegedly well-known proclivity for using his friends 'as instruments, in order to put together some strange, weird comedy, from which he, as spectator, would derive the greatest possible enjoyment'. Praz therefore speaks of Milnes as a 'Virgil', with 'a sting of Mephistophelean malice', knowingly escorting Swinburne 'through the inferno of a library'.[653]

There are many reasons for dismissing this as an over-simplification. It is apparent that Swinburne knew of, and was irretrievably drawn to, the 'treasure-house of erotic and sadistic literature' constituting the Fryston library,[654] but that Milnes was reluctant to grant him access to it. A letter from Swinburne to Milnes in October 1861 includes a reminder of Milnes's promise to allow him to 'look upon the mystic pages of the martyred Marquis de Sade', and of his experience in the meantime of going mad 'with curiosity alone'.[655] It was not until a visit to Fryston in the summer of 1862 that Swinburne, having finally been permitted to flick through *La Nouvelle Justine, ou les Malheurs de la Vertu*, was allowed to take four volumes back home to Cheyne Walk.

Back in London, on 16 August, Swinburne read out extracts in the company of the Pre-Raphaelite painter and poet Dante Gabriel Rossetti and other guests. The young poet was aware by now that de Sade's work was full of absurdity and not as shocking, stimulating or repulsive as he had anticipated.[656] He immediately conveyed his resulting disappointment by letter to Milnes:

> At first, I quite expected to add another to the gifted author's list of victims; I really thought I must have died or split open

> or choked with laughing. I never laughed so much in my life. I went from text to illustrations and back again, till I literally doubled up and fell down with laughter – I regret to add that all the friends to whom I have lent or shown the book were affected in just the same way.[657]

Rooksby suspects that Swinburne's outburst was possibly disingenuous – perhaps 'a rationalization and a defence against the feelings de Sade aroused'.[658] He contends that de Sade's influence soon became apparent in Swinburne's letters of this period. During a subsequent visit to Fryston, for example, Swinburne wrote to Rossetti, informing him that he had been helping Milnes translate a priceless autographed letter from de Sade, and flattering himself that de Sade's handwriting closely resembled his own.[659] Thereafter, as Mitchell points out, 'Swinburne's subsequent letters bubble with open and veiled allusions to [de] Sade';[660] and it becomes clear from them that de Sade's influence encouraged Swinburne's obsession with flagellation to rise to the surface.[661]

Mitchell maintains that Swinburne's preoccupation with flagellation was already an endemic feature of his personality, due to his experience of having been birched at Eton (which was 'vividly and enthusiastically remembered' in his letters to Milnes).[662] Mitchell contends that de Sade's work taught Swinburne not to be ashamed of admitting to these tendencies.[663] Subsequent references to his experience of being flogged certainly came thick and fast. One entry in Milnes's commonplace book, for November 1862, told of an encounter between 'Algernon Swinburne [and] a tutor who flogged him over the fallen trunk of a tree, till the grass was stained with his blood and another time when wet out of the water after bathing: the last much more painful!'[664]

Mitchell emphasises that any part Milnes may have played in encouraging Swinburne's obsession with the works of de Sade or the theme of flagellation was liable to have been unwitting, rather than maliciously contrived. He points to clear evidence that Milnes had been reluctant to lend out *Justine* or *Juliette* to his protégé due to the possibility that they might exert some sort of malign influence.[665] Such evidence also suggests that Swinburne's eventual exposure to these works served merely to satisfy an existing longing to claim de Sade as his role model:

> Swinburne was [de] Sade's enthusiastic champion before he had opened a page of his books. Sir William Hardman, after meeting the twenty-four year old Swinburne in 1861, described him as 'strongly sensual; although almost a boy, he upholds the Marquis de Sade as the acme and apostle of perfection, without (as he says) having read a word of his works'.[666]

In the autumn of 1861, Swinburne wrote a lengthy poem in French, 'Charenton en 1810', which 'takes the form of a pagan hymn to Sade, seeing in his physical features the quintessence of all that can be known or felt about life and death, good and evil'.[667] This, too, predated Swinburne's exposure to de Sade while visiting Fryston.

An altogether separate influence by Milnes on the work of Swinburne has been speculated by Wilson, who maintains that aspects of the poet's early novel *Love's Cross-Currents*, first written in 1861-62 and eventually published in 1905, allude to Milnes and his family.[668] Central to this story is the antagonistic relationship between Captain Harewood and his son, Redgie, a main feature of which is the father's ceaseless flogging of the boy throughout his childhood. Harewood follows this up by writing a stream of 'caustic and cutting letters' to Redgie in the latter's adulthood, which are designed to coerce the son into forging a profession in the Church.[669]

While several of Swinburne's biographers have interpreted this as an autobiographical reference to his relationship with his own father, Wilson detects a possible association between the 'ruthless repression' marking the relationship between Milnes and his father.[670] Wilson regards it as 'inconceivable that Milnes should have omitted mention of this when they exchanged flagellatory confidences',[671] and reckons that the barbed letters sent by Pemberton Milnes to his son acted as a 'stylistic model' for their fictitious counterparts:

> I do not for a moment suggest that Captain Harewood is Robert Pemberton Milnes, for the two are in numerous circumstantial respects quite unlike, but the possibility remains that Milnes' stories of his boyhood influenced Swinburne's novel. Annoyed

> with his own father and wishing to exaggerate his insensitive traits as he wrote, Swinburne may well have assimilated him to the fascinating and terrifying ogre suggested by his friend's anecdotes.[672]

In further evidence of this claim, Wilson invokes Pope-Hennessy's argument that Swinburne's naming and description of the childhood appearance of another central character, Amicia ('Amy') Cheyne, drew on his knowledge of the older of Milnes's two daughters; and that 'the bleak, dank aspect of Fryston in December is to be recognised in Swinburne's description of Captain Harewood's gloomy house, Plessey, where Amicia's half-brother Redgie is brought up'.[673]

Milnes's principal biographer justifiably maintains that, right from the outset, his orientation towards Swinburne was 'helpful and avuncular', and his influence primarily 'constructive'.[674] It may well add the lustre of notoriety to the images of both men to cast Milnes in the role of exploitative svengali, but things were much different in reality. In the early years of their relationship:

> Swinburne's elemental energies needed no human agent to go astray. Though their relationship was never particularly warm, Milnes gave Swinburne confidence in his writing and encouraged him to write only the poetry he could create rather than pastiche medieval lyrics and border ballads, even if this involved more obviously sado-masochistic content. Milnes introduced him to books and people, enabling Swinburne to publish in *The Spectator* in 1862.[675]

Such acts of benevolence (and the degree of suspicion surrounding them) were to continue unchecked as the decade progressed. As we shall see, this trend is exemplified by events surrounding Milnes's vicarious involvement in the American Civil War.

Chapter Fourteen
North and South

Trouble Abroad

It was a rough sea crossing that brought the American Minister Charles Francis Adams and his family across the Atlantic Ocean to Great Britain, where his renowned diplomatic skills would be tested to the full during the American Civil War of 1861 to 1865. Charles Francis was the American equivalent of royalty, being the son of John Quincy Adams, the sixth President, and the grandson of John Adams, the second President of the United States. The ocean had shown no mercy: the Minister, his wife, Abigail, and three of their children (Mary, Amy, and, the oldest of the three, 23-year-old Henry, who was employed as his father's private secretary) had all been severely sea-sick. Their experience was rendered even more unpleasant by the news that greeted them on their arrival (on the night of 13 May 1861) that the British, following the lead of their Foreign Secretary, Lord John Russell, had adopted a position of 'neutrality' vis-a-vis the war. The Minister learned that this stance had been formulated as the result of a meeting between Lord Russell and Confederate emissaries, in which the British recognised the South as 'belligerents in a war', rather than the perpetrators of an illegitimate 'rebellion'.[676]

It is probable that, as Charles Francis Adams privately suspected, the British establishment looked favourably on the prospect of Jefferson Davis forming a 'secessionist' government, which would help suppress the growing potency of a major rival to its global economic superiority.[677] As the conflict wore on, British opposition to the Unionist cause transcended any countervailing antislavery sentiments. This was due to the Unionist's strategy of blockading Southern ports, the impact of which was to starve the Lancashire textile industry of essential supplies of cotton.[678]

Along with a handful of other northern MPs, Richard Monckton Milnes was part of a very small minority of British politicians nailing their colours to the Union mast: 'He warmly supported the cause of the Union, while almost everyone else in London society hoped, and hoped openly, that the reactionary Southerners would win.'[679] It would be disingenuous to pretend that Milnes's contribution to the Union cause was equivalent to that exerted by certain other northern MPs; but it would be equally unwise to underestimate the key part he played in sustaining the morale and fortitude of the American Minister and his son. As we shall see, events occurring at Fryston Hall were central to this momentous period in world history.

Our Friends in the North

While in Britain, the Adamses were extended the courtesy of many invitations to formal dinners and receptions but 'felt they were able to penetrate the English reserve of only four people' (the northern MPs John Bright, Richard Cobden, William E. Forster and Richard Monckton Milnes).[680] According to Monaghan, Bright and Cobden 'were never seen in the best society. In parliament they had only a small radical following.'[681] What the third individual, the rough-looking, Yorkshire-born Forster, lacked in political experience or acumen, he more than made up for in philosophical conviction:

> Except in being a Yorkshireman he was quite the opposite of Milnes. He had at that time no social or political position; he never had a vestige of Milnes's wit or variety; he was a tall, rough, ungainly figure, affecting the singular form of self-defence which the Yorkshiremen and Lancashiremen seem to hold dear – the exterior roughness assumed to cover an internal, emotional, almost sentimental nature [...] Pure gold, without a trace of base metal; honest, unselfish, practical; he took up the Union cause and made himself its champion, as a true Yorkshireman was sure to do, partly because of his Quaker anti-slavery convictions, and partly because it gave him a practical opening in the House. As a new member, he needed a field.[682]

Such family tradition was epitomised by the conduct of his father, who had twice risked life and limb in his two visits to the United States to campaign against slavery.[683]

Forster and Milnes had been old friends for some seven years by the time Forster was elected an MP in February 1861. He had been an MP for a mere nine days when he delivered his maiden speech; Milnes and another MP had risen simultaneously but it was Forster who caught the Speaker's eye.

> Fighting had not yet broken out, but South Carolina had seceded from the Union and in Charleston the issue had come to a head with a demand for British ships to pay harbor duties to secessionary authorities. Forster obtained an assurance from Russell that the British consul had not recognized the legitimacy of the new government. Afterwards Monckton Milnes pointed out to Forster that in his nervousness he had mispronounced 'lamentable' as 'la*ment*able' but introduced his friend 'to old Pam, who was gracious'.[684]

Forster maintained his interventionist attitude by arranging, three months later, for Charles Francis Adams to attend a meeting with himself and other pro-Northern MPs. Adams was disappointed to discover that only seven people had turned up for the meeting, of which three were American. Neither John Bright nor Richard Cobden had accepted Forster's invitation. Of Forster's three parliamentary colleagues present in the room, it was Milnes who 'impressed Adams at once'.[685]

Doubt has been cast in some quarters as to whether Milnes was entirely committed to supporting the Union. Shain detects 'a feeling of reluctant respect for the Confederacy' on Milnes's part.[686] He points in justification to a letter quoted by Pope-Hennessy in which Milnes confided to a friend that he regarded 'the lower civilization, as represented by the South, [as] so much braver & cunninger & daringer than the cultivated shopkeepers of the North'.[687] Such apparent disdain for the two sides in the conflict should not be allowed to detract from Milnes's obvious appreciation of the war's underlying moral and political significance:

> Monckton Milnes was one of very few men in the House of Commons, still more of the landed gentry, to support the North, which he did so loudly and warmly that for the first time in his life he found himself a public hero, with a

> popularity up and down the country which he had never experienced before. He loathed 'the abominable selfishness of the South in breaking up a great country.' He was also automatically against slavery and Confederate reaction. His sympathy with the inhabitants of Leeds, Sheffield and other northern cities led him to understand and share their political views.[688]

Milnes and Forster were the most conspicuous champions of the Northern war effort. Forster's self-appointed role involved keeping a watching brief – making sure that:

> he kept himself diligently well informed as events unfolded, with the help of regular briefing from American allies such as Adams and the historian JL Motley, and showed the Government that the slightest digression from a policy of strict non-intervention would be noticed and challenged.[689]

During the parliamentary recess, he used a series of well-attended public speeches to sway public opinion towards an anti-slavery stance.[690] In the meantime, Milnes 'put himself about' in relevant circles of society, with the intention of helping to sustain the morale of his new-found American friends. This was evident in June 1861, when, along with Charles Francis Adams, he attended a dinner party thrown by Lady Palmerston, who 'had chosen the guest list with care, inviting people who were known friends of the North'.[691]

The Trent Affair

Milnes showed further support in November 1861, when he and Annabel invited the Adamses to stay with them at Fryston Hall. Charles Francis Adams Jnr subsequently asserted that Milnes 'was one of the very few whose sympathies were throughout strongly enlisted in favor of the United States; and he, from the beginning, showed a disposition to be civil'.[692]

Milnes's American guests arrived on 25 November and were evidently unimpressed by Fryston's '"somewhat ancient" decoration and total lack of modern conveniences'.[693] Persistent rainfall forced the large house party – which included pro-Union individuals including the novelist Elizabeth Gaskell, the archaeologist (and, more recently,

Under Secretary for Foreign Affairs) Austen Henry Layard, and the ubiquitous W.E. Forster – to huddle together indoors. Within two days, this experience had become far too much to bear. The group leapt at Milnes's suggestion that they brave the rain and visit the ruins of Pontefract Castle, where Richard II was murdered.[694]

As they set off for Pontefract (on the afternoon of Wednesday, 27 November), no one had any inkling of the potentially 'unmitigated disaster' already unfolding in London during the American Minister's absence.[695] At approximately 12.30pm, the American Legation had received a message, hastily conveyed from Southampton, of a civil war development that would, if allowed to go unchecked, propel Great Britain into direct conflict with the United States of America.

This diplomatic crisis had originated from a maritime incident on 8 November in which Charles Wilkes, captain of a Union warship, *San Jacinto*, had fired on and subsequently boarded a British mail packet, *The Trent*, in the Bahama Channel off the coast of Cuba:

> He had forcibly seized confederate Commissioners James Mason and John Slidell, who were on their way to Britain and France to present the confederate government's case for recognition of its independence, and had ignored the protests of the captain and commissioners, who had 'appealed to the British flag, under which they were sailing, for protection'.[696]

A day later, the two prisoners and their secretaries were whisked away to Boston, Massachusetts, where their arrival on 15 November was gleefully acclaimed, both by the North (who celebrated the capture of two 'secessionist conspirators'), and by the South, who saw this as the possible trigger for war between Great Britain and their Yankee adversaries.[697]

All of this was occurring five years before any Atlantic cable system had been established, meaning that, when news of the *San Jacinto*'s seizure eventually reached London via the steamship *La Planta,* it was already eighteen days out of date. It took very little time for a messenger bearing a telegram from London – 'a horseman bloody with spurring, fiery-hot with haste'[698] – to track down Charles Francis Adams as he was surveying the Pontefract castle ruins:

> The Minister would always remember standing in the persistent drizzle, making polite conversation with his fellow guests, while in his hand he clutched the news about *The Trent*. 'We had a very dark and muddy walk home,' he recorded [...] Dinner that evening was a tortuous affair. No one knew what to say, and Forster's attempts to make conversation were so ham-fisted that Adams could not help commenting in his diary: 'He is no courtier.' In the end, it was left to a local manufacturer, who had been invited to make up the numbers, to fill the void, which he did at great length in a diatribe addressed solely to Adams on the Morrill Tariff.[699]

The Adamses returned to London the following morning, taking a later train than the other guests, such as Layard and Forster: 'Milnes and his wife were so warm and earnest at the parting that Adams felt rather emotional; it seemed at that moment as though no one in England had ever been so kind to him.'

This so-called 'Trent Affair' occurred amidst a very delicate climate of distrust between Britain and America. On the one hand, the British felt resentful that the Union blockade of Southern ports was beginning to deprive the Lancashire cotton industry of its essential raw materials; while on the other, the United States regarded the British definition of the Confederate action as 'belligerency' (rather than rebellion) as an attitude of treachery.[700] The fact that 'This high-handed action touched British pride on the raw' was seen by Northern supporters like Milnes and Forster as 'a time for cool nerves'.[701]

Forster adopted a self-consciously subtle approach, balancing outright denunciation of 'Yankee bullying' tactics and such patriotic gestures as the opening of a barracks for Volunteers in Bradford on 30 November with speeches protesting how it was inconceivable that President Lincoln would stoop to the 'insanity and wickedness' of engaging in war with the British.[702] Such interventionism was rewarded just after Christmas when the US Government acceded to British demands that they, a) condemn Wilkes's action; and, b) return Mason and Slidell into British custody. Moreover, 'Through the difficult years 1861-63, when few people in British politics believed that the South could be defeated, Forster and Bright worked untiringly with Adams to defuse successive crises and to counter the pressure for the Government to recognize the Confederacy or to join Napoleon III in imposing a mediation settlement that would perpetuate the secession.'[703]

Milnes and Forster considered it important to ensure that Adams remained strong and clear-headed to the last; and 'since his strength was theirs, they lost no time in expressing to all the world their estimate of the Minister's character'.[704] In this respect, Adams's son, Henry, raised an interesting conundrum:

> One might discuss long whether, at that moment, Milnes or Forster were the more valuable ally, since they were influences of different kinds. Monckton Milnes was a social power in London [...] A word from him went far. An invitation to his breakfast-table went farther. Behind his almost Falstaffian mask and laugh of Silenus, he carried a fine, broad, and high intelligence which no one questioned [...] Socially, he was one of two or three men who went everywhere, knew everybody, talked of everything, and had the ear of Ministers [...] His breakfasts were famous, and no one liked to decline his invitations, for it was more dangerous to show timidity than to risk a fray. He was a voracious reader, a strong critic, an art connoisseur in certain directions, a collector of books, but above all he was a man of the world by profession, and loved the contacts – perhaps the collisions – of society. [...] Milnes was the good-nature of London; the Gargantuan type of its refinement and coarseness; the most universal figure of May Fair.[705]

There can be no denying that it was Bright and Cobden, 'the hardest hitters in England', who exercised most pro-Union influence in the House of Commons. While Milnes and Forster were 'not exactly light-weights', theirs was a backstage approach to wielding influence. Either way:

> With four such allies as these, Minister Adams stood no longer quite helpless. For the second time the British Ministry felt a little ashamed of itself after the Trent Affair, as well it might, and disposed to wait before moving again. Little by little, friends gathered about the Legation who were no fair-weather companions.[706]

Pope-Hennessy explains how the Trent Affair 'was not the only ominous event of that freezing December 1861, when the cold throughout England was of immemorial intensity and the river Ayre [sic] a sheet of ice on which the people of Ferrybridge and Ferry Fryston could disport'.[707] On the night of 14 December, Queen Victoria's husband and Consort, Prince Albert, died of the typhoid fever he had contracted only a few days earlier.

In the autumn of 1862, all three of Milnes's children were afflicted by illness. Milnes wrote to Charles MacCarthy on 24 October, informing him of their renewed good health, making special reference to Florence:

> We are going on very well domestically, the children recovering fast from the whooping cough, and in good progress of mind and body. The second little girl has developed into a verse-writer of a very curious ability. She began theologically and wrote hymns, which I soon checked on observing that she put together words and sentences out of the sacred verse she knew; and set her to write about things she saw and observed. What she now produces is very like the verse of William Blake, and containing many images that she could never have read of. She cannot write, but she dictates them to her elder sister, who is astonished at the phenomenon. We, of course, do not let her see that it is anything surprising; and the chances are it goes off as she gets older and knows more.[708]

Fryston Hall continued to be a major epicentre of Victorian social and cultural life – no less so than in November 1862 when relations between the Milnes and Adams families were strongly rekindled.

For all his earnest attempts to form new friendships and enlist new converts to the Union cause, 24-year-old Henry Adams was continuing to find London society unwelcoming and his role as his father's secretary tough and unrewarding. Out of the blue, in December 1862, he received an invitation to stay at Fryston.

> Naturally, a dispirited, disheartened private secretary was exceedingly grateful, and never forgot the kindness, but it was chiefly as education that this first country visit had value. Commonly, country visits are much alike, but Monckton

> Milnes was never like anybody, and his country parties served his purpose of mixing strange elements. Fryston was one of a class of houses that no one sought for its natural beauties, and the winter mists of Yorkshire were rather more evident for the absence of the hostess on account of them, so that the singular guests whom Milnes collected to enliven his December had nothing to do but astonish each other, if anything could astonish such men.[709]

Adams arrived at Fryston Hall to find that his host had already been joined by a handful of other guests, all of whom were male. These included the quiet, well-mannered author William Stirling of Keir and the thirty-something Laurence Oliphant, who had just returned from Japan where he had been wounded in the course of an attack on the British Legation. Oliphant had arrived in the company of two other guests: a Hindu barrister from Ceylon by the name of Muthu Coomaraswamy, and 'a little person whom Adams took at first to be a boy'.[710]

Unfortunately, Mr Coomaraswamy found the cold Yorkshire air far too cold to tolerate and was forced to leave prematurely. Coomaraswamy and Monckton Milnes would be used three years later as prototypes of characters appearing in one of Oliphant's novels:

> When *Piccadilly* first appeared in *Blackwood's Magazine* for 1865, it was recognised that Dickiefield, the comfortable country house in which the opening scenes of the entangled plot are laid, and where Lord Frank Vanecourt first meets the determined Hindoo, Juggonath Chundango, was a picture of Fryston Hall, and that the 'warm-hearted and eccentric' host, Lord Dickiefield was a representation of Lord Houghton.[711]

The novel was eventually published by Blackwood in 1870.

It was not Coomaraswamy but the youngest-looking of Milnes's other guests who had the most strikingly profound effect on Adams, due not in the least to his unusual appearance:

> He resembled in action [...] a tropical bird, high-crested, long-beaked, quick-moving, with rapid utterance and screams of humor, quite unlike any English lark or nightingale. One could hardly call him a crimson macaw among owls, and yet

> no ordinary contrast availed. Milnes introduced him as Mr. Algernon Swinburne. The name suggested nothing. Milnes was always unearthing new coins and trying to give them currency.[712]

When the five men sat down to dinner, it was Oliphant who initially took centre stage with his dramatic account of events in Japan. The conversation then meandered before Milnes prompted the 24-year-old Swinburne into action, to unforgettable effect:

> That Swinburne was altogether new to the three types of men-of-the-world before him; that he seemed to them quite original, wildly eccentric, astonishingly gifted, and convulsingly droll, Adams could see; but what more he was, even Milnes hardly dared say. They could not believe his incredible memory and knowledge of literature, classic, mediaeval, and modern; his faculty of reciting a play of Sophocles or a play of Shakespeare, forward or backward, from end to beginning; or Dante, or Villon, or Victor Hugo. They knew not what to make of his rhetorical recitation of his own unpublished ballads – 'Faustine'; the 'Four Boards of the Coffin Lid'; the 'Ballad of Burdens' – which he declaimed as though they were books of the Iliad.[713]

Later that evening, even the normally reserved Stirling was 'ejaculating explosions of wonder', thus reinforcing Adams's conviction that he had 'actually met a real genius'.[714]

On 7 December, Swinburne played the loveable clown in helping to ensure that Florence's seventh-birthday party was successful.[715] Then, two days after Christmas, he wrote to her father, expressing the hope that, 'Florey has not forgotten her conditional engagement to me in ten years' time if I am rich enough to give her a trousseau of rubies.'[716]

In the longer term, Milnes proposed Henry Adams for membership of the prestigious St James' Club. Such acts of patronage and generosity made a lasting impression on young Adams; this good friend of his father contributed inestimably to his personal development and social standing, due not least to the way in which 'he lent to younger Adams some of his own audacity and courage in society. He fed him, talked to him, showed him off, in other words, threw him, good-humouredly, into the social frying pan.'[717]

Turning Point

This is not to pretend that Henry Adams suddenly found himself accepted into the wider elite society. He often found himself reviled or criticised. On 10 January 1862, for example, Adams was subjected to a highly personalised and humiliating attack by John Delane, the leader writer of *The Times,* who lengthily chastised him for having (in a 'diary' published in the *Boston Daily Courier*) conflated the views of the people of Manchester regarding the American conflict with those of London society.

> Even though we speak the same language and belong to a kindred stock he must ever be an outsider in this kind of intercourse [...] Let him but persevere in frequenting the *soirees* and admiring the 'family pictures', which make London society 'a distinct thing' from that of a provincial town, and we shall not despair of reading some day a new diary in the *Boston Daily Courier,* wherein the *amende honorable* will be made to the gay world of the Metropolis.[718]

A crucial turning point in the civil war was reached in July 1863 with the news that the Confederate invasion of the North had been repelled at Gettysburg and the Union army under General Grant had captured Vicksburg. These were arguably the two most telling victories of the war. As Monaghan maintains, 'Payday had come for democracy' and 'The strain at the American Legation in London eased immediately.'[719] Henry Adams wrote a letter to his father on 23 July 1863, explaining how he had received the news via telegram while eating his Sunday breakfast. Adams predicted that this would have a devastating effect on well-heeled English people, who had complacently assumed that Grant was on the point of surrendering.

> And now, the announcement was just as though a bucket of iced water were thrown into their faces. They couldn't and wouldn't believe it. All their settled opinions were overthrown, and they were left dangling in the air. Sunday evening I was

> asked round to Monckton Milnes's to meet a few people. Milnes himself is one of the warmest Americans in the world, and received me with a hug before the astonished company, crowing like a fighting cock. But the rest of the company were very cold.[720]

Of those present, W.H. Russell stood out as someone who was ready to appreciate the gravity of the situation for the South, and did not endeavour 'to turn Lee's defeat into a victory'.[721] Only one day earlier, *The Times* had declared that the Union plight was becoming more helpless by the day. It was therefore with great satisfaction and sense of vindication that, 'at the moment of Milnes's embrace' Adams caught the eye of his erstwhile tormentor, John Delane. In truth:

> Delane probably regarded it as a piece of Milnes's foolery [...] he had no suspicion of the thought floating in the mind of the American Minister's son [...] Even if he had read Adams's thought, he would have felt for it only the usual amused British contempt for all that he had not been taught at school. It needed a whole generation for *The Times* to reach Milnes's standpoint.[722]

After the party, Adams accompanied Milnes to the Cosmopolitan Club, where other members clearly regarded his presence as objectionable in light of such unpleasant news. In his letter to his father, Adams predicted that things were unlikely to improve for them socially and that the Union's success would only attract more hostility towards them. 'Never before since the Trent affair,' he stated, 'has it shown itself so universal and spiteful as now.'[723]

If final proof of Milnes's social and intellectual commitment to the northern cause were needed, it came in the form of a poem, 'England and America', which first appeared in Isa Craig's *Poems: An Offering to Lancashire*, a fundraising volume for the relief of mill workers affected by the 'cotton famine' resulting from the Union blockade of southern ports. The poem then found its way into the 16 April 1864 edition of the American *National Anti-Slavery Standard*. Its chief sentiment was obvious:

> We never thought the jealous gods would store
> For us ill deeds of time-forgotten graves,
> Nor heeded that the May Flower one day bore
> A freight of pilgrims, and another slaves.[724]

By now, Milnes had risen to the peerage, becoming Lord Houghton in the process. There had been a longstanding rumour that Lord Palmerston would exercise his personal prerogative accorded to him by the royal wedding of the Prince of Wales on 10 March 1863 to Princess Alexandra of Prussia at St George's Chapel. Milnes and his sister attended the wedding, while Annabel and their daughter, Amy, avoided the thick London fog by staying indoors all the while.[725] Milnes had found the whole thing tiresome and was therefore relieved to return to Fryston for the summer.

Palmerston included Milnes among those 'eminent commoners' to be elevated to the peerage with a formal announcement appearing in August 1863.[726] As the *Anti-Slavery Standard*, explained:

> He is one of the most respected and beloved noblemen in England, and a man of comprehensive intellect, exquisite culture and refinement. He is distinguished for the sweetness of his character and the unwearied practical beneficence of his life. His friendship to our country has always been strong and steady.[727]

Chapter Fifteen
Cannibals

When Swinburne Met Thackeray?

This chapter focuses on the later stages of the relationship between Algernon Charles Swinburne and Richard Monckton Milnes. Among the main themes to be addressed is the involvement of Milnes and Swinburne in the notorious Cannibal Club, established by Richard Burton. The chapter therefore serves as a corrective to the 'alternative history' constructed by Mark Hodder. The following discussion will also dwell on Milnes's continuing attempts to elevate the public profile of his protégé and enhance his literary reputation. Emphasis will be placed on Swinburne's direct association with Fryston, starting with the intriguing possibility that an oft-cited encounter supposedly occurring between Swinburne and William Makepeace Thackeray never actually took place.

In April 1863, so the story goes, Swinburne returned to Fryston Hall, where he was greeted by a small party of guests who had already arrived. Included in this party were George Stovin Venables, James Spedding, the Archbishop of York, and Thackeray's two daughters (best known by their married names of Lady Anne Ritchie and Mrs Leslie Stephen). The seminal account of this occasion appears in Gosse's biography of Thackeray and is heavily reliant on the testimony of Anne Ritchie, who maintains that her father was also present on this occasion.[728] According to Ritchie, she first caught sight of Swinburne as he advanced 'up the sloping lawn, swinging his hat in his hand, and letting the sunshine flood the bush of his red-gold hair'.[729] She maintains that Thackeray was immediately impressed by the newcomer's conversational wit and underlying wisdom, and that his daughters were instantly captivated by his playful personality.

After dinner, Swinburne was prevailed upon to read some of his poems and controversially chose 'The Leper', which touches on the theme of necrophilia, and 'Les Noyades', which describes the fate of a man and woman who are bound together naked, and drowned.

> At this the Archbishop of York made so shocked a face that Thackeray smiled and whispered to Lord Houghton, while the two young ladies, who had never heard such sentiments expressed before, giggled aloud in their excitement. Their laughter offended the poet, who, however, was soothed by Lady Houghton's tactfully saying, 'Well, Mr. Swinburne, if you will read such extraordinary things, you must expect us to laugh.' 'Les Noyades' was then proceeding on its amazing course, and the Archbishop was looking more and more horrified, when suddenly the butler – 'like an avenging angel', as Lady Ritchie says – 'threw open the door and announced, Prayers! my Lord!'.[730]

Lady Ritchie dwells in her testimony on Swinburne's 'kind and cordial ways', confessing that she had not previously come across anyone 'so disconcerting or so charming'. She confesses to having burst into tears when the time came to bid him farewell. She also recalls that Milnes had shown her father the manuscripts of some of Swinburne's poems. Though Thackeray was greatly impressed by them, he died a few months later, and never got the chance to see them in print.[731]

There is good reason, though, to doubt the veracity of this account. In his retelling of Ritchie's anecdote, Gosse erroneously sets the date of this meeting as the summer of 1862 – an observation fatally contradicted by 'unimpeachable' evidence in the form of an entry in Milnes's diary, which shows that it *actually* took place the following April. This error pales in significance against the possibility that Lady Ritchie may well have been recalling what happened in a similar gathering at Fryston Hall occurring *over two years later* in September 1865. Evidence in support of this latter possibility is provided by Aplin, who refers to a letter sent by 'Annie' to Lady Houghton,[732] in which Thackeray's daughter professes to be 'still recovering' from the impact of meeting Swinburne:

> I have brought some paper & a pen & some ink out into the windy garden to try & say once more thankyou for everything & all the kindness – I don't know what we should have done if we had not come away to a dear sympathetic audience that is not yet tired of hearing every single thing Mr Swinburne said, & all the Archbishop [of York] said and all the names of the books in the library, & everything that happened every day over & over again, & how very very good you & Lord Houghton have been to us for wh I wont say thankyou anymore because it sounds like phrases – It has been like a little awakening to us – all sorts of things which had seemed to cease to concern us almost, have come to us out of our dear little visit, & coming here is like a delightful little moral to it.[733]

Aplin makes the intriguing disclosure that, whilst Ritchie's journal *does* refer to a previous visit to Fryston in 1863 (on which she was accompanied by her father and her sister), there is no suggestion that Swinburne was also present. Aplin therefore concludes that, possibly owing to confusion, Ritchie has compressed details of the two visits into a single all-encompassing narrative.[734] In Aplin's estimation, Gosse's account is 'extraordinarily misleading' to the extent that Ritchie 'assigns to her dead father a wholly imaginary role as chaperon. Praise by "Thackeray" for the young poet's intellect lends respectability to this almost mythic creature whose appearance Annie found so striking.' Regrettably, it seems that, contrary to legend, Thackeray and Swinburne never actually met each other at Fryston Hall (or anywhere else for that matter), even if the former's daughter genuinely imagined that they did.[735]

The Cannibal Club

There are two fundamentally contrasting versions of the origin, nature and purpose of the Cannibal Club, of which Burton, Milnes and Swinburne were principal members. The first of these accounts characterises the club as an intellectually-driven initiative intent on exploring the sexual mores and other aspects of physicality that differentiated particular colonial societies. It was intended as a means, therefore, of addressing the ongoing Victorian debate that focussed on *monogenism* versus *polygenism*. Proponents of monogenism maintained that all of humanity was the product of a common ancestry, while adherents of polygenism insisted that the different races derived from separate origins.[736] Burton had gradually become alienated from the Ethnological Society of London, whose credo was essentially monogenistic. He also argued that the inclusion of female members would inhibit frank discussion:

> In 1863, then, Burton had ample reason to help in establishing the men-only Anthropological Society of London. This new fraternity would allow Burton to explore what most interested him – the new race science – and to do so among an elite of men only, a membership that would permit franker, more radical discussion of 'polygenesis' and, specifically, racial difference with a particular focus on the racialized (and often sexualized) body. This new organization sponsored the club-within-the-club, the Cannibal Club, and there Burton surely felt a deep and energizing freedom, a liberty to do and be what he desired.[737]

An alternative version of this development defines it as a somewhat defiant, frivolous and hedonistic reaction to 'the sexual prudery and religious piety that pervaded polite society'.[738] Burton's alienation from the Church of England and conversion to the Islamic Sufi Brotherhood was indicative of the growing scepticism towards the claims of western Christianity that he shared with Swinburne and other members of the Cannibal Club:

> The club was an irreverent, boisterous gathering over rare wine, steaks, chops, mutton, and all manner of meat at Bertolini's Italian restaurant (the haunt of 'fast men') near the once fashionable but now seedy Leicester Square. He wanted a freewheeling, uncensored forum to discuss the heady topics of the day: sexuality, gender, and, of course, religion. He dubbed it the Cannibal Club as a kind of outrageous joke: what could be more shocking, and blasphemous, than humans eating their own kind?[739]

The ethos of the Cannibal Club was more consistent with this latter version. Its official symbol was that of a mace carved in the shape of an African head gnawing on a thigh-bone.[740]

Bertolini's restaurant was actually a rather seedy place, in which the food was sloppily served and the air was thick with smoke. Amidst an ethos of freedom and conviviality, 'Issues scandalous to the society at large could be explored here without shock or fear of censure (rather, with seriousness, cutting humor, or contrariness but always openly).'[741] Via such rituals, the Cannibal Club 'endorsed a radical code of oppositional identity that, through shared alternative identity, allowed its brethren to reject conformity. It made of estrangement, of ambivalence a mark of distinction.'[742]

This emphasis on identity and distinctiveness resonates with earlier characterisations of the Cambridge Apostles. As in our previous discussion of the Apostles, emphasis here, too, has been thrown onto the sexual proclivities of Milnes and fellow Cannibals:

> Were some of these men 'homosexuals'? Contemporary biographers have argued yes for Swinburne, Burton, Milnes, and [the artist, Simeon] Solomon. They fell into no such categories in their time, though, and it's possible this fluidity of identity left them with a richer continuum of options. Their erotic impulses ranged widely – becoming threaded together with socialism, flagellation, ekphrasis, crafts, anthropology, Christianity, and more. Physicality was part of the fabric, certainly, but a larger field of play had opened up than simply genitals meeting.[743]

It may be overstating matters to assume with Croft-Cook that Milnes's responses to Swinburne's letters were indicative of 'a man of the world indulging a smutty-minded schoolboy'.[744] Croft-Cook compiles evidence to suggests that Milnes was a regular visitor to flagellation brothels in London in the 1860s and 1870s – especially one under the 'governance' of a Mrs Sarah Potter, which had a 'schoolroom' in which clients meted out 'whippings' to 'schoolgirls' sat 'in class'.[745]

Gibson maintains that Milnes was, indeed, the author of the notorious flagellist poem, 'The Rodiad' (1871),[746] which recalls the type of floggings meted out by Eton schoolmasters, sometimes with the help of their accomplices:

> But now for years my chief delight has been
> To scourge the obnoxious stripling of sixteen –
> Horsed at nice angle on the sturdy back
> Of one whose faithful aid I never lack
> My John, who, with his grip and grin, enjoys
> The bounds and twistings of rebellious boys.[747]

Milnes and other Cannibal Club members are alleged to have jointly written pornographic fiction on the basis of a 'round-robin' system in which manuscripts were passed from one author to another or pored over collectively at dinner parties, with actual authorship being unacknowledged or obscured.[748] The seminal *Romance of Lust,* a novel which (in focussing on the erotic history of a 15-year-old boy and his sexual relationships with his governess and two sisters) dealt in unprecedented fashion with the taboo of incest, was initially attributed to William Simpson Potter, though subsequently to the collective efforts of Monckton Milnes, Lord Penzance, George Augustus Sala, and at least three other Cannibals.[749]

Sigel and others conclude that the activities and written work of the Cannibals served to shore up existing sexual and imperialistic hierarchies – that they ideologically endorsed prevailing structures of domination.[750] The men who formed the Cannibal Club believed themselves to be radicals but their radicalism centred on their own personal development rather than widespread political transformations.[751] Moreover, the privileged social location of these men prevented a wider promulgation of their views, insofar as:

> The elite social position of the Cannibals, the limited circulation of their texts, and the meanings they drew from the raw matter of sexuality shifted radicalism from an agent of political change to a means of personal definition.[752]

Lutz attributes a less self-serving motivation to the activities of Milnes, Burton, *et confrere.* She argues that 'Inhabiting a new liberal looseness that pervaded the salons and dinner parties of educated London,' Cannibals Club members:

> revelled in using their iconoclastic, maverick selves to shock their contemporaries out of a certain smug complacency,

> one that tended toward restraint, silence, and conservatism, especially in matters of sexuality and gender.[753]

Gibson further maintains that the Cannibals helped cast a revealing light on the sadomasochism that was endemic to Victorian society.[754] There are clear echoes here of the guiding ethic of the Cambridge Apostles of the late-1820s:

> All of these men felt themselves to be in rebellion against the Establishment of the day in matters of sexual morality, and greatly disliked its hypocrisy and puritanism; all were travellers, linguists and students of foreign literatures, erotic and otherwise; and all of them were obsessed with sexual perversion. As regards flagellation, the documentation which it is possible to put together concerning the group's activities shows that they were far from being unique in their interest in the subject. We can be absolutely certain that their tastes were shared by a great many men from similar backgrounds.[755]

Lutz underlines the point that the club membership comprised notable individuals who were either women's rights activists or openly supportive of women's causes. This included such issues as routine birth control; the reform of divorce laws to allow women to escape abusive marriages; and, in Milnes's case, membership of the Women's Suffrage Society.[756]

Poems and Ballads

The friendship between Milnes and Swinburne peaked in the spring and summer of 1863. From May to July of that year, Swinburne attended five of Milnes's renowned breakfast parties. There, and on subsequent occasions, Milnes strove assiduously to promote the wider appreciation and literary reputation of his protégé. As we shall see, these efforts are regarded in some quarters as an extension of the older man's malicious determination to set up the unsuspecting Swinburne for a fall.

One major act of patronage occurred in July 1863, when Milnes approached Edward Chapman of the publishers Chapman & Hall to try and persuade them to publish Swinburne's poems. Chapman & Hall's list of authors included such leading literary lights as Carlyle,

Clough, Dickens, Thackeray, and the Brownings; it would, therefore, have been greatly beneficial to Swinburne's career to have been included on their list. It so happened that Chapman's impression of Swinburne's poetic prowess had already been prejudiced by feedback from the poet Robert Browning, who had been unimpressed by Swinburne when witnessing one of his recitals while both were guests at Fryston.[757] Responding to Milnes's overtures, Chapman replied that 'the best available opinion, that of Robert Browning, stood flatly against the advisability of taking such a chance'.[758]

Signs of embarrassment and ill-feeling were therefore tangible when Milnes and Browning subsequently came into contact at Fryston Hall on the evening of 6 July 1863:

> The recent performance of Swinburne apparently became the subject of conversation. Suddenly, someone, perhaps Milnes himself, said that Chapman had refused to publish Swinburne, largely because 'You, Mr Browning, [...] disapproved his verses.' Considerably surprised and a little annoyed, Browning evidently offered a heated denial of fault and a circumstantial account of his talk with Chapman. One understands perfectly the annoyance: no matter what was said in extenuation, the impression would remain that an older poet through jealousy, intolerance, or perversity, had placed an obstacle in the way of a young poet.[759]

The matter did not end there. The following evening, Browning wrote in further mitigation to Milnes that he had never personally intended to do anything harmful to Swinburne's career. Browning ventured that Chapman was merely using his opinion as an excuse for not publishing Swinburne's 'highly dubious' poetry. Browning confessed that, with the exception of a poem he had been shown by Rossetti, and the previous night's recital, he knew 'next to nothing' of Swinburne but liked him very much. In his view, the poems constituted 'moral mistakes, redeemed by much intellectual ability'. He went on to say:

> Unluckily the truth is the truth, and one must speak it now and then. It was a shame in this case for Chapman to quote my blame of two or three little pieces – given on a demand

> for unqualified praise which was impossible – as the reason for rejecting a whole bookful of what may be real poetry, for aught I am aware: but as I am in the habit of being as truthful as I like about the quality of certain things which he patronizes, and as I never saw their titles disappear from his advertisements in consequence – I conclude that he only uses my witnessing when he wants to cover his own conviction.[760]

Milnes's patronage of the young poet was just as salient in 1864. That spring, for example, Swinburne accompanied Milnes to Paris, where they visited his friend Sir Charles MacCarthy, who was fatally ill. MacCarthy confessed to being greatly impressed by Swinburne's poetry. Afterwards, Swinburne moved on to Italy where, following an introduction by Milnes, he met Landor. During August, he stayed with Milnes at Fryston. Their friendship appears to have been slightly strained following the publication in November 1864 of Swinburne's third novel, *Chastelard*, which focuses on a sixteenth-century love affair between the ill-fated hero of the title and Mary Stuart. Milnes's review of this work in the *Fortnightly Review* praised Swinburne's characterisation of Chastelard but was less convinced of the way that Mary was used in the plot.[761]

The two nevertheless continued to see each other at regular intervals. During 1865, Swinburne was the guest at the London home of Lord and Lady Houghton on five separate occasions and paid what was to prove his final visit to Fryston that August.[762] On 13 December 1865, Swinburne and Milnes attended a party, given by the publisher Moxon, at which Tennyson was guest of honour. Swinburne was disrespectfully offhand with Tennyson and his flighty behaviour was deemed shockingly inappropriate: 'He entered the room, when the great man's admirers stood respectfully in attendance, exchanged a few words with Tennyson, turned his back on him and hurried off to the next room.'[763]

Afterwards, Milnes rebuked Swinburne for his rudeness towards Tennyson and for possibly jeopardising publication of Swinburne's anthology, *Poems and Ballads*. Swinburne was characteristically unrepentant in a subsequent letter to his mentor:

I am not aware of having retorted by any discourtesy. As the rest of the evening had been spent after the few words of civility that passed between Mr. Tennyson and me, in discussing Blake and Flaxman in the next room with Palgrave and Lewes, I am at a loss to guess what has called down such an avalanche of advice.[764]

Undeterred by Swinburne's attitude, Milnes went to great lengths to secure him the role of principal guest speaker at the Royal Literary Fund dinner on 2 May 1866. The distinguished audience included such great literary figures as Dean Stanley, Charles Kingsley, Henry Reeve, Anthony Trollope, Sir Samuel Baker, Leslie Stephen, Frederick Leighton, and Lord Milton. Swinburne joined Kingsley in responding to the toast delivered by George Stovin Venables to 'The Historical and Imaginative Literature of England'. Meyers quotes from an uncredited newspaper report of this event:

After Mr. Kingsley arose Mr Swinburne. He spoke in such a low voice that I could only see his lips move, and hear no word. But it was enough to see Swinburne's face – especially with his cheek and eye kindled and I shall never forget it. A small, young, even boyish man, with handsome, regular features and smooth skin; with eyes that glitter; with thin, flexible lips, whose coldness is in strange contrast to the passionate intensity of his eyes; with a great deal of reddish hair that surrounds his face like a halo. He seemed to me like some wild bird of rare and beautiful plumage, which has alighted in our uncongenial climate, and who is likely to die before it is acclimatised. No one who has ever looked upon his face would doubt for a moment that he is a man of genius.[765]

The way in which this triumphant performance was almost universally applauded came in stark contrast to the widespread condemnation greeting the subsequent appearance of Swinburne's *Poems and Ballads.* Critical reaction saw Swinburne vilified as 'the libidinous laureate of a pack of satyres', and his poetry condemned as 'recklessly sexual and anti-Christian'.[766] Almost predictably, Milnes has been accused of deliberately 'setting up' Swinburne for such a spectacular fall from grace. According to one early Swinburne biographer, Milnes had peppered his 'advance propaganda' with references to the 'indelicacy' of most of the contents of the volume. He had taken it upon himself to 'drag' Swinburne 'to houses where he felt anything but at home, into a society where he was bored and ill at ease', while his absolute master-stroke 'was to foist a reluctant Swinburne upon an unenthusiastic committee' at the annual gathering of the Royal Literary Fund.[767]

Choosing to ignore his own earlier reference to a statement by Henry Adams – that he had been only one of Milnes's 'whole array of Frystonians' called upon to attend the dinner in support of Swinburne – Meyers is clearly sceptical of the role played by, and underlying motives, of Milnes's seemingly selfless promotion of his protégé:

> One would like to know a good deal more about the evening of May 2, 1866, and especially to know more about the intentions and anticipations not only of Swinburne but also of Lord Houghton, so famed for his experimental combinations of guests on social occasions.[768]

The Ties that Unwind

It has been reported that Milnes became progressively more irritated by Swinburne's increasingly outrageous displays of rudeness and inebriation and that, 'despite his proprietorial interest in Swinburne's poetry, felt little enthusiasm for a continued relationship at close quarters'.[769] The two of them occasionally met up sociably and amicably enough during the late 1860s. By 1867, Swinburne's health was visibly deteriorating. On 2 July, he failed to appear at a dinner-party thrown by Milnes, to which Gladstone had also been invited, but was able to dine with Milnes at Upper Brook Street on 11 July.

Two days later, the poet 'fell down in a fit', having looked 'wretchedly ill' while enjoying breakfast with Milnes, who instantly summoned his own doctor and telegraphed news of what had happened to Swinburne's family. Having thanked Milnes profusely, the poet's father, Admiral Swinburne, removed him to his house in Henley-on-Thames. Five days after suffering his seizure, Swinburne wrote to Milnes to apologise for the trouble he had caused.[770] It was clear, though, that things would never be the same again and is evident, from the younger man's letter to John Morley, objecting to Milnes's assignation as reviewer of *Bothwell* in the *Fortnightly Review*, that their relationship was irreparably fractured. 'I must confess,' wrote Swinburne, 'that I do shrink from the rancid unction of that man's adulation, or patronage, or criticism.'[771]

It was left to Isabel Burton to deplore Swinburne's gross ingratitude. 'I don't like Swinburne for neglecting you,' she told Milnes by letter in 1874. 'He, Richd and I and many others I know, would have remained very much in the background if you had not taken us by the hand and pulled us into notice.'[772]

Chapter Sixteen
Bringing It All Back Home

Man of the People

In the mid-1860s, Lord Houghton (Milnes) remained prominently involved in activities designed to promote the wider social and cultural engagement of previously marginalised sections of society. One such instance occurred in May 1864, when he spoke at the annual prize-giving at the Royal Female School of Art, which was then under the patronage of Queen Victoria and the Princess of Wales. This was one of the few art schools in London to enrol female students in a time when women were not only finding it difficult to attain the formal qualifications to enable them to compete professionally with men but were also debarred from even enrolling at Royal Academy Schools, let alone being accepted as associates or full members.[773]

In paraphrasing Milnes's speech, *The English Woman's Journal* reported that:

> [Milnes] was particularly gratified by the success of this institution, because it proved that the female sex of this country was more and more acquiring that independent position which he believed it was most advantageous for civilization they should occupy.[774]

Devereux makes the point that the public support of this *male* member of the aristocracy not only 'helped lend legitimacy' to the case of aspiring female artists, but also helped campaigning periodicals like *The English Woman's Journal* 'to obtain by subterfuge a foothold in traditionally masculine fields like the fine arts'.[775]

A second example of this kind occurred on 30 August 1865 when Milnes travelled to Wakefield to formally open the town's Industrial and Fine Art Exhibition, held in a newly-built Central

Hall – a large, wooden rectangular structure, flanked on either side by picture galleries. The exhibition, which was the brainchild of a local curate, the Reverend Charles Edward Camidge, placed some 1,400 exhibits by local residents alongside paintings by such grand masters as Constable, Gainsborough, Hogarth, Reynolds and Turner. The objective of the organising committee was to produce a Yorkshire exhibition to rival those of London.[776]

Following, a brief blessing by the Archbishop of York, Milnes delivered an address that celebrated the exhibition as a 'national act of justice that honoured the English artisans' in a context befitting their greatness.

> It was no small consideration that the arts which used to be confined to a few persons – which used to be the mere appendage of the rich and powerful – were now becoming necessarily considered as the due heritage of the mass of the community. They might be thankful indeed that they had lived to see their picture galleries and collections of art and interest, kept not closed up [...] but generally open throughout the country for the public culture of the great people of England.[777]

Milnes exhorted local employers to allow their labourers adequate time off in which to visit the six-week exhibition. This was undoubtedly reflected in attendance figures showing that some 180,000 visitors had passed through.[778] In his formal closing address on 19 October, Milnes urged all present to do their utmost to promote similar exhibitions elsewhere in which all classes of people might come together in the 'common interest and common prosperity' of the nation.[779] He concluded on a poignant note, however, lamenting the passing of the 3rd Viscount Palmerston, who had died in office one day earlier.[780]

This latter occasion exemplifies the fact that Richard and Annabel were now making Fryston and surrounding towns like Wakefield the focus of their existence. They played host in the 1860s and early 1870s to some of the Victorian era's most intriguing poets, novelists and philosophers. Often these were pre-eminent in their field (as in the cases of Wilkie Collins, Thomas Carlyle and Anthony Trollope);

while other visitors, like the poet Robert Buchanan, were far lesser known, and typically in need of an urgent helping hand. This was a decade that also saw the demise of arguably Britain's greatest ever novelist, Charles Dickens. As we shall see, Richard and Annabel Milnes renewed a longstanding relationship with Dickens only weeks before his death, and Milnes played a significant part in ensuring a fitting memorial to the greatest author of the age.

Wilkie Collins Comes to 'Frizinghall'

In the summer of 1864, a visit was paid to Fryston Hall by Wilkie Collins, the acclaimed Victorian author of books like the *The Woman in White* (1859-60), *Armadale* (1864-66) and *The Moonstone* (1868). Collins travelled up to Yarmouth, partly to watch the sailing, but also to gather background material for his novel, *Armadale*. He planned to go on from there to spend the weekend at Fryston, his visit being one of a series of social engagements, including similar stays with Dickens and Nina and Frederick Lehmanns at Franklin on the Isle of Wight.[781]

Collins had already received – but declined – several invitations to visit Fryston. He appears to have attended once previously – on 16 August 1860, when he complained in a letter to Mrs Procter about his inability to read Milnes's handwritten letter of invitation.[782] This second excursion to Fryston, on 9 August, is the only one for which any details have been recorded. They show that Collins travelled across via Peterborough, where he was scheduled to switch vehicles. A delay in the connecting train forced him to take refuge at a neighbouring inn where, as fate would have it, he met Martha Rudd, the woman who would, in due course, become his lover and mother of his children.[783]

Little is known about the events of the weekend, save that:

> [Collins] later described his hosts' house as 'delightfully comfortable, with palatial rooms, a fine park and perpetual company' [...] [and that] he met one of Garibaldi's sons: 'A remarkably stupid boy' [...] [A]nd, no doubt after a stimulating weekend with the Monckton Milnes's wide circle of literary and political friends (Algernon Swinburne was staying there at the time), returned to Norfolk where he planned to find 'some quiet sensible place on the east coast' to go on with his work.[784]

One lasting legacy of the visit is that Collins appears to have used his experience of the palatial surroundings of Fryston Hall as the setting of *The Moonstone*, a novel in which a 'magnificent gem' of that name is bequeathed to Rachel Verinder by her uncle and delivered to her on her eighteenth birthday at her family's 'sumptuous country house in Yorkshire' (the revealingly named 'Frizinghall') by her cousin.[785] The disappearance of the stone from Rachel's bathroom kickstarts the gripping criminal investigation comprising the novel's central plot. Several components of *The Moonstone* were to become endemic to the genre:

> Many features of Collins's fictional detective, Sergeant Cuff – his eccentric nature, his outsider status, his extramural hobby, his intent focus, his ability to deal with different classes of people with charm – would become regular elements of the genre. Sherlock Holmes, Lord Peter Wimsey and Hercule Poirot are among Cuff's many literary descendants (albeit those three are amateurs).[786]

Trollope's Visit to Fryston

The novelist Anthony Trollope and his wife, Rose, were invited to stay at Fryston Hall in mid-January 1866: 'It would give Lady Houghton and myself much pleasure,' wrote Milnes, 'if you and Mrs Trollope would pay us a visit here on the 15th of Jnry [sic] & remain as much of the week as your occupation permits. You can come here in the composition of a chapter – &, when here, you can have all your time to yourself, when not eating or talking.'[787]

Anthony Trollope had already been the beneficiary of Milnes's influence and patronage when Milnes successfully nominated him in April 1861 for membership of the Cosmopolitan Club, an institution which, as Super points out, became the prototype for the 'Universe Club' featured in Trollope's 1873 novel, *Phineas Redux*.[788] Milnes and Trollope had dined together previously, as had their wives, albeit on a separate occasion.

The few existing details of the visit to Fryston Hall reveal that:

> Also at the house party was Lady Rose Fane, daughter of the Earl of Westmoreland, who wrote to her mother, 'I wish I

> had never seen Mr Trollope; I think he is detestable – vulgar, noisy & domineering – a mixture of Dickens [sic] vulgarity and Mr Burtons [sic] selfsufficiency [sic] – as unlike his books as possible.'[789]

Such an impression was contradicted, eighteen months later, by Barry Cornwall's widow, Anne Procter, who informed Milnes that she had bumped into the Trollopes at the Knebworth home of Bulwer-Lytton and 'found Trollope very pleasant'.[790]

Thereafter, Milnes and Trollope enjoyed an enduring and mutually beneficial relationship. In the late summer of 1866, Trollope presented Milnes with a first edition copy (one of only 750 published) of *The Warden*.[791] Three years later, Trollope joined Milnes as a co-treasurer of the Royal Literary Fund, where Milnes introduced him to his extensive network of contacts – most notably Tennyson, who became a regular dinner guest of the *Chronicler of Barsetshire*.[792]

Carlyle's Second Coming

Third in this sequence of great Victorian writers to visit Fryston was Thomas Carlyle. Kaplan makes the point that, by the mid-1850s, Carlyle and Milnes had almost ceased seeing one another.[793] They hardly corresponded, either. 'Are not you a shocking fellow,' Carlyle chided in a letter from mid-1860, 'never to ask once this year whether I am alive or dead.'[794] Milnes actually kept up a stream of invitations in the years that followed but it was not until March 1866 that Carlyle made his second and final visit to Fryston.

Carlyle had succeeded Gladstone as Rector of the University of Edinburgh, where students had voted for Carlyle by a ratio of 2:1 (657 to 310) over his rival candidate, Benjamin Disraeli. Thus, on Thursday 29 March, Carlyle started out for Edinburgh and his formal instigation as rector, having accepted an invitation to stop off, *en route*, and spend two nights at Fryston. The journey was scheduled to be undertaken without Jane, who had written to Milnes earlier that month to explain why she would not be accompanying her husband:

> I had visions of his breaking down in his address! of his lying ill with fuss and dinners! of his going to wreck and ruin in every possible way! [...] When he is gone out of my sight I

> shall calm down. But if I should prolong the nervousness of these days, going with him and the others to Fryston, I should get no good of Fryston, and risk a spell of illness. I want to go to Fryston (it would be the first time, remember) in a state of mind that would not interfere with my enjoyment of it.[795]

Carlyle *was* accompanied on his journey by his friend, the scientist John Tyndall, who was to receive an honorary LL.D. at the same ceremony. The pair set out for Fryston with Carlyle clutching a flask of Scottish brandy, prepared for him by Jane. On reaching Fryston Hall, they were cordially received by Lord and Lady Houghton and then introduced to several other invitees, including another renowned scientist, Professor Thomas Huxley. Dinner was served later than anticipated. The lateness of the meal and the effort expended in a spirited discussion left Carlyle feeling restless by the time he went to bed. Fryston was now on the route of several railway journeys, and the regular whistling of passing trains compounded his notorious insomnia.

The following morning, Tyndall paid a visit to Carlyle's bedroom to discover him 'wild with his sufferings' and adamant that to spend another night at Fryston might kill him. Though disappointed at this development, Milnes wholeheartedly agreed that Carlyle and Tyndall should set off as soon as possible for Edinburgh. During breakfast, Carlyle helped himself to a bowl of milk and tea, supplemented by a raw egg. The rejuvenating effect of this simple meal not only raised Carlyle's spirits but induced him into changing his mind about leaving so early. Tyndall therefore suggested that he and his fellow guest take off for an all-day ride around the neighbouring countryside – a tiring but relaxing activity that would help him to sleep more peacefully throughout the second night.

Two horses were duly prepared by Lord Houghton's stable staff, whereupon Carlyle and Tyndall navigated their way across local fields, down connecting lanes and high roads in the course of a five-hour, mud-spattered ride. Once back at the hall, Carlyle rescued his 'churchwarden' pipe from his bedroom and began smoking it contentedly by the fire, where he also downed a soothing tumbler of pale brandy and soda. Dinner was served at the more reasonable hour of 6 o'clock and Tyndall managed to steer Carlyle well clear of any serious discussion, before seeing him safely to his bedroom, 'every chink and fissure of which had been closed to stop out both light and sound'.[796]

Carlyle was still pessimistic about his chances of achieving a good night's sleep. Tyndall was more optimistic, based on the supposition that local railway traffic was bound to subside since it was Good Friday. This optimism was well-founded: it was not until 9am that Carlyle was overheard getting dressed in his bedroom. 'The change from the previous morning was astonishing,' said Tyndall. 'Never before or afterwards did I see Carlyle's countenance glow with such happiness. It was seraphic.'[797]

Later that day, a suitably cheerful Carlyle was joined on the Edinburgh-bound train by Tyndall, Huxley, and Milnes, with the latter stepping off at York. Two days later, Carlyle was so overcome by nerves that he feared he might be incapable of speaking at his own inauguration.[798] The University Principal was alarmed to discover that Carlyle had not even written a speech and privately feared he might say something deemed offensive by the students. He need never have worried:

> For an hour and a half Carlyle spoke without using a single note and when he sat down Conway thought he heard 'an audible sound, as of breath long held, by all present.' Then a cry of exultation rose from the students. Many were waving their arms; some pressed forward and attempted to embrace the orator; others were weeping.[799]

Tyndall immediately telegraphed Jane Carlyle to tell her that the speech had been 'A perfect triumph'.[800] Later that evening she drove to Forster's for dinner, where other guests, including Charles Dickens and Wilkie Collins, drank her husband's health.[801]

Buchanan's Journey into Darkness

In November 1868, Robert William Buchanan, the Scottish poet, biographer and close friend of David Gray, visited Fryston Hall at Milnes's invitation. Buchanan's recollections of his visit and, in particular, his first, unforgettable encounter with W.E. Forster were set out in a touching tribute to the eminent Yorkshire Quaker politician, published in the 9 April edition of the *Pall Mall Gazette*.[802]

Buchanan begins the article by recalling how, having travelled down by train, he somehow alighted at the wrong railway station. Realising that the carriage that should have been there to meet him had presumably been sent elsewhere, he set off walking into the darkness of a 'wild and windy night', portmanteau on shoulder, in desperate search of Fryston Hall. As luck would have it, he came across a country cart, whose occupants (two small boys) nervously agreed to give him a lift. The lads eventually admitted they were lost and Buchanan was forced to conclude his journey alone – on foot and in total darkness:

> After diverse adventures, with which I need not weary the reader, I at last gained the gates of the park, and, still laden with my portmanteau, struggled in to the hall door – much to the astonishment of my host, who had given me up for the night. I dined alone, and after dinner went into the drawing-room, where one of the first persons to greet me was Mr. Forster, who had already been made acquainted with my adventures, and was ready with many a rough, good-humoured joke at my expense.[803]

The remainder of the article constitutes a warm insight into Forster's essential character. Buchanan states how he could easily have taken the craggy-faced Forster for 'some yeoman farmer' or a 'herdsman of the dales'. The young Scot was clearly enchanted by Forster's 'utter freedom from affectation, his bluff, uncompromising honesty, and his grim sense of humour'. Despite the difference between their ages and standing in society, Buchanan was treated entirely as an equal by Milnes's more exalted fellow guest. Better still, insofar as Buchanan was concerned, Forster was clearly familiar with the details of Buchanan's literary career, especially his relationship with David Gray.

On the following day, Buchanan joined Forster, Milnes and the other guests on a 'ramble' through the Fryston park and home farm. Here, too, Forster revealed himself to be 'completely without false pretence'; and whilst his general knowledge was vast, he freely

Fryston Hall, the country seat of the Milnes family from 1786 to 1905.

A view of Fryston Hall from the surrounding park and woodlands.

The much-acclaimed politician and landowner, Robert Pemberton Milnes, who famously declined the offer of a peerage, much to the chagrin of his son, Richard Monckton Milnes.

Richard Monckton Milnes, the 1st Lord Houghton, pictured in 1851.

A drawing of the youthful Annabel Crewe, the future Lady Houghton.

An early photograph (circa 1861) of the couple's two daughters, Amicia (left) and Florence (right).

A portrait of their son, Robert, as a boy, from a painting by Chapman at West Horsley Place.

Alfred Lord Tennyson.

Thomas Carlyle.

William Makepeace Thackeray.

Wilkie Collins.

Elizabeth Gaskell.

Anthony Trollope.

Henry James.

Great literary figures who visited Fryston Hall: the Poet Laureate, Alfred Lord Tennyson; Scottish philosopher, Thomas Carlyle; English novelists, William Makepeace Thackeray, Wilkie Collins, Elizabeth Gaskell and Anthony Trollope; and the American author, Henry James.

Another distinguished guest at Fryston Hall was the great Victorian novelist and politician, Benjamin Disraeli. He and Richard Monckton Milnes made their maiden parliamentary speeches within a day of each other and actively disliked one another from the outset.

Lord Palmerston.

W.E. Forster.

Charles Francis Adams.

Henry Adams.

Some of the eminent political figures who came to Fryston: the Liberal prime minister, Lord Palmerston; the anti-slavery campaigner and Liberal MP, W.E. Forster; the American Minister to Britain in the early 1860s, Charles Francis Adams; and his son, Henry, who was serving as his secretary.

Florence Nightingale.

Algernon Charles Swinburne.

Sir Richard Francis Burton.

Lady Isabel Burton.

Three of the most famous personalities of the Victorian era were featured alongside Richard Monckton Milnes in the 'alternative history' series of novels by Mark Hodder, and all three figured prominently in his life. These were: Nurse Florence Nightingale ('The Lady with the Lamp'); the wildly eccentric and controversial poet, Algernon Charles Swinburne; and the charismatic soldier, explorer and adventurer, Sir Richard Francis Burton. Completing the set of portraits is a photograph of Burton's wife, Lady Isabel Burton, who was a writer and, like her husband, a good friend of Monckton Milnes.

Sibyl, first wife of Robert Offley Ashburton Milnes (Lord Crewe). She died young, having contracted scarlet fever.

A photographic portrait of Lord Crewe, taken in his early middle age.

A family photograph taken beneath the porticos of Fryston Hall around 1873. Richard Monckton Milnes (by now, Lord Houghton) is stood (hands clasped) on the left of the steps, while his brother-in-law, Lord Hungerford Crewe, is standing just behind him. Lady Houghton is seated on the steps, while Amicia and Florence are seated in the phaeton carriage.

Two late-period portraits of Richard Monckton Milnes. The first of these is a drawing from 1878, while the second is a caricature drawn by the famous Victorian cartoonist, Ward, in 1882.

The last known portrait of Richard Monckton Milnes (Lord Houghton), in the form of a painting from 1883.

Pictured on the left is the novelist, animal rights activist and society hostess, Florence Ellen Hungerford Henniker, younger daughter of the first Lord Houghton. Her husband, Arthur Henniker, was a commanding officer in the Coldstream Guards. He figured prominently in the second Anglo-Boer War (October 1899 to May 1902).

The main photograph depicts the Viceregal Lodge in Dublin, residence of the 2nd Lord Houghton during his period of tenure as Viceroy of Ireland. He was assisted in the role by his sister, Florence, who acted as his hostess while her soldier husband, Arthur Henniker, was posted on military duties elsewhere. It was while occupying this role that Ms Henniker came into contact with the famous author, Thomas Hardy (bottom left), and the Irish Nationalist politician, John Dillon MP (bottom right).

The Prince of Wales (future Edward VII) is pictured with his Derby and St Leger winning horse, Persimmon. Edward was staying as the guest of Lord Crewe at Fryston Hall for St Leger week in 1896 when Persimmon romped home, leaving the rest of the field in his wake.

Afterwards, Edward led a shooting party through the woods around Fryston Hall. He is rumoured to have sprayed local 'game-beaters' with pellets from his shotgun – an accusation he strongly refuted.

The wedding of the year, 1899. Pictured top left is the popular Liberal politician, Lord Rosebery. It was Margaret ('Peggy') Primrose (top right), daughter of Lord Rosebery and the wealthy heiress, Hannah de Rothschild, to whom Lord Crewe was married in London. The event was witnessed by huge crowds of well-wishers and commemorated in numerous magazine articles of the day (e.g. bottom left and right).

The bitterly contested Wheldale-Fryston strike lasted from October 1902 to January 1904. The top photograph shows Fryston strikers marching alongside other members of the Yorkshire Miners' Association in the annual miners' 'demonstration' (gala), held in Castleford in 1903. The remaining photographs depict two locally-born national union officials, Benjamin Pickard (left), and Herbert Smith (right), each of whom negotiated on behalf of the Wheldale and Fryston miners during the lengthy and ultimately ill-fated dispute.

During the brief Edwardian era of 1901 to 1910, Lord Crewe quickly established himself as a major political figure and member of the nation's elite social circles. In the top picture he forms part of a royal party hosted by Lord and Lady Londonderry at Wynyard Park, Northumbria, in 1903. Crewe is standing five in from the left, while King Edward VII is positioned three places to his left. Peggy, Countess of Crewe, is seated three in from the left. The second picture shows Crewe in conversation with Winston Churchill. Both men had already begun to play prominent parts in the key political developments of the twentieth century.

admitted to lacking any insight on particular subjects, and displayed a disarmingly modest eagerness to learn. Following this first meeting, Buchanan and Forster often corresponded and met up from time to time in London, with the older man ever willing to offer friendly advice. According to Buchanan, 'the fearless honesty, the unassuming manliness, and the perfect independence of Mr Forster were born of the same nature which endowed him with such great moral and physical courage'.[804]

Nothing is mentioned by Buchanan of any interaction with Milnes, although we do know that Milnes extended him a loan of £100. Shortly after the meeting, Buchanan wrote to Milnes in diplomatic fashion to take issue with his patronage of Swinburne:

> I far too thoroughly disagree with you in matters of taste to feel with you on literary questions or to be influenced by your dictum [...] I think it has been a dictum for evil in Swinburne's case. You will not misconceive me! I regard you with admiration and even affection, and shall be grieved if you felt hurt by my words; but I cannot in honesty conceal my feeling that many of your views would be fatal were they not counteracted in your case by a heart so infinitely more noble than themselves [...] Regret nothing that you did for David Gray! God will remember that.[805]

The Death of Charles Dickens

Milnes's son Robert once maintained that his parents might most accurately be described as 'outer acquaintances' of the great Charles Dickens. Although they were on 'pleasant and intimate' terms, they seldom met each other and Robert was 'pretty sure' that Dickens never came to Fryston.[806] There was no denying, however, that, 'Dickens had a very high regard for Milnes as a literary man, as an enlightened and Liberal politician, as a champion of the oppressed, and as a man of very exceptional charm.'[807] Dickens had been hugely complimentary in his assessment of Milnes's *Palm Leaves*, which he referred to, in a letter dated 1844, as a work of 'elegance, tenderness and thoughtful fancy'.[808] Dickens also exchanged letters with Annabel in July 1862, thanking her for praising *David Copperfield*.[809]

Improbable as it may seem, Dickens's grandmother, Elizabeth, was housekeeper at Crewe Hall when Annabel, her sister Henrietta and brother Hungerford came to live with their grandfather following the death of Annabel's mother. Annabel maintained that her greatest treat as a child was when Mrs Dickens (who was an 'inimitable storyteller') surrounded herself with the three children and proceeded to 'beguile them, not only with fairy tales, but with reminiscences of her own, and stories from the page of history'.[810] It has been speculated that Elizabeth was the prototype for the character of Mrs Rouncewell in her grandson's novel, *Bleak House*.[811]

Dickens died in June 1870. One year earlier, Milnes had spoken in tribute of the novelist at a banquet held in Dickens's honour in Liverpool and, allegedly:

> expressed regret that Dickens abstained from public life, and (in Forster's words) 'half reproached him for alleged unkindly sentiments to the House of Lords.' Dickens waxed rather vehement in denying the latter charge [...] Then he took up the other charge, prefacing his reply with 'here I am more serious.' The reply was that well-known passage in which he declared his life-long determination that literature should be his sole profession by which he would stand or fall. Commenting on this, Forster says: 'Here, however, he probably failed to see the entire meaning of Lord Houghton's regret, which would seem to have been meant to say in more polite form, that to have taken some part in public affairs might have shown him the difficulty in a free state of providing remedies very swiftly for evils of long growth.' That difficulty Dickens never seems fully to have realised.[812]

The last time Milnes and Annabel saw Dickens was on 24 May 1870. Two weeks earlier, on 7 May, Dickens had been complaining of appalling pains in his feet (requiring nightly doses of laudanum), while conducting a reading of the fifth episode of *Edwin Drood* at W.E. Forster's house.[813] The famous Victorian caricaturist Leslie Ward undoubtedly had this occasion in mind when he said that he was accompanied by his father to Dickens's last reading. Included in the reception was a virtuoso performance by the great Jewish-Hungarian violinist Joseph Joachim.

> That evening Joachim gave us an exhibition of his incomparable art. Lord Houghton, who was as absent-minded in his way as his brother-in-law, Lord Crewe, was one of the guests. He fell asleep during Joachim's recital, and snored. As the exquisite chords from the violin rose on the air, Lord Houghton's snores sounded loudly in opposition, sometimes drowning a delicate passage, and at others lost in a passionate rush of melody from the player, who must have needed all his composure to prevent him waking the slumbering lord.[814]

Dickens was well enough to dine with Forster at Hyde Park Place on 22 May; and two days later, he had dinner with the Milneses in the company of Leopold II of Belgium and the Prince of Wales, who had asked to be introduced to him.[815] Crippled by gout, 'Dickens was unable to mount the staircase, and the Royal guests came down to him, in the dining-room where the presentation took place.'[816] Richard and Annabel made a point of bringing their children downstairs to meet him, and one of the daughters asked him to autograph her album.[817]

Milnes had one more act of tribute and benevolence to bestow. Shortly after Dickens's death on 9 June, Milnes received a letter from the Dean of Westminster Abbey, explaining that, whilst he had not received any approach from the novelist's family to have Dickens buried in the Abbey, he felt that there was a strong public desire to have him interred in this way. Knowing that such a burial could only be transacted on the basis of a direct request from the deceased's family, Dean Stanley asked of Milnes, 'Will you kindly act as you think best?'[818] Milnes acted with due regard to the 'almost passionate outcry from all classes of the community for this last tribute of honour to one to whom the whole race felt grateful' and spoke to Dickens's family.[819] As a result, the legendary author's funeral was carried out in private but his body was laid to rest in Poets' Corner.[820]

Chapter Seventeen
The Coming of Coal: Industrial Relations (1860-1873)

Industrial Development in the West Riding

As the 1860s dawned, the Yorkshire coalfield spurted into a period of growth that led its transformation into the largest and most diverse of the British coal mining regions.[821] The coalfield's prior economic *raison d'être* had been to satisfy the local demand for household coal and service the industrial requirements of the wool textiles and metal trades. This all changed with the introduction of local coke-producing capacity, which enabled Yorkshire collieries to capitalise on the great iron boom of the early 1870s and to challenge the monopoly hitherto enjoyed by coking plants in Durham. Surplus capacity in the post-boom era of the mid-1870s forced the coal owners to seek out fresh markets:

> That they should have looked to exports and coastwise shipments was largely the result of the fact that much of the recently created capacity was in the eastward extension of the coalfield, nearer to Hull, Goole and Grimsby than the older exploited mines.[822]

It was in this highly propitious context that the inception of deep coal mining at Fryston occurred. The *Wakefield Express* reported how:

> On Saturday, the Hon. Robert Offley Ashburton Milnes, son and heir of Lord Houghton, turned the first sod of an intended coal pit, situate on the Fryston Estate, which is the nearest pit to the port of Hull and the German Ocean.[823]

Bearing the headline 'First Sod Cut', the article explained that the 'Fryston Coal Company' was leasing 2,000 acres from Lord Houghton, with the intention of yielding coal reserves lying 150 yards from the surface. The coal seam in question was reputed to be five-foot thick, and it was hoped that, by using state-of-the-art machinery, annual production would reach 300,000 tons.

'The Hon. Robert', who was presented with a silver spade and mahogany wheelbarrow to acknowledge the great significance of the occasion, was clearly ahead of his time in desiring 'to see the day when colliers' labour might be considerably lessened and this he hoped might be realised when the newly-invented cutting machine could be brought into active play'. He also emphasised the importance of proprietors doing their utmost to reduce the effects of local smoke pollution. In economic terms, Robert regarded the new undertaking as an opportunity to increase the 'activity and comfort' of local people and the north-east section of the West Riding more generally.

This industrial and commercial innovation had corresponding implications for the development of a village community close to Fryston Hall. As one future female resident of Fryston explained in interview:

> I am the last surviving granddaughter of Charles Poundford, who came as a shaft sinker to Fryston along with his brothers Sam and George. They came from Kingswinford, Stourbridge, Staffordshire. Along with two other brothers by the name of Bilton, they sunk the shaft for Fryston Colliery. There was no Fryston village as such at that time – not as we know it – but there were several cottages down by the riverside [i.e. the River Aire] and the Biltons were allocated one of them. After sinking the pit, they eventually moved to America. But Grandfather Poundford, they gave he and his wife a house in Denton Terrace, which is the other side of Castleford Cemetery, and thus he had to walk from there down the lane and cross at what is now known as 'Screw Bridge', but what was a wooden bridge at the time, to cross the railway down where the Wheldale sewerage works are now and collect these two Bilton men from their cottage and go into Fryston. The village was then developed to accommodate the influx of labourers brought in to work at the colliery.[824]

'The Hon. Robert' had also expressed the sincerest hope 'that the proprietors of that colliery would show the surrounding collieries an example of how to work amicably with their men'.[825] In order to trace the ongoing development of worker-owner relations at Fryston *per se*, it is necessary to understand the way that industrial relations and trade union organisation had evolved in the preceding decades. While this chapter is concerned with relevant trends occurring in the county as a whole, particular emphasis will be placed on the experience of the Castleford-based Allerton Collieries (especially Bowers Row), which, as we shall soon see, had powerful knock-on implications for the workers and residents of Fryston.

The Evolution of Organised Trade Unionism

The commercial development of the early 1860s onwards was accompanied by the corresponding growth of trade union organisation in Fryston, as in other Yorkshire mining communities. Prior to this, there had been few instances of any such organisation, despite the fact that the majority of mineworkers shared any number of serious grievances. One major reason for this was that the coalfield consisted of small, geographically dispersed mines, which hampered attempts to organise.

> But of more importance was the ruthless opposition of the employers to trade unionism. They invoked the aid of the law when it suited them to do so; introduced blacksheep and starved the colliers into submission when there was a strike or lock-out, except in periods of good trade; and ejected the miners, their families and household goods into the street when other methods failed or if the houses were required for blacksheep.[826]

Even in the early 1860s, the union suffered a loss of hard-won membership whenever they entered into strike action. By the end of the decade, however, the nascent West Yorkshire Miners' Association (WYMA) began a vigorous recruiting campaign that gained further momentum due to a marked upturn in trade. Eleven of the Association's thirteen lodges voted to press for wage increases and deputations were organised with the intention of speaking to managers at each of the relevant collieries. The WYMA's Secretary, John Dixon, urged the lodges not to proceed with threatened strike action as any concerted effort might cause a depletion of hard-earned union funds. As a result, all lodges bar one were persuaded to withdraw their notices and carry on working. The exception was the small group of Allerton Collieries, owned by Messrs. Bowers, where 463 miners downed tools on 26 January, 1870. The Bowers workforce argued that, if they were to succeed in their action, other coal owners would think twice before refusing to increase wages.

The WYMA did not share this optimism. Having failed to induce the men to withdraw their demands for an increase in wages, the union pushed for an immediate resolution. When all forms of persuasion and proposed arbitration failed to move the owners, a long and bitter conflict inevitably ensued:

> It was an inopportune time to press for an advance in wages and the miners had sadly underrated the nature of the opposition, the quality of which was quickly revealed when Bowers declared his intention to destroy the trade union, refused to give his men clearance notes without which they could not obtain work at any other colliery in the area, and began to introduce blacksheep. Dixon now had no option but to fight.[827]

In addition to a three-shillings per week levy imposed on members of other lodges, the strikers were well-supported by the South Yorkshire Miners' Association, which awarded several grants; the Committee of the Glass Bottle Trade, who made eight donations of 800 loaves of bread; and the Rothwell Scrap Society, which made a donation of eighty stones of flour. The company, meanwhile, brought in 'new hands' from Derbyshire and Staffordshire, some of whom returned home once they learned that they had been enlisted as strikebreakers. By August (the seventh month of the dispute), 38 families had been ejected from their homes to make way for imported blacksheep.[828]

When Dixon spoke directly to the owners on 24 September, he was told that there was no chance of any 'old hands' being re-employed unless they agreed to sign a written pledge committing them to relinquishing their trade union membership and never engaging in future union activities. By the end of October (the fortieth week of the strike), the number of WYMA lodges had withered away to six, leaving a total membership of only 480 men. The onset of winter proved decisive: by December, some 200 workers had left the area entirely, while all but a handful of the remainder were driven back to work by cold, hunger and privation.[829]

Fortune swung back, just as quickly, in the workers' favour. An 'unusual increase' in the demand for coal occurring in the late summer of 1871 led to increased wages, which were sustained at a comparatively high level for three more years. Union membership increased accordingly, partly in response to an assiduous membership drive. That said:

> Although there [had] been a striking increase in the numerical and financial strength of the trade union, and although the miners had recovered their fighting spirit, there were coal owners whose dislike of trade unionism was so intense that they were still prepared to challenge the Association, despite the fact that economic conditions favoured the miners.[830]

A singular case in point was that of the Altofts collieries, near Normanton, West Yorkshire, owned by Pope and Pearson. The experience of one Altofts miner and his family at this point in time would, as we shall later discover, have great relevance for the unfolding history of Fryston.

From Altofts to Bowers Row

The future manager of Fryston colliery and founder of the British Association of Colliery Management (BACM), Jim Bullock, recalls the day he was told by his uncle (his mother's eldest brother) about the time he had first clapped eyes on Jim's father, William, who was only 20 years old and standing in the pit yard at one of Pope and Pearson's Altofts collieries:

> He was stripped to the waist stood outside the colliery offices at Popes and Pearsons, offering to fight any man for his wages. Miners could never resist a challenge and that day I saw him have three fights and he took three men's wages. We saw his possibilities and a few of us formed a syndicate to back him and arrange fights for him, not boxing as you know it, sheer all-in fighting. He never lost.[831]

William Bullock had actually started his mining career at the tender age of ten years old. He had good reason to count his blessings for both his parents had gone down the mines aged eight, and his grandparents when they were only six. At Altofts, his job was that of 'horse breaker'.

This was a colliery that, despite a relatively low rate of union organisation, had seen numerous disputes in the past twenty years. Encouraged by the onset of higher wages and the work of local activists, the union had commenced a recruitment drive that, so far, had yielded a membership of 300. In their corresponding determination to sabotage the union campaign, the company had sacked over seventy of those driving it. Similarly, when the union set up a procedure for setting on two checkweighmen, the company responded by ordering the 'appointees' to leave the colliery. One of this pair was arrested for resisting expulsion by a West Riding police constable who Pope and Pearson's had brought in to maintain order.[832] At a crowded meeting in Normanton on 20 November 1872, the men were pledged the support of the Miners' National Union, who had 90,000 members and a fund of £50,000 at their disposal.

> It was now clear that the Association meant business and that the men were determined to exercise rights which, according to Dixon, were then denied at few collieries in Yorkshire. The demand for coal was still increasing and, had a strike taken place, the employers, if they had persisted in their attitude, would have suffered considerable losses. Accordingly, next morning they capitulated. A notice was 'stuck on the pit gates' by the owners telling the miners they could become members of the Association and elect checkweighmen. Nearly all the men who had been dismissed were re-engaged.[833]

In this context, William Bullock decided to leave Altofts and work, instead, at the nearby Bowers colliery. His motives were primarily romantic. He had gone one day into his future wife's home, on the invitation of her eldest brother who was intent on having him sign a contract for another fight. While negotiations were in progress, a 'bonny lass of sixteen' walked into the kitchen. Bullock took one look at her and asked, 'Is tha spokken for, lass?' The young woman replied, 'No, I'm not,' to which Bullock declared: 'Then tha is now.'[834] The girl's father, who was also present, took immediate exception, angrily insisting: 'We're having no prize-fighters in this family, we are good living Baptists.' Bullock stormed off in a rage, only to return six months later for a second attempt at winning the father's consent. The old man was resolutely unconvinced. 'We are contractors, you are only a horse breaker,' he declared. 'You cannot give her the standard of life she is accustomed to.'[835] William Bullock adopted the do-or-die strategy of securing a job as contractor at Bowers Row pit, eight miles away. As his son Jim recalls:

> Within six months my father was contracted to this pit making a new pit bottom and within twelve months my grandfather and my uncles were working for my father and a few months later my mother and father were married, living in a little miner's cottage [with] two bedrooms, one room and a kitchen downstairs, bare walls, no water, no lights, no sanitation. It was in a long row of thirty other houses just like it.[836]

Now aged 24, William Bullock and his 17-year-old bride transported all of their worldly belongings to 'Bowers' on the back of a horse-drawn cart. They were given a key (which opened all the houses in the village) and told to pick whichever vacant property most took their fancy. Bullock's wage was 25 shillings a week (with one ton of concessionary unscreened coal every month), and their weekly rent was 3s 5d. This was the house in which every one of their children would subsequently be born, of which Jim Bullock was the youngest.

In the meantime, the boom period for the market for coal had encouraged an increase in the WYMA's membership and financial stability. The need for another full-time official to join John Dixon opened the door for the appointment of the 31-year-old Benjamin Pickard, who entered the role in March 1873. There had been four other candidates against him, but the vote in Pickard's favour was so overwhelming that the union eventually gave up counting.[837]

The following section incorporates brief biographical sketches of Pickard and a second future national mining trade union leader, Herbert Smith. Both Kippax-born individuals were destined to play a key part in an epic early twentieth-century dispute, which, as we are about to discover, permanently transformed the demographic profile and culture of Fryston village.

Made in Kippax: the 'Iron Man' and the 'Man in the Cap'

Benjamin ('Ben') Pickard came to the forefront of mining trade unionism in 1873 when elected as Assistant Secretary of the WYMA before being elected as Secretary three years later. Pickard was born on 28 February 1842 in the village of Kippax on the outskirts of Castleford town centre. He was educated at Kippax Grammar (elementary) School, before joining his father as a 'hurrier' at the local pit. Pickard was soon active in trade union affairs, becoming his local lodge secretary at just eighteen.[838]

Not one to suffer fools gladly, Pickard possessed a 'considerable intellect' and unrivalled knowledge of the mining industry. He 'deprecated political ideology in general', placing common sense and pragmatism higher in his estimation than simple 'idealism'.[839] 'What was prickly intransigence to some was to others a sign of staunch integrity and dogged perseverance to obtain what he regarded as right.'[840] With his outlook on life underscored by religious conviction, even his most ardent adversaries did not dare question his redoubtable honesty:

> Brought up in the Wesleyan Connection and having had a yearning for its ministry, he was a strict Protestant, a pillar of the Lord's Rest Day Association, and for the greater part of his life a rigid teetotaller and non-smoker. He was 'stubborn as a mule' and had no end of courage. 'There could not,' says one account, 'have been more of a fighter for the miners. He knew what he was after, and he was stubborn.' This obstinate man was at the same time a most skilled negotiator. Unlike most trade union leaders, there was nothing 'free and easy' about Pickard. He held aloof, permitted no familiarities. Whoever stood in his path was likely to rue it. Many years afterwards, Herbert Smith, fourth President of the M.F.G.B., recalled the memory of Pickard, 'the iron man.' For that was the name the miners gave him in his own county.[841]

One year earlier, in July 1872, a small, but already chunky, thick-set ten-year-old called Herbert Smith was making his way with his adoptive father to start work on the 5am ('morning') shift at Glasshoughton colliery. Herbert Smith was born on 17 July 1862 in the parish of Preston, just on the outskirts of the same Kippax village whence Ben Pickard hailed. Tragically, Smith's biological father had been killed in a mining accident only a few days earlier, and it was not long afterwards that his mother died as well.[842] His early childhood was therefore spent in a workhouse, an experience which, according to his biographer, had a profoundly formative effect:

> He only lived there a few years, but long enough to light the fires of hatred of all coldness, indifference, and hardness to inoffensive children. That experience made him one with them [...] As men boast their high lineage, Herbert Smith, in his manhood, proclaimed his relationship to the afflicted; belligerently challenging the self-righteous. He was an aristocrat of the afflicted.[843]

Smith was still scarcely more than an infant – his precise age at the time is uncertain – when he was adopted by a childless couple living nearby, who went coincidentally by the names of Charlotte and Samuel Smith. Thereafter, the boy was raised in a cosy, loving home. The family moved briefly into the Durham coalfield, only to return to Castleford, where they settled in Glasshoughton via a short stay in the town centre. There was no compulsory education in those days, but his parents paid tuppence a week for him to attend the Dame's School in Glasshoughton, followed by the British School in Pontefract, which required a daily three-mile walk. Thus, by the time he joined his father at the pit, he had developed the capacity to 'read, write and figure'.[844]

For Smith's father, Samuel, 'trade unionism was a Faith in a world set against him and his kind. And he brought his son up in the Faith',[845] and ensured that Smith joined the union on the day he started work. Charlotte Smith was an immensely kind, 'strong-minded religious' woman who also helped shape Smith's outlook on life, as did his direct experience of mining work. Whilst scarcely in his teens, for example, Smith witnessed the death underground of a 15-year-old friend. Consequently:

> Steeped in the ways of the pit, experience emphasized by that of his father and his fellow workers, Herbert Smith began early to look on the ruling class with hostile eyes. Though he had throughout his life a contempt for theorizing, the fact remains he was emphatically class conscious. To have said he was 'Miner-conscious' would have pleased him most. He would have understood that better. Miners are real: classes are abstract – and Herbert Smith had no room for abstractions.[846]

Smith entered manhood a muscular, powerful, hard-working but blunt-speaking individual; but as Bellamy and Saville point out, it would be some years before the man who was to become synonymous with his trademark cloth cap showed signs of becoming 'one of the best-loved leaders in the history of the British miners'.[847]

Out of the Frying Pan…

For William Bullock, the move from Altofts provided no respite from the type of industrial relations conflict he was already accustomed to. Unlike his kind, sympathetic and friendly new bride (who 'had soothing hands and a quiet voice'), William Bullock was 'a thick-set man of fiery temper [...] full of fight, particularly against the bosses, fighting them at work and in chapel. He was a man who never gave in.'[848]

Following the dispute of 1870, Bowers had vowed never to permit trade union organisation at their collieries.

> But as wages rose and the Association became stronger Dixon, in 1872, paid as much attention to the recruitment of members at Bowers' pits as at other collieries. Before the year was out some of the miners employed joined the Society and, early in March 1873, it was reported that about two hundred had done so, and that a lodge had been established. The following month, when a committee was appointed to try and increase membership, it was decided to elect three checkweighmen, Bowers would not let the men do so and suggested that if the miners put forward twelve names he himself would select the checkweighmen, a proposal which the miners, with the support of the Association, rejected.[849]

Even though the Bowers miners had received identical wage rises to those negotiated on behalf of colleagues in the same district since

October 1871, the concessions they had been forced to make in 1870 had left their wages lagging some ten per cent behind those being paid at neighbouring pits. Thus, in October 1871, emboldened by a thriving lodge membership, the Bowers miners pressed for the discrepancy to be mended. Once more, the owners were steadfastly opposed and took the belligerent step of dismissing all members of a delegation who tried to address this issue with the pit manager. A strike was called, but Dixon persuaded the men to return to work once Bowers agreed to refer the dispute to arbitration. The ruling that followed fell in the miners' favour: on discovering that Bowers men were being paid a lower tonnage rate than miners at surrounding collieries who were working at identical or similar seams, the Arbitrator granted them a 7.5 per cent increase on existing wages.[850]

So it was that, by the time Fryston Colliery was sunk in 1873, trade union organisation had survived an early onslaught and become an integral feature of the West Riding mining industry. Each of the significant individuals identified in this chapter – Ben Pickard, Herbert Smith and William Bullock, would play pivotal roles in shaping the destiny and character of Fryston village and its mine. We shall resume their story in Chapter 21, but only after briefly refocusing on the corresponding experience of the local landed gentry.

Chapter Eighteen
'Once More Towards the Setting Sun'

Lady Houghton's Farewell

The five years spanning 1873 to 1877 constituted a bitter-sweet period in Milnes's lifetime. While the celebrity he enjoyed by virtue of his longstanding political and literary careers, and his regular philanthropic activities, was considerably enhanced, he also experienced the tragic loss of his wife, and witnessed the partial devastation of his mansion.

The beginning of the period was immensely satisfying. In the spring of 1873, Milnes consolidated his literary renown following the publication of his *Monographs Personal and Social* – a series of essays on some of the more interesting and invariably obscure friendships formed in the course of his varied and distinguished life. Included here were portraits of Suleiman Pasha, Alexander von Humboldt, Cardinal Wiseman, Walter Savage Landor, the Berrys, Harriet Lady Ashburton, the Reverend Sydney Smith, and an essay on 'The Last Days of Heinrich Heine'. The inclusion of unedited versions of Lucie Duff Gordon's letters, recalling how she had visited the poet on his sickbed, distinguished Milnes's essay on Heine from his earlier piece in the *Edinburgh Review*.

The highlight of Milnes's involvement in parliamentary affairs was his intervention in the debate regarding the Marriage with a Deceased Wife's Sister Bill, which sought to lift the existing prohibition on such a relationship. Biblical references condemning marriages of this nature were invoked alongside the more secular argument that the proposed new law risked destroying the *cordon sanitaire*, which preserved 'the dignity and purity of family life'. More specifically, 'Opponents of the bill took for granted that a man would lust for his wife's sister if their relationship were not tabooed.'[851]

In moving a Second Reading of the Bill, Milnes stated that it was only in this country that 'scriptural ordinance' was used to deny this right of marriage. Previously, 'when the Church of Rome was the Established Church of England', such marriages were permitted – a state of affairs that remained characteristic of practically every other nation in the world. Moreover, in Britain's major colonies of Canada and the United States of America, marriages between a man and his late wife's sister were strongly regarded as 'a means of binding family ties still closer'.[852] Milnes would not live to see the eventual passage of the 'Wife's Sister Bill' on 29 August 1907, but it was typical of him to have been such an ardent and persistent proponent during his lifetime.[853]

By the post-summer London season of 1873, the lease on 16 Upper Brook Street had lapsed, necessitating a move to a furnished house at 27 Berkeley Square. Milnes was by now susceptible to recurring attacks of the gout, and his wife's health was increasingly volatile. Without realising it, their family life was entering an extremely crucial phase:

> Here, during [what proved to be] the last London season of her life, that of 1873, Lady Houghton did her best to amuse Amy, who was 'out', and Florence, who had not yet been presented. She planned Amy's clothes, taking her to the Queen's Drawing-room on one occasion in 'pale green and white, decked with white narcissus,' on another in a dress of faint lilac colour decorated with sprigs of white lilac flowers [...] She would also take the girls about to draughty country-houses – to stay with the Fitzwilliams in 'the grand and gloomy Wentworth,' or to Trentham, and of course to Crewe. One day she drove Florence over from Crewe for her first sight of Madeley Manor, walking with her nineteen-year-old daughter round the Bryn where she herself had walked each morning before breakfast as a girl. At Fryston (still subject to white fogs which did not lift till mid-day and in winter were so thick that you could not see an inch before you, and when out riding the girls would lose each other in the woods; and where the frost blackened the geraniums in the garden) Lady Houghton gave up her big cold bedroom and settled cosily in her boudoir on a 'sofa-bed'.[854]

Following the crushing defeat of Gladstone's Liberal government in the general election of February 1874, Milnes hosted a 'post mortem' discussion involving leading Yorkshire Liberals at Fryston. Milnes's biographer, Thomas Wemyss Reid, was one of those present. He observed that there was nothing to suggest at this point that Lady Houghton's health should have given any obvious cause for concern. She had taken 'the head of the table' in her customary manner 'and delighted her guests by her bright conversation, by the vividness of her reminiscences of bygone celebrities, and the sympathetic tact with which she brought persons of very opposite opinions and characteristics into friendly intercourse'.[855]

Wemyss Reid recalls that this was the occasion on which Lady Houghton recounted her childhood relationship with the grandmother of Charles Dickens. It was to prove the last time that she felt capable of dining with her family. On the following day (24 February), her slight cold developed into a fatal congestion of the lungs.[856] Milnes and their daughters were present at her passing but their son, Robert, was unable to return from Harrow in time to see her before she died.

Lady Houghton's funeral took place less than one week later, the sombre black cortege passing through the gates and the end of the long elm-lined avenue of Fryston Hall and into St. Andrew's Church at Ferry Fryston. There, the coffin was lowered into the Milnes family vault. As Pope-Hennessy told it most evocatively, 'The mourners sorrowfully retraced their steps to the great empty house, and to that weary sense of inexplicable absence that death brings.'[857]

The Conquest of America

It had been with the intention of 'comforting or distracting' Amy, Florence and Robert following the death of their mother that Milnes took his children on a round of visits later that autumn to friends in Scotland, including Lady Ashburton, who traditionally spent this time of the year in her lodge on the banks of Loch Luichart. Amy used the opportunity to recover from recent illness, while Robert did some shooting and their father took gentle rides out on a pony.[858]

The following spring, Milnes spent time in London, where he resumed entertaining a variety of guests to his now-famous breakfasts. One of these, on Sunday 7 March 1875, brought together a diverse group, including the Liberal politician Henry Cowper, the American poet Joaquin Miller, and the biographer and travel writer, Augustus Hare. It was Hare who subsequently recalled how:

> There was a young man there whom I did not notice much at first, but I soon found that he was very remarkable, and then that he was very charming indeed. It was Lord Rosebery. He has a most sweet gravity almost always, but when his expression does light up, it is more than an illumination – it is a conflagration, at which all around him take light. Joaquin Miller would have been thought insufferably vulgar if he had not been a notoriety: as it was, every one paid court to him. However, I ought not to abuse him, as he suddenly turned round to me and said, 'Do you know, I'm glad to meet you, for you write books that I can read.'[859]

Having first sought out and introduced himself to Miller (the 'Poet of the Sierras') two years earlier, Milnes had gradually eased the maverick poet into fashionable London society. Milnes was sometimes critical of his protégé's verses and Miller was unceremoniously refused when making a romantic approach to a relative of Lady Houghton's.[860] This was in no way detrimental to their friendship. As one unspecified London daily newspaper wrote in its gossip column, it was typical of:

> [Milnes] that graceful poet and entertainer that he should have shown such warm hospitality to Miller. Indeed, a notion prevails amongst some of our Transatlantic cousins that Lord Houghton was raised to the peerage on the understanding that he would promote kindly feelings between the great Republic and the 'Old Country' by giving breakfasts and dinners to celebrities in London hailing from the other side of the great ocean.[861]

Later that year, Milnes yielded to the 'burden of celebrity' by embarking on a tour of North America along with Robert: 'Easily the most popular man in England with visiting Americans, [Milnes] had long wished to travel in the United States, and "as old age approached, a desire had entered his breast to turn his footsteps once more towards the setting sun"'.[862] Milnes and his son spent an initial ten days in Canada, where they landed on 16 August. They visited such major cities as Quebec, Montreal and Toronto, where Milnes found his hosts 'kind and welcoming, but not especially interesting', and considered the Niagara Falls and the Lachine Rapids far less fascinating than the floating icebergs they had sidestepped while crossing the Atlantic.[863] The American leg of the journey proceeded via Buffalo, followed by one-week stays in Chicago and St Louis. Also included in the four-month tour were visits to Washington, D.C., various stop-off points in New England (e.g. Quincey, Cambridge, Concord and Boston) and two lengthy stays in New York City.

While in St Louis, Milnes and Robert were given a tour of the city and its parklands by the Union civil war hero General William Tecumseh Sherman, who also invited them to dinner. This was clearly the highlight of the trip in Robert's estimation, as he confessed in his diary:

> After dinner we sat and talked in the General's room; he talked of the war which, as his son-in-law said, he very rarely did, giving us an account of Macpherson's death and the March to the Sea. He is a dear old boy, the sort of man one would be proud to serve under and die for, tall with a close-cut beard and moustache, and a short soldierly almost nervous manner of speaking. He gave Father a handsome map and me some photos writing our names upon each [...] I shall never forget the evening, Sherman is the man of all others that I wanted to see, & feel most admiration for.[864]

Among the great literary figures Milnes renewed his friendships with were Bret Harte, Longfellow and Emerson; he also took time out to visit the grave of his old friend, Nathaniel Hawthorne. Generally speaking, 'The American people treated him as one of themselves, and, from the President downwards, made him free of their homes.'[865] Early in the visit, on 15 September, the American Secretary of State had sent a telegram to President Ulysses S. Grant, enclosing a letter of introduction from General Badeau, the US Minister in Brussels, recommending that the president host a reception for Milnes in recognition of the Englishman's 'warm support of our cause during the rebellion'.[866] Milnes was duly received by the President and First Lady, Julia Dent Grant, in Washington, D.C. on 13 November. While there is no record of this meeting, Wemyss Reid reports that Grant 'showed [Milnes] exceptional marks of attention'.[867]

Milnes was accorded a further distinction by the dinner given in his honour by the Lotos Club on 21 November. The declared aim of the club (established five years earlier) was 'to promote social intercourse among journalists, literary men, artists and members of the musical and dramatic professions, and such merchants and professional gentlemen of artistic tastes and inclinations as would naturally be attracted by such a club'.[868] In the course of an enthusiastically received speech to a 'great gathering of literary men', Milnes spoke in glowing terms of the promise being shown by the Liberal politician Lord Rosebery, and quoted the poetry of his friends and protégés, Joaquin Miller and Algernon Charles Swinburne.[869]

This was a resounding success by any possible criteria:

> This visit to America, indeed, might be regarded as an epitome of his whole life, seeing that it illustrated the breadth of his sympathies, the universality of his curiosity, his social gifts and his kindness of heart, the keenness of his interest in literature and men of letters, and the genuine attachment which he always felt to those social and political movements that promised to make for good in the world.[870]

It was only after two postponed departures, designed to accommodate the ceaseless flow of invitations extended to Milnes, that he and Robert were finally able to return to England at the end of November.

Fire and Burns

Travel continued to be the best therapy for Milnes and his family, though this was famously not the case when, twelve months after returning from America, he was staying with Robert at the Shelbourne Hotel in Dublin on 17 November 1876. It was there that Milnes received an urgent telegram from the housekeeper at Fryston Hall, conveying the horrendous news that the building was being destroyed by fire. The conflagration, whose origins were unknown, had been ignited in the tower in the top bedroom of the house.

> Messengers were at once despatched to Pontefract, Wakefield, and Whitwood, for the fire brigades, and speedily the Pontefract engine was on the spot. Unfortunately the engine could not be got to work for some time, owing to scarcity of piping to connect the engine with the fishpond south of the hall, and in the meantime the fire was spreading rapidly along the upper range of bed rooms in the front portion of the hall. Ultimately the engine being brought into the stable yard was connected to a well, but in some fifteen minutes this was pumped dry. The roof fell about four o'clock yesterday morning. In the meantime more assistance had arrived from Castleford and Whitwood, and the fire engine from the former place was at once connected with the river Aire, north of the hall, and may fairly be said to have saved the older portion of the hall in the rear.[871]

At approximately seven o'clock, a third fire engine arrived from Wakefield, having been initially transported to Knottingley by special train, and drawn from there by horses from the Fryston stables. Works of art and the contents of the famous library were twice rescued by farm-hands and tenants who had rallied to the cause.

Milnes hurriedly returned home, leaving Robert, who was seriously ill, behind. He quickly discovered that the fire damage was every bit as extensive as he had feared. The morning-room, drawing room and hall of the old house had been burnt out by the blaze, along with the bedrooms located above them.[872] Due to the fact that the salvaged books had been deposited outside on the lawn, many of them were, in Milnes's own words, 'wetted, knocked about'. It was suspected that some of the many onlookers had helped themselves to 'mementoes' of the fire. There was some consolation in the fact that the back rooms of the hall remained habitable, giving Milnes sufficient incentive to begin the long process of restoration – even though 'it was weary work for an old man, and expensive too'.[873]

It probably came as a welcome distraction for Milnes – and further proof of the esteem and affection in which he was held by the British public – when, appropriately enough, on 'Burns Night' of 25 January 1877, he travelled to Glasgow and, in the presence of tens of thousands of people, unveiled a statue in honour of the country's greatest poet, Robert Burns.[874] Milnes's beneficence towards the 'Scottish Baird' had first been revealed as long ago as 1842 when, along with Thomas Carlyle and Robert Chambers, he set up a relief fund to provide financial support in old age for Isabella Begg, a former schoolmistress and sister of Robert Burns, whose husband had died in 1813, having been thrown from a horse.[875] Now it was Milnes's turn to honour Isabella's brother. In addressing the crowd, Milnes maintained in typical fashion how:

> The songs composed for the merriment of an obscure tavern club have set millions of tables singing with delight; the natural yearnings of his affections have become the stimulus and interpreter of youthful passion in ten thousand breasts; and the religious bickerings of a remote province have been made vocal with the most stirring tones of civil and religious liberty.[876]

It was with some irony that, some four months later, Milnes also suffered a nasty accident in falling from a horse in Hyde Park, 'when the loose curb rein of "a Miss Farquhar" caught his leg in the jam of riders and dragged him off his pony: he fell on his face and retired to bed for a week, later emerging in a carrying chair to dine at the Roxburghe Club'.[877]

The accident did not impair his capacity to entertain. On 30 May, for example, he hosted 'a pleasant party', consisting chiefly of poets including Algernon Swinburne, Violet Fane and Sir Francis Doyle, and other writers including Augustus Hare, Henry James and William Mallock, whose *The New Republic* had recently appeared in print.[878] It was not long afterwards that Milnes played host to a far more remarkable and momentous gathering.

President Grant and the Jersey Lily

In May 1877, as the curtain came down on his second term in office, President Ulysses S. Grant embarked on an extensive, two-and-a-half-year tour of Europe, Asia and Africa. His first 'port' of call was Liverpool, followed by visits to other large English cities, including Manchester, Newcastle, Southampton and London. Massive cheering crowds lined the docks, streets and railway stations everywhere the President and First Lady visited, no less so than when he arrived at St Pancras Station on 1 June, to be greeted by the American Minister and a range of English dignitaries. He drove off from there in a horse drawn carriage to be introduced, later that afternoon, to the Prince of Wales.[879]

On the following day, Grant accompanied the Prince and a large party, including the German Ambassador, by rail to the Epsom race meeting; and later that night, the Duke of Wellington held a banquet in the President's honour. On 3 June, Grant attended a divine service at Westminster Abbey, at which Dean Stanley described him in the course of his sermon as the man 'who had restored unity to his country'.[880]

Milnes joined such eminent fellow-Victorians as William Gladstone and Julia Ward Howe at a large reception given by the American Minister on 5 June. Two nights later, Milnes was given the opportunity of returning the favour extended to him two years earlier by hosting a large dinner party for the President and First Lady, followed by a more intimate reception.[881]

The after-dinner reception was noteworthy for the unlikely encounter between the President and Lady Emily Charlotte le Breton, who was soon to become better known by her stage name of Lillie Langtry. The 'Jersey Lily' had arrived late to Milnes's Arlington Street address with her husband but was surprised to find herself seated side-by-side with the President and with Julia Ward Howe positioned directly opposite. Milnes introduced them by 'making a gallant remark on the *rencontre* of "Mars and Venus"'.[882] For the most part, Grant hardly spoke to Langtry, having been tied up in conversation with another guest, Sir Garnet Wolseley, who confessed to having a high regard for Grant's chief adversary, General Robert E. Lee.[883] Langtry professed to having forgotten what she and Grant eventually said to one another:

> I am sorry that I cannot remember details of our conversation. The only recollection I have is of a rather abrupt, soldier-like man, who had seen great happenings, done great things, and to whom social functions must, perforce, seem small. A man, I thought, young as I was, whose authority was great and whose word could be trusted – a man to give one a sense of security. Like many others in England at the time, I knew little of the history of the United States, and I am not sure that it even

> occurred to me that he had been its President. A great general he was, that I knew, and he looked it.[884]

It seems possible that Langtry was trying to conceal a major faux pas she had famously committed. As Bogar explains, in 'fumbling for conversation', Ms Langtry 'brought the table to stunned silence when she asked, "What have you done since your Civil War, General?" Grant, humor gleaming from his soft blue eyes, replied, "Well, I've served two terms as President of the United States."'[885] Langtry also engaged in precious little conversation with the First Lady. President Grant had the good grace to introduce her to his wife, but (as Langtry recalls) 'as I had little or no conversation with her, I retain her in my memory only as a rather stout figure, in a black gown, with very fat arms'.[886]

Langtry was also introduced by Milnes to Joaquin Miller, a man she refers to as 'a child of nature and perhaps the most picturesque personality of the literary world'.[887] The introduction occurred after Langtry had chanced upon a book of Milnes's poetry and playfully approached him as follows: 'I laughingly asked my host if I couldn't inspire him sufficiently to write *me* one. He looked at me whimsically, a wee bit pathetically, and said, "My dear, I am too old".'[888] By way of consolation, Milnes subsequently presented Langtry to 'a very tall, lean man, with a pale intellectual face, yellow hair so long that it lay in curls about his shoulders, a closely cropped beard, and a dreamy expression in his light eyes'. It took only a short while for this unconventionally attired, 'strange' man to disappear, only for him to suddenly return with a torn sheet of paper from which he read off the following verse:

> *To the Jersey Lily:*
>
> If all God's world a garden were,
> And women were but flowers,
> If men were bees that busied there
> Through endless summer hours,
> O! I would hum God's garden through
> For honey till I came to you.[889]

At this, Miller gave off a final, dramatic gesture, and stated: 'Let this verse stand; it's the only one I ever wrote to a living woman.'[890]

Langtry speaks very warmly of Milnes in her autobiography, describing him as 'the most delightful host of his time in London [...] [exhibiting] a mode of entertainment [that] seemed so easy and so comprehending'.[891] She credits Milnes with a great capacity for spotting and encouraging the talent of other people and for having an unrivalled knowledge of New World literature, which meant that 'no American of note, or colonial cousin, passed through London without being welcome and feted in that large, yet cozy Arlington Street house'.[892]

Wilde Flowers

Less than two weeks after entertaining the US President, Milnes received a letter (dated 16 June 1877) from another eminent Victorian whose name is inexorably linked to that of Lillie Langtry: the controversial poet and socialite Oscar Wilde. Wilde had recently written in the *Irish Monthly* of the feelings of disappointment and distaste he had experienced on entering the Roman cemetery in which the tomb of John Keats is located. Wilde had discovered to his horror that, not only was the tomb overgrown with wild flowers, but it was also decorated with a medallion-type commemorative portrait of Keats, which constituted an ugly and inaccurate misrepresentation of the poet's features.[893]

Part of Wilde's stated objective in writing was to draw Milnes's attention to the following sonnet, which he had been inspired to write while standing at Keats's graveside:

> Keats' Grave
>
> Rid of the world's injustice and its pain
> He rests at last beneath God's veil of blue;
> Taken from life while life and love were new
> The youngest of the Martyrs here is lain,
> Fair as Sebastian and as foully slain.
> No cypress shades his tomb, nor funeral yew,
> But red-lipped daisies, violets drenched with dew,
> And sleepy poppies, catch the evening rain.
> O proudest heart that broke for misery!
> O saddest poet that the world hath seen!

O sweetest singer of our English land!
Thy name was writ in water on the sand,
But our tears shall keep thy memory green,
And make it flourish like a Basil-tree.[894]

Wilde maintained that, whilst he 'should be very glad to know if you see any beauty or stuff' in the sonnet, his principal reason for writing was to enlist Milnes's help in having something done about the monument. In repeating the objection he raised in the course of his *Irish Monthly* article, Wilde complained that the medallion profile 'exaggerates his facial angle so as almost to give him a hatchet-face and instead of the finely cut nostril, and Greek sensuous delicate lips that he had, gives him thick almost negro lips and nose'.[895] Wilde maintained that the memorial ought to be replaced by a more fitting 'tinted bust of Keats', similar to the one dedicated to the Rajah of Koolapoor in Florence.

It was here that Milnes's help might prove invaluable: 'Your influence and great name could achieve anything and everything in the matter,' Wilde deferentially observed. He felt certain that, with his name heading a list of donors, 'the ugly libel of Keats could be taken down' and replaced by a fittingly beautiful memorial. While there is no record of any reply by Milnes, or of any initiative arising from Wilde's solicitation, this episode is a testament to Milnes's reputation, both as the foremost biographer of the great English poet, and as a redoubtable patron of the arts and a great philanthropist.

Chapter Nineteen
Crossing the Floor

Henry James: A London Life and Other Tales

Milnes's final years were mainly spent at Fryston Hall, where he continued to play host to established and rising literary and political figures. Notable among these was the American writer Henry James, who was already established in this country. It was also a period in which his children married and, especially in the cases of Robert and Florence, embarked on their own distinguished careers. Commentators on this period continue to speak of Milnes as a scheming, manipulative and curmudgeonly figure – a view certainly not shared, as we shall see, by the likes of Henry James.

Cynthia Gamble, a recent biographer of Henry James, is among the most prominent critics of Milnes, whom she describes as 'a flamboyant, temperamental character who enjoyed the domineering and controlling role of patron of budding writers – *provided they accepted his conditions*'.[896] Milnes was equally renowned, according to Gamble, 'for his trenchant wit, malicious gossip and sexual excesses'.[897] He was, as Gamble puts it, as much a collector of people as an avid collector of books; to this end, he made James the centrepiece of his literary breakfasts and dinners, and eventually established him as a guest at Fryston Hall.[898]

It is evident from surviving letters to friends and family that James harboured no such cynicism towards his English mentor and benefactor. In one early example, Henry wrote to his brother William on 29 March 1877, enthusiastically informing him about the breakfasts to which Milnes 'invites me most dotingly'.[899] James refers in this letter to a dinner, hosted by Lord Houghton, at which Gladstone and other men of 'high culture' were also present. The young James was seated in close proximity to one of Milnes's fellow-Apostles, the poet laureate, Alfred Tennyson:

> I sat next but one to the Bard and heard most of his talk, which was all about port wine and tobacco: he seems to know much about them, and can drink a whole bottle of port at a sitting with no incommodity. He is very swarthy and scraggy, and strikes one at first as much less handsome than his photos: but gradually you see that it's a face of genius. He had I know not what simplicity, speaks with a strange rustic accent, and seemed altogether like some creature of a primordial English stock, a thousand miles away from American manufacture.[900]

After dinner, James conversed 'affably' with Gladstone, 'not by my own seeking, but by the almost importune affection of Lord H'. (Milnes), whom he regarded as 'fascinating' and someone with the eye of 'a man of genius'.

In another letter (dated 5 May 1877), this time to Henry Adams, a fellow-American who, as we know, had also benefited from Milnes's patronage, James acknowledged unequivocally the debt he felt to Milnes:

> Lord Houghton has been my guide, philosopher and friend – he has breakfasted me, dined me, conversationalized me, absolutely caressed me. He has really been most kind and paternal, and I have seen, under his wing, a great variety of interesting and remarkable people. He has invited me to an evening party tonight (but you see I prefer to sit here and scribble to you; it's half past 11) and to a 6th or 8th breakfast next week. So you will perceive he has done very handsomely and I will defend him with my last breath![901]

Adams had been responsible for introducing James to one of Milnes's relatives – the former Conservative MP for the Borough of Wenlock – Charles Milnes Gaskell. Gaskell invited James to the family estate in Shropshire and, thereafter, to spend an English Christmas with them at Thornes House in Westgate, Wakefield, in 1878.[902] Hearing of this arrangement, Milnes asked James if he might join him at Fryston Hall for a New Year celebration.

The West Riding landscape that Christmas was thickly covered with snow, though this did not deter James from accompanying Lady Catherine Milnes Gaskell to a local workhouse, where they dropped off a Christmas tree and distributed toys to 150 grateful children.[903]

After Christmas, James travelled the twelve miles from Thornes House to Fryston Hall. On New Year's Eve, he wrote to his sister, Alice, while sitting by a warming bedroom fire. Dinner was due in an hour but, as James reported to Alice:

> Lord H. has just come into my room to know why I haven't come to afternoon tea, and, plumping himself into my armchair, is apparently lapsing into sociable slumber. He is a very odd old fellow – extremely fidgety and eccentric; but full of sociable and friendly instincts, and with a strong streak of humanity and democratic feeling. He has begun to snore violently and I must follow my letter as I can.[904]

James explained to his sister how, one day earlier, Milnes had taken him on an excursion to York Minster, after calling in on the Duchess of Somerset the previous day. Back at Fryston Hall, the small party consisted largely of Milnes family members, with the exception of Mrs Procter and her daughter. James portrayed Milnes's sister, Lady Galway, as 'a rather unattractive old woman, whose lightest observations exasperate her brother', but was far more complimentary about the Milnes children: 'The Miss Milnes's [sic], in fact, are charming girls, and the Hon. Robert is a very intelligent and clever young fellow for whose coming of age, a week or two hence, an extensive fête is being prepared.'[905]

On 4 January, James wrote a further letter to his friend Grace Norton, in which he praised Mrs Procter as a 'singularly delightful old woman' (of 82), and 'the best talker, in a certain way, I have met in England'.[906] He also spoke, affectionately again, on the subject of his host and his two daughters:

> Of Lord Houghton you have comparatively recent impressions. He is a battered and world-wrinkled old mortal, with a restless and fidgety vanity, but with an immense fund of real kindness and humane feeling. He is not personally fascinating, though as a general thing he talks very well, but I like his social, democratic, sympathetic, inquisitive old temperament. Half the human race, certainly everyone that one has ever heard of, appears sooner or later to have staid [sic] at Fryston. (I saw this in looking over the 'visitors books' of the house.) This represents an immense expenditure of hospitality and

> curiosity, trouble and general benevolence (especially as he is not very rich.) His daughters are very nice and rather clever girls, who appear like most of the English of both sexes to much greater advantage in their native element, the country than amid the odious social scramble of London.[907]

Robert Comes of Age

Milnes's son, Robert, was making a brief return to Fryston from Trinity College, Cambridge. Pope-Hennessy informs us that Robert's undergraduate days of the late 1870s 'sped along expected and conventional lines', and that the only obstacle to his eventual acquisition of a BA degree was his father's hollow threat to cease financially supporting him were he to continue 'eating and drinking more expensively than he could afford'.[908] At this stage of his life, Robert was leading a relatively free-spirited social existence, regularly attending the London theatres, going to balls and dinner parties, and accepting invitations to visit the most splendid English country houses.[909] Concurrently, Milnes was busily engaged in the expensive task of renovating a family home recently ravaged by fire. Thus:

> While flitting from country-house to country-house Robert was pursued by anxious letters from his father, increasingly illegible owing to gout in the hands, describing the progress of the rebuilding of Fryston and the extremities – such as the sale of the carriage-horses – to which the old man was at times driven by lack of ready coin. All the same, Lord Houghton somehow managed to go on hiring houses in Mayfair for the Season [...] Yet, despite all their father's earnest efforts, the Milnes sisters seemed to remain resolute spinsters and in point of fact the London houses were taken quite as much for their father's benefit as for their own. A stooping old man, in a black skull cap, Lord Houghton still entertained at his *omnium gatherum* parties, and was still to be seen everywhere in London, too often leaning with bibulous geniality upon the arm of his tall, elegant young son, who must have silently suffered much embarrassment as he guided his parent's unsteady steps out through some drawing-room door.[910]

On 6 January 1879, Milnes hosted a dinner party at Fryston Hall of 'friends old and new', including Mrs Procter and George Venables, to celebrate the re-opening of the section of the house that had been destroyed by fire.[911] Six days later, a tenants' ball was held at Fryston to celebrate Robert's coming of age.[912] This was the prelude to momentous changes in the young man's life. In June 1879, he unexpectedly announced his engagement to Sibyl Marcia Graham, the daughter of a north-country baronet. The prospective bride and groom were extremely young-looking 21-year-olds, he having 'no job and no prospects to speak of'.[913] Nevertheless, the couple were married one year later. Among those offering their heartiest congratulations to the father of the groom was his old friend, Florence Nightingale.[914]

Striking a Sour Note

Pope-Hennessy paints a very vivid image of Milnes in his final years:

> The object of deep affection to his own friends, of curiosity to those of his children, Richard Monckton Milnes was now become a gouty, stooping old man, with white whiskers, and fronds of white hair curling out from under the black skull-cap worn well back on his head [...] Benevolent, humorous, anecdotal, he was also very short-tempered, and had a tendency to go suddenly to sleep. He had always been gluttonous [...] and this characteristic, like his love of wine, became the solace of his old age. The very young no longer understood him. They did not understand his paradoxes, nor his habit of quizzing their remarks: for in age Lord Houghton continued his life-long occupation of watching the idiosyncrasies of others [...] and of commenting them in an irreverent way.[915]

This tendency towards irreverence and irascibility was exemplified by a well-documented occasion, on 14 February 1880, when Milnes was guest speaker at a dinner in celebration of the hundredth performance of Shakespeare's *Merchant of Venice* at London's Lyceum Theatre. The play had been universally regarded as a triumph for the celebrated actor-manager, Henry (later, Sir Henry) Irving, who not only occupied the major role of Shylock, but also took on principal responsibility for set design, lighting, direction and casting, in the course of a run eventually stretching to 250 consecutive nights.[916]

Milnes and Irving had first met almost exactly one year earlier at a dinner party in London at which Richard Burton was also present, and where the conversation focused on Shakespeare, Byron and sword-fencing.[917] At a subsequent party, held six days later to commemorate the anniversary of the publication of Isabel Burton's travel book, *AEI* (Arabia, Egypt, India), Irving was seated between Burton and Milnes, who good-naturedly speculated on the whereabouts of the grave of Moses.[918]

The 300-350 guests gathered in celebration on the stage of the Lyceum comprised the cream of London's artistic, literary and fashionable society. As Bingham points out, it must have been most satisfying for the great Victorian actor to survey the hundreds of candlelit guests assembled in his honour. There was, however, 'a skeleton at this feast' – in the form of Richard Monckton Milnes, who rose to propose a toast to 'The health of Mr Henry Irving and the Lyceum Theatre'.[919]

Unexpectedly, and with questionable taste in light of the occasion, Milnes delivered a speech that was 'flippant in tone and lukewarm in its praise'.[920] He began by launching 'an all-out attack on long runs', and bemoaned the passing of the old custom whereby productions were limited to no more than two performances per week.[921] Milnes partially redeemed himself by observing that men like Irving (who came from 'families of condition' with traditions of 'good breeding and high conduct') were helping to cleanse the acting profession of the 'impurity and scandal' previously associated with it.[922]

Having delivered this backhanded compliment, Milnes nonetheless lambasted Irving for having misinterpreted the role of Shylock. He equated the actor-manager with the type of historian who had sanitised the reputations of such 'great villains of the world' as Nero, Napoleon, Richard III and Robespierre:

> While upon that stage they had seen a rehabilitation of something of the same nature, for the old Jew, Shylock, who was regarded usually as a ferocious monster, whose sole desire was to avenge himself in the most brutal manner on the Christians of his neighbourhood, had become a gentleman of the Hebrew persuasion, with the manners of Rothschild.[923]

Irving responded to the speech with his characteristic good humour and strove to defuse the situation, though not without jibing that, while those 'who did not know better might cling to their outworn notions', his own characterisation of Shylock 'had the endorsement of the intelligent public'.[924] Afterwards, as the gentlemen guests retired to brandy and cigars, the actor-manager's old friend and fellow-actor J.L. O'Toole made a cheery speech that succeeded most effectively in removing 'the sour note from the evening's entertainment'.[925]

Houghton: The Decadent Lord Surbiton?

Milnes's reputation ran the risk of being tarnished when he became associated with a controversial book, *A Romance of the Nineteenth Century* (1881) by the novelist and economist William Hurrell Mallock. It takes as its central plot 'the systematic debauching of a young girl by a middle-aged libertine', Colonel Stapleton, who is a close friend of her family.[926] This theme was widely criticised for what was regarded as its gratuitously licentious subject matter.[927] Both Lucas and Yarker maintain that a salient theme of this and Mallock's previous novels is an emphasis on the growing decadence and religious and spiritual detachment of well-heeled Victorian society. Through two of Stapleton's associates, the Duchess and Lord Surbiton, Mallock 'tries most forcefully to reveal the squalor and *ennui* of society life'.[928] Even more to the point is Lucas's assertion that Lord Surbiton's character is based 'without doubt' on Milnes.[929]

Mallock discloses how he had been a visitor (on some unspecified date) not only to Fryston but also to the Blands' mansion at nearby Kippax. He recalls how Fryston was well-stocked with books and 'constantly filled with celebrities, generally of a miscellaneous, sometimes of an incongruous, kind'.[930] In this, as in other contexts, it was Lord Houghton's 'peculiar mixture' of talents that set him apart amidst 'any company which his ubiquitous presence animated'.[931]

Lucas highlights Mallock's description of Surbiton as a 'poet, diplomat and dandy', with a tendency to suffer indigestion from over-eating, and observes its strong resonance with Milnes's career interests and appetites. He reads further significance in the fact that, while Milnes owned a vast collection of erotica, Surbiton was not only renowned for his 'conversational freedom' but was also 'repeatedly shown to be a connoisseur of women and erotic customs'.[932] Lucas also maintains that certain of Stapleton's references (e.g to his witnessing of 'a certain dance in Damascus') are 'plainly alluding to Houghton's friendship with Richard Burton and their mutual passion for erotica, especially the sexual customs of the Middle East, on which Burton was an expert'.[933] Finally, Lucas believes it 'even possible' that Stapleton's character was based on the real-life prototype of 'Burton's crony' – the Colonel Studholme Hodgson referred to in Chapter 12.

Lucas considers it feasible that Mallock could easily have met Hodgson in the context of one of Burton and Milnes's many 'bachelor evenings'. True or not, 'Surbiton and Stapleton represent cynicism and profligacy; they are products of a failed faith, and they are meant to suggest the moral decadence beginning to overtake England.'[934]

Typically, Milnes proved to be one of the 'stoutest defenders' of Mallock's heavily-criticised novel. Showing uncanny insight, he was completely accurate in surmising the identity of the prototype of Colonel Stapleton: 'You have made only one mistake in it,' he playfully chided Mallock. 'The conduct of the colonel in one way would have differed from that which you ascribe to him.'[935]

Daughters and Marriage

In the autumn and winter of 1880-81, Amicia Milnes had embarked on a tour of Palestine and Egypt with her Aunt Harriette. While she was abroad, her father wrote to her (on 8 February 1881), informing her of the death of Thomas Carlyle. He also told her:

> We thought of you in your pleasant sunshine in our long snows that we have here at Fryston. We bore the storm very well; no pipes burst, and the drawing-room kept very warm and comfortable. The air was very equable and fairly warm.[936]

It is probable that Amicia's mind was otherwise distracted. While in Cairo, she had met and formed a match with the Irish Catholic Gerald FitzGerald, a member of the Indian Civil Service, who had been seconded at the time to the Egyptian Department of Finance. The couple sought Milnes's permission to become engaged and were duly married later that summer. It was 'one of the last occasions on which Lord Houghton succeeded in bringing around him a great gathering of the friends of his lifetime'.[937] Friends from all corners of society congregated for what was a remarkable celebration, even by London's standards:

> It was [...] the last occasion on which Lord Houghton played the host on a large scale in that London which he knew so well [...] one for which the moment aroused mingled feelings in his own mind, as he saw the daughter who since his wife's death had been his most constant companion, transferred from English life to a distant country, but which more and more, as his few remaining years passed, he recognised as a blessing, both for himself and her.[938]

In January 1882, Milnes sailed out to Egypt to pay a visit to his daughter and son-in-law. Whilst there, he observed the initial phases of a momentous revolution, led by Arabi Pasha. Two months later, during a stop-over in Athens on the journey home, Milnes suffered an apoplectic stroke that resulted in the paralysis of his left-hand side. Robert and his aunt, Lady Galway, set out immediately to his aid, only to be reproached by him over the cost of their journey.[939] Nevertheless, the three relatives returned home well in time for the Easter wedding between the younger of Milnes's two daughters, Florence, and the Honourable Arthur Henry ('Arty') Henniker, 'a somewhat impecunious younger son of the fourth Lord Henniker of Thornham Hall, Suffolk'.[940]

At 27 years old (the same age as his bride), Henniker occupied the relatively lowly rank of adjutant in the Coldstream Guards. Milnes was reputed to be disappointed with the match:

> The seat, Tudor with later additions, had descended to his [Lord Henniker's] father through two heiress sisters, the Duchess of Chandos and Baroness Henniker of Worlingworth Hall. But good blood and ancient lineage were not enough for Baron Houghton. What he had wanted for his pretty, eligible daughter was *money*. He sourly confessed that he had been paid back for his mercenary motives [...] he was forced to admit that he had been disappointed over Florence's marriage settlement.[941]

Once more, Florence Nightingale wrote to him (in a letter dated Easter Day, 1882), explaining that she and her family had been concerned to hear of his recent illness, but nonetheless asking him to pass on her blessings to Florence 'from her old namesake'. Nightingale commiserated with Houghton in the knowledge that Florence was due to escort her new husband on his re-posting to Ireland, adding: 'May all success attend her with a good soldier of professional enthusiasm, which is the right thing. The woes of Ireland almost surpass those of India with which I am always occupied.'[942]

Joining the Majority

In April 1883, Robert secured his first form of employment – as Assistant Private Secretary to Lord Granville in the Foreign Office. He and the majority of his colleagues were aristocratic by birth and the work they carried out was invariably non-arduous.[943] Things changed in the first month of the New Year when the Liberal government sent out General Gordon to supervise the evacuation of Khartoum, an undertaking that ended disastrously, one year later, in the killing of Gordon and the fall of the city. It also contributed to the growing unpopularity of the Gladstonian regime.

> These events provided [Robert] Milnes, at the age of twenty-six, with his first glimpse of politics and diplomacy from the inside. Already capable of judging a situation without party prejudice, and with a cool head and a calm eye, he privately disagreed with Granville's handling of the Sudanese crisis while realising the reasons for it.[944]

Having quickly decided that he was not cut out for a diplomatic career, Robert set about standing for parliament. In 1884, he and another young man put themselves forward for the newly-created Barnsley Division of the West Riding. The road to selection looked all the more straightforward when the rival candidate moved across to the neighbouring Rotherham Division. His political ambition was never realised, however, due to his father's death on 11 August 1885.[945]

In spite of being prone to illness, Milnes had paid visits to Cannes and Rome in 1883 before travelling once more to Cairo to see his daughter and son-in-law in March 1884. For the remainder of that year, he had devoted his time to rearranging those papers and books that had survived the fire. According to his close friend and biographer, he appeared to know by now that his death was close at hand:

> It was towards the close of August that, going to see him at Fryston, I heard him, almost for the first time, complain of being very ill. 'What is the matter?' I asked. He looked up quickly with a flash of intelligence in his eyes. 'Death,' he answered gravely; 'that is what is the matter with me; I am going to die.' And then the face was illuminated by the beautiful smile which those who loved him knew so well. 'I am going over to the majority,' he added, 'and, you know, I have always preferred the minority.'[946]

Such a realisation did not deter him from engaging in a typically active social life. A month later, he hosted the 'last large party' ever to be assembled at Fryston, which brought together guests who had earlier attended a massive Liberal demonstration in Pontefract.[947] A major mishap occurred a few weeks later when he fell out of his bed and fractured a collar-bone while staying at Lord Rosebery's home near Epsom. He had dreamt at the time that he was being chased by a hansom cab containing Mr Gladstone.[948] It was a measure of his resilience that, later in December, he gave a small dinner party at Fryston, which included Sir Frederick Pollock, James Payn, and the ubiquitous Wemyss Reid among the guests. 'None of us who were present on that occasion,' wrote Wemyss Reid, 'will forget his high spirits or the delightful flow of conversation, full of reminiscences of bygone celebrities, which made the evening pass so quickly.'[949]

Following a short trip to Naples with his sister in the spring of 1885, Milnes made two of his last major public appearances: the first, at the unveiling of a bust of Coleridge at Westminster Abbey on 7 May; and then when he unveiled one of David Gray at Cambridge nineteen days later. His final speech was delivered on 8 July, when he spoke with characteristic warmth at the annual meeting of the Wordsworth Society, which was held at his sister's house in Rutland Gardens. Later that month, he met up with her in Vichy on 8 August, where they both revelled in the opportunity to reunite with close friends. Two days later, Milnes appeared to be in the best of spirits, as he extolled the virtues of the Prince of Wales to a party of French citizens. Nevertheless:

> A few hours later the end came. Shortly after he had wished his sister good-night, he came to her room, breathing with difficulty. A violent thunderstorm was raging, and no medical man could be induced to come to the hotel. No remedy that could be applied restored him even momentarily; and his strength swiftly ebbed away [...] On the morning on which [Milnes's body] left London for Fryston a service was held in St. Margaret's church, Westminster, at which many of those who had known him in his later days, as well as one or two of his oldest friends, were present. On Thursday, August 20th, Milnes was laid by the side of his wife in the little churchyard at Fryston. The Archbishop of York, who had known them both throughout their married life, and whose warm affection for them had never changed, conducted the service. All the members of the family were present, as well as a great company of his Yorkshire friends and neighbours, to all of whom he had shown the unvarying kindness which was characteristic of the man.[950]

The sense of loss pervading all those who knew Lord Houghton was encapsulated in the words of Mrs Procter, who wrote: 'He was to me the best company I had. He knew so much. He had seen so much. The World never did him justice.'[951]

Chapter Twenty
Upholding Family Traditions

The Second Lord Houghton

Milnes's death had profound implications, of course, for his son, Robert. It transformed him into a landowner and a young peer, committed to a 'sacred creed of Gladstonian Liberalism' that countered the opposition of other Whig peers who were openly disparaging of Gladstone's attitude to Irish Home Rule.[952] Robert (hereafter 'Houghton') and his wife spent the remainder of 1885 with their four children (three girls, of which two were twins, and a boy called Richard or 'Dicky' after his paternal grandfather) settling in at Fryston Hall. From this vantage point, Houghton keenly observed the outcome of the 1885 election, which brought Gladstone into office. Any resulting euphoria Houghton may have felt was short-lived: he had only recently accepted one of the posts of Whips in the House of Lords when, in the autumn of 1886, majority parliamentary opposition to Gladstone's Home Rule and Irish Land Bills brought the government down. Following Gladstone's resignation and a subsequent general election, the Tories returned to power.

As 1887 unfolded, Houghton and his family were due to travel to India on the invitation of the Viceroy and Vicereine. They spent much of the late summer at home in Fryston, where all four children suffered bouts of scarlet fever. In September, the second Lady Houghton and her children temporarily relocated to Crewe Hall with the intention of convalescing in the company of 'Uncle Crewe'. Most tragically and unexpectedly, however, Lady Houghton not only contracted the same disease but died of it within a few short days: 'The youth and gaiety, good looks and popularity of the Houghtons made this death particularly shocking to their friends, all of whom sympathised with a young widower left with four small children to bring up on his own.'[953]

Incapable of carrying out his political responsibilities, let alone re-entering life in London, Houghton distracted himself from his grief by undertaking a course in agricultural studies at the Royal Agricultural College, Cirencester, aiming to prepare himself for managing the land surrounding Fryston Hall and the larger Cheshire and Staffordshire estates that he would one day inherit from his late wife's uncle. He was forced to abandon this plan, however, due to recurring problems with his lungs, which forced him into resigning his place on the course and travelling to Egypt to stay with his older sister, Amy Fitzgerald.[954] An even greater tragedy then followed:

> His only son, Dick, a child of eight years old, became gradually more and more gravely ill. The best doctors and nursing could not help him, and when in the winter of 1889 Houghton was himself once more ordered abroad by his medical adviser and unwillingly set off for Madeira and Capetown with his brother-in-law, the Duke of Montrose, he knew that he would not again see the boy alive. It was in March 1890, at Capetown, that he received a telegram announcing his child's death.[955]

Houghton coped with this second bereavement by immersing himself in his political work – primarily by serving on a 'notoriously dull committee' concerned with Railway Rates. Five months after his son's demise, he was profoundly dismayed to hear of the sudden death of the wife of his longstanding friend, the Liberal peer, Lord Rosebery: 'Like [Houghton], Rosebery was left a widower with a family of young children. [Houghton's] senior by eleven years, Rosebery, as a young man, had been an amused friend of [Houghton's] father.'[956]

Milnes had confidently (and accurately) predicted that Rosebery would one day rise to the position of Prime Minister.

As we shall see, Rosebery was destined to become closely related to Houghton by marriage. He was also set to play an important role in shaping the direction of industrial relations in the mining industry. During his lifetime, Rosebery was one of the nation's most renowned and popular politicians: his fame and celebrity multiplied in consequence of the great success he enjoyed as a racehorse owner, and his marriage into the famous Rothschild family added further wealth and lustre to his name. Such is his relevance to our wider narrative that it is imperative that we examine his background and nature.

Enter Lord Rosebery

Archibald Philip Primrose (Rosebery) was born on 7 May 1847 in Mayfair, London. His father, also Archibald Primrose, Lord Dalmeny, was, at the time of his son's birth, not only MP for Stirling but also the son and heir apparent to the 4th Earl of Rosebery. His mother was Lady Catherine Lucy Wilhelmina Stanhope, daughter of the 4th Earl Stanhope, and an eminent historian in her own right. When Lord Dalmeny died prematurely in 1851, his title and place as heir apparent were passed onto the four-year-old Rosebery. Three years later, the boy's mother was remarried to the 4th Duke of Cleveland (thus becoming the Duchess of Cleveland).[957]

The future Earl attended Eton and Christ Church College, Oxford, though he abandoned his studies in 1868, when, having been presented with an ultimatum that required him either to get rid of a racehorse he had purchased in contravention of college rules, or to keep the horse and abandon his education. He opted for the latter and thus embarked on a long career as a successful racehorse owner. Following his grandfather's death (also in 1868), he became 5th Earl of Rosebery, whereupon he allegedly stated that he harboured three aims in life: to own a Derby winner, to marry an heiress, and to become the British Prime Minister. He would ultimately achieve all three.[958]

Despite being blessed with famously handsome features, Rosebery was reputedly very shy and privately doubted whether he had the right aptitude for the responsibility of marriage. This all changed in 1877 when he appeared to have found someone who was likely to 'enhance rather than reduce his tranquility'.[959] Almost inevitably, Rosebery met his future wife, Hannah de Rothschild, when, as a mere 17-year-old, she was accompanying her father, Baron Mayer de Rothschild, to the Newmarket races.

> [Mayer] was the sixth of seven children born to the remarkable Nathan Meyer [sic] de Rothschild who arrived in Manchester in 1799 as a cloth merchant and, through diligence and acumen, extended the family banking house into England, created a financial empire and established the Rothschilds'

> influence at the heart of British society. Baron Meyer [sic] – the title derived from an Austrian barony conferred on his father – used his inheritance to build Mentmore, one of the most imposing houses in England, on a 700-acre estate in Buckinghamshire.[960]

The Rothschilds included the Prince of Wales (the future King Edward VII) among their circle of friends. It was rumoured that they not only advised the Prince on his financial investments, but also sometimes bailed him out of debt.

Aside from steadily accumulating a fantastic art collection, Baron Mayer de Rothschild also established Mentmore as a successful stud farm, which soon gave rise to a string of notable victories on the turf: in 1871 alone, he recorded victories in the One Thousand Guineas (which he also won on two subsequent occasions), the Derby, the Oaks and St Leger. Though serving a fifteen-year stint as MP for Hyde, he spent most of his time at his stables in Newmarket, and invested a large part of his fortune in improving his horse racing stock.

Mayer's marriage to his cousin, Juliana Cohen, produced a daughter, Hannah, in 1851, who turned out to be their only child.[961] When Mayer died in 1874, followed soon after by his wife, it was Hannah who inherited, not only Mentmore Towers and its horse racing empire, but also two million pounds in cash.[962] It was somewhat predictable that someone of Rosebery's social standing and love of the turf should have been drawn into Baron Mayer's society of friends.[963] But while it has been unkindly alleged that Hannah was by no means 'ravishing' in appearance,[964] Rosebery clearly held her in high regard:

> Deprived of maternal affection throughout his young life, he needed a warm-hearted, emotionally generous woman who would give him unconditional love rather than disapproving lectures. Furthermore, it would be a mistake to exaggerate Hannah's plainness, for contemporary pictures reveal a quality of voluptuous serenity about her.[965]

Following the death of Hannah's parents and Rosebery's commitment to consoling her, the couple's relationship flourished and they were married on 20 March 1878. Opposition to the union came from Rosebery's mother, an ardent anti-Semite. Though not so openly hostile, the Rothschild family also registered some qualms about a mixed marriage. Outrage was also expressed in sections of Jewish society that Hannah was deserting her faith.

However, it was by all accounts a very happy marriage, in which they had four children: two daughters, Sybil (1879) and Margaret or 'Peggy' (1881); and two sons, Harry and Neil (both 1882). This contented family life, in which Rosebery enjoyed the staunch encouragement and support of his wife, was fundamental to the steady development of his political career. It was shortly after the couple's marriage that Rosebery persuaded the former Liberal Prime Minister, Lord Gladstone, to come out of retirement following his 1874 election defeat and stand for the Midlothian seat that incorporated Rosebery's Dalmeny estate. Rosebery and Hannah have been credited with managing the successful campaign that saw Gladstone duly elected as MP and returned to the position of prime minister amidst a resounding Liberal victory.

Rosebery's personal and political relationships with Gladstone became notoriously lukewarm. He was disappointed not to be included in Gladstone's new cabinet, and it was with great reluctance that he accepted the consolation prize of a junior position in the Home Office. Having quickly resigned this post in disillusionment, Rosebery was offered the newly-created post of Scottish Secretary, but rejected it because it did not qualify the holder for a place in the cabinet. He eventually entered the cabinet in January 1885 as the relatively lowly First Commissioner of Works; but a real turning point arrived in 1886 when, in the process of forming his third administration, Gladstone appointed Rosebery to the enviable position of Foreign Secretary, which he carried out with great distinction:

> Although the administration only lasted five months, Rosebery won golden opinion for his skilful conduct of diplomacy. He defused a dangerous crisis in the Balkans, consolidated the British position in Egypt, and stood up to both Russia and Germany when they threatened British interests, while doing nothing which might risk war.[966]

In the next three to four years, Rosebery put his personal stamp on British politics, principally due to his assiduous lobbying for the reform of the House of Lords on the grounds that the hereditary peerage system was outdated and illegitimate. In 1888, he set out to renounce his peerage and stand for the House of Commons, only to be told that such a move was legally inadmissible. He therefore stood, one year later, in elections for the newly created London County Council, in which he not only won his seat but was immediately elected as Chair. During his eighteen-month tenure, the Council made fantastic progress in building new schools, clearing slum housing and implementing a raft of health reforms. It was at this point, however, that Rosebery's political career was derailed by the death of his wife. His life shattered, Rosebery immediately retired from politics. However, less than two years later (in August 1892), he was persuaded to resume his position as Foreign Secretary in Gladstone's fourth administration. This time, his political activity proved more controversial: he successfully lobbied for an expansion of the naval fleet, although many doubted that the country could afford it. He was also less than wholehearted in his support of Gladstone's campaign to introduce Home Rule for the Irish.

In the meantime, the second Lord Houghton had been treading political water, although, in May 1891, the public was served with a reminder of his literary prowess with the publication of *Stray Verses*, a small volume of the occasional poems he had started to accumulate in Egypt. Some of these poems touched on his travels to Italy, and others to specific pieces of literature, like Zola's *La Terre* and Tolstoy's *Anna Karenina*; most touching of all was the poem 'Seven Years', a tribute to his late wife:

> To join the ages they have gone
> Those seven years, –
> Receding as the months roll on;
> Yet very oft my fancy hears
> Your voice, – 'twas music to my ears
> Those seven years.
>
> How perchance, do they seem to you,
> Those seven years,
> Spirit-free in the wider blue?

When time in Eternity disappears,
What if all that you have learned but the more endears
Those seven years?[967]

Among the many friends and acquaintances who sent their congratulations or expressions of approval were Robert Browning and Lord Gladstone.[968]

Houghton's relationship with Gladstone was more cordial and benevolent than Rosebery's. Gladstone had been a good friend of Houghton's father, and was a regular visitor to Fryston. A degree of nepotism may, therefore, have been involved when Gladstone offered (and Houghton promptly accepted) the Viceroyalty of Ireland. Pope-Hennessy points out that, in reality, it was the Chief Secretary (a cabinet member destined to spend more time in London than anywhere else) who was the *actual* ruler of the country. Thus, 'While not exactly a sinecure, the post of Lord-Lieutenant of Ireland was largely a shop-window one.'[969] It nonetheless represented a major fillip to Houghton's public career, though, as a widower, he would need the support of a hostess to help him expedite that role. There was no one better suited than his sister Florence.

Soldier's Wife

The second Lord Houghton's sister Florence, and her soldier husband, Arthur, were both rising to positions of social and professional prominence at this time. In the fourteen years after the war in Egypt, the Coldstream Guards had not directly engaged in battle, their role having been primarily ceremonial. The 2nd Battalion, in which Henniker had now risen to second in command, was based at Chelsea Barracks. Both battalions of the Guards had been present at Jubilee celebrations in 1887, the 2nd Battalion taking part in a spectacular military tattoo at Windsor Castle on 19 June and forming a Guard of Honour at a Thanksgiving Service at St Paul's Cathedral three days later. Finally, both battalions turned out in Aldershot on 1 July when Queen Victoria reviewed her troops.[970]

Two years later, on 6 April 1889, the Duchess of Cambridge died in her 92nd year. Her husband had been a popular Colonel of the Coldstream Guards for almost 50 years:

> Accordingly, on the 14th April 1889, the day of the funeral, the coffin was borne by twelve men of the 2nd Battalion, commanded by Lieut. H.C. Sutton, from Cambridge Cottage to the church, where a Guard of Honour had been mounted under the command of Major Hon. A.H. Henniker, the remainder of the battalion under Col. J.B. Sterling being employed in lining the route and in keeping the ground in the vicinity of the church. In the course of the service, which was attended by Her Majesty Queen Victoria, the coffin was taken by its bearers to the reredos and lowered into the mausoleum.[971]

Novelist

In the meantime, Florence Henniker was in the process of gathering considerable social esteem, both as a novelist of some distinction and as a hostess of equivalent reputation. By 1893, Henniker had published five major poems, collectively entitled 'Poesies from Abroad', and three novels: *Sir George*, *Bid Me Good-bye* and *Foiled*.[972] There has been an overriding tendency within her own family and in the wider circle of literary criticism to regard these works as somehow lightweight and lacking in substance.

Her future sister-in-law contends, for example, that Florence actually 'accomplished little worth recognition beyond her association with the distinguished men in her life', and that, notwithstanding the occasional exception, 'her literary accomplishments are forgotten'.[973] It may be that Stewart's characterisation of Henniker as the writer 'of very mildly talented novels of high life'[974] is symptomatic of a wider inclination to devalue more popular forms of art, such as the romantic fiction she was principally famous for. Whatever the actual reason for these attitudes, Sylvia considers her work to have been deserving of more serious attention and respect than it received while she was alive:

> Henniker's novels present the conventional habits and rituals of upper-class society but also its dark confusions; her fictions are deeply colored by the horrors of incest, paedophilia, suicide, and despair. Although on the surface everything comes out fine, the status quo maintaining its authority over her characters' actions, Henniker's treatment of society exposes a world of moral and spiritual decay and questions the allure of property, privilege, and, finally, love itself.[975]

Sylvia's critical overview of the three novels above contributes immeasurably to our appreciation of the ways in which Florence's relations with her father and the nature of her upbringing at Fryston, not only influenced her written style, but also provided the basis of some major characterisations. Sylvia considers it important that Florence came into contact with her father's wide circle of political and literary associates, 'was thrilled by the quasi-Bohemian atmosphere at Fryston', comfortable in masculine company, and well-schooled in the art of intellectual discussion.[976] These and other more specific family reference points, such as the fact that her father, a dandy, married relatively late on in life, are reflected in the recurring motifs underpinning these works, e.g. relationships between older men and younger women, and the primacy of homosocial (and, sometimes, homoerotic) over heterosexual relationships. Nevertheless:

> Just as likely to have influenced Henniker as her family history is her understanding of the role of women in a world controlled by men. She consistently infantilizes women and wives in her novels as a sign of their dependence on men who, like Sir George and Harold, are more interested in their relationship to each other than in accepting their heterosexual duty to family and state (i.e., courtship, marriage, procreation).[977]

These themes appear most explicitly in *Sir George* and *Foiled*, two novels that exemplify a cultural commitment to 'male bonding' (or 'men loving men') and the need to constantly reassert masculine control over women and property, even when the men concerned are rivals. In the earlier of the two novels, the Sir George of the title is a retired military officer, country squire, and guardian of a nephew and heir called Harold. When Harold sets off to serve his country in India, he is forced to leave behind his sweetheart, Olive, an orphan who is far too ill with tuberculosis to travel with him. Left in the care of Harold's uncle, Olive develops mutually strong feelings for the older man:

> The major motif of this melodrama – an older man's love for a much younger woman and the suggestion of incest and paedophilia underpinning it – returns in *Bid Me Good-bye* and *Foiled*, Henniker's next two novels, as well; indeed, it is so insistent in her work, it takes on the guise of an obsession,

> which I believe originates in Henniker's family situation and cultural milieu. Her father, Monckton Milnes, was himself late to marry and – something of a dandy – sensitive about getting older; in his poem 'The Flight of Youth,' love alone can compensate for the loss of youth.[978]

Harold's eventual return soon leads to his discovery of Olive's and Sir George's feelings for one another. But rather than addressing the situation directly, they go their separate ways: 'Olive to suffer alone and die; Harold to marry a good woman for whom he does not "burn"; and Sir George to flee his estate – his birthright – and to finish his days on the continent.'[979]

Afterwards, however, Sir George is blinded in a hunting accident and further afflicted by a stroke. He decides belatedly to visit Olive's grave, where he unexpectedly meets Harold, triggering an emotional reconciliation and the perpetuation of conventional property rights.[980]

Foiled focuses on events occurring at country mansions in Yorkshire (Ledsham Towers) and Scotland (Strathrowan) belonging to the central character, Frank Hesseltine, or at the country estates of his wealthy friends: 'Henniker incorporates into the plot detailed descriptions of events closely associated with upper-class privilege: the country house visit, breakfasts, dinners, teas, dances, hunts, steeplechases, picnics, shooting lessons, as well as church socials, London balls and society weddings.'[981] She harks back nostalgically to an era predating the blighting of the countryside by the escalating Industrial Revolution:

> Indeed, the view from Hesseltine's Yorkshire property is ruined by the 'chimneys and coalmines that hemmed in one side,' and his guests have to cross a 'stagnant black river' to reach it by coach. Such a compromised view dominated at Fryston Hall, the Yorkshire estate of Henniker's father, Monckton Milnes, which suggests that Henniker uses her own experience of upper-class privilege in *Foiled* more closely than she had in her two previous novels. Ironically, Hesseltine, one of the richest of the rich commoners who put their money into country estates in the second half of the century, owns collieries (the Milnes family money came from the mines as well), so he is personally responsible for diminishing the value of the grandest sign of his acquired privilege – the countryside itself.[982]

Henniker's use of familial touchstones is apparent in her creation of Hesseltine as 'a popular host to his quirky friends' and a Liberal MP, *à la* Richard Monckton Milnes. Sylvia's contention that 'Henniker takes a careful look back at the men she knew best when creating Frank Hesseltine'[983] is underscored by the way in which she '"feminises" Hesseltine with traits and behaviors associated with women', in such a way as to evoke comparison with her father.[984] There may be some resonance, too, in her depiction of Frank Hesseltine as a possible misogynist who prefers the company of men. Indeed, Henniker 'moves the homosocial to the homosexual' by 'eroticising' the relationship between Hesseltine (who harbours an ambivalent attitude to women) and his friend Charles Marsham (who is enduring an unhappy marriage). Hesseltine, we learn, often gazes 'lovingly' at his friend, while, on one visit to Ledsham Towers, the latter deliberately shuns his wife by preferring to sleep in the same wing as their host.[985]

Sylvia concludes by confidently declaring that Henniker was far from being a 'lightweight literary lady of the 1890s with nothing better to do than to write silly books (i.e., romance novels)'. Indeed, closer analysis than is customarily accorded to her work (up until 1893 at least) undoubtedly reveals that:

> Her novels are serious attempts to picture truthfully the fashionable world she knew so well, a world both defined and limited by its highly conventional forms of behavior. Beneath the respectable demeanor of her characters, confusion, pain, and despair dominate. For some, Henniker's treatment of those, who, like Frank Hesseltine, sense the abyss and yet cling to the status quo for support, will seem too gentle, too accommodating [...] She offers no vision of a new, liberated world. Yet for its sensitive honesty, the troubling depiction of homosocial desire and romance, most especially in *Foiled*, merits careful critical attention.[986]

Hostess

Alongside her growing prowess as a novelist, Florence was also establishing a considerable reputation as a societal and literary hostess. This emergence is exemplified by her association with the great American writer and diplomat, Bret Harte.

Harte was a renowned poet and author of short stories, but it was during his tenure as United States Consul, based in Glasgow in the early 1880s, that he became a regular fixture at the first Lord Houghton's London breakfast parties. It was Milnes who not only guaranteed Harte's access to elite English literary society, but also publicly defended him when most others were cynical of his tendency to 'escape' from his responsibilities in Glasgow in preference for the literary and aristocratic adulation awaiting him in London and Paris.[987]

Long after his days as a public official had ceased, Harte continued to cut a ubiquitous figure. Milnes's death did not deter him from developing a close correspondence and, eventually, firm friendship with Milnes's daughter, which originated from their first meeting at the home of a mutual friend in Ripon in January 1890.[988] Soon afterwards, they began writing to one another and were often to be found in each other's company.[989]

By September 1890, Harte was advising Henniker on how to refine her romance, *Mary Garnett.* They exchanged views regarding the merits of Henniker's friend, the literary giant Rudyard Kipling, especially in relation to *Plain Tales from the Hills* (1888), which Harte had read on Henniker's recommendation.[990] Harte strove as ardently as possible to secure American publishers for Henniker's work. She, in turn, dedicated her novel *Foiled* to him in acknowledgement of his friendship and support.[991] It was, however, in the confines of Florence Henniker's increasingly renowned London salon that the relationship between the pair was most frequently in evidence. As one of her father's staunchest friends maintained in this regard:

> There is one house in London which, somehow, I especially associate with recollections of Bret Harte [...] I am speaking of the house which has for its gifted and charming hostess my friend Mrs Henniker, [who] is, as everyone knows, an authoress of rare gifts, a writer of delightful stories; like her brother she inherits from her father a rich poetic endowment. She is also one of the hostesses, not very common in our days, who, if she had lived in Paris at a former time, would have been famous as the presiding genius of a salon where wit and humour, literature and art, science and statesmanship found congenial welcome.[992]

It has been said that, 'With memories of her childhood and girlhood in her father's open houses in Upper Brook Street, London, and Fryston, Yorkshire [...] it was to be expected that Florence Henniker would one day have a coterie of her own literary and political friends, inheriting as she did, many of her father's tastes and characteristics.'[993] There are intriguing (but, alas, under-developed) references, for example, to an Easter party in March 1892, in which Tennyson sang at the piano and read aloud 'The Passing of Arthur' to Florence and her brother, Robert.[994]

It was this consummate skill as a hostess that Florence Henniker would soon employ in support of the political and diplomatic career of her brother. Being erect in posture, having grey-blue eyes and chestnut hair, Ms Henniker bore an alert, good-natured expression as if permanently ready to be amused. She 'was also gay and worldly, to the extent of liking pretty clothes and accepting, if not courting, admiration', and particularly 'enjoyed the company and minds of men'.[995] Such gaiety of appearance concealed an underlying emotional and moral abhorrence of suffering and brutality.

The recurring themes of tragedy, drama, and pathos that featured in her work reflected a generally pessimistic outlook, particularly towards the institution of marriage, even though her own and those of her immediate relatives were reputedly very happy.[996] These were among the qualities and values she would display in the process of renewing the acquaintanceship of Henry James and the close friendship of Bret Harte, and as she forged famously productive and controversial personal and literary alliances with perhaps the most celebrated English novelist of the era, Thomas Hardy.

Chapter Twenty-One
Stirrings: Industrial Relations (1876-1894)

The Changing Balance of Power

In this chapter, we return to our theme of the development of industrial relations in the coal industry at national and local levels. By the mid-1870s, the balance of industrial power was tilting back in favour of the employers. Jim Bullock observed that his father always said 1873-6 were very important years.[997] The WYMA had moved its headquarters from Normanton to Arundel Street, Wakefield in 1875. Following the death of John Dixon in April 1876, Ben Pickard was elevated to the position of the WYMA Secretary:

> Almost immediately he had to meet the renewed challenge of the employers who, as conditions worsened, became more ruthless and aggressive. Over the next few years the Association found no firm ground on which it could rest and recover. Maybe it was the hammering he received during this period which, as much as anything else, made Pickard the man he became.[998]

In May 1876, the Yorkshire coal owners predictably returned to the attack. Miners in South Yorkshire were locked out and their resistance to large wage cuts was eventually overcome. A Yorkshire-wide meeting of employers and the union held on 27 June agreed to a reduction of 12.5%. Though this agreement was generally accepted by the membership, some activists responded by gate-crashing a Joint Council meeting and hurling abuse at Pickard. At a handful of Yorkshire pits, the men chose to stop working, invariably to their eventual detriment. Such was the case at the Bowers collieries, where a five-week strike was defeated. Ever since the long stoppage of 1870, the Bowers mines had become 'one of the storm centres in West Yorkshire' with a constant potential for conflict.[999]

Earlier that year, Bowers had unilaterally decided to introduce safety lamps into one of their mines, with no compensatory increase in the miners' pay. The Bowers men felt entitled to such an increase because they had traditionally used candles for illumination, which they simply re-lit whenever the flame went out. With safety lamps, the miners were forced into the time-consuming requirement of tracking down a deputy each time their lamps needed re-lighting. They therefore came out on strike, based on the claim that the use of lamps would stifle their output and produce a corresponding reduction in pay. Though a joint committee was set up to investigate the claim, it failed to achieve a consensus. Despite the fact that miners at a neighbouring pit were awarded an extra penny per ton of coal when safety lamps were introduced, the Bowers owners were unyielding.

In fact, the owners' onslaught was unrelenting. In the early spring of 1878, miners at Bowers' Victoria Colliery were locked out until they consented to a wage reduction of 12.5%.[1000] Then, in May of that year, a dispute arose over the re-introduction of 'riddles' (hand held meshes for 'sizing' pieces of coal). This was a constant sore point among miners of the Victorian era:

> When trade was good, and all the coal produced could be sold, riddles were withdrawn from the pits, when while trade was bad and the consumer demanded cleaner and larger coal for his money, riddles were taken back into the pits and slack was left underground or, if sent to the surface, might be wasted or used for some other purpose than fuel.[1001]

This issue became the focal point of a strike by 800 workers at the five Bowers pits.

> The dispute, as far as the Association was concerned, ended on 6 May 1878, when a 'winding up order' was made for the collieries. The miners concerned were then unemployed and not on strike or locked-out and, according to the rules of the Association, were no longer entitled to pay from the funds [...] In May, 1879, an unsuccessful attempt was made by Messrs. Bowers to sell their collieries which were not re-opened until August of that year. A little more than twelve months later, in October 1880, it was reported that the men at these pits were

> unorganised, and that their wages were lower than elsewhere in West Yorkshire, and that Bowers were thus able to undersell other collieries.[1002]

As Jim Bullock stated in his memoirs, 'To my father's everlasting credit, he joined the union when it first started and stuck to his guns ever after. Even today I feel very proud of that.'[1003]

Growing Militancy at Fryston and Wheldale

The late 1870s and early 1880s saw a sustained counter-attack by Yorkshire coal owners in response to trade union attempts to introduce the office of checkweighman at collieries throughout the county. Such opposition was hardly surprising: in addition to being trade union sponsored, the checkweighman was also invariably Secretary of the local miners' lodge. It was thus firmly in his interests to use his sharpened negotiating skills both to protect his members' interests and maintain local solidarity. In so doing, 'He must not only see that coal which came from the pit was properly weighed, and that corves which contained only a moderate amount of dirt were not confiscated, he must also protest if the employer violated an agreement [and] try to secure prompt and just remedies for the grievances of the men.'[1004] Employers typically resented this undermining of their authority as well as the fact that it obliged them to increase their wage bill.[1005]

Fryston Colliery was directly affected by this issue. The first evidence of its increasing local salience emerged early in 1879, when the workforce was dismissed and then re-engaged on condition that they dispense with the services of their checkweighman.[1006] This issue resurfaced in spectacular style some six years later. While the checkweighman position had been reinstated in the interim, the coal owners unilaterally decided to derecognise it, which provoked a lengthy strike.

Twenty-three weeks into the dispute, the *Leeds Mercury* scotched an unfounded rumour that a settlement had been arrived at. The *Mercury* reported that, whilst around 25 men (mostly 'new hands') were working in the pit, 200 colliers remained out on strike, with a number of these having been evicted from their cottages. A roughly equal number of men had chosen to leave the district in search of work elsewhere. Those on strike were receiving strike pay of up to

9 shillings and 6 pence per head for their children, but were chiefly relying on public support to sustain them.[1007]

Three weeks later, the *Mercury* reported on the trial at Sherburn Petty Sessions of two striking Fryston miners (one of them being the checkweighman at the centre of the dispute) who had been charged with 'besetting' the house of one of their non-striking counterparts:

> The case for the prosecution was that the complainant was in the employ of the Fryston Colliery Company, and in consequence of the strike at their collieries had been into Staffordshire to employ hands to work the colliery. On the morning in question, at about four o'clock, the defendants went to Jones's house, and, knocking him up, asked where the Staffordshire men were, and made use of threats towards him, stating that they would not allow him or them to go to work. There were about 200 persons outside on the road at the time, and the three defendants were amongst those who went to the door of Jones's house and made use of the threats. The defence was a denial that any threats were used, and it was urged by Mr Hall [acting on behalf of defendants] that all the men who were out on strike went to Jones's house [to] have a conversation with the Staffordshire men, and [dissuade] them from commencing work.[1008]

The defendants received fines of £1 each and were required to pay costs, but the strike action was far from losing steam. The climactic episode of the dispute occurred on 17 January 1886, by which time the importation of dozens of 'blacksheep' from Staffordshire and Denaby Main colliery had guaranteed that, 'A great deal of ill-feeling existed between the new and the old hands and many summonses for assault had been issued.'[1009] With the strike now forty-three weeks old, a 'serious affray' was said to have occurred in the nearby village of Brotherton.[1010] Most of the estimated sixty or so blacksheep now working at the colliery were housed in a makeshift shed (or 'barracks'), located on the colliery premises; but it was the handful of strikebreakers residing over the river in Newton who were most vulnerable to the resentment of those on strike.

It was in Newton that a forty- to fifty-strong delegation of former Staffordshire miners collectively decided that they had had enough of being on the receiving end of threats and intimidation, and therefore marched, 'cudgels, pokers and rifles' in hand, into Brotherton (within three miles of Fryston), which represented the stronghold of the strike.

> On entering [Brotherton] the police endeavoured to prevent the 'black sheep' from creating a disturbance, but were helpless. A desperate struggle took place between the strike hands and the 'black sheep'. The sergeant of police was shot at, and had a hole knocked through his helmet; a police-constable was shot through the arm; three men on strike were shot; John Grace, knuckle blown away on holding his hand up to protect his face; and another man named Grace had a shot wound inflicted on his body. Several others were seriously injured. Of the injuries to the 'black sheep' only one serious case is reported – that of John Jones of Newton, who was so badly hurt that he is confined to his bed. Most of the 'black sheep' have absconded, and the greatest excitement prevails.[1011]

A settlement of the strike was finally achieved in February 1886. Following a meeting between a delegation of union officials led by Ben Pickard, and Messrs Blockby and Oldroyd for the coal owners, a set of terms for ending the dispute (including the reinstatement of the checkweighman) was arrived at. The basis of this agreement was put before a meeting of the senior union members in Barnsley on 15 February, where delegates were also informed how:

> These [conditions] were afterwards laid before the men, and accepted by them with the result that work was resumed yesterday by a section of the miners, and others will follow as soon as the places can be prepared for them. Satisfaction was expressed at the settlement, and a vote of thanks was moved to Mr Pickard and the deputation for the manner in which they had settled the dispute, which has been in existence since last year.[1012]

Cometh the Iron Man

Meanwhile, mining trade unions had been forced to box clever *region wide* in response to the employers' onslaught, choosing carefully when to strike in order to show that they were not prepared to take things lying down, but also realising when such action might prove self-defeating. In March 1879, for example, Fryston and Wheldale miners were instructed by the Association to withdraw their threatened strike action in support of a pay increase for the additional task of riddling coal.[1013] One obvious solution was to join forces. Thus, on 25 April 1881, an amalgamation of the South and West Yorkshire Associations was agreed at a meeting of their two Executives. A new headquarters was opened in Barnsley, with Pickard elected as Secretary and Edward Cowey (erstwhile President of the WYMA) as President of the newly-formed Yorkshire Miners' Association (YMA).[1014]

In the seven lean years that followed, the YMA continued to operate cautiously, occasionally enduring setbacks – as in 1885 when a nine-week strike in opposition to a 10% wage cut was resoundingly defeated. The union's fortunes changed in the autumn of 1888, which saw an increase in the selling price of coal:

> All over the Central Coal-fields the colliers began to stir for an increase. The Yorkshiremen had gone forward on their own in March and had met with a refusal. Thus rebuffed, they began to think of banding themselves together with the men of other counties. At the same time (summer 1888), Lancashire had decided to move for a National Conference on the wages question. The actual initiative was taken by Yorkshire in a circular sent out by Ben Pickard on September 10, 1888, in which he invited 'all miners now free from sliding scales' to attend a conference for the purpose of considering the best means of securing a 10% advance in wages and of trying to find common ground for action.[1015]

By the time the relevant meetings were convened in Manchester and Derby (in September and October 1888, respectively), the 10% increase had been achieved everywhere with the exception of Derbyshire and Yorkshire. Although the pay rise had also been conceded in some pockets of these two counties, the decision by most coal owners to stand their ground resulted in 30,000 Yorkshire and 6,000 Derbyshire miners coming out on strike. The owners eventually yielded to this moral and economic pressure, and Pickard's stock rose immeasurably in consequence: 'The battle had indeed been successful. It had brought not merely a 10% advance in wages, but a sense of common interest which was soon to take shape as a permanent Federation.'[1016] On 26 November 1889, scores of union delegates met in Newport, South Wales to agree to form a Miners' Federation of Great Britain (MFGB). Three days later, on Friday, 29 November, they reconvened to elect officers and committee members. It was the 'Iron Man', Ben Pickard, who, according to Page Arnot, 'was the dominating personality of the Conference'.[1017]

The 1893 Lockout

The founding fathers of the MFGB could count themselves fortunate that their membership was initially drawn from those mining areas sharing a common commitment to winning coal for the home market. This 'natural' basis of unity gave thousands of mineworkers a 'new powerful voice' and enabled Pickard to launch a campaign in (1890) for a statutory eight-hour working day, and to have the confidence to resist any proposed wage reductions that might have compromised the hallowed principle of a consistent 'living wage'. This latter issue was central to the monumental lockout of 1893:

> By 1893 the price of coal was thirty-five per cent lower than it had been in 1890, and it was clear that the colliery owners would seek to restore their profits by demanding a substantial reduction in wage rates. From the outset the MFGB and the YMA were determined to maintain the 40% advance on the 1888 wage rates which the Federation had secured between 1889 and 1890 [...] The employers were equally determined to enforce a reduction and on 30 June 1893 they formally demanded a 25% cut in the 1888 wage rates. This demand was vociferously opposed by both the Yorkshire miners and the MFGB, and at the end of July the majority of the 80,000 colliers employed in the West Riding's 253 pits were locked out, together with their fellow workers throughout the Federated area.[1018]

From an initially peaceful outset, the dispute became progressively marked by violence, typically associated with those mines where strikebreakers were known or suspected to be entering, or where stockpiles of coal were being shipped out by the owners. By the beginning of September, the violence (especially in the strike's epicentre of the West Riding of Yorkshire) was perceived to have grown so far out of hand that hundreds of troops and police reinforcements (including 400 officers from the Metropolitan Police Constabulary) were brought into the county. The troops' arrival was like a red rag to a bull.

This was no more so than in the small town of Featherstone, near Pontefract, where there were repeated confrontations involving strikers seeking to prevent the loading of 'smudge' waggons and troops brought in by train from outside of the mining areas. One such detachment of army personnel found themselves heavily besieged and under bombardment in a colliery engine-house. Clearly intent on saving their skins, the commanding officer offered to withdraw his soldiers on condition that the men refrain from any further destruction. Once the troops had evacuated the engine-house, however, the strikers began using wooden pit props and other combustible materials with which to set fire to buildings. The soldiers quickly returned; and when the strikers refused to disperse they were read the Riot Act:

> The soldiers attempted to disperse the crowd by advancing with fixed bayonets and when this did not work by firing a warning volley into the ground. Ultimately the soldiers, who had been stoned by the crowd for some time, were given the order to fire directly and at point blank range into the mass confronting them [...] [T]his action resulted in two [men] being killed outright and some fourteen others being injured.[1019]

Neville reports that, as word of the troops' arrival spread outside of Featherstone, huge beacons were sympathetically ignited which lit up the skies in the nearby villages and towns of Sharlston, Normanton, Loscoe, Castleford and Pontefract, drawing people to their local collieries.[1020] Strikers at Featherstone's Ackton Hall set fire to a number of colliery waggons and set about felling a tall chimney stack. It soon became clear that these miners and their supporters were by no means isolated in their opposition. There were rumours of similar attacks having been made at the Glasshoughton and Fryston collieries, with the result that, 'Detachments of soldiers and police are at both these places, and similar defence is provided at Sharlston Colliery, where some riotous proceedings are reported.'[1021]

Adding to the repressive control to which they were subjected was the 'human misery' experienced by mining communities, which became even more acute after 30 September 1893 when the YMA relief fund reached the point of exhaustion, leaving thousands of those affected in conditions of 'appalling hunger and poverty'.[1022] As the biographer of one eminent YMA and MFGB leader stated:

> Herbert Smith now had three young children. In common with the rest who were on strike, he got no help – the money from the Federation Fund and other sources being negligible. The Poor Law for such purposes, did not exist. The sick got nothing. How anybody lived under the conditions would be a mystery to any but those who have learned to live on little.[1023]

It was against this background that the intervention, in mid-November, of the Liberal Foreign Secretary, Lord Rosebery, as 'independent arbitrator' in the strike, was heralded with such universal enthusiasm within the mining communities.[1024]

Lord Rosebery's Mediation

At this political juncture, Lord Rosebery and Gladstone were almost permanently at loggerheads. The Foreign Secretary regarded the Premier as 'condescending and interfering', while Gladstone viewed Rosebery as 'aloof in manner and aggressive in policy' and lacking in sound judgement.[1025] The Prime Minister went so far as to confide to one colleague that he had been disappointed right from the outset in Rosebery's performance as Foreign Secretary.[1026] In November 1893, however, an unexpected opportunity arose for Rosebery to 'recover his Midas touch' and redeem himself in Gladstone's eyes while confirming 'his reputation as a constructive Radical'.[1027]

What McKinstry refers to as 'Traditional Gladstonian Liberalism' seemed ill-equipped to find a solution to the strike wave of 1893, of which the miners' stoppage was the most troubling and perplexing instance. As the strike became increasingly protracted, and mining families began to endure hardship and starvation, Liberal backbenchers publicly vented their concern and grew more visibly partisan. On 1 November, for example, the National Liberal Club expressed wholehearted support for the miners.[1028] Following prior discussion with Asquith and the Education Minister, Arthur Acland, Gladstone settled on an unprecedented interventionist approach, according to which Rosebery would act as an independent moderator (a Chairman only, with no casting vote) between the two conflicting factions.

Rosebery initially confided in Queen Victoria that he was ignorant of the main issues framing the dispute;[1029] but in reality, he was 'admirably suited by his prestige as Foreign Secretary to be an impartial chairman – and still more by his own fervent belief in the mission of the nobility to compose differences between the lower order of manufacturers and workpeople'.[1030] The strategy adopted came all too easily to Rosebery. In short, 'He charmed both sides and lunched them well.'[1031] The two sides duly assembled at the Foreign Office on 17 November, with Rosebery supported in the role of Chair by Llewellyn Smith, a Labour Department official, who acted as his secretary.

> For several hours the negotiations appeared to be going nowhere, until Rosebery put forward the idea of creating a Board of Conciliation, with 14 representatives on each side, to meet in a month's time. The employers then disappeared for two hours to discuss the proposal over a cold luncheon that Rosebery had provided in another room at the Foreign Office; the miners were much more businesslike, spending only twenty minutes over their meal. By late afternoon both sides were ready to accept Rosebery's proposition, and at 5.20 agreement was formally reached. After sixteen weeks the strike was over. Rosebery's tact and shrewdness had enabled him to pull off a magnificent coup.[1032]

An ensuing feeling of euphoria immediately gripped the nation. Rosebery chose to dine alone that night, stating with obvious satisfaction in his diary that, 'It would have been a good day to die on.'[1033]

In the Wake of the Lockout

The 1893 lockout had been the first 'severe test' that the MFGB had faced. Pickard had been its staunch and redoubtable leader, 'and its successful conclusion further strengthened his already powerful hold over the affairs of the Federation'.[1034] His almost impregnable position of authority within the MFGB was soon to be reflected and reinforced in the Attercliffe (Sheffield) by-election of 1894.

As Church and Outram put it, Pickard was the ideal type of 'the Liberal mining trade unionist', his views very much conforming with the party's political and economic policies. His commitment to using the party political system as a vehicle of industrial reform was reflected in his election as MP for Normanton in 1885.[1035] His vehement opposition to socialism per se (with its allegedly abstract and over-idealistic trappings) was reflected in his outright opposition to the Independent Labour Party (ILP) candidate in the electoral campaign at Attercliffe near Sheffield.

The by-election was called due to the fact that the incumbent Liberal MP Bernard Coleridge had been elevated to the peerage. Local labour institutions, notably the Sheffield Federated Trades Council, lobbied hard for Charles Hobson, a local trade union leader and local councillor, to be put forward as Liberal candidate in what was fundamentally a working-class constituency. The nomination, instead, of the middle-class J. Batty Langley, a local timber merchant and former mayor, produced local outrage and alienation, which quickly manifested in the introduction of an ILP 'protest candidate' (Frank Smith) in opposition to the Liberals.[1036]

While many prominent Labour figures went into Attercliffe to voice their support for Smith and opposition to Langley, Ben Pickard went against the grain by publicly denouncing the ILP and urging local miners and trade unionists to vote for Langley. Pickard's endorsement was undoubtedly a major factor in Langley's eventual success, but it will be argued in Chapter 26 that his personal involvement in this, and in a second high-profile by-election three years afterwards, may have served to undermine his longer term credibility and authority as YMA and MFGB leader and figurehead.

A contrasting case can be made regarding the reputation of Herbert Smith, which was significantly enhanced by the lockout. The 1893 dispute has been listed as one of the 'important' influences on his outlook and style.[1037] In the lead-up to the lockout, his progress within the YMA had been steady. As an existing member of two years' standing of the Glasshoughton branch committee, he was elected (in 1891) onto the Glasshoughton School Board, ostensibly to help establish the content of local religious teaching but with the broader remit of furthering the educational prospects of mining families. One year later, he was elected as his pit's delegate to the YMA. As two commentators noted of Smith's progress to this point:

> He grew to manhood noted for his self-reliance and fearlessness, the epitome of Yorkshire bluntness and toughness. He was a good workman and a good trade unionist but until he was nearly thirty there was little sign of the future miners' leader. His experiences in coal-mining shaped and moulded the man who was to become one of the best-loved leaders in the history of the British miners.[1038]

It is hardly coincidental that, within one year of the lockout, he was elected as checkweighman for the Haigh Moor seam at Glasshoughton, as a local parish councillor, and as Pontefract district councillor. Within another two years, he was elected president of Castleford Trades Council.[1039]

At this particular juncture, 'Rosebery was by far the most popular politician in the country, a man who apparently could do no wrong.'[1040] His robust but essentially disarming intervention represented a ground-breaking approach to governmental involvement in industrial relations, which was consolidated two years later when a new Conciliation Act allowed the Board of Trade a more participatory role in industrial disputes.[1041] His popularity was paramount in the coalfields.

In his presidential address at the 1894 MFGB conference, Ben Pickard heaped considerable praise on Rosebery. 'Whatever we may have thought before entering that room,' Pickard told the delegates, 'we were not long in it before we found that we had a gentleman to deal with who would strike the balance fairly.' The suggestions for a resolution put forward by Rosebery gained the immediate approval of the 28 representatives present. Far from seeing anything to complain about, Pickard ventured that 'every praise and credit is due to his Lordship for conducting the business in such a way as to bring about such a peaceable settlement of one of the most awful and protracted lockouts during this century'.[1042]

Chapter Twenty-Two
Viceroy of Ireland

The Viceregal Role and its Symbolism

The role of Viceroy of Ireland which the second Lord Houghton took on in 1893 was ostensibly that of representing the queen, as a quasi-royal personage, during her physical absence from the country. In reality, however, the viceregal court served the controversial function of setting 'a standard and pattern of social, cultural and manners' for an essentially British world-view.[1043] This archaic institution formed part of an overarching representation of a 'loyal Ireland', which was symbolically underlined by the naming of Dublin streets, hospitals and bridges, and by the nature of its monuments (e.g. those of such British icons as Lord Nelson and Lord Wellington).[1044]

Of key symbolic significance within this synecdochical array was Dublin Castle, home of the throne room and 'offices dealing with instances of rebellion, agrarian crime and popular agitation'.[1045] The physical positioning of this massively ostentatious building in one of the city's most downtrodden areas courted inevitable controversy: 'The exercise of viceregal pretensions amid some of the worst slum areas of any city in the empire spoke metaphorical volumes about the relationship between the viceregal system and the mass of the ruled.'[1046]

Notwithstanding the viceroy's direct link to the queen, 'It was plain that the source of [his] authority resided, not in royal origins, but in the elected government that had appointed him and whose departure from office terminated his own.'[1047]

The major implication of this was that the viceregal court – and all the rituals it entailed – became a significant 'arena of conflict'. This was starkly illustrated with the return of the Gladstone government, which – according to the opinion polls of the day – appeared to have been given a mandate for the introduction of Home Rule. The Irish Unionist elite immediately embarked on a campaign of determined resistance to this possibility:

> They resolved not to touch Gladstone or his noble representative with a fortyfoot [sic] pole, and, numbering in their ranks the majority of the gentry and nobility, their decision to boycott the incoming viceroy meant much more than it appeared on the surface.[1048]

Appraising Houghton's Period in Office

As Loughlin points out, the second Lord Houghton's predecessor as viceroy, Lord Aberdeen, had striven to reassure and align himself with the Irish non-nationalist community. 'This meant that it was now necessary to redress the balance and establish a position of equidistance between the country's political groups.'[1049] In contrast to the deliberately engaging and self-consciously influential style associated with Aberdeen, Houghton adopted a more objective, formally direct and neutrally forthright approach, reflecting the strict requirements of his official role.[1050]

There is no doubt that Houghton's sympathies were fundamentally in favour of Home Rule (and therefore at odds with those of his monarch); but as Loughlin points out, 'with the Aberdeen viceroyalty as the standard nationalists had come to accept from a Liberal government a sense of alienation found expression'.[1051] In its extreme form, this alienation was manifested in bomb explosions, notably on Christmas Eve 1892, when a police constable was 'blown to pieces' close to the castle wall, and in May 1893, when the windows of Dublin Law Courts were shattered – thankfully, with no resulting loss of life.[1052]

In the words of O'Mahony, 'The position [of viceroy], certainly, was most difficult, and abler men than Lord Houghton would have failed.'[1053] It was widely felt that large part of the problem was bound up in Houghton's own underlying attitudes and personality. In short:

> He could not forget his own dignity, and therefore never attempted to conciliate the Opposition. The distrust of the Nationalists must have struck him as savouring of ingratitude,

> and as every Liberal viceroy has found it, Lord Houghton was an object of suspicion and distrust to all Irishmen.[1054]

The main upshot of this was that all sections of Irish society ostentatiously boycotted the viceroy and his office. Invitations to attend Dublin Castle and the Viceregal Lodge were summarily declined or, worse still, totally ignored. Party political issues were undoubtedly at issue, but the situation was not helped by Houghton's characteristic aloofness of character:

> In some ways this stiffness, very evident in all the official photographs taken of him in Dublin at this time, was what was wanted. No amount of carefree charm would be likely to placate or mollify the natives of this occupied territory, and a fine show-piece like Lord Houghton, who was tall and handsome, could ride a horse to perfection, sit erect in a state carriage, 'kiss a regiment of women' on presentation nights, and make a good bow, was a suitable and decorative symbol of English rule.[1055]

The fact that the responsibility for entertaining the viceroy's guests rested largely on the shoulders of Houghton's sister Florence reinforced the overall impression that his office was 'a sham' and that the entire political system was 'destitute of honour and honesty'.[1056] In consequence:

> Wherever the viceroy went he was received in silence; there were no popular demonstrations in town or country. Ireland was in the position of the beggar who awaits charity with curses ready on her tongue in the case of refusal or dissatisfaction.[1057]

The occasional respite Houghton enjoyed, principally by attending the many race meetings occurring within close proximity of Dublin (e.g. Baldoyle, Leopardstown and, especially, the Curragh), scarcely compensated for the difficulties he habitually encountered. Also included here was the onerous responsibility of writing confidential letters to Queen Victoria in such a way as to circumvent the fact that even the most ardent loyalists were highly critical of the monarchy's continuing neglect of Ireland.[1058] In their vain attempt to pretend that a happy consensus pervaded all Ireland, and to protect the viceregal institution from utter collapse, Houghton and his sister were reduced to inviting (and, sometimes, cajoling) high-profile 'imported' guests to visit Dublin Castle.

Entertaining the Literary Giants

The visits paid to Dublin Castle by two of the greatest literary figures of the nineteenth century, Thomas Hardy (in 1893) and Henry James (in 1895), certainly fit this mould. Details of each visit are fortunately well-documented. Each of these authors had been a personal friend of Houghton's father. Their visits therefore represented a rekindling of each writer's relationship with the Fryston dynasty. Details of the visit by Henry James provide an extremely close insight into the way that Houghton fared in the role of viceroy. We begin, however, by focusing on the earlier of the two visits, in which Thomas Hardy established a highly significant personal and literary relationship with Florence Henniker.

Thomas Hardy, 1893

Thomas Hardy had been a good friend of Milnes since 1880, at which point he had declined a visit to Fryston due to the sudden onset of serious illness. The two men had often met in the intervening years (sometimes in the company of Hardy's wife, Emma), usually at Milnes's London residence. Following Milnes's death in 1885, and the subsequent passing of Robert's wife, Sibyl, in 1887, it was not until the summer of 1892 that Mr and Mrs Hardy received their second invitation to Fryston. Houghton had intimated in his invitation that his sister Florence would also be staying at Fryston Hall.

> It is clear from this and a subsequent letter that Mrs Henniker, who had by this time completed two novels and was naturally not without literary ambition, was especially eager to meet the author who, after the publication of *Tess of the d'Urbervilles*, was rapidly becoming the most famous writer of his time. After the death of Hardy's father in July, the invitation was renewed for August. Once again the anticipated meeting had to be deferred, when Lord Houghton accepted the Viceroyalty of Ireland from Gladstone. In January 1893 he sent a copy of his

> *Stray Verses* to Hardy, who, thanking him in reply, expressed the hope that Mrs Henniker's second novel (*Bid Me Good-bye*) had sold out. The following April the Hardys were invited to stay at Vice-regal Lodge, Dublin, during Whitsuntide, when Phoenix Park would be in 'full beauty'.[1059]

Earlier that spring, Thomas and Emma had chosen to rent a house in London's Maida Vale. It was indicative of their growing celebrity and wealth following the publication of *Tess of the d'Urbervilles* (1891) that they were able to move all their servants up from their family home at Max Gate.[1060] On 18 May, they set out for Ireland, via an overnight stay in Llandudno. Once in Dublin, they were greeted at the Viceregal Lodge by Florence Henniker. This appears to have been the first ever meeting between the novelist and the younger of Milnes's two daughters.

This was, as Pinion explains, 'an important occasion' for the viceroy, inasmuch as John Morley, the Chief Secretary for Ireland, was among the principal guests.[1061] In the lulls of an otherwise busy schedule, Hardy and his wife found time to visit principal Dublin landmarks, including the site of the Phoenix Park murders. The final day of their visit was spent with other guests on a tour of Guinness's brewery. Time and time again, it was Mrs Henniker who, whether by playing the zither at dinner, or being splashed with ale or dirty water while on the brewery's miniature train, repeatedly captured Hardy's attention. As if somehow preordained, on the ferry back to Holyhead, Hardy 'found on board' Mrs Henniker, who happened to be making her way back to Southsea, close to Portsmouth, where her husband was stationed.[1062]

Pinion further emphasises that the circumstances were undoubtedly ripe for Henniker to make a lasting impression on the older man.[1063] Hardy's marriage to Emma was clearly unfulfilling:

> He had for some time been looking for someone to fall in love with and, in effect, 'chose' Mrs Henniker with little if any encouragement on her part and little initial realization of what was going on.[1064]

It is commonly accepted that Hardy was immediately attracted to Henniker (a 'charming, intuitive woman apparently', was how he described her on the basis of that first meeting).[1065] Though fantastically well-connected, and capable of drawing Hardy into the upper echelons of Victorian society, she was not *too* wealthy to be entirely out of Hardy's reach.[1066] Physically, it was no contest: 'Though not exactly a beauty, [Henniker] was handsome, assured, and elegantly dressed – in sharp contrast to Emma, who is said to have appeared in Dublin in an outfit of muslin and blue ribbon ludicrously inappropriate to her fifty-two years.'[1067]

Henry James, 1895

The acclaimed American novelist, Henry James, had twice previously visited Ireland: the first time when, en route to America in 1882, he stopped off at Cork and travelled across country; and then again in 1891 when, during a two-month stay, he managed to write two short stories, 'The Private Life' and 'The Chaperon', while recovering from a bout of influenza.[1068] His third and final visit occurred in March 1895, when his professional life was in the doldrums: two months earlier, he had been booed off the stage following a performance of his heavily criticised *Guy Domville*, which was unceremoniously replaced by Oscar Wilde's *The Importance of Being Earnest.* It did not help James's mood that he 'disliked Wilde's work, despising its cheapness and facility [and] was jealous of the Irishman's success in London and despondent at his own failure'.[1069]

It was against this sorry background that Houghton invited James to Dublin Castle as part of his bid to face down the Unionist boycott. It was evident from the outset that 'Henry did not take well to being imported'.[1070] After a brief and enjoyable stay with Houghton's private secretary, Herbert Jekyll, in his lodge in Phoenix Park, he progressed to Dublin Castle. His account of subsequent events shows how James was unrelentingly scornful of the viceroy and the institution he represented.

As James made out in a letter (dated 28 March 1895) to his brother and sister-in-law, his six-day stay in Dublin constituted a 'gorgeous bore', and the viceregal society 'a weariness alike to flesh and spirit':

> Young Lord Houghton, the Viceroy 'does it' as they say here, very handsomely and sumptuously (having inherited

> just in time his uncle, Lord Crewe's, great property); but he takes himself much too seriously as a representative of royalty, and his complete Home Rule – or rather hate-Home Rule boycotting by the whole landlord and 'nobility and gentry' class (including all Trinity College, Dublin) leaves his materials for a 'court', and for entertaining generally, in a beggarly condition. He had four balls in the six days I was there and a gorgeous banquet every night – but the bare official and military class peopled them, with the aid of a very dull and second-rate, though large, house-party from England. His English friends fail him – won't come because they know to what he is reduced; and altogether he is quite a pathetic and desolate and impossible young man [...] but he doesn't matter; and the sense of the lavish extravagance of the castle, with the beggary and squalor of Ireland at the very gates, was a most depressing, haunting discomfort.[1071]

Such uninhibited derision also pervaded a letter sent to his friend, Theodora Sedgwick two days later, in which James described his six days in Dublin as a 'Purgatorio'. He was not 'made', he protested, for 'viceregal "courts", especially in countries distraught with social hatreds'. His host, he acknowledged, 'is very good looking, rich, gentle, well-meaning, widowed (with three girls), and grabbed at, but he is too conscious a representative of royalty to be even a tolerable host; and his "court" is moreover so deserted (he is *absolutely*, by the fine folks, boycotted) that it was grandeur terribly in the void'.[1072] This 'deadly correctness' on Houghton's part was attributed by James as an attempt by the viceroy to 'make up' for 'the amiable *désinvolture* of his father – which [...] he hated and was humiliated by'.[1073]

It was with some considerable relief, therefore, that James, having awkwardly bade farewell to Houghton, eagerly crossed the city to take up an earlier invitation to stay with his friends, Lord and Lady Wolseley, (the former being Commander of the Forces in Ireland) at their Royal Hospital residence.[1074]

Beating a Retreat

As stated in the introduction to this chapter, the period of tenure allowed to any given viceroy of Ireland depended on the electoral fortunes of the government that had sponsored him. In Houghton's case, his fortunes were linked to the rise and fall of his future father-in-law, Lord Rosebery.

Rosebery's political ascendancy was meteoric but short-lived. Even as he was brokering the settlement of the 1893 lockout referred to in Chapter 21, monumental events were occurring elsewhere in the parliamentary process – uppermost amongst which was the resignation as prime minister of Gladstone, whose attempt to push through the Home Rule Bill was rejected by the House of Lords. The strong favourite to replace Gladstone was the then Chancellor of the Exchequer and deputy Prime Minister, Sir William Harcourt, who was nonetheless considered too overbearing by his fellow Liberals, many of whom would have preferred not to serve under him. Though relatively inexperienced, Rosebery was undoubtedly more popular with his colleagues and the general public alike; he had made a good job of being Foreign Secretary; and perhaps most crucially, he was the candidate favoured by Queen Victoria.[1075]

It was in such ostensibly favourable circumstances that Rosebery achieved the second of his three great aims in life by becoming British Prime Minister. It did not take long, however, for even Rosebery himself to realise that the 'Midas touch' had just as swiftly deserted him. It was none other than Sir William Harcourt, the man whose political ambitions he had thwarted, who set Rosebery on an inexorable route to failure: first by introducing (as Chancellor of the Exchequer) an unpopular system of graduated death duties to pay for the planned naval expansion; and then by leading cabinet objection to an exchange of territory with the Belgian Congo which would have provided Britain with free trade passage to key African destinations. The achievement of Rosebery's third great aim occurred in June 1894, with the victory of Ladas II in the Derby. But by this time his premiership was continuing to unravel. That same month, the government's loss of a vote on the relatively innocuous issue of army supply became the pretext for an increasingly disenchanted Rosebery and his ministers to tender their resignations to the queen.[1076]

It is possible that Rosebery's morale and appetite for the premiership were being sapped by an ongoing scandal that was coincidentally starting to emerge. Central to this controversy was a campaign of harassment mounted against Rosebery by John Douglas, 9th Marquess of Queensberry:

> On becoming Foreign Secretary in 1892 he had appointed Queensbury's heir [Francis Douglas, Viscount Drumlanrig], a handsome charmer, his private secretary; and only a few months later he arranged for Drumlanrig, who was twenty-six and yet to demonstrate any outstanding talents, to be made a junior member of the government, with a seat in the House of Lords. This enraged Queensberry, who was not entitled himself to sit in the upper chamber. He suspected Rosebery of having sexual relations with his son, and expressed these suspicions in intemperate letters to various personages including the Queen. In August 1893 Queensberry followed Rosebery to Bad Homburg, where he was taking a cure, with the declared intention of giving him a horse-whipping, and had to be dissuaded by the Prince of Wales who was also staying there. This behaviour could be dismissed as the ravings of a madman; but in October 1894, the eighth month of Rosebery's premiership, Drumlanrig, who was staying with a family to whose daughter he had recently become engaged, detached himself from a shooting party and proceeded to kill himself by firing his gun through the roof of his mouth.[1077]

A subsequent inquest verdict of accidental death was insufficient to scotch the rumours that Drumlanrig had resorted firstly to the pursuit of a sham marriage, and thence to desperate suicide in a bid to protect his famous lover.[1078] The debate continues to this day as to whether Rosebery was, in fact, a closet homosexual.[1079]

The general election of 1895 was an utter debacle for the Liberals, whose internal disarray was exemplified by the fact that, while Rosebery regarded the reformation of the House of Lords as the main issue to put before the country, many prominent colleagues either undermined his position, or placed more attention on other more distracting and potentially destructive matters like Home Rule. The outcome was a 'fat majority' for the Unionists. Rosebery hung around for another year as Liberal leader before quitting politics for good.[1080]

'Heroically enough', as O'Mahony put it, 'the viceroy [had] agreed to continue in office when Lord Rosebery was unexpectedly given the premiership'.[1081] A year or two earlier, Rosebery had visited Houghton in Dublin as Foreign Secretary in Gladstone's cabinet. On rising to the rank of Prime Minister, Rosebery insisted that Houghton send him regular updates on relevant Irish affairs: 'I make the suggestion that when you feel disposed, or even when you don't, you should fire off a letter to me for my benefit: not as Lord-Lieutenant to First Lord, but as Irish mouse to town mouse.'[1082]

There is no doubt that the Liberal defeat helped put Houghton out of his misery. The second Lord Houghton is said to have found the business of saying goodbye to his staff and the place in general a 'depressing affair';[1083] but there can be no disputing that he 'left Dublin as glad to be out of the country as the country was as pleased to see the last of him'.[1084]

Houghton's life had its consolations. As Henry James mentioned in his letter of 28 March 1895, his host had recently (i.e. in January 1894) inherited Crewe Hall and the massive estates formerly belonging to his now deceased uncle. One of Rosebery's final acts as Prime Minister was to ask Queen Victoria to confer an earldom on Houghton, who thus became known as the Earl of Crewe (and is therefore referred to hereafter as 'Crewe'). Following a brief period of reflection, and with a sense of liberation resulting from his loss of office, the new earl presented his views on the future of Ireland in the form of an article called 'The Outlook for Ireland', which appeared in the September 1895 edition of *The North American Review.* The article reiterated what Pope-Hennessy refers to as Crewe's 'staunch and unshakable belief in the logic and the inevitability' of Home Rule for the Irish.[1085] There was always a tendency, he ventured, for the Conservatives to return to the exasperating methods of coercion, and to the 'weary see-saw of repression and reprisals'; but he also acknowledged that he and other Liberals 'frankly admit that Ireland cannot be permanently ruled by Englishmen of any party according to Irish ideas'. The chief virtue of *his* party was that it could at least be relied upon to conduct the governance of Ireland 'in a more sympathetic and less alien spirit' than its rivals.[1086]

Chapter Twenty-Three
'A Rare, Fair Woman': Florence Henniker and Thomas Hardy

Hardy's Unrequited Passion

Pinion discloses how a passage deliberately excluded from Florence Hardy's *The Life of Thomas Hardy, 1840-1928*[1087] conceded that 'the chief significance of his visit to Dublin was his meeting Mrs Henniker, who became "one of his closest and most valued friends, remaining so until her death many years after"'.[1088] This was only a fraction of their story. Aside from being the only person Hardy ever collaborated with on a short story, there is copious and plausible evidence to support the assumption that Henniker became the muse for various examples of the writer's poetry and prose. This chapter is devoted to explaining Henniker's crucial relevance to Hardy's personal and professional lives, starting from the possibility that they were engaged in a full-blown romantic liaison.

There is no doubt that Hardy was instantaneously bowled over on first meeting Florence Henniker at the Viceregal Lodge. Throughout the following summer there was no let-up in his affection; the behaviour he exhibited towards her on returning to England became 'almost manic' in nature.[1089] There is every indication that, while 'Outwardly, it was a harmless, slightly quaint and middle-aged excursion. Inwardly, it was traumatic.'[1090]

Having returned from Dublin to London, Hardy and his wife, Emma, entered a busy round of social engagements, including a visit to the theatre to watch Ibsen's *The Master Builder.* They were joined at the theatre by Florence Henniker (who was briefly in the capital); her sister, Amy; and her brother-in-law, Sir Gerald Fitzgerald. Millgate maintains that Hardy somehow found room on this occasion to make 'a declaration of affection' towards Henniker.[1091] Apparently not easily deterred by the 'distinct coolness' with which this preliminary manoeuvre was received, Hardy quickly followed up with a sequence of letters in June, which were 'nakedly exploitative of whatever links – as substantial as literature or as tenuous as architectural history – might be established between them'.[1092] By the end of the month, Hardy had read through and commented favourably on Henniker's third novel, *Foiled*, pronouncing it 'far superior to more highly-rated novels such as *The Heavenly Twins*'. He also showed a rare favouritism towards her by confidentially disclosing 'the true names of the places' in her copy of *Tess*.[1093]

Hardy's conviction that he and Henniker were 'kindred souls' was reinforced by his discovery that they were coincidentally reading Shelley's 'Epipsychidion', a revelation which appeared to confirm for him the unconventional and liberal-minded nature of her character.[1094] In essence:

> What drew him to her was the belief that understanding between them would be effortless, and as easy as her own actions would be spontaneous and natural. He thought he had found in her the purity of Tess – purity that did not mean chastity so much as purity of heart – and found it combined with all the charming elegance of a cultivated woman. Florence Henniker seemed to possess the simplicity of heart which allowed one to know one's instincts and to follow them. That appearance [...] held the promise for Hardy of an erotic relation that was 'pure', as he understood that word. Because of their intuitive understanding, the relationship could never degenerate into heartless flirtation and in addition it would remain pure even if it were consummated – even if, that is to say, they committed adultery together.[1095]

Henniker was obviously aware of Hardy's towering literary reputation, and of the degree to which such a relationship might prove beneficial to her career. It is nonetheless clear from the content of his letters to her 'that she was keeping him very much at arm's length, declining to be drawn into exchanges of a romantic or potentially physical nature'.[1096] At the end of June, Henniker included in one letter to Hardy some translations of French and Spanish verse whose connotations could be interpreted as 'coquettish, or cruelly teasing', depending on the audience. In a later item of correspondence (10 July), she also engaged in 'a gratifying (if mock-serious) display of jealousy' when Hardy playfully 'threatened' to use his architectural knowledge for the benefit of other women.[1097]

The sternness of Hardy's comments reveal that he was already feeling frustrated that Henniker's moral code was far too conventional to permit a sexual relationship between them. Their simultaneous reading of Shelley now struck Hardy as a disappointing red herring – something he made plain to her by letter:

> I had a regret in reading it at thinking that one who is preeminently the child of the Shelleyan tradition – whom one would have expected to be an ardent disciple of his school and views – should have allowed herself to be enfeebled to a belief in ritualistic ecclesiasticism. My impression is that you do not know your own views. You feel the need of emotional expression of some sort, and being surrounded by the conventional society form of such expression you have mechanically adopted it. Is this the daughter of the man who went from Cambridge to Oxford on the now historic errand![1098]

Hardy and Henniker continued to see each other during July 1893, largely at Hardy's instigation. It was on 8 August, though, that the defining moment of their relationship occurred as they set out together on the excursion to Winchester mentioned in Chapter 1. Shortly after they met at the Eastleigh railway junction outside Southampton, Henniker seems 'immediately to have made it clear, once and for all, that things could not be as Hardy wished'.[1099] They then had lunch at the George Inn in Winchester and walked via the cathedral to the out-of-town location from which Angel and Liza-Lu witnessed the raising of the black flag in *Tess* which confirmed the eponymous heroine's execution. It was, as Millgate points out, 'a pilgrimage sadly appropriate to Hardy's mood'.[1100]

This did not prevent them from remaining friends, even though Henniker 'never responded to him quite as he wanted her to'.[1101] Later that autumn, they began collaborating on a short story, 'The Spectre of the Real'. The accusation has been levelled that Florence Henniker was fundamentally selfish and hard-hearted, 'and she does indeed seem – for all her charm and passionate advocacy of humanitarian causes – to have been a little lacking in personal warmth'.[1102] From this perspective, her attempt to salvage the situation by sending Hardy a present of a silver inkstand, inscribed 'T.H. from F.H.', followed by some photographic portraits of herself, may have seemed like rubbing salt into Hardy's wounds. However, Pite has defended this as 'less flirtatious than perhaps it may appear', suggesting that the inkstand was a coded message that they should concentrate on their professional relationship, and that there was nothing unusual in the exchanging of photographs between friends.[1103]

Stewart is succinct in his analysis of Hardy's relationship with Henniker: 'To me, at least, the Henniker affair suggests itself as being compounded out of middle-aged sentiment and a little sex-in-the-head.'[1104] Ultimately, the mutual attraction and abiding loyalty between them was founded on 'a strong affinity, steady affection, high personal regard, keenly shared interests, and – perhaps the most critical factor of all in the long run – susceptibility to, and respect for, their differences of outlook'.[1105] While Hardy may have yearned for a sexual consummation of his relationship with this apparently liberated 'new' woman, she harboured no corresponding sexual attraction: 'In spite of all his literary advice and an offer of a guide to architecture which would take the form of "oral instruction in actual buildings", and in spite of her teasing him by sending him photographs and romantic translations of romantic verses, she was no more in love with him than Bathsheba was with Boldwood.'[1106] This is not to deny that, as Hardy's letters indicate, 'this was the most important and fascinating of all his friendships'.[1107]

The Spectre of the Real

It is commonly accepted that Hardy first mooted the idea of a literary collaboration with Henniker as early as July 1893. Even by then, 'Mrs Henniker's more consistent emphasis upon their shared literary interests had been largely motivated by her eagerness to deflect Hardy from his pursuit of other forms of attachment.' It is possible that Hardy, in turn:

> seriously took up the idea of their collaboration only as a kind of last resort following their trip to Winchester on 8 August

> [...] A literary partnership would at least provide an excuse for meetings and correspondence and Hardy may still have hoped that friendship might eventually lead to something more.[1108]

Whatever their actual motives, the collaboration eventually resulted in the publication, in the 17 November 1894 edition of *To-Day*, of a short story, 'The Spectre of the Real', which represents the *only* officially acknowledged collaborative work bearing the name of Thomas Hardy.[1109]

Surviving typescripts of initial drafts and a corrected set of proofs constitute a testament to the fact that Henniker's role in the collaboration was more substantial than originally supposed.[1110] The plot was quintessentially Hardy's:

> The story has familiar features, the clandestine romance and marriage of a 'noble lady' and a poor officer, the return of the vanished husband on the eve of his wife's remarriage, the removal of a troublesome character by drowning in a water-meadow.[1111]

But the composition was a far from easy. Henniker showed an acute sensitivity to Hardy's criticisms and, as the author of three reasonably successful novels, was less inclined than his earlier protégées to be cast in the role of obedient 'pupil'.[1112] It is generally agreed that Hardy played the dominant role in the composition:

> It can be summarised thus: after discussing the project, including potential plots, with Henniker, Hardy sent her two outlines; she selected one and wrote it up as a scenario which he altered slightly; she then wrote out the story in full and sent the manuscript to Hardy, who extensively revised it and completely rewrote the conclusion before dispatching it to be typed; after she had lightly corrected that first typescript he altered it substantially, had a second typescript made, revised it, sent it to *To-Day*, and finally corrected the proofs when they arrived.[1113]

According to Dutta, Henniker got so upset by Hardy's attempt to edit out some of her descriptive passages, which he found superfluous and/or cliché-ridden, that he reluctantly reinstated them. There was, he felt, an over-usage of such 'stock phrases' as 'velvet-like skies' and 'cheeks pink and eyes shining':[1114]

> That the descriptive passages were finally included is evidence not only of Henniker's strength of will but also of Hardy's willingness to accommodate her – and by extension the depth of his feelings – even at some cost to his professional integrity, for the details are essentially superfluous, contributing little or nothing to the story in terms of imagery, theme, mood, or even local colour. As such they are typical of Henniker's work: all her stories contain obtrusive description for its own sake, usually involving birds, occasionally butterflies and small animals. The style, too, is essentially Henniker's, prosaic and thick with clichés.[1115]

It remains debatable whether this ultimately negative experience was sufficient to cure Hardy's infatuation with Henniker, but there is no doubt that it dissuaded him from entering into any further collaborations of this nature.[1116] Henniker's assertiveness and spirit of independence was evident when she included a revamped version of 'The Spectre' in her book of short stories, *In Scarlet and Grey*,[1117] in which she had made a number of 'verbal alterations' and several other editorial interventions on matters of 'taste' (e.g. by de-emphasising the sexual nature of the heroine's attraction to her husband, an issue over which she had originally disagreed with Hardy).[1118] She may have been vindicated by the fact that critics generally considered 'Spectre of the Real' as inferior to the bulk of the other chapters in the volume (the majority of which she had written alone).[1119]

Hardy's Muse

Harvey highlights the extent to which the 'emotional summer of 1893' was the well-spring for a number of publications by Hardy in which the influence of his relationship with Henniker is manifest.[1120] This emotional entanglement is clearly embodied in a number of his poems, most notably 'At an Inn', 'A Thunderstorm in Town', 'In Death Divided', 'The Division', 'A Broken Appointment', and 'Wessex Heights', in which she is famously characterised as 'one rare fair woman'; and in a short story, 'An Imaginative Woman', published in the *The Pall Mall Magazine* in April 1894. Lastly:

> Hardy's final, great tragic novel, *Jude the Obscure*, bears the mark of Florence Henniker in the characterisation of its heroine, Sue Bridehead, whose full name is Susanna Florence Mary Bridehead. Sue's sexual unresponsiveness, ecclesiastical interests, and intellectual gifts all point to Florence Henniker as a model.[1121]

It is clearly imperative that we explore Henniker's relevance to these works in more detail, starting with his poetry.

Henniker's Place in Hardy's Poetry

Pinion remarks that Hardy told his second wife that two of his poems, 'A Thunderstorm in Town' and 'A Broken Appointment', were directly related to Henniker.[1122] The title of the former is even followed in parentheses by 'A Reminiscence: 1893', an obvious clue to Henniker's relevance.[1123] The actual words have a telling resonance with the fateful day in Winchester:

> She wore a new 'terra-cotta' dress,
> And we stayed, because of the pelting storm,
> Within the hansom's dry recess,
> Though the horse had stopped; yea, motionless
> We sat on, snug and warm.
>
> Then the downpour ceased, to my sharp sad pain
> And the glass that had screened our forms before
> Flew up, and out she sprang to her door:
> I should have kissed her if the rain
> Had lasted a minute more.[1124]

Millgate maintains that 'A Broken Appointment' is the most moving of all of Hardy's 'Henniker poems', and is 'certainly eloquent of Hardy's longer view of the relationship'.[1125] The second stanza is especially revealing:

> You love not me.
> And love alone can lend you loyalty;
> – I know and knew it. But, unto the store
> Of human deeds divine in all but name,
> Was it not worth a little hour or more

To add yet this: Once you, a woman, came
To soothe a time-torn man; even though it be
You love not me?[1126]

In Gibson's estimation, there has been no better poem written about the disappointment of being 'stood-up', and the four short lines mark the clock's striking of the quarter hour as the 'time-torn-man waits in vain'.[1127] For Gibson, this forms part of a quartet of Hardy's poems (along with 'A Thunderstorm in Town', 'The Division' and 'At an Inn') which lament his losing of a 'prize' in Florence Henniker.

The last-named of these four poems 'painfully suggests' a meeting which, while outwardly appearing like a 'lovers' tryst', is actually far more demoralising.[1128] Clearly recalling their time together in Winchester (where, on entering the George Inn, Hardy and Henniker were taken for a married couple and shown into the same bedroom), it is a commentary on the anti-climax experienced by the author:

And we were left alone
As Love's own pair;
Yet never the love-light shone
Between us there![1129]

Finally, and perhaps most sadly of all, Hardy's 'Wessex Heights' marks the point that Hardy finally became reconciled to the fact that his devotion to Henniker was entirely unrequited and that it was time to 'let her go':

As for one rare fair woman, I am now but a thought of hers,
I enter her mind and another thought succeeds that she prefers;
Yet my love for her in its fulness she herself even did not know;
Well, time cures hearts of tenderness, and now I can let her go.[1130]

An Imaginative Woman

There are clear traces of Hardy's relationship with Henniker in his short story, 'An Imaginative Woman', which was written during the summer and autumn following their meeting in Ireland and her subsequent rejection of him as a suitor.

Ella Marchmill, the central character, is an 'emotionally repressed' poet (who writes under the pseudonym, 'John Ivy') and wife of a Midlands-based gun manufacturer.[1131] The plot focuses on a holiday the couple take at 'Solentsea', in rooms previously occupied by a poet, Robert Trewe, whose work Ella has long cherished. Following an unsuccessful attempt to meet the poet (who has gone off to the Isle of Wight), Ella takes, somewhat bizarrely, to dressing up in his hat and mackintosh and obsessively referring to his photograph, which she keeps secretly by her bedside. On returning home, she starts to correspond with Trewe, using her poetic pseudonym, but eventually reads in the newspapers of his suicide and of the subsequent reference at his inquest to the inspiration of an imaginary woman.[1132]

On learning of all this, 'Ivy' requests, and receives, a lock of Trewe's hair from his landlady, and visits his graveside, where she is caught in the act by her husband. Mrs Marchmill subsequently dies in childbirth. Two years later, as her husband is preparing for remarriage, he comes across Trewe's photograph and lock of hair, and immediately observes that there are close resemblances between the poet and the Marchmills' son. Concluding that the child must have been conceived by Ella and Trewe during their brief stay in Solentsea, Marchmill angrily rejects the boy.[1133]

Several commentators have pointed to numerous possible allusions to Henniker in 'An Imaginative Woman'.[1134] The very name of the 'imaginative woman' appears to have been derived from Henniker's second name, Ellen, and her maiden name, Milnes. Earlier manuscripts of the story also reveal that Trewe started out as 'Crewe', which is, of course, the surname of Henniker's mother's side of the family. A further association is apparent in the fact that Arthur Henniker-Major has a shared military interest with the gunmaker Marchmill; and it seems more than mere coincidence that, while the Hennikers lived on South Parade, Southsea, Robert Trewe resided on the similarly named *New Parade, Solentsea*. A final, loose connection is discernible in the fact that, just as Ella kept a lock of her hero's hair, Henniker's father, Richard Monckton Milnes, possessed a similar keepsake of Keats's in his Fryston library.

A deeper allegorical resonance with the Hardy-Henniker relationship has been conjectured, notably by Pite, who reckons that the entire story constituted Hardy's bitter and punitive response to Henniker's rejection:

> She could not have missed the allusions to herself. As Ella Marchmill, she is depicted as an affected person, superficial and mediocre as a writer, and foolishly impressionable as a person. Trewe, the equivalent to Hardy, is by contrast a genuine artist and an innocent victim. His truth (declared by his name) encounters her falsity – her use of a pseudonym and her choice of one that implies something parasitic and exploitative. That he is true and she is false is then made part of the story: the narrator explains that Trewe's suicide came about because he never found a devoted woman he could love. By using her pseudonym in their correspondence, Ella prevented him from finding her so that her professional disguise is made responsible for his death.[1135]

Pite maintains that, even if such 'oblique attacks' on Henniker were not sufficiently hurtful in themselves, they were matched in vitriol and intent by Hardy's 'mean depiction of Ella's husband, as first a boor and later a bad father'.[1136] If, as Pite suspects, Hardy had Arthur Henniker in his sights, there is no doubt that Florence would have been wounded by such a 'caricature'. This may help to explain why there was such a long gap in her correspondence with Hardy, lasting from January 1894 to the summer of 1895.[1137]

Jude the Obscure

Perhaps the 'greatest literary influence' of Florence Henniker on Thomas Hardy concerns his characterisation of Sue Bridehead, the heroine of his final novel, *Jude the Obscure.*[1138] It was in 1896 that Hardy confided in his friend Edward Clodd that Henniker had been his model for Sue (something also confirmed by Hardy's second wife, Florence).[1139] Hardy's depiction of Sue 'as an epicene intellectual, sexually cold and fastidious but tantalizingly attractive' squares up with his slightly embittered view of Henniker.[1140] Pettit contends that Hardy associated a 'Shelleyan idealism' with Henniker, 'as with Sue Bridehead, whose character Mrs Henniker influenced',[1141] while Bullen makes the general observation that the emotional turmoil and romantic ambitions exercising Hardy's imagination were reflected in his casting of the relationship between Sue and Jude.[1142]

There are clear echoes of Hardy's relationship with Henniker in the book's central premise that, while Jude devotes himself, body and soul, to Sue, she cannot commit herself so wholeheartedly. The accusation levelled by Hardy is that Sue stands guilty 'of secret indifference and exploitativeness – of not knowing how to handle an honest man'.[1143] It is this 'faithlessness' of Sue Bridehead to the 'Shelleyan ideal of transgression', her inability to go beyond the conservative and the conventional, that Hardy sees fit to 'punish' in describing Sue's '"cowardly" betrayal and abandonment of Jude'.[1144] In this way, he is also referring to the 'treachery' perpetrated by Henniker:

> Hardy placed great faith in his 'Shelleyan' relationship with Mrs. Henniker, as his letters to her attest [...] he could not understand why the daughter of one so closely connected to the Shelley heritage and so imbued with Shelleyan creeds of free love would not desire to consummate their affair, as Mrs Henniker did not [...] Hardy's disillusionment at her refusal is the historic source of Sue's 'failure' as a type of Veiled Maiden. Henniker's weak Shelleyan character becomes Sue's; Henniker's miming of Shelleyan possibilities for romantic transgression becomes Sue's demanding that Jude see her 'as exactly like' the intellectual beauty in Shelley's poetry. Read in the light of biography, *Jude* is an instrument of Hardy's revenge upon Mrs. Henniker for not fully practising what she preached.[1145]

The relationship between Hardy and Henniker survived this perceived 'treachery' on her part, however. Ironically, it took a short story by Henniker to redefine the parameters of their personal and professional associations. 'The Colour Sergeant' is seen by some commentators as occupying a significant part in their story, insofar as it not only rebukes Hardy for his attitude toward his protégé (and requires him to maintain more social and professional distance), but also helps consolidate the theory that Hardy may have had a serious rival for her affection.

Chapter Twenty-Four
The Heart of the Colour Sergeant

Retelling Their Relationship?

Florence Henniker's book of short stories *In Scarlet and Grey* was published in 1896. While it is commonly assumed that Thomas Hardy advised her on the writing of some of these tales, this was certainly not the case for the opening story of the collection, 'The Heart of the Colour Sergeant'. As Pite explains, this particular work 'had never been mentioned between them and it reads in some ways like a retelling, from Florence's point of view, of her relationship with Hardy'.[1146]

In 'Colour Sergeant', the main female character, Kitty Malone, is about to marry an ordinary-looking soldier, who happens to be the son of a wealthy peer. Before getting married, Kitty meets a sergeant whose life has 'gone downhill' due to the fact that he has ceased mixing with members of his own class and has been deprived of a meaningful relationship with a woman. It soon becomes clear that he is immensely grateful to Kitty for the attention, sensitivity and understanding she has shown him. Both the sergeant and Kitty's soldier-husband are consigned to a military expedition in Egypt in 1893. Before setting off, the sergeant asks Kitty to give him a nosegay of forget-me-nots as a keepsake of their relationship. In a dramatic display of heroism, Kitty's fiancé saves the sergeant's life, but the sergeant is so badly wounded that he is forced to return home. Kitty's husband and her father-in-law dissuade her from visiting him directly, but in a final act of compassion she sends him another posy, which he is clutching when he dies.

Pite endeavours to unravel the moral of this story and observes that Kitty learns the importance of the dubious morality of consorting with the sergeant and encouraging his romantic feelings towards her.

Her actions, which risked going too far for comfort, are ultimately excused within a narrative that acknowledges that her conduct was designed to help 'redeem a fallen man'. In this way, 'A married woman's kindliness to other men is vindicated (even when it makes them fall in love with her); simultaneously, its limits are defined.'[1147]

It is probably significant that *In Scarlet and Grey* was dedicated to Florence Henniker's husband. Certainly, Pite regards 'The Heart of the Colour Sergeant' as a tribute to Arthur Henniker's military heroism and his 'delicacy and sensitivity too'.[1148]

> Moreover, if the story is seen as in part a response to Hardy's feelings for Florence, it comes across as more self-defining and less complacent. Hardy had asked to be pitied and comforted; the story agrees to that and sets terms. Florence, like Kitty, will do what she can and no more, because she does sincerely wish to help him, but it would be wrong for him to ask her to do more than she should. Similarly, and perhaps in reply to 'An Imaginative Woman', the story rebukes Hardy's contempt for commonplace men – for Ella Marchmill's husband, Kitty Malone's and, behind them both, for Florence's own. Florence must keep herself properly restrained and Hardy must learn to be more roundedly kind. It is the proper way forward for them both.[1149]

It seems that this publication may well have accelerated a change of direction in the Hardy-Henniker relationship, in which she became more independent of his patronage and he became more resigned to the fact that they could never have a romantic relationship. They would, however, remain 'close and trusted friends';[1150] and, as we shall see, Hardy continued to grow increasingly fond of Arthur Henniker. It has been postulated elsewhere, however, that, far from being an oblique reference to her relationship with Hardy, Henniker's short story strongly hints of her attraction to an altogether different man.

The John Dillon 'Affair'

Hardy and Pinion described how, presumably as a result of her supportive role towards her brother when he served as Viceroy of Ireland, Florence Henniker befriended many leading Irish MPs, including T.P. O'Connor, J.G. Swift MacNeill and John Dillon.[1151]

Her relationship with Dillon requires some discussion – partly because of its probable relevance to the content of 'Colour Sergeant', but principally because of the intriguing new perspective it creates for our understanding of why Henniker was so resistant to Hardy's romantic overtures. As one leading authority on Hardy has contended:

> Scholars have assumed that while Henniker did not reciprocate Hardy's feelings, she eagerly accepted his attention and help, but the first story of the collection, 'The Heart of the Colour Sergeant', together with thirty-five unpublished letters from Henniker to John Dillon, indicate that during the years of Hardy's most ardent interest in her, she was working through other interests – Dillon in particular. Her letters to Dillon indicate that she not only became a serious student of Irish politics under his tutelage, but also, was tempted by the prospect of an exciting, deeply personal friendship.[1152]

According to Sylvia's interpretation, Henniker's rejection of Hardy 'was not so much callous towards him as struggling with her attraction to another man, John Dillon'.[1153]

The third child and second son of John Blake Dillon (a lawyer, Irish nationalist and, as of 1865, MP for Tipperary), John Dillon was born in Blackrock, Co. Dublin, in September 1851. Following the deaths of his father in 1866 and mother six years later, Dillon spent parts of his late youth and early adulthood living with his maternal uncle at 2 North Gt. George's Street, Dublin, which eventually became his permanent residence. Dillon was privately educated until his teens, then briefly attended the University School in Harcourt Street, before moving on to the Catholic University, where he studied art from 1865 to 1870. Following an ill-considered and abortive apprenticeship with a Mancunian cotton-broker, he entered the Catholic University medical school, where he obtained a degree from the College of Surgeons.[1154]

It was none other than Richard Monckton Milnes's lifelong friend Justin McCarthy, who referred to 'John Dillon the elder' as 'in every way a remarkable man'.[1155] McCarthy outlines Dillon Snr's role in the abortive Irish 'rising' of 1848, the quelling of which saw Dillon make his escape via France to America, where he spent the next several years serving at the Bar. He only returned to Ireland after the declaration of amnesty in 1854. 'The younger Dillon' was, according to McCarthy, 'not likely having been brought up by such a father, to keep comfortably out of the field of Irish politics.'[1156]

An elected MP in the British House of Commons for two spells (1880-1883 and 1885-1918), Dillon is best remembered as an original committee member of the Irish National Land League, which fought tenaciously for fixed tenure, fair rents and the free sale of Irish land in the face of opposition from exploitative landlords. He was imprisoned on six separate occasions for playing leading parts in such campaigns, and temporarily fled – like his father – to New York in 1890 to evade one such term of imprisonment. Dillon was in America when news of a scandal broke out in which the prominent Irish Nationalist leader, Charles Stewart Parnell, was cited as correspondent in a divorce case. Hitherto regarded as one of Parnell's close political allies, Dillon subsequently distanced himself from his compatriot to avoid any possible political fallout.[1157]

Between 1886 and 1890, Dillon joined William O'Brien at the forefront of the 'Plan of Campaign', in which scores of impoverished tenants collectively refused to pay their rents unless substantial reductions were agreed, and any tenants previously evicted were duly re-instated.[1158] During one such rent strike protest organised by Dillon and O'Brien at Mitchelstown in 1887, the police shot dead two civilian protesters and wounded several others:

> And it was only after Dillon had gone himself to the barracks to restrain them that further bloodshed was avoided, though what had already happened was to echo and re-echo through English and Irish politics for many years to come.[1159]

McCarthy paid tribute to Dillon's commitment and integrity: 'I have never met a man more thoroughly single-minded. I have never met one of whom I could more firmly believe that his actions and his words were invariably dictated by a sense of public duty.'[1160]

Dillon's biographer has explained how, 'For most of his early career John Dillon had seemed an extreme example of the patriot so dedicated to the cause as to have crushed out of existence all the appetites and passions the flesh is heir to.'[1161]

Alongside the unremitting intensity of his political activity, Dillon suffered from tuberculosis and lacked independent wealth to fall back on. It would have been fair, therefore, to disregard him as a good marriage prospect:

> Yet no doubt there were many who were prepared to take the risk. When he first entered public life, and indeed for a long time afterwards, he was a striking figure. Tall, slender, olive-skinned, with black hair and beard and dark, burning eyes, he was undeniably handsome. The touch of extremism in his nature, his courage, his sincerity, his obvious compassion for the poor, the very fact that he belonged to a revolutionary tradition – these things made him at once conspicuous and desirable. And, such is human nature, his remoteness from human contacts, his dedication to politics, even the periodic rumours that the family curse of consumption was about to claim him – all increased rather than diminished his appeal.[1162]

Sylvia uses the contents of the thirty-five unpublished letters Henniker wrote to Dillon (covering the period from 16 October 1894 to 17 March 1896) as evidence of her growing fascination with him. Sylvia maintains that Henniker employed the novel political perspective she acquired from this correspondence to frame the narrative of 'Colour Sergeant' in such a way as to 'challenge ethnic stereotypes and to explore Anglo-Irish tensions'. He further contends that this correspondence also serves to unmask Dillon as a 'third party' in the 'Henniker/Hardy affair'.[1163]

Sylvia acknowledges from the outset that nothing in these letters suggests that, for all their enforced spells of separation, there was any sign of marital unhappiness between Henniker and her husband. On the contrary, the surviving correspondence reveals an enduring tenderness between them.[1164] Dillon was, at this time, already involved in a longstanding relationship with Elizabeth Mathew, a young woman of shared political affinity and impressive intellect, who was also the grandniece of the well-known temperance apostle Father Mathew and the daughter of the London-based High Court judge Sir James Mathew. She was well-educated, widely travelled and fluent in several languages. Her devout Catholicism was reflected in her committed charitable work and her political commitment (which, like her father's, was sympathetic to Home Rule). She and Dillon obviously had a lot in common.

The couple first met in Killiney, Co. Dublin in 1886, by which time Mathew was already an ardent admirer of Dillon. It was customary for her family to spend part of her father's long annual vacation in Ireland, and on this occasion they rented Killiney Castle. During their stay, a pair of mutual family friends arranged for Dillon, Elizabeth and her sister, May, to have lunch together. An avid diarist (there are thirty-nine volumes of her journals among the Dillon Papers in Trinity College, Dublin), Elizabeth confessed on the eve of their meeting that she and her sister were in 'desperate excitement' at the prospect of meeting someone of 'Mr Dillon's fame and handsomeness'. She was already positive that 'great numbers of young ladies are in love with him',[1165] and was certainly not disappointed if the evidence of their initial encounter is anything to go by.

On meeting Dillon, Mathew quickly found that he was open, unaffected and earnest in character. His conversation was unselfconscious and devoid of hidden agenda.

> His manner is quite different to anyone else's; he evidently does not care a bit whether people are impressed with him or not, nor does he desire to make himself agreeable to them. He knows about everything, but does not start a conversation on anything; we did not refer to a single subject last night on which he could not give us the fullest information; who wrote a book, what opera a song came from, the climate of a foreign country, the different dialects of Italy, the peculiarities of American speech, the resources of the colonies, statistics of every kind; and then at last he began to tell us about the evictions on the Clanricarde property and the history of the landlord oppression in that part of the country, and then his eyes glistened and his voice rose to that softly eloquent tone I have heard in the House, and we listened quite breathlessly; he had quite ceased to be 'languid' then.[1166]

This was the start of a relationship that would eventually see Dillon and Mathew get married and have seven children together by the time of her premature death from pneumonia at age forty-two. It was a prolonged courtship, nonetheless, and they were only married after Dillon was pushed into proposing in October 1895.

Sylvia maintains that it is clear from Henniker's first known correspondence that, 'at the very peak of Hardy's ardor, she was pursuing Dillon's attention'.[1167] It was, indeed:

> During those years when Hardy's affection for Henniker was most keen [...] [that she] was becoming a serious student of Irish politics under the tutelage of Dillon, asking him to recommend reading on the history of Irish Nationalism and its heroes and to comment on current debates.[1168]

She also attended relevant debates in parliament; and whenever Dillon's busy schedule permitted it, she entertained him in her London home.[1169]

Judging by a letter dated 3 December 1894, Henniker was clearly becoming increasingly sympathetic to Dillon's perspective. She contrasted the staunchly pro-Home Rule standpoint of her brother, Crewe, with that of the 'rigidly Unionist' position adopted by her sister Amicia's husband, Sir Gerald Fitzgerald, of whom she said, 'I am sure he is one of the kindest of people, but he cannot realize all the terrible cases – or a hundredth part of them, of the sufferings of the tenants.'[1170] Sylvia points out that, as is so often the case in these letters, Henniker concludes by seeking a meeting with Dillon: 'I do so wish I could see you soon, & talk to you about these things.'[1171]

Sylvia maintains that it was the 'The Heart of the Colour Sergeant' that enabled Henniker to give free-rein to her bourgeoning interest in Irish affairs. The plot focuses, it may be recalled, on the experiences of Kitty Malone who becomes drawn to a dashing Colour Sergeant Rhodes, even though she is already engaged to someone else. Sylvia speculates that Kitty may have been a name appropriated from 'Kitty O'Shea', who had gained notoriety in 1890s as the adulterous lover (and eventual wife) of Charles Stewart Parnell, alluded to above. He also hypothesises that John Dillon (with his private school education, university degree, chronic ill-health and susceptibility to dark moods) was a 'likely possibility' as the prototype for the 'mysterious' Colour Sergeant.

This supposition that Dillon had a discernible influence of

Henniker's fiction writing is ultimately all speculative. So, too, is the possibility of any tangible romantic attachment between them. Letters dated as late as September 1895 suggest an eagerness by both parties to see one another. On one occasion, Dillon's planned visit is thwarted by Henniker's illness and she invites him instead to see her play the zither. A letter of 23 September smacks of some possible intimacy between them:

> I hear that the 'Hamburg' is shut up. Where shall we have dinner? Will you suggest a place? We might perhaps go to Kinger, or to the Kursaal. I should like to know what you think. I should be very sorry if you did not dine with us on our last evg [sic].[1172]

In the final analysis, it remains true, as Sylvia conceded, that 'Since only one side of the correspondence survives, the exact nature of their developing friendship is difficult to establish – beyond her insistent requests for contact and Dillon's remarkably prompt willingness to respond.'[1173]

Perhaps the reason that Henniker was able to capture so much of Dillon's attention at a time of great 'tumultuous political activity' is because of her readiness to patronise the Lord Lieutenant. Alternatively, it may have been 'a testament to her special ability to attract to her circle people of interest, importance and energy'.[1174]

Sylvia maintains that, irrespective of whatever bond may have existed beforehand, Dillon's marriage to Mathew completely transformed the nature of his relationship with Henniker. Henceforward, Henniker's letters were more aloof and less 'ardent', as if she was aware that Dillon might share the contents with his wife. For Sylvia, Hardy's lines in 'Wessex Heights' – 'As for one rare fair woman, I am now but a thought of hers, I enter her mind and another thought succeeds me that she prefers' – suggest that he 'knew of her passion for Dillon, knew that he had a rival in these early years of their friendship, and that she, too, ironically, suffered an affair of "one-sidedness"'. It is therefore ironic that, whilst both Hardy and Henniker may have simultaneously experienced 'the pain of unrequited love', it was not with one another.[1175]

Chapter Twenty-Five
A Right Royal Finale

A Seat of Social Extravagance

Pope-Hennessy observes that, on returning to England in 1895 from his three-year stay in Ireland, Lord Crewe preferred to live *in* Crewe, making only short visits to Fryston Hall, 'where he stayed for Doncaster Race Meetings and, from time to time, entertained shooting parties'.[1176] While in Cheshire, he indulged in his passions for hunting and riding, and developed his stables of horse racing stock.

> Crewe was devoted to horses, and his outdoor relaxations were almost entirely concerned with them. He hunted as much as possible in Ireland and in Cheshire until about 1900, when he gave it up. In the meantime he had built some paddocks at Crewe and had bought a few brood mares, whose produce were trained by John Porter at Kingsclere. He had a few winners, but none of them of much merit, the best being St. Lundi.[1177]

Fryston Hall continued to be a seat of social extravagance, where Crewe's sister Florence remained ever-willing to play the role of hostess on his behalf. In this chapter, we focus on two such occasions of note, occurring in December 1895 and September 1896. The first involves the joint visit paid to Fryston by two acclaimed American writers – the British-born Frances Hodgson Burnett (author of the children's novel, *Little Lord Fauntleroy*) and Bret Harte, a close friend of the first Lord Houghton and his daughter. The second saw Fryston playing host to a party led by the Prince of Wales, the future King Edward VII.

Last Suppers

Hodgson Burnett first met Crewe in July 1894 when, as Lord Lieutenant of Ireland, he represented his father at the unveiling of a Keats memorial in Hampstead Parish Church. 'That had been an occasion,' her biographer ironically maintains.[1178] The unveiling was preceded by a celebratory luncheon hosted by the author Walter Besant, who was also a founder of the Society of Authors. The subsequent memorial service was led by an officiating parson and hymns delivered by a surpliced choir.

The poet W.S. Blunt described what he witnessed as a 'curious ceremony', to which the biographer Edmund Gosse and Crewe were the principal of several contributors: 'Gosse, who presided, made a dull, platitudinous oration in the tone of a sermon [...] and the others were even duller. [Crewe] alone was brief and to the point.'[1179]

Once unveiled, the poet's bust was decorated by laurels hung by Gosse's children[1180] and, 'When all was over the worthy vicar consoled himself with some prayers and an anthem.'[1181] Blunt's 'meagre approval' of Crewe[1182] was in sharp contrast to Hodgson Burnett's impression of him as 'a charming, modest and lovable young giant'.[1183]

It was owing to his enduring friendship with Florence Henniker that Bret Harte was introduced to numerous aristocratic friends and acquaintances, such as Lord and Lady Compton, whose country estate he visited in June 1894. Also on this list was Henniker's brother. Harte had been enthusiastic for some time to make Crewe's acquaintance, but it was not until Christmas of 1895 that he was able to accept an invitation to Fryston Hall, a place he had never visited when the first Lord Houghton was alive.[1184] Even so, it was apparent from a letter (dated 18 December 1895) sent to 'Nan' from Fryston Hall that his acceptance of Crewe's invitation had been subject to one condition:

> I am here on a visit to the Earl of Crew [sic] – the son of the late Lord Houghton, whom you remember breakfasted with us once at Eliza's in Fifth Avenue; and though I have often been invited before I have never yet succeeded in effecting my intention. Even now, I have only come on the promise of Lord Crew [sic] that I should be allowed to work while here, and I have brought with me some unfinished manuscripts which I want to complete by Christmas, if I consent to stay during the holidays.[1185]

Other guests included the Irish politician and newspaper editor T.P. O'Connor and the writer Edith Sichel, whose *Catherine de' Medici and the French Reformation* had the distinction of having been reviewed by

Virginia Woolf for the *Times Literary Supplement.* Hodgson Burnett wrote to one (unnamed) correspondent that Harte and 'Mrs T.P. O'Connor' were out walking while 'the great T.P. is doubtless at work upon a thundering leader'.[1186] Harte further revealed in his letter to Nan how British feathers had been ruffled by the US President Grover Cleveland's insistence that America should have a say in an ongoing 'boundary dispute' between Britain and Venezuela, in which the British were claiming territory as part of British Guiana.

> Everybody here is very much excited over the President's Message, which they all believe means war between the two countries! Heaven forbid! – for all reasons – and not the least, the selfish one that it would be ruinous to my future, for I should, of course, no longer remain in England – the only place where I could earn my daily bread. For much as I love my own country – it does not love me sufficiently to enable me to support myself there by my pen.[1187]

Thwaite reports that Harte was ill-tempered during his visit to Fryston, and 'had to be calmed with lemon tea'.[1188] This was in contrast to Hodgson Burnett, who was obviously enchanted by the whole occasion. 'She enjoyed everything,' according to her biographer – the rare books and manuscripts, the works of art, and even the spectacle of 'Lady Celia, one of the twins, tearing up the avenue on her horse "like a little witch"'.[1189] It was Crewe, though, that Hodgson Burnett was so clearly captivated by. He was, she ventured, 'the most beautiful Earl in England', and there was something touching about the fact that he had been left with three young daughters after only seven years of marriage.[1190] At dinner, his Lordship was 'entertaining rather than touching', in reciting a throwaway verse he once heard Tennyson quote as the 'finest poem of its kind':

> Mrs Boem wrote a poem
> In praise of Tynemouth air;
> Mr Boem read the poem
> And built a cottage there.[1191]

For Hodgson Burnett, Crewe 'was everything an earl should be'. She regarded him as 'exquisite and lovable and perfect-natured and of finer clay than the rest of the world'.[1192] It has since been speculated that Crewe subsequently became the inspiration for Archibald Craven, in what is arguably Hodgson Burnett's most famous novel, *The Secret Garden*, which was eventually published in 1911.

The Context of the Prince's Visit to Fryston, 1896

The most illustrious of all the grand occasions ever witnessed at Fryston Hall was the visit of Edward, Prince of Wales (by now, a close friend of Crewe's) to Fryston in September 1896. The main purpose of the future King Edward VII's visit to Yorkshire was to attend the race meeting in nearby Doncaster, where the pride of his stables (and already that year's Derby winner), Persimmon, was clear favourite to win the season's latest 'classic', the St Leger Stakes. It was inevitable, however, that Prince Edward would also seize the opportunity to go out hunting in Fryston woods, thus satisfying the passion he shared with his host.

The name of Edward VII is synonymous with horse racing: it is uncontested that he did more than anyone to elevate to the unrivalled stature of the 'sport of Kings'.[1193] The future monarch first developed his passion for horse racing in the 1860s, when he frequently attended flat and steeplechase meetings in defiance of his mother, Queen Victoria. His appetite for the sport was substantially reinforced during a lengthy stay in Ireland in 1868; and following his return to England, Edward revived the traditional royal procession at Ascot. His mother continued to argue that the 'shiftless lifestyle' associated with attending and gambling on such meetings would leave him 'vulnerable to scandal' – a position she deemed vindicated when 'Bertie' was called to give evidence in a divorce case concerning the legitimacy of a child: 'His mother felt that, guilty of fathering [the] baby or not, it was his lifestyle that had got him involved in the case in the first place.'[1194]

Edward was not only able to resist his mother's objections (with the support of the Princess of Wales, who was also a keen race-goer), but also went on to establish himself as an owner in 1875. His disastrous first race, in which the winner outstripped Bertie's Arab horse by 30 lengths, set the scene for the relatively inauspicious next few years. However, the decision in 1892 to move 'all the future King's horses' from Kingsclere to the Newmarket (Suffolk) stables owned by the renowned trainer Richard Marsh was a key turning point.[1195]

In 1894, it was Marsh who took in hand the Prince's treasured new acquisition, the fabled Persimmon, whose sire was the undefeated St Simon. The Prince bought Persimmon on the advice of his trainer, John Porter.[1196] Already regarded as a colt of outstanding promise, 'In appearance, Persimmon was a lengthy bay, just a shade on the leg in his early days, with a bold head, slightly lop ears, perfect shoulder and immense power behind the saddle. He was thoroughly genuine but high-mettled and could be difficult when in the mood.'[1197] The horse was run only sparingly – a mere nine times in the course of a career that lasted from 1895 to 1897. His first three outings were victorious; but in his only other race as a two-year-old, he finished third behind his future great rival, St Frusquin (another fine colt, owned by Leopold de Rothschild), and a fast-moving filly called Omladina, who had recently won the Champagne Stakes at Doncaster.

> Persimmon had in fact been coughing not long before the Middle Park and Marsh had not wanted to run him. He was overruled, though, by the Prince's racing manager, Lord Marcus Beresford. The race could have done Persimmon considerable harm but luckily Jack Watts had the sense to drop his hands as soon as he realized Persimmon had no hope of defeating St. Frusquin.[1198]

The horse's return to full health was so slow that Marsh refused to enter him in the April 1896 Two Thousand Guineas, which was easily won by St Frusquin. Persimmon's next outing saw him come home labouring in fourth place. By the time of his 'final gallop', the horse was showing considerable enough improvement to suggest to his owner that he might well win the Derby. On the day of the race, Persimmon was sweating profusely and seemed disconcertingly irritable. There seemed no obvious reason to question the bookmakers' odds, which made St Frusquin the hot favourite at 13-8 on, with Persimmon a less-fancied 5-1. These expectations were resoundingly confounded, though, when, from a quarter of a mile out, Persimmon gradually closed the gap on the favourite, before the jockey, Jack Watts, 'drove him home as hard as he could to win a wonderful race by a neck'.

One month later, St Frusquin gained some revenge by beating

Persimmon by half a length in the Princess of Wales's Stakes, though Persimmon carried a 3lb disadvantage. Persimmon was withdrawn from the subsequent Eclipse Stakes, which was easily won by his main rival. Strong anticipation now focused on the next major showdown of the two horses at the Doncaster St Leger. However, a massive anti-climax arose when it was revealed that St Frusquin would have to be withdrawn due to a leg injury. Not surprisingly, the build-up to the race generated little excitement outside of Yorkshire, due to the fact that a virtual walkover was being predicted. Within Yorkshire, however, the prospect of cheering on a popular royal victory was greatly relished:

> Persimmon, the hero of the Derby, will on Wednesday endeavour to win for his Royal owner the valuable and time-honoured St. Leger Stakes, and it is a matter of great satisfaction to thousands upon thousands of Yorkshiremen that the Prince will be present to witness the triumph of his magnificent thoroughbred. For every one seems to take it for granted that the son of St. Simon will be acclaimed the victor. It may be they are rash in so doing. There is no such thing as a certainty in horse-racing [...] and if by any chance Persimmon should find a conqueror at Doncaster, the upset will prove the wettest of wet blankets. On the contrary, the success of the Royal colours will be the signal for an outburst of loyal enthusiasm that will rival the exciting scene witnessed on Epsom Downs on the occasion of 'The Prince's Derby'.[1199]

The *Mercury* further explained that the Prince's host in Yorkshire, Lord Crewe, was a 'noble sportsman' in his own right – the possessor of several 'useful racers', and a future owner of a Derby winner in the making.

Details of the Visit

It was a couple of days prior to the St Leger that the Prince of Wales arrived on Yorkshire soil:

> The Royal train steamed into Ferrybridge at 6.27 p.m., punctual to the second. Lord Crewe, who had driven up a few minutes before, received his Royal visitor, who shook him cordially by the hand as he descended from the carriage.

> As soon as his Royal Highness stepped on to the carpeted platform, Lord Crewe handed him a wire, which the Prince immediately opened, and as he perused the telegram a smile broke over his face; and the few spectators who had been privileged to go on the platform were pleased to think it contained a good report from Persimmon's trainer. The Prince wore a brown hat, brown frieze overcoat, and brown boots – the garb of a country gentleman. A closed landau, horsed by a magnificent pair of black chargers, awaited the Prince at the foot of the station slopes, in charge of Mr Isles, head coachman to Earl Crewe, and the cover of the carriage having been let down, the Royal visitor drove off with Earl Crewe.[1200]

While making his way through Ferrybridge to Fryston, the Prince repeatedly raised his hat in acknowledgement of the large crowds of bystanders cheerfully lining his route. That evening, Ferrybridge continued to be a hive of activity as large crowds gathered to greet Lord Crewe's house guests for the occasion. One notable absentee was the great racegoer and owner Lord Rosebery. Crewe was, by this time, a regular visitor to Rosebery's palatial residencies, including the Durdans at Epsom and at Dalmeny on the banks of the Firth, and stayed with him at the Rothschild Estate at Mentmore. But he could not 'lure' his Lordship to Fryston, even for the St Leger: 'If I go to Doncaster I shall only do so for a day to a pothouse in the town,' Rosebery replied to one of Crewe's invitations. 'The noise, stench and villainy of the town of Doncaster are essentially a part of the entertainment.'[1201]

The St Leger classic turned out to be the foregone conclusion that virtually everyone had prophesied. Persimmon came to the starter's post as 11-2 on favourite in a field of only seven horses. The Duke of Westminster's colt, Labrador, was second favourite at 6-1, with the rest of the field starting at 66-1. Amidst scenes of excitement and jubilation superseding those witnessed at the Derby, 'Watts settled the colt in fourth place in the early stages, before moving him up to dispute the lead with Labrador entering the straight. He pulled ahead to win easily by one and a half lengths amid great cheering.'[1202]

Now it was time to relax. The following Saturday, a shooting party set out from Fryston Hall at half-past-ten and did not return until six that evening, by which time they had killed almost 3,000 rabbits.[1203]

Among the nine gunners were the Prince, Lord Crewe, Sir H. Keppel and Lord Londonderry. The event proved most controversial due to subsequent reports that 'one of His Royal Highness's shots struck some iron railings, and rebounded with great force into the faces of five of the beaters, who were ranging bushes nearby. Fortunately nothing very serious resulted.'[1204]

According to one local report, 'The Prince was evidently cognisant of the mishap.' Subsequently, however, Edward, acting on the advice of Lord Rosebery, 'officially denied' that the incident had ever occurred.[1205] Either way, the incident was not taken any further. Although one of the beaters was said to have taken the majority of the rebounding pellets in his face, the others, 'glad that they escaped further injury, [spoke] of being shot by the Heir-Apparent to the English throne with a considerable degree of pleasure, and retain[ed] the small pellets taken from various parts of their persons as interesting relics of the incident'.[1206]

Echoing this evidence of Edward's reckless targeting of game, the future king was subsequently alleged to have shot down a protected species of owl as part of a shooting party attending Lord and Lady Londonderry's stately home of Wynyard Park (County Durham) later in September 1896. Lord and Lady Crewe were also present on this occasion. As at Fryston, the king's representatives strongly refuted any such misdemeanour on his part.[1207]

A lasting legacy of the relationship between the Houghton family and the town of Castleford, and of their allegiance to the royal family, was created in 1897 with the opening of Queen's Park, a huge recreational area in the Redhill district of the town. Built on thirteen acres of farmland jointly donated by Crewe and the Bland family of Kippax, the park consisted of elaborate floral gardens, shrubs and native and non-native trees, all rendered accessible by miles of pedestrian walkways. In due course, it would showcase an impressive bandstand, public library, tennis courts and bowling green.[1208] Castleford District Council originally intended to open the park in 1887, in commemoration of Queen Victoria's Golden Jubilee, but delays in planning and development forced a postponement of the project until the Diamond Jubilee of 1897.[1209] Ironically, this consolidation of the link between the Houghton family and Castleford occurred just when Crewe was in the process of disconnecting this century-old relationship.

Chapter Twenty-Six
Transition and Disconnection

Local Evolution and Change

The title of this chapter alludes to two major changes in the late 1890s which were particularly significant in the evolution of the Fryston Hall estate, the local colliery and its associated village. The process of *transition* is evident in three important social adjustments: the shifting power and influence of trade union officials like Ben Pickard and Herbert Smith; the changing ownership and management structures of the mine; and the altering demography of the village, following protracted industrial conflict. These developments are explored in the first three sections of this chapter. The corresponding process of *disconnection* refers to the rupturing of the historical link between the Milnes family and Fryston Hall, consequent on the marriage of Lord Crewe to the daughter of Lord Rosebery in 1899. This marriage and its implications are described in the final section.

The Barnsley By-election, 1897

Crucial to this process of transition are events surrounding the political ruction elsewhere in the West Riding of Yorkshire. In this particular episode, the wrath of YMA leaders like Pickard and Cowey was thoroughly roused when they discovered that the Independent Labour Party (ILP) was putting up a candidate in the Barnsley by-election of 1897. Not content in having recently contested by-elections in East Bradford and Halifax, the ILP was intent on creating a three-cornered fight in the pro-Liberal 'headquarters of the Yorkshire Miners, the capital city of the Miners' Federation of Great Britain'.[1210] Exemplified by the powerful and charismatic Ben Pickard, Secretary of the YMA and President of the MFGB, and also the recently re-elected (in 1895) MP for Normanton:

> The adherence of trade unionists to Liberalism was particularly strong among miners. The leaders of the Yorkshire miners were among the most powerful and vocal of working-class Liberals. The Liberal Party claimed to stand for the right to vote, the right to form trade unions, the advance of popular education, the working man's means of obtaining elective office, and a measure of equality of opportunity which would reward those who practised self-help and weaken the caste-like social distinctions of late-Victorian England.[1211]

Such tenets clearly resonated with a prevailing working-class ideology maintaining that the interests and objectives of manufacturers and workers were not too dissimilar and were in definite contradistinction to the 'parasitic' hereditary land owners who were the undeserving recipients of large mineral royalties.[1212]

It scarcely seemed to matter that the YMA-endorsed Liberal candidate, Joseph Walton, happened to be a Durham-based coal-owner (who belatedly admitted to having sent coal into Yorkshire during the national stoppage of 1893). The rival Tory candidate was James Blyth, a London-based captain of the Oxfordshire Light Infantry, while the ILP representative was Pete Curran, a Fabian Society member and national organiser of the National Union of Gas Workers and General Labourers.

Right from the outset, campaigning focused disproportionately on one particular issue:

> Walton's campaign centred round the legal eight-hour day for miners, the legislative demand which was at the heart of the miners' programme and which was rightly called 'the alpha and omega of the contest'. Walton did not support the legal eight-hour day for all workers, as Curran did, but this lost him no support among the miners' leaders; Pickard termed him as or more radical than he was himself, and said that Walton put 'Labour first, and Liberal after'.[1213]

By contrast, Blyth was totally opposed to the introduction of the eight-hour day.

Among the social measures Walton advocated were the appointment of worker representatives to factory and mines inspectorships and the introduction of state-aided old-age pensions. However, Curran roundly attacked him for not sufficiently endorsing the miners' national programme, which included the nationalisation of the mines, land and railways. In addition to promoting a universal eight-hour day and arguing for nationalisation, Curran further advocated such measures as school meals for needy children and Home Rule for the Irish.[1214]

Taken overall, Curran's agenda was that of 'the trade unionist rather than the socialist'.[1215] This did not deter the YMA leaders – Pickard in particular – from mercilessly castigating Curran's political perspective (and that of the ILP more generally) for being far too abstract and over-idealistic. Pickard accused Curran of working alongside Blyth to deliver a death blow to the YMA and MFGB 'because the knee is not bowed to Independent Labourism'.[1216] Pickard ruthlessly exploited his great personal power and prestige to crush the ILP campaign: 'Even in an age accustomed to vigorous cut and thrust in its political campaigns, the fury of Pickard's onslaught against fellow trade unionists was extraordinary.'[1217] Without directly advocating violence, he recommended that any ILP-ers roaming the district should be treated in the same way as 'non-unionist miners on the pit bank'.[1218]

At the final count, Walton achieved 6,744 (59.7%) of the votes cast, followed by Blythe with 3,454 (30.6%), and Curran with 1,091 (9.7%). It is possible that the size of the ILP vote was enhanced by the fact that many male residents of the local villages of Hemsworth and Kinsley had been involved in a long and bitter stoppage at the nearby South Kirkby mine, which had resulted in some strikers receiving jail sentences for breach of contract.[1219]

One of the most striking characteristics of the by-election was the conspicuous stance adopted by Herbert Smith, who supported Curran in open defiance of the pro-Liberal position adopted by Pickard and other YMA officials. Smith saw in the ILP candidate someone who, unlike his Liberal counterparts, was wholeheartedly and vociferously committed to achieving the eight-hour day, which he regarded as essential to the industrial unity of all the British miners. In so doing, he 'burnt his boats and took his place with those who stood for a separate political party which was pledged to pursue working-class interests irrespective of both great parties'.[1220] Opposing the likes of Pickard in this way 'was not an easy thing to do when such leaders were so popular',[1221] but it was a development carrying huge implications for the reputations of the main protagonists.

Enter Percy Greaves

The strong historical link between Fryston and the city of Wakefield was reinforced in early 1897 by the involvement in the colliery's affairs of the nationally renowned mining engineer Percy Christian Greaves. Greaves's father, John Oldroyd Greaves, was already acting as Lord Crewe's mineral manager and had been responsible for negotiating the Dewsbury Mill Owners' lease of the Fryston Hall Estate. Born on Christmas Day 1868, Greaves had been forced to leave school aged 17 (and to abandon plans to go to Cambridge University) in order to assume the responsibility for running the family business as land agents, mining engineers and colliery proprietors from his seriously ailing father. This included the day-to-day running of the Roundwood colliery in Ossett, Wakefield.

Having obtained a first-class certificate as a colliery manager in July 1892 and successfully overseen the sinking of a new shaft at Roundwood three years earlier, Greaves could boast peerless mining credentials. According to *The Times*:

> comparatively few days passed when he was not to be seen at the pit-head or down the shaft of one of his own collieries or one of those of the many people who readily consulted him as, perhaps, the best known mining engineer in the north.[1222]

Greaves took a pioneering approach to new methods of improving safety and efficiency, and obtained great satisfaction from the fact that no miners at collieries in his portfolio had ever gone out on strike.[1223]

John Oldroyd Greaves had been in the process of establishing Percy and a second son, John Henry (born 1871), as partners in the family business when he found it necessary to contact Lord Crewe on a matter of urgent commercial necessity regarding the future of Fryston colliery. Percy Greaves recalls in his autobiography that:

> The concern was not well managed and, about 1897, they experienced great need of cash. The directors came to my father to ascertain if Lord [Crewe], now Marquis of Crewe,

> would advance £10,000 to keep them going [...] Lord [Crewe] was, at that time, spending week-ends at Fryston, and part of his holidays, too. The company had a capable underground manager, Mr H.G. Soar, whom [Crewe] got to know very well, and they had many conversations of a private nature together.[1224]

Crewe agreed to extend the loan but only on condition that Greaves was accepted as his personal nominee onto the Board of Directors. At Crewe's request, Greaves also took on the position of consulting engineer at Madeley colliery in Staffordshire. According to Greaves, Crewe's loan 'undoubtedly saved the pit', and Greaves was 'practically put in charge' of a pit with which he was fortunate to be so familiar.

This soon proved a daunting task, not least because 'the commercial policy was unsound, and the directors quarrelled among themselves, which made the outlook distinctly unpromising'.[1225] Additionally, coal prices were extremely low and orders hard to obtain. Greaves had succeeded against all odds in securing a yearly contract with a Belgian customer for coal to be supplied via Goole – a contract never completed due to the onset of an eighteen-month strike – the most protracted dispute so far experienced at Fryston.

The Fryston Safety Lamp Dispute (1897-1899)

Among the most 'troubled branches' in the West Riding coalfield of the mid-to-late 1890s were Glasshoughton, Hemsworth and Fryston, where major disputes had occurred in 1895 and 1896.[1226] The local trade union militancy was invariably related to a problematic management style:

> Branches appearing militant may have been those most subject to frequent provocation or perhaps to managerial clumsiness. It is certainly the case that most grievances were defensive, involving protests at changes in working conditions or wages which involved relative disadvantage over what had maintained previously.[1227]

While the majority of colliery owners had accepted – however reluctantly – the legitimacy of the YMA, some continued to regard the union as 'an irritant', refused to participate in orderly negotiations, and sought to replace their workforce with non-unionised labour. At the YMA's annual gala of 1897, Ben Pickard characterised the owners of the Glasshoughton, Fox Holes (Altofts) and Fryston in this vein, endorsing Greaves's contention that the Fryston enterprise was badly managed.

The hostile relations between the Fryston owners and their men came to a head in the summer of 1897, when the company insisted on introducing safety lamps for all workers. The men objected to this innovation on the basis that the lamps not only physically hampered the winning of coal (thus reducing their earning capacity), but also made it more difficult to inspect the roofs. Almost all employers in the district conceded it necessary to pay out compensatory 'lamp money' allowance. The exceptions were the colliery owners at Fryston and Micklefield (near Leeds). As one local newspaper explained:

> The main feature of the dispute relates to the payment of an extra penny a ton upon the introduction into the pit of a safety lamp. Hitherto the Fryston pit was what is known as a mixed light pit, in which candles predominated. The men hold that if they are compelled to use safety lamps it will mean a distinct loss to them. Should their light go out by some means or other, they might be compelled to walk a couple of miles to find the deputy to relight it, instead of which, under the old system, they could light their candle at that of their 'marrow'.[1228]

A four-day strike ensued at Micklefield, where a compromise solution was reached in which the employer agreed to pay for explosives, provide picks, hammers and shovels, and to install an extra lamp for each stall. At Fryston, management was not so conciliatory. They were encouraged to stand firm by the West Yorkshire Coal Owners' Association who feared that any failure to do so might create an unwanted precedent to be followed by other branches. Faced with such resistance, 950 Fryston workers engaged in a strike which lasted from mid-July 1897 to early 1899.

At length, Management inevitably adopted a widespread programme of evictions. The *Yorkshire Evening Post* reported that Fryston seemed to have been deserted: 'At no time does it boast of more than perhaps a thousand inhabitants, but now that over one hundred houses are shut up, there is a graveyard quiet about it.'[1229] As many as fifty employees had been served with eviction notices several days earlier. Some erstwhile Fryston miners had chosen to abandon the strike by re-entering work at neighbouring collieries, like Wheldale.

There had been few signs of violence or misconduct relating to the strike, however. It had not been necessary to draft in extra police and relations between the strikers and colliery management remained extremely cordial:

> Mr Soar, the manager, informed our representative that not the slightest disturbance is apprehended. It is purely a matter resting between the two Associations, and not one in which any ill-feeling exists between himself and the men. Indeed he and the men who remain in the village have from the first been on a most friendly footing. And it is the fact also, that during this unfortunate dispute Mrs Soar has been unremitting in her attentions to the more destitute of the strikers' families. Undoubtedly the greatest part of the men would have been at work long before this had it not been for the tyranny of their Association.[1230]

By the following Christmas, as many as 150 miners were employed at the Fryston coal face: 'But rather than form a break in the ranks of those still out, this had been achieved by recruitment from other counties, which the YMA proved unable to stem.'[1231] It was equally problematic for the union that the owners of the Wheldale and Micklefield collieries had heeded a request by the Fryston Board to dismiss any recent refugees from the Fryston strike. Moreover, 'character certificates' were routinely being employed throughout the district to ensure that strikers would be 'blacked' in their attempts to gain alternative employment, a policy the YMA castigated as 'the most foolish, ill-natured and most provocative of mischief ever known in the county'.[1232]

The YMA also heard reports that Fryston's owners were 'sending men to other counties to obtain blacklegs'.[1233] Intriguingly, local school records show how:

> A large number of the children from Newton [situated across the river from Fryston] had to leave school in the November

> when their parents were turned out of their houses as a consequence of a strike at Fryston Colliery which had been going on several months. A sequel to this was the arrival of the children of strike-breakers from the Black Country who had lately come to reside at Newton and exhibited a deplorable state of ignorance: not one knew their multiplication tables.[1234]

'Indigenous' Fryston miners may well have felt that justice was subsequently served when supplementary records further revealed that these incoming pupils soon left school, 'owing to Mr Bland of Kippax Park refusing any longer to let the cottages belonging to the [Allerton Coal] company'.[1235]

The *Yorkshire Herald* reported that the dispute had been settled the day before, with 'the miners having been met half-way by the masters'.[1236] However, of the 800 miners formerly employed by the colliery, 'only three hundred now remain in the district'. The *Sheffield and Rotherham Independent* subsequently maintained:

> It is satisfying to hear of the settlement of the Fryston (near Pontefract) Colliery dispute on terms favourable to the men [...] after they have been out for a year and a half. The claim of the men was for 1d. per ton for lamps, and the arbitrators, two representing each side, have granted the men's demand. On the other hand the men had conceded some small points, and have now returned to work. But it ought not to have taken 83 weeks to get the contending parties represented at the arbitrators' table.[1237]

Aside from its impact on the demography of the village population and its possible implications for future industrial relations, another legacy of the strike induced a new form of ownership. Even while the stoppage was in progress, Greaves was approached by the Wheldale Board, which was seeking to purchase Fryston coal reserves because their own reserves were approaching exhaustion. Greaves conferred at this point with Mark (soon to become 'Sir' Mark) Oldroyd, Fryston's biggest shareholder. According to Greaves, 'Mr Oldroyd [...] was an able man, but his best friend could not call him a negotiator. He was too dogmatic and had very strong views on certain subjects, particularly on politics and religion.'[1238] Oldroyd had previously been on Fryston's Board of Directors, only to resign his position due to disagreements over matters of policy.[1239] He had also owned shares in Wheldale, which he relinquished in the wake of a serious underground fire. It is possible that such prior affinities influenced his decision to follow Greaves by not merely selling off Fryston's coal reserves, but the colliery *per se*.[1240]

Tying and Untying the Knot

No sooner had the strike ended than an event took place of monumental significance, both for the people of Fryston and the nation. In April 1899, the people of Britain rejoiced over the marriage at Westminster Abbey of Lord Crewe to Margaret Etrenne Hannah (better known as 'Peggy') Primrose, the daughter of Lord Rosebery and the Countess of Rosebery (formerly Hannah de Rothschild). Aside from being of noble birth, Peggy Primrose had posed for a painting as a three-year-old girl by the famous artist Sir John Millais, which became a popular feature at the 1885 Academy Exhibition.[1241]

Pope-Hennessy remarks how it was:

> indeed apparent that a wealthy and personable young widower with great possessions, rare qualities of distinctions and sensibility, and a mental capacity which marked him down for high public office would be a target for many mothers with a daughter to marry.[1242]

Eleven years had elapsed since the death of his first wife, Sibyl, with Crewe remaining an apparently 'unconsoled' widower. It was only now that he, having turned 41, had fallen in love with a young woman who was only 18 years old.

The bride-to-be subsequently recalled her first encounter with her eventual husband:

> It was years after the Viceroyalty in Ireland that we met at a dinner-party at the Asquiths, though I had known him at a distance as a child. We talked at dinner and the rest of the evening, and Margot Asquith said afterwards that she immediately prophesied our marriage.[1243]

The couple announced their engagement at the coming-out ball in honour of Crewe's daughter Annabel, who was only eight months her future stepmother's junior. (Crewe's twin daughters, Celia Hermione and Helen Cynthia, were fifteen.) The marriage was initially opposed by Peggy's grandmother (Lord Rosebery's mother), the Duchess of Cleveland, who regarded the considerable age gap and the existence of three stepdaughters as 'insuperable obstacles to married happiness'.[1244] Crewe's prospective father-in-law had no such qualms to speak of. Indeed:

> Rosebery disagreed with the Duchess. He told the Queen, 'I like him very much and he is all that I could wish for, for I think nothing of the obvious difference in age, as it seems to me that such marriages are often the happiest.' With his blessing, therefore, the wedding went ahead on 20 April, inspiring an outburst of public enthusiasm such as only the late Jubilee could be said to rival.[1245]

It has been maintained that the massive outpouring of public goodwill and euphoria on the day of the marriage was largely a reflection of Lord Rosebery's universal popularity. Well before the service, thousands of sightseers crammed into Parliament Square and into the vicinity of the Abbey. Traffic was completely log-jammed, while young boys climbed trees and lampposts in search of a better view, and street vendors peddled bucket-loads of artificial primroses in tribute to the bride.[1246] Inside the Abbey, the aisle was bordered by banks of lilies and marguerites, the latter in deliberate reference to the bride's first name.[1247]

The arrival of Lord Rosebery and his daughter at half-past one was greeted by 'roar upon roar of cheering'.[1248] The bride was dressed in a gown of snowy white, with the procession of ten bridesmaids decked out in pale primrose.

> As they came slowly on, the bride's hand passed through her father's arm, we could see her hand was slightly trembling and that her lips were firmly set in the effort of self-command. The bridegroom, who with his best man, Lord Chesterfield, had been talking with his friends, made a step towards Lady Margaret as she advanced, and she gave him a quivering little

smile as she reached his side, but her sweet face grew more serious again as the service began.[1249]

The bride and groom both stood tall and erect, she at five-foot nine and he some four inches taller. One observer complimented the groom on account of his bride's 'very fine figure', 'beautiful line of chest and shoulder', and 'gentle face with its large, clear, candid blue eyes'.[1250] Just as impressive was the way she deported herself in public – with a 'quiet dignity' and 'self-possession', which was refreshingly 'in contrast with the loud, gushing self-assertiveness of the majority of modern maidens'.[1251] The groom, meanwhile, was considered relatively slight of build and 'very good looking, with large, expressive grey eyes, and a refined contour of the face, the brow high and broad, the lower part of the face clear cut, without the smallest hint of heaviness'.[1252]

Following the exchange of vows, the newlyweds were immediately congratulated by the principal guest, the Prince of Wales, who formed part of the procession that made its way into the vestry. This party also comprised the clergy, the Duke of Cambridge, the bride, groom and ten bridesmaids. Last of all, came the somewhat ailing Duchess of Cleveland, patiently and touchingly supported by her son, the Earl of Rosebery.[1253] The Prince of Wales's wedding gift took the form of a diamond caduceus with a cabochon emerald at the top and a fine pearl below. The gift was presented in a shagreen case, accompanied by a card bearing the hand-written inscription, 'With very best wishes for dear little Peggy's happiness, from Alexandra and Albert Edward.'

Returning from a honeymoon by the Italian Lakes and in Venice, the Crewes initially settled down in the Berkeley Square residence Crewe had inherited from his uncle. Remaining links with Fryston Hall had now become extremely tenuous. *The Times* reported that 'Lord Crewe has let Fryston for five years to Sir John Austin, as he intends to make Crewe Hall his only country residence in future. Sir John Austin takes the place furnished from Michaelmas, together with the shooting.'[1254]

The wealthy owner of a malting firm, Sir John was born in March 1824 and grew up and was educated in Kippax. His forebears had arrived in Yorkshire from Scotland sometime in the eighteenth century. After a brief period at Owens College in Manchester, Sir John returned to the Castleford area and resided there from 1853 onwards, firstly at Kippax House and then Red Hill House (which was built in 1882), on the edge of Castleford town centre.[1255]

Austin had been elected Liberal Member of Parliament for Osgoldcross in 1886. His first major speech (in March 1887) related to a Bill advocating the tighter prevention and punishment of 'crime' in Ireland where political disorder was pervasive. A devout Catholic, Austin spoke passionately in opposition to the Bill and in favour of a more humanitarian approach to the country's social problems. Austin was re-elected in 1892 and 1895, and created Baronet of Red Hill in 1894. On 10 January 1894, he rose in the House of Commons to demand that compensation be given to the families of two men gunned down in the Featherstone shootings of the previous year, and to the other men who were wounded in the incident.[1256]

In 1899, however, Austin courted controversy by distancing himself from such locally salient matters as a proposed Local Veto (which allowed local authorities to suppress liquor sales in an attempt to deal with drunkenness), by siding with the government in favour of the Boer War, and by opposing his party's pro-Home Rule position. He responded to a vote of censure by the Osgoldcoss Liberal Association by resigning his seat and standing in the resulting by-election as an 'Independent Liberal'. His political stance on the above issues earned him the support of the Osgoldcross Conservative Association, which encouraged its members to lend him their votes. He was able to count on the backing of the mining sections of his constituency, who were conscious of his support for the eight-hour day and of his attitude to the Featherstone shootings. It was therefore no surprise when he was re-elected, having secured 66.8% of the vote.[1257]

By 1901, the Crewes had purchased the seventeen-bedroom Wharncliffe House on Curzon Street in London's Mayfair. The house was renovated and extended into the former stables and laundry room, whereupon it was re-named 'Crewe House'. Pope-Hennessy explains how:

> In this house, as well as Crewe Hall – a much more intractable proposition – Lady Crewe was for the first time able to give

> play to her peculiar gift for arranging houses so that they retain their own strong personality, but seem living, pleasant and happy.[1258]

Her grandmother's misgivings about the marriage were soon proven groundless. 'She [the Duchess of Cleveland] did not know that age does not affect affinity,' Peggy reflected, 'and as for the three step-daughters, they became my dearest friends. They had, besides intelligence, that rarest of qualities, heart – and another – loyalty.'[1259]

Chapter Twenty-Seven
War Horse

The Anglo-Boer War (1899-1902)

The British war against the two South African republics of Transvaal and the Orange Free State (commonly known as the Anglo-Boer War) was officially declared on 11 October 1899. The British objective was to gain ownership and mastery of the country's mineral wealth, whilst the relevant Boer republics were determined to maintain their independence.[1260] The patriotic fervour and 'jingoism' gripping the British nation encouraged expectations that a military walkover was all but inevitable.[1261] The enemy was deemed inferior, both in number, and in military experience and organisation:

> The armed forces of the South African Republic (usually known by its older title of the Transvaal) and Orange Free State, created by the Afrikaner descendants of European colonists, included a few professional corps such as the artillery, and some overseas volunteers or mercenaries, but were largely composed of locally raised units (the word 'Boer' means farmer) between company and battalion size, known as Commandos and acting as mounted riflemen. The Boers 'on commando' were legally obliged to serve, elected their lower-ranking officers, and had their supplies and transport provided at first by their extended families, including Africans known as *agterryers* ('after-riders'). Against these Commando forces, numbering perhaps 65,000 at the war's start, the British Army pitted eventually 256,000 regular soldiers supplemented by 210,000 volunteers.[1262]

Such gross initial optimism was speedily confounded by a series of early setbacks in battle, notably in the second week of December 1899 ('Black Week'), in which the full extent of the 'inadequate [British] combat preparation' was shockingly exposed.[1263] Following the capture of around 600 British troops at Stormberg on 10 December, soldiers under Lord Methuen were heavily defeated at Magersfontein a day later. Worse still, on 15 December, Buller's forces were routed near Ladysmith, where some 1125 casualties were incurred.[1264]

In the following twelve months, British troops under Roberts and then Lord Kitchener progressively undermined Boer resistance through a series of conventional 'set piece' confrontations, which included the capture of the two state capitals of Bloemfontein and Pretoria.[1265] Premature notions of outright victory were rudely dispelled at the end of 1900, however, when there was a resurgence of Boer resistance in the form of guerrilla warfare, involving sudden raids and 'cat and mouse' activities by mobile units of Commandos:

> The British response was to remove sources of food and shelter, implementing a devastating scorched-earth policy. Farms were destroyed, and large numbers of both the Boer and African civilian population were relocated into concentration camps.[1266]

Other controversial British tactics included the transportation of Boer prisoners of war and the execution of Cape Colony rebels.[1267] Though equally protracted, this second phase of the war concluded with the Boer surrender on May 1902.

In this chapter, we track the conduct of the war from the personal perspective of Arthur Henniker – husband of the first Lord Houghton's second daughter, Florence – who, as we shall see, played extremely significant strategic and tactical roles in the conventional and guerrilla warfare phases of the conflict and in the highly controversial trials and execution of senior Boer commanding officers. This intimate account of the conflict is complemented in Chapter 28 by a discussion of corresponding activities undertaken on the 'home front' by Florence Henniker and Thomas Hardy. The chapter will focus on Florence Henniker's attempts to offset or relieve the suffering of horses deployed in the conflict, the wartime correspondence between Hardy and Ms Henniker, and on the extent to which the 'war poems' of Thomas Hardy appear to allude to Arthur Henniker's experience.

Embarcation and Early Campaign

With the exception of annual training manoeuvres staged on such locations as Salisbury Plains, Arthur Henniker's Coldstream Guards had undertaken no advance war preparations. The Coldstreams formed part of an army corps of three divisions, including a cavalry division and eight battalions, which was sent out to join army personnel already based in South Africa (a grand total of approximately 100,000 men). On 20 October, the 2nd Battalion of the guards was inspected by the Duke of Cambridge; and the following day, they marched 'amidst cheering crowds' to Nine Elms Station and took the train to Southampton, from where they set sail aboard the *Gascon*. Each battalion of the Guards consisted of 30 officers (including a medical officer) and 1,080 NCOs and men, with an average service of six years. The ship was crowded, but the journey was generally 'uneventful', with few rough seas to contend with.[1268] The Battalion arrived safely at the Cape on 12 November 1899.

Within two weeks of landing, the 2nd Battalion was propelled into the thick of the action, forming part of Lord Methuen's advance on Kimberley. This operation was obstructed by a force of approximately 3,000 Boers positioned to the east of the town of Belmont. It was imperative that the enemy be dislodged, and soldiers under Henniker's command proved strategic to this task:

> They had not advanced more than a quarter of a mile across the plateau between 'Gun Hill' and 'Table Mountain' before they came upon the first signs of the fighting which, in this quarter of the field, had been going on since dawn. To their left front were numerous groups of men who had lost their different units and were now retreating. On seeing them, Major Henniker made a slight change of direction which, by bringing him immediately in their rear, had the effect of pushing them forward. In this manner he pressed on steadily, until he reached the extreme northern edge of 'Table Mountain'. By that time the Boers, after a gallant defence, had been compelled to abandon the position.[1269]

Henniker's cool-headedness was also in evidence during the next notable instance of hostilities later that November. While marching to the Modder River, the 2nd Battalion came under intense enemy fire.

This was followed by heavy shelling, and Lieutenant H.R. Stopford was one of the ten members of the 2nd to be killed (with 56 more being wounded) that day. The British were in temporary disarray and by nightfall found themselves seriously dispirited and lacking food and water. A proposed night-time attack on the Boer position was rejected due to thirst, hunger and exhaustion. It was at this point that Henniker stood tall:

> Darkness had come on and strange rumours were flying about. On such occasions even highly disciplined troops may degenerate into a mob. But suddenly Major Henniker's well-known word of command rang out, reviving memories of the barrack square at home. 'All Guardsmen to fall in and number from the right.' The effect was instantaneous. The symptoms of unsteadiness disappeared. The men fell in in silence, and were marched about a mile and a half along the railway to the neighbourhood of the Guards Field Hospital, where there was a small well and where Major Henniker decided to bivouac.[1270]

The next day, the British discovered that the Boers had vacated the area overnight and there were no further hostilities. The 2nd Battalion enjoyed a brief respite before next doing battle, during which time Henniker took over as commanding officer from Stopford and was promoted to Lieutenant-Colonel.

It was at Magersfontein on 11 December 1899 that Henniker and his Battalion experienced their first taste of defeat. Lord Methuen had chosen to lay siege to Boer positions at Magersfontein Hill. The enemy had been subjected to a softening up process by the British artillery, and it was up to the Coldstreams to provide support for the Highlanders who had been fighting for the previous four hours. Henniker soon found himself in a horrible dilemma: such was the volume and intensity of the enemy fire that the Coldstreams were instructed not to become too readily engaged; he soon learned, however, that the beleaguered Highlanders were facing total destruction. By way of compromise, Henniker ordered half a company of men under Lieutenant Studd to go off in support of the Highlanders. These soldiers managed to get within sixty yards of the Boer trenches, where they were greeted with a 'feeble' welcoming cheer by a small group of Highlanders. However, there was no question of proceeding any further: 'Lieut. Studd therefore ordered his men to lie down and sent back a written message to Col. Henniker asking for support. Until reinforcements should come up there was nothing to be done.'[1271]

Henniker and his troops had only made a mile's progress when they, too, came across Highlanders who had just been ambushed and were looking harassed and dejected. The cover provided by dense scrubland completely screened the Boers from view, so they could fire without reply. In the meantime, Henniker was urged by his Brigadier to link up with the hapless Highlanders. In order to resolve the situation, he ordered part of the personnel at his disposal to engage Boers in the thick scrub and higher on the ridge: 'This order was duly carried out, with the result that the pressure on the troops covering the battery was greatly relieved.'[1272] The remaining companies could then push on up Magersfontein Hill in line with the Brigadier's objective. A temporary respite occurred when the Boers raised a white flag with the intention of clearing their dead and wounded. Optimism that this might be the prelude to a full withdrawal proved unfounded, however, and it was the British who mounted a tactical retreat. Morale was soon further depleted by similar setbacks at Eastern Cape Colony and Ladysmith.

The British response was to send in Lord Kitchener as supreme commander, which was the prelude to an upturn in British fortunes. It was a measure of Henniker's growing importance within the army that he was invited on 22 February 1900 to dine with Kitchener at a small house on the bank of the local river. Kitchener had stopped off at Klip Kraal while en route to Naauwpoort, and was delighted to convey the very welcome news to Henniker that Piet Cronjé, the Boer General (and commander of the sieges of Kimberley and Mafeking), was currently surrounded by British troops and would find it impossible to escape:

> That that was his situation had been rumoured for some time past, but it was gratifying to have it confirmed from so high a source. Col. Henniker for his part seized the opportunity of drawing his host's attention to the crying need for boots. He recounted how, when the brigade marched off from Modder River, he had been obliged to leave behind sixteen of his men who were absolutely bootless.[1273]

Cronjé's subsequent surrender, combined with the recapture of Ladysmith, revived hopes of a quick end to the war. Such optimism increased in March, when the British surrounded Bloemfontein and forced the Boers to capitulate. Henniker's Guards were also part of the operation to capture Pretoria in early March. The Coldstreams were among those Battalions who, once again, tightly surrounded the enemy, eventually enforcing another unconditional surrender.[1274]

The pace and intensity of warfare slackened for a while in correlation with these British successes. On 24 May, it befell Henniker, as senior Coldstream Officer in South Africa, to send a telegram to Queen Victoria, congratulating her on her birthday. The Colonel incurred an injury while losing his footing in battle several weeks later, during an otherwise successful attempt to rid Boers from a chain of hills skirting part of Pretoria. He was sufficiently recovered by 18 July to be able to participate in an 'Eton rules' football match between officers of the 1st and 2nd Battalions. One month later, Henniker's was one of a pair of Battalions brought in to restore local unrest and quell intermittent sniper fire in the recently-taken village of Waterval Onder.

Henniker received a similar assignment the following November, when, after a month's stay in Pretoria, he moved on to Potchefstroom, seventy miles south-west of Johannesburg. Shortly after arriving, he was having dinner with other senior officers when they suddenly came under fire by 'hostile bands' which had recently been operating in the vicinity. Following house-to-house searches to emphasise the British resolve, Henniker acted as press-censor within a system of benevolent despotism used to 'police' the local population in a firm but not overly-coercive manner.[1275]

As the year drew to a close, Henniker and his Battalion moved south to Bloemfontein, where he had another meeting with Lord Kitchener, whom he described as 'in good form and full of fight'.[1276] Shortly after, he travelled on with his troops to Orange River Station – which, 'After many months of nearly uninterrupted bivouacking [...] was almost a return to civilisation.'[1277] The emphasis henceforward was on pursuing the mobile commando units currently running amok.

Guerilla Warfare

The guerrilla phase of the war commenced in mid-December 1900, when some 1,000 Commandos led by the Boer general and future Prime Minister of the Union of South Africa, J.B.M. Hertzog, and a second Commando unit of 700 men under the leadership of P.H. Kritzinger, made separate crossings of the Orange River and invaded the northern Cape Colony. Among other notable Commando leaders involved in these missions were Wynand Malan, Gideon Scheepers, J.C. Lötter and Willem D Fouché, all of whom would gain prominence in what remained of the campaign.[1278]

The principal objectives of the Boer commandos were to disrupt the enemy lines of communication by blowing up railway lines and wrecking trains, to encourage Cape Colonials to join their cause, and to burn down the houses of any Afrikaners thought to have collaborated with the enemy.[1279] In the process, 'The commandos harassed the British troops constantly, capturing their trains and wagon convoys, taking what they needed – horses, weapons, ammunition, blankets, saddlebags, riding breeches, boots and hats – and destroying the rest.'[1280]

In his eagerness to quell these activities and suppress any spreading disaffection, Kitchener declared a state of martial law and made arrangements for the pursuit and capture of the raiding parties. He therefore established two mobile columns of guards along the Orange River under Lieutenant-Colonels Crabbe and Henniker. Henniker thus found himself located in De Aar, where he had 815 men drawn from the 1st and 2nd Coldstream Guards under his command. These were later substituted by 850 Victorian Imperial Riflemen (VIR).[1281]

Henniker's activities in the early weeks of this second phase involved checking Hertzog's progress by blocking the Roggeveld Mountain passes in the vicinity of Matjiesfontein. This objective was more easily achieved than had been anticipated. Indeed:

> At Matjesfontein itself Col. Henniker found, once his men had settled down in their camps, that he had so much free time that he could play lawn-tennis and indulge in a little rat-hunting. The business which gave him the most trouble was the administration of martial law, which by the middle of January [1901] was proclaimed over the whole colony with the

> exception of the ports. Cases of open rebellion were rare, for only a few of the Karroo farmers or their sons actually joined the invaders, but instances of disloyal conduct, especially in the matter of supplying the enemy with information, were very numerous.[1282]

It was here, on the 23 January 1901, that news arrived of Queen Victoria's death. That evening, Henniker led a parade in her honour: 'After resting on their arms reversed while the drums played the "Dead March", the men saluted and marched off in slow time with arms reversed.'[1283]

Henniker's guards were put back on alert when, with most British eyes focused on Hertzog, De Wet entered the fray. From February 1901, Kitchener made it a strategic priority to keep De Wet out of the Cape Colony. Later that month, Henniker joined Crabbe in providing support for Plumer, who was giving chase to De Wet at Houtkraal. On 23 February, just as the British supplies of food and water were reaching the point of exhaustion, De Wet's rearguard was sighted. It soon became apparent that De Wet's men were even more exhausted and lacked the stomach for a fight. Henniker's mounted troops swept up scores of enemy soldiers all too willing to surrender and easily dispersed the rest.

It was fair to say that the 'expulsion' of Hertzog and De Wet before the end of February had 'averted a great peril and banished any immediate fear of a general rebellion in Cape Colony';[1284] but it was equally true that the likes of Kritzinger and other supremely able junior commanders including Scheepers, Fouché and Malan remained dedicated to the creation of military mayhem.[1285] Henniker's attempts to track down Commando units took him initially to Grahamstown and Tweefontein, where, in mid-March, his advanced troops came into headlong collision with a strong force of Boers under the leadership of Lötter. Henniker's mounted troops intercepted the enemy but eventually lost them after a long but fruitless pursuit.[1286]

Following a brief period of inaction, Henniker and his command headed off in April for Aberdeen, where he joined up with Colonel Scobell with the intention of tracking down Malan and Scheepers. Henniker's most sustained engagement of the second phase got underway at dawn on 22 April. Having reached their anticipated resting place in the hills skirting Middelwater, his troops were subjected to a sudden outburst of fire by a well-established contingent of 200 Boers led by Malan. When Henniker led a counter-attack with the backing of heavy gunfire, the Boers hastily retreated, bringing an end to the matter.[1287] This was at the height of the South African winter. Thereafter, the extreme cold and precipitous terrain made it difficult for Henniker's troops – particularly the Australians, who were unaccustomed to these levels of frost and snow. In the meantime, Malan and Scheepers 'showed great resourcefulness, and aided, without doubt, by the "amiable disloyalty" of the inhabitants, dodged their pursuers with complete success'.[1288] Thus, by 2 May, Malan had relocated to the north-west, while Scheepers had moved in the opposite direction to the south-east.

Acting on orders to pursue and capture Scheepers, Henniker and his followers marched on Thorngrove, where Scheepers was said to be occupying a strong strategic position on the Fish River. On the morning of 8 May, Henniker began moving his guns into position, only to find that Scheepers was already retreating. After two consecutive days of hard fighting, Scheepers managed to escape from a perilous situation under the cover of 'a terrific snowstorm which raged through the night of the 13th May'.[1289] The following day, Henniker's VIR repeatedly harried Scheepers into taking up fresh positions. Eventually, however, the Boers broke out with the intention of fleeing to the south. The VIR set off in pursuit. Meanwhile, Major Crawley's Yeomanry were given orders to circle round to Marais siding, with the intention of intercepting the enemy in flight.

> But here again Henniker's hopes were disappointed. Scheepers not only eluded the trap which had been laid for him, but, crossing the railway three miles to the south of Marais siding, held up and burnt a passenger train. From the railway he headed for the north-west, and disappeared, about the 23rd May, amidst the vastness of the Camdedoo Mountains. This brought the operations to a close.[1290]

While Scheepers's numerical strength was gradually being depleted in consequence of the Commandos' 'hair-breadth escapes' from

Henniker and his men, the enemy had the good fortune to be replenished by seventy new recruits who joined up when their own commander had been shot dead in battle.[1291] Henceforward, Scheepers would conform to a 'policy of mischief rather than one of open aggression'. Henniker, meanwhile, was ordered to take his column to Graaff-Reinet, where, 'being sorely in need of rest', he was to oversee the Graaff-Reinet and Aberdeen districts.[1292] His dealings with Scheepers and Kritzinger were to enter an even more controversial phase.

Trials and Executions

Far from being a quiet backwater in which to enjoy a peaceful respite from the war, Henniker's new command introduced him to arguably greater levels of stress and controversy. Graaff-Reinet was the location of numerous high-profile trials of rebel leaders, of which those of Lötter and Scheepers (who were two of eight men to be sentenced to death) received the most publicity.[1293]

Of these two trials, the court martial and execution of Commandant Johannes Lötter was by far the least contentious. He and his notoriously brutal and undisciplined Commando unit were taken captive at Paardefontein in 1901. Among the charges brought against him were those of treason, the murder of defenceless scouts, the flogging of a pair of Afrikaners, and the destruction of a railway line. The level of proof against him was too compelling to resist. He was duly executed in Middelburg on 12 October 1901.[1294]

The second of these executions, that of the 'young, handsome, dashing' Gideon Jacobus Scheepers on 18 January 1902, 'most stirred the hearts of men and women around the world'.[1295] Scheepers had been taken prisoner the day of Lötter's execution. In the preceding months, Scheepers had been defying Kritzinger's orders not to burn farm dwellings (which was setting potentially pro-British Afrikaners permanently against them) by setting farmhouses alight in places like Aberdeen. Scheepers was suddenly stricken with fever and therefore could not ride. On 10 October, he informed his men that he was too sick to continue in their company and they reluctantly departed without him. Two days later, he was discovered in his sickbed at a farmhouse in Kopjeskraal, where he surrendered to officers of the

10th Hussars and was taken immediately to Graaff-Reinet.[1296] The involvement of Arthur Henniker became crucial at this point.

Afrikaner folklore maintains that, just prior to his capture, Scheepers 'sent word' to Colonel Henniker, informing him 'that he was coming into town and he would hang Henniker from the nearest telegraph pole'.[1297] Ironically, it fell upon Henniker to chair a three-man jury in a court martial brought to consider the various charges (including seven allegations of murder, one of attempted murder, one of ill-treating prisoners, three of flogging, one of destroying railways, one of train-wrecking, and numerous cases of arson) levelled against Scheepers. Asked at the trial if he objected to the presence of any of the officers before him, Scheepers replied: 'No, not one, but the whole court. I am a prisoner of war and should be treated as such.'[1298]

In the course of conducting his own defence, Scheepers contended that some of the men had been shot legitimately, having been exposed as spies in the course of court martial. He further maintained that the destruction of railways, the wrecking of trains and the burning of farms had been carried out in accordance with the instructions of superior officers, and vehemently refuted the accusation that he had ill-treated his prisoners.[1299] A written declaration to this effect was sent by De Wet to Lord Kitchener, to which Kitchener replied that individual Boer officers must take responsibility for their own actions. Scheepers was found guilty of all but one of the charges and sentenced to death. The sentence was confirmed by Lord Kitchener two weeks later and set for 18 January, 1902.[1300]

On 17 January, Scheepers was taken to Church Square where most of the townsfolk of Graaff-Reinet had assembled:

> There Colonel Arthur Henniker-Major read the death sentence and announced that Kitchener had confirmed it. It was reported that Colonel Henniker-Major's whole body trembled as he read and that it almost seemed as if he rather than the condemned man would collapse.[1301]

Scheepers was then taken to a secret location out of town, where he was tied to a chair and shot. Ivie H. Allan – a British-born resident of Graaff-Reinet credited with taking an iconic photograph of Scheepers slumped dead in his chair – professes to have personally witnessed the execution. According to Allan's version, Scheepers wanted to be shot standing up but was bound instead to a chair and, therefore, 'not allowed to die as a soldier.'[1302] Following his execution, Scheepers's body and the broken up chair were lowered on a blanket into a waiting grave and sprinkled all over with quick lime.[1303]

As Farwell points out, 'Scheepers was dead and buried, and the British had done their best to make certain there would be neither relics nor shrine.'[1304] But scarcely a week after Scheepers's execution, Commandant Kritzinger was badly wounded in the course of a Commando mission and taken prisoner by crew members of an armoured train who had found him lying wounded by the track. The Boer leader was initially taken to Naauwpoort.

> In a short time, however, he was transferred to the hospital at Graaff-Reinet, and here both Col. Henniker and Major Shute paid him frequent visits. He had always been regarded as a worthy adversary and, in addition, on the night of his capture, he was known to have returned to assist some of his wounded followers and generally to have displayed courage of a high order. It was consequently, with deep regret that both these officers learnt he had been sent to Graaff-Reinet, because it was the intention at headquarters to prefer charges against him similar to those which had been brought against Scheepers.[1305]

The political climate of opinion had now shifted in Kritzinger's favour. Scheepers's execution had raised concern about the way that this and other court martials appeared to have been conducted. Heart-rending accounts of the execution were repeated in parliament and Kitchener was harried into accounting for the fact that the presiding officers – a lieutenant-colonel (i.e. Henniker), a captain and a subaltern – were not all of equal or superior rank to the accused. Notwithstanding Henniker's reassurance (as officer conducting the execution) that 'Scheepers was composed, he did not need help to walk to the chair and everything was done quickly', pressure was being exerted on Kitchener to adopt a softer attitude towards the trial of Kritzinger:

> The British government was now very cool towards the idea of inflicting the death penalty and Kitchener was informed that

> 'if an acquittal results, no harm will be done'. Unsurprisingly, perhaps, Kritzinger was subsequently acquitted.[1306]

There is no doubt that Arthur Henniker would have been delighted with this outcome. The emotion he exhibited in announcing Scheepers's execution and the cordiality he expressed towards the captive Kritzinger underline the type of affection and respect for their Boer counterparts that was commonplace among the British officer class.

The South African enemy was felt to epitomise a noble code of life that was regrettably disappearing with the onset of the industrial revolution.[1307] As one unnamed fellow-officer, who professed to know Henniker 'intimately' pointed out, he 'was of a most kindly disposition'.[1308] Thus, when Kritzinger visited London once the war was over, he was invited to have lunch with Henniker and other British Army officers at Henniker's home on Stratford Place, off Oxford Street, even though the Boer had supposedly 'only [been] thought fit for execution a few months before'.[1309]

Chapter Twenty-Eight
The Home Front

The Plight of Horses in the War

The South African War exacted a heavy toll on the animals involved: on the British side alone, 326,073 horses and 51,399 mules perished in the conflict – representing 66.88% and 35.37% respectively of the livestock deployed, 'proportionally the most devastating waste of horseflesh in military history up until that time'.[1310] Yet, only 163 of these animals died in battle of bullet wounds, and another three of shellfire. The vast majority were the victims of disease, neglect, lack of food, or, failing that, sheer exhaustion.[1311]

Preliminary problems were caused by poor transport conditions. Once on board ship, horses were required to stand for weeks at a time in tight, poorly ventilated stalls. There was inadequate space for stretching out or lying down, or for their handlers to effectively muck out the 'decaying dung and excoriating urine'.[1312] Not surprisingly, some 13,144 (3.7%) of the 352,353 horses sent to South Africa failed to survive the arduous journey:

> It was not so much the voyage that killed them but its aftermath: its debilitating effects coupled with the absence of an acclimatization period. In the absence of acclimatization depots, horses would arrive incapacitated – dehydrated, malnourished, and their immune systems severely compromised – and instead of having the weeks or months needed to revive, they would be transported to the front almost at once. There were insufficient supplies, which entrenched constant low-level malnutrition.[1313]

Prior ignorance of local conditions (e.g. ambient temperature and sources of disease) was a costly related factor. Horses arriving from England in their December winter coats immediately found the intense South African heat insufferable.[1314] Local grasslands were a notorious source of biliary or tick-bite fever, caused by a parasite that gets into the red blood cells, picked up from tick bites when the animals were grazing. This was not the only concern. Mange, which is highly contagious, affected over 20,000 horses, while 'strangles' (a disease of the respiratory system), equine influenza and pneumonia all proliferated among animals rendered even more vulnerable by the stress of transportation and the poor conditions in which they were kept.[1315]

Vulnerability to disease was further compounded by the inhumane workloads demanded of such creatures. Chronically underfed cavalry horses already exhausted from carrying up to 300 pounds of baggage across endless rough terrain, and with their backs rubbed raw by unsuitable saddles that no longer fitted their shrinking frames, were suddenly required to break into a charge.[1316] By contrast, the Boers tended to ride much smaller ponies that were already accustomed to long hunting expeditions and herding cattle. These were hardier than their British counterparts, capable of surviving on eight pounds of grain per day and a modicum of grazing.[1317]

The British Army faced a huge crisis from October 1899, when both the horse population of South Africa and the cereal and grassland required to nourish them were inadequate to sustain the war effort. By 6 November, the standard horse ration had been reduced to twelve pounds of oats a day (dropping down to eight when grazing was available). Worse was to follow: in the four days after the relief of Kimberley, French's cavalry horses received nothing at all to eat. On the fifth day, they received five pounds of grain, but only one pound after that. It took several weeks before their already inadequate threshold of eight pounds per day was restored.[1318]

By mid-1900, horses were being exported to South Africa from such faraway places as Hungary, Argentina, India and Australia. These, too, were given no time to acclimatise. Exposed to the same problems endured by the British horses, they were thrust into 'a vicious form of natural selection', in which injured or ailing animals were instantly put down when they might easily have recovered if given the proper treatment. The veterinary and remount services were numerically inadequate for the workload involved,[1319] even if the British Army Veterinary Department (AVD) had been sufficiently experienced, well-trained or specialised in equine care to do a competent job in the first place. Among the catastrophic decisions they made was the decision to pen contagiously diseased horses together such that widespread epidemics soon arrived.[1320]

Attempts to Relieve the Suffering

There is no doubt that Thomas Hardy and Arthur and Florence Henniker were passionately concerned for the wellbeing of the horses and mules deployed in South Africa. Florence Henniker, in particular, strove persistently throughout the war to alleviate the suffering of these animals. The Hennikers could point to a long family tradition of practical intervention in promotion of animal welfare – most notably in 1875 when Arthur Henniker's brother presented a bill to the British Parliament calling for the regulation of animal experiments, rather than simply giving scientists carte blanche to operate as they saw fit.[1321] In keeping with such tradition, Arthur and Florence Henniker did their utmost to relieve the suffering and prolong the lives of the thousands of horses involved in the South African War.[1322] There is also some evidence to suggest that Thomas Hardy was supportive (both in principle and practice) of Florence Henniker's work on behalf of the animals destined for the battlefields.[1323]

Sylvia draws on a collection of unpublished letters between Florence Henniker and representatives of the British government (housed as part of the Henniker family archive in the Suffolk County Record Office in Ipswich), which describe her part in a concerted RSPCA campaign for the introduction of a special service corps to care for or destroy sick and wounded horses in the war. Henniker's letters were primarily written during the winter of 1899-1900. Her efforts were designed to explain the plight of the horses to members of the War Office and to appeal for urgent action to be undertaken on their behalf. She also corresponded with her fellow RSPCA member Laurence Pike, who used letters to *The Times* to bring greater public pressure to bear with the ultimate aim of securing an amendment to the Geneva Convention, such that members of the special corps would be protected from enemy fire while attending to wounded animals. Their letters show that Henniker and Pike liaised very closely on matters of strategy.

Hardy's role in this process was far from negligible. It was he who first introduced Pike (a Dorset friend and neighbour) to Henniker. Hardy and Henniker's mutual concern for the plight of the horses was evident in a letter dated 11 October 1899, in which Hardy talks of the 'suffering', 'hardship' and 'exposure' being experienced by the animals. It hardly seems coincidental that Henniker's diplomatic efforts coincided with the publication in newspapers and periodicals of the verses by Hardy that were subsequently collected in the 'War Poems' section of his 1901 book *Poems of the Past and the Present*.[1324] There has been much speculation surrounding one of Hardy's most famous poems, 'Horses Abroad', that his commitment to the animals' cause was perhaps more circumspect than Florence Henniker's.

As Sylvia makes clear, it is difficult to escape the impression that the poem is anything but a reference to the Boer War:

> They are horses of war,
> And are going to where there is fighting afar;
> But they gaze through their eyeholes unwitting they are,
> And that in some wilderness, gaunt and ghast,
> Their bones will bleach ere a year has passed,
> And the item be as 'war-waste' classed. –
> And when the band booms, and the folk say 'Goodbye!'
> And the shore slides astern, they appear wrenched awry
> From the scheme Nature planned for them, – wondering why.[1325]

Sylvia is also personally convinced that the poem was written in the course of the war. If that was the case, it becomes pertinent to ask why Hardy delayed its publication until some two decades later in 1925. While undoubtedly regretting the 'sufferings of the horses in war', he was nonetheless keen to get the campaign over and done with. Sylvia is therefore obliged to ask, 'Was Hardy, then, ambivalent enough about the sacrifice of animal life in the war effort to suppress "Horses Abroad"?'[1326]

Henniker's efforts were complemented by her husband's, whose direct experience of animal suffering in the war instilled in him a resolve to do something practical to relieve their plight, which was realised in his creation of a horse sanctuary during his spell at Graaff-Reinet:

> It was due to the foresight of Colonel Henniker in starting a rest camp that thousands of horses and mules were saved from death on the veldt. He started this camp soon after he was appointed to command at Graaff-Reinet, and all sick and exhausted animals were taken over from columns that passed through or near Graaff-Reinet, and were looked after until fit for re-issue. I believe that the number of issues from this rest camp was about 3000 animals in about twelve months. The total cost of the camp was the forage bill, and the wages of one white superintendent and about ten natives.[1327]

The continuation of immense animal suffering and sacrifice indicates that Florence Henniker's efforts were unsuccessful in altering attitudes and conduct during the Anglo-Boer War. However, it is nonetheless plausible that:

> Thanks in part to Henniker's efforts, the devastating loss of horses in the Boer War led to reforms that greatly reduced the loss in World War I, though she has never been recognized for it. Hilda Kean claims that it was Ernest Bell and H. Baille-Weaver, with their 1912 publication of the pamphlet, *Horses in Warfare*, who 'called for the extension of the Geneva Convention to horses', but, of course, the call went out much earlier than that, the proof of which lies in the Henniker family archive.[1328]

Hardy's War Poetry and Letters

Thomas Hardy's small collection of poems on the South African conflict is habitually taken as indicative of his 'lifelong abhorrence of war'. King and Morgan nonetheless maintain that such characterisation of this work not only represents an oversimplification of the poems' inherent meanings, but also under-emphasises contradictions in his attitudes to conflict of this nature:[1329]

> He did condemn war as futile, stupid, and barbaric, but he was never simply or clearly the pacifist sometimes encountered in Hardy criticism. War always both intrigued and revolted him, and he reluctantly admitted that it was sometimes a practical necessity. And though he condemned the Boer war in the abstract, he did not directly oppose it.[1330]

Hardy's relationship with Florence Henniker (and, less directly, with her husband, Arthur) adds an important dimension to this debate: the letters passing between them (from the immediate prelude of the conflict to its aftermath) not only highlight the enduring ambivalence of Hardy's moral and intellectual perspectives on the war, but also emphasise how his oppositional attitude may have been attenuated by his relationship with the Hennikers.

The earliest of Hardy's 'war letters' to Florence Henniker certainly demonstrate that he regarded resorting to war as a deplorably outdated course of action. A letter dated 17 September 1899 considered it to be 'a justification of the extremest pessimism that at the end of the 19th cent[ur]y we settle an argument by the sword, just as they w[oul]d have done in the 19th cent[ur]y B.C.'[1331]

This theme was put more concretely in Hardy's letter of 11 October: 'I constantly deplore the fact that "civilized" nations have not learnt some more excellent and apostolic way of settling disputes than the old and barbarous one, after all these centuries.'[1332]

Signs of the underlying contradictions referred to by King and Morgan are already evident, however, as Hardy also admits that 'few persons are more martial' than himself, or apt to show more relish for the opportunity to write about war in one way or another.[1333]

Hardy was certainly quick out of the trap once the war was underway. He cycled all the way to Southampton on Friday 20 October, with the intention of personally witnessing the departure of the troops to South Africa. He later said that he would have preferred to convey his best wishes to Arthur Henniker face-to-face; but on discovering that the Coldstreams were not due to depart until the following day, Hardy 'roused up [his nephew] Gordon Gifford at an early hour, made him some fortifying cocoa, and sent him off on his bicycle to observe the scene and deliver the letter to Major Henniker by hand'.[1334] The letter was exceedingly warm and complimentary, with Hardy referring to Henniker as 'the most perfect type of the practical soldier' that he knew, and wishing him 'good fortune' and a 'speedy return'.[1335]

A mere four days later, Hardy's poem 'Departure' – later re-titled 'Embarcation (Southampton Docks: October 1899)' – appeared in the *Daily Chronicle* of 25 October.

Yellow as autumn leaves, alive as spring;
And as each host draws out upon the sea
Beyond which lies the tragical To-be,
None dubious of the cause, none murmuring,

Wives, sisters, parents, wave white hands and smile,
As if they knew not that they weep the while.[1336]

It is at this point that some of the problems and dilemmas resulting from Hardy's relationship with the Hennikers emerge. It was entirely predictable that, given Hardy's oppositional stance, his poetry should leave no space for the celebration of military bravery and heroism.[1337] It could scarcely have been anticipated, though, that, 'on the Boer War's causes, its key protagonists, its pivotal moments, its battle scenes, and even its outcome, his poetry stays silent [...] [it] concerns itself almost exclusively with departures, burials, returns, and the women left behind'.[1338] The main difficulty confronting Hardy was constantly having to contend with the fact that, as long as he remained in contact with Florence Henniker – 'a woman condemned to endure the emotional complexities of what he simplistically imagines',[1339] and someone whose husband is away risking his life on the battlefield – his commentaries ran the risk of being considered trite, inauthentic or, at worst, plainly disrespectful.

One prominent device Hardy uses to resolve this dilemma is the persistent assertion of his 'credentials as witness'.[1340] Tellingly, the first three poems in the 'War Poems' section of the *Poems of the Past and Present* anthology of 1901 are all subtitled, 'Southampton Docks: October 1899'; a fourth, 'The Going of the Battery', is dated 2 November 1899, as if to stamp it with a hallmark of authenticity. Kendall suggests that, in emphasising the 'eye-witness' nature of his poetry, Hardy was hoping to avoid any charges of exploiting other people's grief.[1341]

The tension between Hardy's value system and his sensitivity to Florence Henniker's feelings and beliefs becomes most salient in his direct references to her husband. His letters exhibit an apparently genuine interest in Major Henniker's activities and well-being, exemplified by the following reference to his participation in the Battle of Belmont:

> It was with the keenest interest and anxiety as you will readily imagine, that I opened the *Times* this morning and read that the Coldstreams had been engaged with the Boers at Belmont. They are pushing on more rapidly than the Natal force, don't you think? Did you know any of the wounded?[1342]

Subsequent correspondence extends into a minor show of sympathy for the major, but stops short of a resounding endorsement of his role: 'There seems soon a likelihood of a turn of affairs in S. Africa. Have you heard lately from Major H[ennike]r? Is his health good? What a stress it must have been to stand fire for 12 hours and more!'[1343]

Hardy later entered into more critical discussion of British war activities. In a letter dated 25 February 1900, he speaks disapprovingly of the British defeat of Boers under the command of Piet Cronjé: 'How horrible it all is: they say that his wife and other women are in that river-bed with his unfortunate army: and the mangled animals too, must have terror superadded to their physical sufferings.'[1344]

Hardy then explains to Henniker that he follows war with the same sort of regard as he would a game of chess. His primary personal interest is for the deeper humanitarian issues. As if in deference to his friend, he adds the crucial disclaimer that 'I do not, of course, refer to this particular war, and the precise shade of blame or otherwise which attaches to us'. Finally, he asks with almost matter-of-fact politeness: 'I wonder if you have had a cablegram from Major Henniker lately? He must be in Kimberley by this time, must he not? I wonder if he suffers much from the heat. But I think he likes hot weather.'[1345]

The clearest expression of Hardy's ambivalence is contained in his letter dated 22 October 1900, where his 'interest' in Major Henniker, concern for 'humanitarian' issues (but not for acts of heroism), and sensitivity to Florence Henniker's emotional involvement in the war are uncomfortably juxtaposed:

> I should imagine that he is nearly tired of the campaign by this time, and all of them. It is sad, or not, as you look at it, to think that 40,000 will have found their rest there. Could we ask them if they wish to wake up again, would they say Yes, do you think?
>
> However, I was not meaning to write like that, and you must forgive me. What have you yourself been doing?[1346]

Finding himself hampered by an incapacity to praise Arthur Henniker's military exploits and heroism, Hardy obliquely signals his respect for the major's role in the war, not only by sending him a goodwill letter prior to his departure, but also by requesting a recent photograph of him ('In uniform preferred; and the *latest*') from his wife. 'I can't possibly get it signed, of course, now,' laments Hardy, 'but unsigned will do. He is going to be framed with the other celebrities.'[1347]

With the war finally over, Hardy was not so reluctant to show his affection and respect for Colonel Henniker:

> I saw in the papers a few days ago that Col. Henniker had sailed for home, and was so glad to think that he had at last reached that stage of his long campaign of three years, without being, as I suppose and hope, much the worse for it. It will be a great pleasure to see him again when I come to London; and also to see you, for I have thought of you since the death of Lady Fitzgerald more than you may suppose from my silence. I hope you are as well as we can be in this sorry world.[1348]

In a subsequent letter, dated 28 November 1902, Hardy applauded the fact that the couple's Suffolk parishioners had accorded the Colonel the warmest of homecoming receptions. It was, Hardy ventured to suggest, 'not more than he deserved', but only according to 'what a long service over there his has been', and not on the basis of his repeated acts of bravery or heroism.[1349]

Chapter Twenty-Nine
Cataclysm: The Wheldale-Fryston Strike (1902-04)

The Context of the Strike

One major economic effect of the Boer War was to stimulate a temporary increase in the market price of coal. Unfortunately, it also created a misplaced sense of optimism among British miners. Whilst the MFGB had managed to secure a 10% advance on wages in early 1901, a steep drop in the price of coal within the next twelve months led the coal owners to demand an equivalent across-the-board reduction of miners' wages.[1350] The national Conciliation Board broadly endorsed this application by recommending a 5% reduction in June 1902, followed by a further 5% in August.[1351] The MFGB Executive's recommendation that the men accept this offer was rejected by all districts of the union. This provoked a ruling by the independent Chairman (a former Conservative Chancellor of the Duchy of Lancaster) that sanctioned the full wages reduction.[1352] This was a further blow to the credibility and popularity of the MFGB national leadership.

Taylor argues that Herbert Smith and Ben Pickard were likeminded in their passionate commitment to using the unity and solidarity of union members as the surest means of improving the miners' lot.[1353] Such commitment 'inclined both men towards an aggressive, often authoritarian, leadership style in which they identified their preferences with the interests of the union and its members';[1354] but there is no doubt that they differed significantly in their willingness to sanction industrial opposition, and in the extent to which they now commanded the confidence and support of their members.

Pickard's previously uncontested authority over the rank-and-file was beginning to unravel.[1355] One contributing factor to this was the vocal attitude of a 'small nucleus' of lodges in the West Riding (e.g. Rothwell, Middleton, Glasshoughton and Hemsworth), which were generally critical of the MFGB leadership. In such places, the influence of young ILP advocates like Will Lunn at Rothwell and Middleton, and (more significantly for our purposes) Herbert Smith at Glasshoughton, was paramount. Howell asserts that such figures were not only adept at shaping local industrial and political perspectives, but also able to rely on strong local support and loyalty.[1356]

This growing sense of rank-and-file alienation became manifest in an outbreak of 'strike mania' in Yorkshire at the turn of the century,[1357] to which Pickard's attitude was highly circumspect:

> While not suggesting that any of these were necessarily avoidable, Pickard urged caution and care so that strikes only occur 'when it becomes a matter of what might be called life or death in regard to the members of the branches'.[1358]

Herbert Smith followed the more nuanced approach of encouraging or endorsing industrial action wherever the depreciation of miners' wages or conditions was at issue, while urging restraint whenever trade union unity and solidarity risked being undermined. In 1901, for example, Smith argued tenaciously alongside William Lincoln, his fellow YMA representative on the Joint Committee, for strikers at the Raventhorpe colliery to be paid extra for each ton of coal due to the thinness of local seams. Under their stewardship the dispute was referred to arbitration, which found in favour of the men. The coal owner remained steadfastly uncooperative. Egged on and financially supported by the West Yorkshire Coal Owners' Association, he brought in new machinery, recruited non-union labour, and re-employed those strikers willing to accept the former price lists in breaking the two-year strike.[1359]

An even more interventionist approach was evident in Smith's handling of a coalfield-wide 'pit lads' strike in 1902, in opposition to a planned 10% reduction in their wages. A co-ordinated series of stoppages were called that July by 'lads' (the term conventionally applied to trainee miners recently entering the industry) at Glasshoughton, Ackton Hall, Wheldale, Fryston, and other Yorkshire mines. The knock-on effect was that 6,000 other miners in Castleford and Pontefract alone (and an estimated 15,000 across the whole county) could not continue working.[1360] Mindful of the possibility of disunity, Smith addressed a long meeting of the lads at the Castleford Salvation Army Barracks on 25 July, and eventually persuaded them to return to work by promising that the union would investigate and resolve all 'errors complained of'.[1361]

By now, an altogether higher-profile dispute was monopolising the MFGB's attention. Strike action was being undertaken by workers at the Cadeby and Denaby collieries in South Yorkshire in support of a demand for extra payments for having to remove 'bag muck' from the coal they were producing:

> 'Bag muck' was an uneven layer of rock running through the Barnsley Bed seam of coal. When it was soft and thin it was unimportant, but when it was hard to get down and relatively thick it cost the collier time and effort. At the time of the 'bag muck' strike the issue was said to concern only about 100 men out of a total labour force of 2,700, but the miners took a strong view of the question and thought they should get extra payment for getting it down.[1362]

Both pits had balloted for strike action in September 1901, but the union had not achieved the necessary two-thirds majority. The owners adopted the provocative stance of not only employing additional workers to remove the bag dirt, but paying them out of deductions from the existing workers' wages. Following a failed attempt by the union to sue the company over this action, a further strike ballot was undertaken in July 1902 that, this time, easily achieved the requisite majority in favour.

A bitter and protracted strike ensued in which the owners employed strikebreakers (brought in from Staffordshire) and evicted miners and their families from company-owned properties to break the strikers' resolve. Neville maintains that the 'principal reason' for the strike's failure was legal action against the YMA and its trustees by a Cadeby miner, William Henry Howden, who not only succeeded in having the strike declared unofficial and illegal, but also secured a crippling injunction prohibiting the union from distributing strike pay.[1363] It subsequently emerged that Mr Howden's legal fees had been covered by the company.

Though permanently beset by illness, Ben Pickard strove hard to obtain a peaceful settlement, but the owners were in no mood to compromise. The company's hand was undoubtedly strengthened by the recent passing of the so-called 'Taff Vale Judgement' – named for the successful outcome of a suit brought by the Taff Vale Railway Company against the Amalgamated Society of Railway Servants (ASRS) in which it was legally decreed that a trade union could be sued for damages resulting from the actions of its officials in the course of an industrial dispute. Henceforward, picketing would be rendered illegal: 'And, even if by some chance a strike were to be effective, the employer was bound to emerge unscathed because he could then sue the union for whatever the strike had cost him.'[1364]

Baylies observes that the Taff Vale Judgement was 'very much in the minds of district officials' from the outset of the Bag Muck strike.[1365] The combined effect of the Howden case and the Taff Vale outcome was to make the mining union hierarchy 'prudent of its funds and, as a direct corollary, more conservative in its actions than its members would have wished [...] In short, the strike led to a further widening of the division between leaders and led within the union.'[1366]

Denaby was not especially well-noted for having a poor industrial relations record, its recent history being 'not as fraught as such other Yorkshire pits as Frystone [sic], Glasshoughton or Hemsworth'.[1367] However, it would not be long before workers at these branches would face a managerial attack on their wages and/or conditions, while they were represented by a more belligerent leader like Herbert Smith.

Instigation and Early Development

In October 1902, Fryston miners struck in support of their fellow-workers at Wheldale Colliery, where, like colleagues at Cadeby and Denaby, miners were unhappy that, whilst the coal seams they were working were getting progressively thinner, the amount of dirt (or 'muck') in such seams was correspondingly increasing, forcing them to toil much harder for diminishing returns. The men's grievance was referred to the West Yorkshire joint committee, but the owners' section stuck resolutely to their argument that, although wages had admittedly declined, the earnings of Wheldale miners were still above-average for the West Riding as a whole.[1368]

Following an apparent deadlock in negotiations, the Wheldale branch voted 840 to 46 to give notice to strike in August 1902; at Fryston, miners voted 645 to 47 in favour of supporting them. The *Express* reported that:

> A ballot of both pits [...] favours a strike if terms cannot be arranged, and the Miners' Union Council may be appealed to for sanctions to put in notice on. The management having heard rumblings of a storm for two years do not attach any importance to the present agitation.[1369]

Such complacency may have been linked to the obvious hesitancy exhibited by union officials. Although a meeting of the YMA council had registered a small majority in favour of authorising the planned strike (69 votes to 62), 'At this same meeting, branches were issued with a general warning to exercise caution in bringing out any more men in the prevailing circumstances.'[1370]

This was one of several signs that a stoppage was not inevitable. At the start of October, management asked for a two-week extension of the notice of strike action. Thus, according to the *Express*, 'It was expected that in the meantime something would be done to obviate a strike.'[1371] These expectations were confounded when a meeting of the Joint Board in Leeds on Tuesday 14 October failed to resolve the deadlock. The following day, some 2,000 employees downed tools. 'So far as we could learn yesterday,' the *Express* ominously declared, 'there seems every probability of a long struggle.'[1372] This piece was unerringly prophetic. The Fryston and Wheldale miners had embarked on a bruising seventeen-month stoppage. In the following section, we examine the conduct of the strike, firstly in terms of the experience of one participating family, then in terms of the company's attempts to break the stoppage and of the impact of these tactics on the strikers and their families.

One Family's Dispute

A rare insight into the lifestyle of families involved in the Wheldale-Fryston strike draws on biographies of the world-famous, Castleford-born sculptor, Henry Moore, whose father worked at Wheldale. Moore was born the seventh of a family of eight children on 30

July 1898 in a two-bedroom terrace house in Roundhill Road, Castleford. His Lincolnshire-born father, Raymond Moore, had left school at nine and initially worked on the land, before moving north in order to escape the penury of farm work by going down the mines.[1373] Moore's mother, Mary, was the daughter of a Staffordshire miner. She and Raymond were married when they were 27 and 35 years old respectively. Raymond was fifty by the time his seventh son was born.

Moore has remarked on the 'absolutely feminine, womanly, motherly' nature of his mother, who was so hard-working and constantly supportive of her husband and children that 'he could not recall seeing her rest'.[1374] Raymond, meanwhile, was the archetypal Victorian father, seated in exalted fashion by the fire, where woe-betide anyone who had the temerity to disturb him:

> Raymond Moore was one of a proud generation of self-taught miners [...] He had read the works of Shakespeare, taught himself the violin (later inflicting violin lessons on his protesting youngest son) and enough mathematics and engineering to qualify first as pit deputy, then as an under-manager. But an injury to his eyes in a pit accident, probably a gas explosion, prevented him from taking up this position, and he focused his ambitions on his children the more fiercely. He had almost certainly worked at the coal-face as a young man: a surviving photograph of him, aged about twenty-two, suggests a powerful physique and no lack of self-confidence [...] but by the time [Henry] was a small boy, his father had [...] become a lamp-man, responsible for maintaining and distributing those vital items of equipment.[1375]

It is likely that the political and intellectual outlooks of father and son alike were shaped by the arduous and austere conditions in which they lived. The cramped and extremely basic nature of the 'two up, two down' terraced house on Roundhill Road did not extend to running water, which had to be drawn from an outside pump. Daily ablutions were carried out in a tin bath in front of the coal fire, while human waste was deposited down the chute of a 'dry' outside toilet, where it rested alongside ashes and general household refuse to await weekly collection.

'It was in character with this exacting, vicariously ambitious Victorian paterfamilias that [Raymond] should have been an early trade unionist and friend of Herbert Smith.'[1376] Smith was later to become a governor of the Castleford Secondary School, which Henry Moore attended alongside Smith's own son.[1377] Henry Moore later recalled how his father 'was politically active and used to hold meetings in our front room. It was, I suppose, about the setting up of a kind of trade union. It must have been 1906 or thereabouts.'[1378]

Such resilience and political commitment were contributing factors to the determination and adaptability of Raymond Moore and his family, and many others like them during the course of the 68-week strike.

> Henry recalled that his father bought an iron last to save money by mending the shoes first of his extensive family (by no means an unusual practice in those days) and then, to earn something extra, of several neighbours. During this hard period, Mary Moore did some additional domestic work for the Clokies who owned one of the town's main potteries. They must have been decent folk, since Henry was sometimes asked to stay to tea when he went along with his mother.[1379]

The 'Denaby Programme Repeated'?

In several respects the anti-strike tactics used by the Wheldale and Fryston Coal Company were redolent of those employed in the Cadeby-Denaby stoppage. The familiar tactic of mass eviction emerged, for example, in June 1903, when some sixty Fryston miners were served with 'notices to quit' their tied accommodation.[1380] Included among the company's 250-strong portfolio of housing stock was virtually every building in the village of Fryston (the exceptions being the Board Schools, Wesleyan Chapel, and a smattering of houses occupied by employees of the North Eastern Railway Company), a further twenty-four houses in the village of Fairburn, and approximately fifty more lining the main entrance route of Wheldon Road.[1381] By this time, some fifty houses were standing empty, their erstwhile tenants having left the village to take on alternative jobs. Another fifty were currently occupied by pit deputies or 'topmen' who were not participating in strike action.[1382]

The *Express* reported that, with the strike entering its 35th week, there had been no drift back to work following the company's decision to open the pit gates eleven days previously.[1383] The *Yorkshire Evening Post* observed that striking miners and their families were managing to survive on the strength of nine shillings per week strike pay, supplemented by various forms of public benevolence – e.g. boot funds for women and children.[1384] There was a surprising air of normality about the place:

> As recently as Thursday, the village showed little evidence of the silent struggle which has lasted for nearly nine months, but as has been the case throughout was very peaceable and quiet. It is reported that the approaches to the village are picketed to intercept aliens.[1385]

Noting that that miners from 'outside districts' were now being set on, the *Express* ominously concluded that, 'Considering all the circumstances, it looks like the "Denaby" programme is going to be repeated.'

Later that month, the *Express* reported that the company had successfully applied to the Castleford Magistrates' Court for seventeen more eviction orders.[1386] A spokesman maintained that, 'The Company had no vindictive feeling against the men.' It was 'only a question of right between landlord and tenant. If they did not pay the rent they must leave for those who would pay.' The same article revealed that, in the previous week, 'a few more men' had commenced working at Fryston.

Another long piece was devoted to the occurrence in Castleford town centre of the annual YMA Gala, which had been attended earlier that week by 95 branches and 60 brass bands. Commencing at noon from the iconic lamppost in Bridge Street (a symbolic focal point for local political activism), this 'great procession' of miners, their families and supporters, worked its way through the town centre to assemble on the rugby playing fields located over the river in Lock Lane. The number of women in the procession supporting the membership of their husbands, fathers or sweethearts, was a remarkable feature, and in one instance two women went still further and supported the drum. The large trade union banners – some requiring up to eight men to carry them – featured portraits of famous leaders of the miners' association and prominent Liberal politicians, such as Lord Rosebery.

By the first week of September (the 48th week of the dispute), 1,200 men remained on strike but sufficient 'new hands' had been employed to ensure that 2,000 tons of coal were being drawn at Fryston. None was being produced at Wheldale, however, which was significantly 'not so privately situated'.[1387] Extra police were drafted in 'on account of several scenes which have occurred lately'.[1388] This was the prelude to an intensification of conflict associated with the accelerating influx of strikebreakers and a more pervasive police presence.

On 29 September 1903, the *Sheffield Daily Telegraph* reported that:

> From the first, moderate counsels have prevailed, and although much misery has been entailed, especially upon the womenfolk and children of the strikers, anything approaching serious trouble has been averted until quite recently, when more new hands have been imported into the district, and set to work at the old rates of pay. At the present time the Fryston pit is almost, if not quite, completely manned, and it is only the lack of cottage accommodation which has presented, so it is said, the Wheldale pit, which lies nearer to Castleford, being also fully set to work.[1389]

The *Telegraph* observed how there had been a proliferation of 'minor collisions' between strikers and the 'black sheep' brought in to take their places.[1390] In one such instance, two striking miners, claiming to be taking a short cut through Fryston village to Fairburn, aroused the suspicion of their working counterparts. On the return leg of their journey, the pair were apprehended by a decidedly unfriendly cluster:

> Strangely enough, they found a few sympathisers and the words which had freely flown from the time of the first impact gradually gave way to more forcible 'arguments', until at length stones began to fly, and a battle royal appeared imminent. Fortunately, the police at Fairburn were on the 'qui vive', and in response to urgent messages a number of constables reached the scene from several quarters on bicycles. By that time matters had assumed a very ugly aspect, for several revolver

> shots had been fired, and it was evident that a very serious conflict was developing in the midst of the several hundred angry men who lined the river banks. The presence of an increasing force of police, however, had a soothing effect upon the combatants; but although they gradually dispersed it is not unlikely that a number of charges may be brought as a result of the melee. Yesterday the resident police force in the district was greatly strengthened.[1391]

The parts played by the police and courts in 'breaking' the Wheldale-Fryston strike were most apparent in the late autumn of 1903. The *Leeds Mercury* reported how one striker had delivered a 'blackleg' a blow on the head with a heavy stick, an incident directly observed by three police officers lying in wait as the result of a tip-off.[1392] In sentencing the offender to two-months in prison, the Chairman of the Bench described the offence as 'an attempt to terrorise and coerce people and prevent them doing what they had a perfect right to do'. He sent out a general warning to all strikers that, should the punishment prove insufficient to deter further violence of this nature, 'the imprisonment meted out would be heavier each time until the maximum period was reached'.[1393]

The Parts Played by Smith and Pickard

The stoppage still had three more months to run but defeat already seemed inevitable. Previously, the owners had grudgingly made concessions which the union side, led until now by Herbert Smith, persistently derided as unacceptable:

> In March 1903, while not moving on the tonnage rate, the owners confirmed that they would offer other concessions equivalent to 1½d per ton. When the men refused, the offer was dropped, but in May the company offered a tonnage rate of 1s 6d which represented a substantial concession over previous prices. Again the men refused. And at a joint committee meeting on 15 September 1903, Sir Joseph Rymer, speaking for the company, stated that 'the Wheldale people had been most anxious that this Strike, which never ought to have been begun, should be terminated as soon as possible'. Toward this end previously offered concessions were again put on the table. But none of these were regarded as sufficient by the workers.[1394]

Baylies maintains that some of the owners' representatives 'were particularly disdainful in their assessment of the role played by Herbert Smith, one of the YMA's representatives to the joint committee specifically assigned to the case'.[1395] This was exemplified by the scathing comments made by Mr Oldroyd at a meeting held at the Great Northern Station Hotel, Leeds, on 20 October 1903:

> The whole dispute arose in a most unbusinesslike way [said Oldroyd]. They told us at the time – they told their own men at the time, they couldn't afford to make any concessions. Notwithstanding that statement, which was absolutely true, they did make concessions which he stated at the beginning. They had no right to make those concessions, but they made them. They were scornfully and disdainfully rejected by Mr Smith. Their offer that referred to End and Bord were scornfully rejected by Mr Smith, and he would never forget the flash of his eye, and on his shoulders he put the responsibility of the whole business [...] If the men were foolish to begin a fight under those conditions it was not their fault. These men were ill led by men of weak judgement, and they had to pay for it.[1396]

Ben Pickard's first major contribution had occurred one month earlier at the joint committee meeting of 15 September 1903, when he appealed to the owners to show a clement and humanitarian attitude. Responding to Sir Joseph Rymer's assertion that there had been too large a loss of trade for the company to put previously proposed concessions back on the table, Pickard pleaded with the owners to demonstrate that 'all the humanity had not left them' by recognising that 'there had not been a better set of men, a more hard-working set of men in Yorkshire for the last 30 years' than their own workers.[1397] He further exhorted the owners to imagine the type of suffering being endured by the wives and families of the strikers. Similar sentiments were expressed at the meeting of 20 October, when Pickard implored the owners to 'act the Good Samaritan'. It was all to no avail. Sensing the virtual infallibility of their position, the owners refused to concede another inch and the strike began to crumble.

Surrender

It is evident from an *Express* article for 9 January 1904 that the company was showing no let-up in its pressure. A legal representative of the Wheldale strikers appealed in the Castleford Court for ejectment orders to be deferred on practical and compassionate grounds:

> He said that about 160 men were served with notice to quit three weeks ago. A large majority had already gone out, and all had made every possible effort to get out, but the Bench would understand the difficulty of those who were out of work being able to get houses anywhere. They could if they wished suggest that they were not carried out until the expiration of 10 days. An attempt was to be made that day to get an amicable settlement between masters and men. He thought the Colliery Company did not really need the homes, and no harm would be done to anyone by granting his application, and it might prevent some distressing scenes in the way of evictions, as the people would remove as early as possible.[1398]

A representative for the company counter-argued that, whilst they would have no objection to extensions in the cases of any residents currently suffering ill-health, the directors and management would consider it 'remiss' of themselves not to execute the order made by the Bench. The Chairman of the Bench instructed the local superintendent of police to 'delay evictions as much as possible'.[1399]

It was reported in the same edition that strikers attending a two-hour mass meeting of Fryston and Wheldale miners at the Salvation Army Barracks in Castleford had resolved not to abandon their action;[1400] but at a subsequent mass meeting three weeks later, over 900 men voted (albeit by a narrow majority of 18) to 'present themselves at the pits for work in a body, prepared to resume on the same terms as those on which they came out'. They also resolved that any workers re-employed by the company would contribute to a levy for those not taken back on.[1401]

It soon became apparent, though, that company policy was to ignore pleas by the YMA for 'old hands' to be taken back in preference to 'strangers':

> The settlement of the strike has been so long delayed – this being about the 68th week – that it is more than probable only a proportion of the men can be set on, and it is apparent, therefore, that many will have to seek employment in other districts [...] The Collieries are now drawing nearly two-thirds of their maximum output before the strike commenced. Two of the three seams at the Wheldale Colliery are nearly fully manned, and in the other pit applications for work have come in, and men have been set on as rapidly as places could be opened out. At the Fryston Colliery one seam is employing as many men as there is accommodation for and the other has been filling up. In general terms, about two-thirds of the full complement of men necessary to work all the pits at their maximum output are now working, and they are chiefly new hands, though many of the old employees have already returned to work.[1402]

There are close similarities (in terms of the underlying causes, duration, managerial tactics employed and eventual outcomes) of the Wheldale-Fryston and Cadeby-Denaby disputes. The main distinguishing feature is that there were several junctures in the former dispute where the owners seemed ready to make concessions. Additionally, the Wheldale-Fryston miners were led by Herbert Smith, who was a more pugnacious and populist trade union representative whose oppositional style resonated with contemporary rank-and-file disaffection.

In January 1904, just as the dispute was drawing to its conclusion, Smith was elected Vice-President of the YMA. It has been claimed that the death of Ben Pickard (on 3 February in London, where he was presenting evidence to a Board of Trade Inquiry into the Cadeby-Denaby strike) was caused by the stress of handling that dispute.[1403] It is possible that the Wheldale-Fryston stoppage contributed in similar manner to his demise. His body was brought back to Yorkshire and he was buried in Barnsley Cemetery.[1404] The iron man had finally been broken.

Chapter Thirty
Forward, Into the Past

Echoes of Fryston Hall: Lord Houghton and His Children

The larger-than-life figure of Richard Monckton Milnes, the first Lord Houghton, is predominant in most of the history retraced in this volume. Milnes was one of the best-known figures of nineteenth-century British life, but his literary and political merits have only grudgingly been acknowledged and said to bear the stigma of underachievement.[1405] These casually dismissive attitudes are forgetful of the plaudits Milnes received on the publication of the first major (and most transformative) biography of the poet John Keats. They do scant justice to the reformist exploits of a man who pushed, earnestly and tenaciously, in beneficence of workers in the factories and mines, on behalf of divorced women and those campaigning for female suffrage, in the interests of Irish peasants, of those awaiting the death penalty, and of juvenile offenders. Perhaps his greatest virtue was never to take himself too seriously: 'He, unlike the other Cambridge Apostles, never regarded himself as a great being set apart for a great mission.'[1406]

Often derided, and occasionally reviled, as a sinister, Machiavellian predator with obsessive interests in pornography and flagellation (and simultaneously accused of constantly stirring up social controversy for his own amusement), Milnes supposedly 'corrupted' the youthful Swinburne by exposing him to the 'vile' works of the Marquis de Sade and by placing him in the reckless hands of the explorer Sir Richard Burton. This overlooks the fact that Swinburne had a longstanding prior fascination with de Sade and was not diverted from this trajectory either by Milnes's reluctance to grant him access to the Marquis's books, or by Milnes's entreaty to tread carefully in his relationship with Burton.

While Milnes's collection of erotic literature was reputedly unrivalled, it only formed a small part of one of the most diverse privately-owned libraries in Europe. Far from representing a peculiar sexual perversion, the Victorian obsession with flagellation, pornography and taboo subjects like incest was a shared feature of elite homosocial gatherings. Observing how two recent commentaries had referred to Milnes's interest in erotica as 'unedifying', Pope-Hennessy was reconciled to the fact that, 'To prudish and illiberal persons his [Milnes's] name has become a bogey, to the prurient a decoy.'[1407]

An unfortunate side effect of the demonisation of Milnes has been to detract from his unrivalled acts of philanthropy. He may well have lacked true political or literary genius:

> But his *häusliche Thätigkeit* was in itself a kind of genius – a genius that manifested itself in beautifully appointed dinners for exiled princes and for struggling young poets, as well as for the high and mighty of all lands; and his *Sentimentalität* was of that sublime variety which impelled him to canvass London for subscribers to the lectures of the needy and little known Carlyle, to carry jellies and custards to consumptive David Gray, and to aid the dying Hood with money and anonymous contributions to *Hood's Magazine*. It was this sort of philanthropy that Milnes was engaged in all his life, and those in need of his assistance had only to make known their wants to gain his unstinted and invariably efficient aid.[1408]

From his welcoming and unpretentious country seat of Fryston, Milnes 'reigned as literary host to all of England for almost fifty years'.[1409] Standing at the entrance of Fryston Hall, he greeted great Victorian philosophers, poets and novelists of the calibre of Carlyle, Collins, Gaskell, Thackeray, Tennyson, Trollope, Browning and Spedding; famous politicians like Disraeli, Forster and Palmerston; and other highly-reputed figures, such as the explorers Burton and Vámbéry. Whether in Yorkshire or one of his London homes, Milnes extended a similar hand of friendship and moral, financial, and practical support to visiting American writers such as Emerson, Hawthorne and Miller, and to transatlantic politicians like Charles Francis Adams (the American Minister during the American Civil War). He was cordially received, in turn, by the two most celebrated

Union Generals, Grant and Sherman, while visiting America, and was honoured by a visit from Grant during Grant's post-presidential tour of Europe. Such accolades recognised Milnes's conspicuous support of the North during the American Civil War.

Milnes is, understandably, best-remembered as the one-time suitor of Florence Nightingale, whose misinterpretation of Nightingale's true feelings may have resulted in the breakdown of their relationship and clinched her decision to travel to the Crimean war front, where she became immortalised as the 'Lady with the Lamp'. Milnes later worked, conspicuously and assiduously, in support of the Nightingale Foundation and could just as easily be relied upon to champion the inception of Free Libraries and countless other humanitarian causes. It is a measure of Milnes's ubiquity and the magnitude of his personality that his persona was borrowed or caricatured during his lifetime in novels by Collins, Disraeli, Oliphant and Thackeray, and recently resurrected, as we know, in Mark Hodder's alternative histories.

Following his death in 1885, Milnes's political, social, literary and philanthropic mantles were passed on to two of his three children, both of whom benefitted greatly from their affluent social position, the extensive networks they already enjoyed access to, and from their exposure to a vibrant and gregarious way of life in which the talented and highly-esteemed were commonplace. The oldest of Milnes's three children, Amicia ('Amy') – arguably the most gifted and doted upon – chose to immerse herself in married life. It was her younger sister, Florence (named after her godmother, Florence Nightingale), who followed imitatively in her father's footsteps, becoming a novelist (albeit of modest acclaim) and society hostess of distinction. Her life was forever transformed when she entered the latter role on behalf of her brother and younger sibling, Houghton, during his ill-fated tenure as Viceroy of Ireland.

Following the tragically early death of Sibyl, the mother of his four children (one of whom died in his youth), Houghton entered politics as a parliamentary private secretary. The second Lord Houghton objected to his father's irrepressible flamboyance. He was also aware of how his father's inherently gossipy and indiscrete nature had earmarked him as an 'impossible candidate for office'.[1410] Maybe it was this, in conjunction with an in-built reticence and tendency to stammer, that gave Houghton such a reserved and aloof, but nonetheless reliable political disposition,[1411] even if characteristics were not ideal for his role as viceroy when Irish unionists and republicans were equally disenchanted with the British government.

It would have been impossible for Houghton to have contemplated such a role without his sister Florence acting as hostess at the Viceregal Court. Florence's involvement was made less complicated by the regular absence of her husband, Arthur Henniker, an officer in the Coldstream Guards who was often posted elsewhere in the UK or overseas. Florence revelled in the opportunity of meeting such important literary figures as Henry James and Thomas Hardy.

It was Hardy's unrequited passion for Florence Henniker that made her the muse for several of his poems, the central character of a short story ('An Imaginative Woman'), and for Sue Bridehead in Hardy's final and arguably greatest work, *Jude the Obscure.* Hardy and Henniker collaborated, with some difficulty, on a short story ('The Spectre of the Real'), and it is speculated that Henniker wrote a short story of her own ('The Colour Sergeant') to set the record straight with Hardy – though some have surmised that it is an oblique reference to the radical Irish politician John Dillon, to whom she was allegedly attracted.

Florence's husband, Arthur, played a conspicuously brave and controversial part in the Anglo-Boer War, and is said to have inspired several of Hardy's 'War Poems' and was also the regular subject of Hardy's ongoing correspondence with Florence. During the war, Hardy played a minor role in Florence's campaign to promote the welfare and relieve the suffering of the horses and mules deployed in the conflict.

By this time, Houghton (now Lord Crewe) had achieved a position of great prosperity and social standing. He had not only inherited the title, wealth and estates bequeathed to him by his uncle, but in 1899 also married Peggy Primrose, the daughter of Lord Rosebery and Hannah de Rothschild. The Milneses' links to Fryston Hall were now extremely tenuous (and soon to be severed when Sir John Austin bought it outright in 1905). For the duration of the 1902-04 Wheldale-Fryston strike, Crewe and Peggy remained distanced from the conflict playing out in close proximity of his former ancestral seat. In the winter of 1902-03, they were guests at Lord Curzon's

Dunbar celebrations in India, an experience that proved vital in preparing Crewe for his forthcoming five-year tenure as Viceroy of India.[1412] Crewe was already closely connected to the British royal family. Having entered the House of Lords, he was now destined for a glittering political career. It was Peggy who claimed to having 'heard it said that the son had all the success for which the father longed'.[1413] It is in the aftermath of the two-year strike that we now re-join the story of his progress.

The Entertainers

Crewe House, Lord and Lady Crewe's seventeen-bedroom mansion on Curzon Street, soon became a major hub of London society, the type of which the first Lord Houghton would have relished owning. It was during the summer season of 1904 that Winston Churchill was invited to a ball at Crewe House. Five years earlier, Churchill had resigned his commission as a dashing cavalry officer in the 4th Hussars and was elected Member of Parliament for Oldham in the autumn of 1900. By 1904, he had written six critically acclaimed books and it was already apparent that a substantial literary and political career lay before him. However, Churchill became embroiled in a major political controversy that spring, when, objecting to his party's commitment to Tariff Reform and its implications for Free Trade, he 'crossed the House' to join the Liberal benches. The consequences of this were far-reaching:

> Politics were more vehement in those days, and permeated social life to a marked degree. Since Winston's defection the doors of nearly all Conservative houses were closed to him. But he was welcome at Crewe House, since Lord Crewe was a prominent member of the Liberal Party.[1414]

The 30-year-old Churchill attended the ball with his mother, Lady Randolph, and was captivated by the sight of a beautiful young woman standing alone in a doorway. Lady Randolph soon established that the person in question was 19-year-old Clementine Hozier, the daughter of an old friend.[1415] It was therefore perfectly legitimate for Lady Randolph to introduce Ms Hozier to her son.

> Their first meeting was, however, brief and unpropitious – for, upon his mother's introducing him, instead of asking Clementine to dance, Winston stood rooted to the spot, staring at the vision which had so powerfully beguiled him. Clementine felt embarrassed by his scrutiny and, far from thinking that this strange, intent young man had asked to to be introduced to her, imagined that Lady Randolph had noticed that she was without a partner and, taking pity on her plight, had out of kindness introduced her son. Moreover, Clementine had heard about Winston Churchill; she had heard him discussed on several occasions, and she was not at all favourably disposed towards him. Now his gauche, singular behaviour settled the matter.[1416]

Knowing of Churchill's reputation, Clementine had taken the precaution of having a male friend position himself nearby. Following a discreet, pre-arranged hand signal, he stepped forward to 'rescue' her.[1417]

The significance of this debacle was only apparent in hindsight: it left no lasting impression on either of the parties involved and it was four more years before their paths crossed again. Yet Lord and Lady Crewe could take credit for indirectly drawing together one of Britain's greatest historical figures and his future wife. The occasion was another step in the development of an inter-family relationship that would see descendants of Lord and Lady Crewe play enormous (if primarily *covert*) roles in the conduct of the Second World War and in Churchill's post-war tenure as Prime Minister.

In the short term, both Crewe and Churchill were to emerge unscathed from the 'chaos' inflicted on the Liberal Party by the downfall of the Rosebery administration. Following brief periods under the ineffectual leadership of Harcourt and Morley, the Liberals rallied under Sir Henry Campbell-Bannerman, who took office as Prime Minister in December 1905. Crewe was neither a close friend nor a particular admirer of Campbell-Bannerman, who, in his opinion, had insufficient experience of travelling overseas to be capable of understanding the British Empire, let alone wider world affairs.[1418] It was therefore ironic that, in forming his new administration, Campbell-Bannerman elevated Crewe to the position of Lord President of the Council, a post which, if admittedly ill-defined and not especially taxing, placed him in the cabinet.[1419] This post had the additional advantage of bringing its occupant into regular contact with the Sovereign:

> Ever since the days when he used to shoot at Fryston, King Edward had liked Crewe personally, for they had one passion in common – racing. On one or two occasions the King and Queen actually dined at Crewe House, while Crewe was often at Windsor and Balmoral. The King did not, of course, feel any sympathy for Crewe's politics. Although he had many Liberal friends [...] King Edward was fundamentally as reactionary as his mother had been – a somewhat natural tendency in monarchs. King Edward would sometimes use Crewe when he wished to express disapproval to the Cabinet of the actions or speeches of one of its members.[1420]

The subsequent death of Campbell-Bannerman in March 1908, and the succession of Asquith as Prime Minister one month later, saw Churchill rise from the position of Under-Secretary of State for the Colonies to President of the Board of Trade; Crewe, meanwhile, replaced Lord Elgin as Secretary of State for the Colonies. Within one week of this appointment, the resignation, due to ill-health, of Lord Ripon resulted in Crewe taking over the Leadership of the House of Lords. Six months after that, Crewe also succeeded Ripon as Lord Privy Seal. Thus, before 1908 was out:

> Crewe found himself in charge of the Colonial Empire at a period of great delicacy in its history, Leader of the small and often disunited band of Government supporters in the House of Lords and holder of the ancient and honourable position of Lord Privy Seal.[1421]

Crewe was now on the brink of political greatness: for him 'the year 1908 – in which he celebrated his fiftieth birthday – was thus the threshold to a period of strenuous and responsible work which did not cease until his resignation from the Government in 1916'.[1422] Over the next two decades, he would rise to become Leader of the Liberal Peers in the House of Lords, Secretary of State for India, and the British Ambassador to Paris. During this period, he would play extremely significant parts in such major political issues of the day as the reform of the House of Lords, Home Rule for the Irish, the inception of the female vote, British relations with India and South Africa, the establishment of the state of Israel, British strategy in World War I, and key diplomatic issues following this conflict in relation to Britain's erstwhile allies and opponents (principally, France and Germany). Speaking of this period, Lord Samuel would eventually reflect how:

> Lord Crewe held an [sic] unique position in the Cabinet. This was not on account of any pre-eminence in Parliament, or in the country, or in the counsels of the Party, but through an almost uncanny soundness of judgement. In any difficult situation, where pros and cons were nicely balanced, it was Crewe, more than any other colleague, that the Prime Minister was accustomed to consult. He was always ready indeed to help any of us with our problems. His great experience made him an invaluable counsellor [...] We could be sure that any opinion he offered would be as clear-cut as the conditions allowed, and bear the stamp of that wisdom which was his outstanding quality.[1423]

Needless to say, the second volume of this history will partly be devoted to describing the many contributions made by the Marquess of Crewe to British cultural and political life of the twentieth century.

The Crewe Dynasty

Equally important – insofar as the content of our second volume is concerned – is the emergence of new generations of Crewe's children and grandchildren, whose impact on cultural, political and, indeed, royal matters was of considerable significance. As we shall see in Volume Two, Crewe's political and aristocratic networks were crucial to this emergence.

Of the three surviving children from Crewe's marriage to Sibyl, Lady Cynthia was to become a well-known campaigner for improvements in health provision for women, the poor, and Woman of the Bedchamber for Queen Mary. Cynthia was the mother of John ('Jock') Colville, who would become Private Secretary to Neville Chamberlain, Winston Churchill and Clement Attlee. During the Second World War, he broke off temporarily to become an RAF fighter pilot. Afterwards, he would play a controversial and constitutionally dubious role in helping distract attention from the fact that Churchill was seriously ill while in office.

Lady Annabel had married Arthur O'Neill, the Northern Irish MP for Mid Antrim. Tragically, he was to be the first Member of Parliament to be killed in action during World War I. Their third son, Terence, became Prime Minister of Northern Ireland and would become centrally embroiled in the escalation of the 'Troubles' occurring in the late 1960s. Terence's half-brother Quentin (one of the children from Annabel's second marriage) was to become a well-known writer and socialite. In his youth, Quentin entered a relationship with the daughter of the Prime Minister, Harold Macmillan, and was socially close enough to witness a scandalous extra-marital affair. Subsequently, he became the close friend and confidant of Princess Margaret's husband, Lord Snowdon. Jock's wife, Lady Meg Colville, would become Lady in Waiting for Princess Elizabeth (the future queen) for a three-year period, before spending a decade as Woman of the Bedchamber for the Queen Mother.

Of the two children issuing from the marriage of Crewe and Peggy Primrose, a son, Richard, would die in 1922, leaving Lady Mary Evelyn Hungerford Crewe as sole survivor. A goddaughter of King George V, Mary was married to the 9th Duke of Roxburgh. This marriage would be destined for an acrimonious and well-publicised break up during the 1950s, in which Mary locked herself in her bedroom in defiance of her husband's attempts to oust her from the property. Mary eventually took possession of her mother's mansion at West Horsley Place, near Leatherhead in Surrey. The mansion, its accompanying 400-acre estate, and a prized art collection (constituting all that was left of the Crewe fortune) passed in to the hands of her godson, who was, as we shall see, a famous television personality. The story of Lady Mary and other members of the Crewe dynasty, and of their various contributions to British social, political and cultural life, will be expanded on in our second volume.

Trade Union and Political Developments

Simultaneous developments in mineworker politics would help set the direction of industrial relations activity in the first three decades of the twentieth century. Prominent in these events was the pugnacious figure of Herbert Smith, whose political ambitions were thwarted but whose trade union career was ascendant.

By the end of the Wheldale-Fryston strike, and with the Denaby-Cadeby 'Bag Muck' strike still fresh in the memory, rank-and-file disaffection towards the MFGB leadership was paramount. The wholesale transformation of the YMA leadership following the deaths of Pickard and other diehard Liberals between December 1903 and February 1904 induced a slackening of rank-and-file commitment to the Liberal Party[1424] and 'eased the psychological inhibitions on the expression of dissent in the YMA'.[1425]

A clear focus was given to their anger when the miners were locked out of Hemsworth near Pontefract in August 1904, which developed, predictably, into a programme of widespread evictions by the company. The growing radicalism of local activists, like the Hemsworth checkweighman John Potts and his colleague W.O. Bull, was reflected in increased coalfield support for the ILP.[1426] As Baylies points out, the ILP leader, Keir Hardie, was a guest speaker at the union's annual demonstration of 1904, 'an event scarcely imaginable during Pickard's lifetime'.[1427] This changing mood was not immediately reflected in forthcoming general elections.

At the MFGB conference in the autumn of 1900, Ben Pickard's proposal that the union set up an election fund had been approved by vote of 168,000 to 68,000. Henceforward, all members would pay a shilling a year into a Labour political fund to cover the general election expenses and annual salary of political candidates nominated by the union. This policy reflected Pickard's view that the eight-hour day could only be achieved by retuning a Liberal government. It was far better for the miners, he maintained, to set about 'permeating and eventually dominating the Liberal Party', rather than seeking to establish a socialist party of their own.[1428] One problem here was (as Herbert Smith was soon to discover to his cost) that the Liberal Party was not always willing to stand their preferred candidate aside in favour of the miners' nominee.

Following his death, Pickard was succeeded by Parrott as MP for Normanton. Soon after, the YMA put forward five nominees (including Smith) to contest any further seats that might otherwise become available. It was not long before the seats of Osgoldcross (including Fryston) and Hallamshire (Sheffield) came up. In each case the sitting Liberal MPs (including Sir John Austin) were not seeking re-election. In Osgoldcross, however, the YMA's ambitions were thwarted as the Liberal Association had already approached J. Compton-Rickett, a London-born ex-novelist and coal merchant, to be their candidate.

Since 1895, Compton-Rickett had been the Liberal MP for Scarborough, where his credentials as a Quaker lay preacher stood him in good stead amidst an overwhelmingly Nonconformist constituency.[1429] During this time, he helped found the Coal Trade Benevolent Association (which offered financial support to non-manual workers in the coal trade who may have fallen on hard times) and argued successfully in favour of the Checkweighman's Bill (which guaranteed greater employment protection for such officials and made their wages more secure) being placed on the Statute Book.[1430]

In the summer of 1905, the MFGB instructed Fryston and other branches in Osgoldcross to nominate their own representative, and they selected Fred Hall as their candidate. When Compton-Rickett refused to make way, Hall began canvassing in anticipation of a three-cornered fight. The impasse broke in November 1905 when Parrott's death enabled Hall to contest the 'safer' Normanton seat instead. It had been hitherto assumed that Herbert Smith would contest Normanton on behalf of the YMA, albeit as an ILP representative, but Hall's change of candidacy forced a ballot of local miners, which produced a 652 to 435 majority in favour of Hall. The ILP-ers within the union regarded Hall's move as treacherous:

> Had the original arrangements remained intact, Hall [...] would have stayed in Osgoldcross [...] and the choice of candidate for Normanton would have been confined to Smith [and two potential rivals], in which case Herbert Smith would almost certainly have been selected.[1431]

Even if, as Hall's selection suggests, the majority of YMA members were still reluctant to endorse the ILP over the Liberals, they showed no such reticence in promoting ILP advocates within their own union. Far from stymieing his progress, Smith's 'incendiary decision' to support the ILP in the Barnsley by-election was consistent with the growing coalfield militancy.[1432] It came as no surprise when he was elected vice-president of the YMA in 1904 and president in January 1906.[1433] Smith's political influence thereafter was tangible: Taylor maintains that 'the core of the labour movement's doctrine and ethos for the next seventy years [found] visible expression in the substantial shape of Herbert Smith'.[1434]

Yet, Smith was first and foremost a miner rather than a socialist and 'his political militancy never matched his industrial militancy'.[1435] Smith was driven primarily by a determination to improve the miners' lot via the unity, solidarity and collective strength of the trade union. He exemplified a 'moderate Labourism', whose central logic was the unification of mineworkers from different areas of Great Britain and with differing roles above and below ground as 'men within a common industry'. This corps would be capable of acting not only in their own collective interests but also 'as the shock troops for a whole class'.[1436] Smith was purpose-built for this task:

> Epitomising the colliers, his origins were also distinctive: an orphan born in the workhouse at Kippax, near Leeds, he found his family among the miners. Starting work at ten in 1872 and on the coalface at seventeen, Smith represented the generation which had founded modern mining trade unionism and which combined a deep attachment to district organization with implacable determination to organize nationally. He was steeled in conflict. In 1893, with three young children, he was locked out for thirteen weeks, and *his tenacity, stamina and perhaps inflexibility as a negotiator were honed in stand-offs such as the fourteen-month Wheldale[-Fryston] strike which ran from 1902 to 1904.*[1437]

Smith's role in the Wheldale-Fryston dispute validated the enduring impression that, 'Unyielding, uncompromising, preferring to be beaten rather than make terms which went against the grain of his nature and his sense of justice to those whose livelihood was hardly and dangerously won,' he commanded the loyalty of, and held an 'unrivalled supremacy of influence' over, even those 'whose interests suffered from his too inflexible resolution'.[1438] These characterisations were reflected in and reinforced by the Wheldale-Fryston strike and would help shape the behaviour, experience and ultimate fate of Fryston people with regard to the eight-hour working day, the ownership and management of the industry, and the volatile nature of their wages.

A 'New' Fryston

The demographic and cultural characteristics of Fryston village were continuing to change. The strikes of 1897-99 and 1902-04 had transformed the village population. Some long-established residents, such as the colliery manager George Soar and his family, and the Whetton family, of which John Thomas (born 1894) was the youngest of thirteen children, had been on 'different sides' in the disputes. Others were brought into the village to act – consciously or not – as strikebreakers. Some of these, like the family of John ('Jackie') Kriens crossed the river from nearby Newton to settle in Fryston, where the 17-year-old Jackie was taken on as a pony driver. Still more came from far afield: my maternal grandfather, Samuel Holmes, arrived as a 9-year-old with his older sister and four brothers in 1902 from Madeley in Shropshire, following a stopover in rural Nottinghamshire; and Barbara Stewart's ancestors arrived in 1903 from Beighton, near Chesterfield, to occupy a village terrace. 'Only colliery employees were allowed to live in the houses,' she maintains: 'Leave the pit, leave the house. Get behind with the rent, be evicted. Those who were evicted would move into huts on Wheldale Road [sic] and manage as best they could.'[1439]

There is strong anecdotal evidence of an influx into Fryston village (around 1902-03) of dozens of Staffordshire miners and their families from places like Fenton and Pelsall.[1440] A female descendant of one longstanding Fryston family remembers how she arrived in the village from Fenton as a three-year-old in 1903, four months after her father who had resided in lodgings until a back-to-back house eventually became vacant. Some confusion surrounds the arrival of the parents of the celebrated amateur photographer Jack Hulme in Fryston. Hulme disclosed in interview how his family had transferred from Fenton in 1903,[1441] though this contradicted his earlier assertion that his father (a miner) and mother (a pottery painter) had first settled 'in the year that Queen Victoria died' (1901).[1442] Once established, this migratory trend was continued by other Staffordshire families, including the Astburys, who also sought to seize this opportunity to carve out a new life:

> All my relatives worked down Fryston Pit. My dad was an Irishman, but I think he came to Fryston from having previously settled in Castleford. My mother's side were all from Staffordshire. They came from somewhere near Pelsall. At one time, I should think there were more Staffordshire people in Fryston than anybody else. My mother was thirteen when she came. She's been dead twenty years and she died when she was 72. So, it would have been 1907 when she came to Fryston.[1443]

These examples have deliberately been chosen because of the relevance of the individuals or families concerned to events of major significance in the twentieth-century history of Fryston, as will be recounted in our second volume. Of particular significance to the creation and telling of Fryston's twentieth-century history is the memoir of the immensely charismatic and high-profile Fryston colliery manager Jim Bullock OBE. Bullock's colourful autobiographical account states that this sixth son and youngest of twelve surviving children was born in nearby Bowers Row in 1903. His parents were William and Naomi Bullock, whose lives we traced in earlier chapters.

Bullock's earliest recollections include 'the warmth of the house, the comforting presence of my mother, a certain awe of my father, but above all I remember the companionship of a large family'.[1444] The front bedroom of the two-up-two down terraced house referred to in Chapter 17 contained, not only the 'parental bed' but another one opposite, in which all the girls slept. The back bedroom contained two very large beds pressed tightly together, leaving just enough room to escape to the top of the stairs. These beds accommodated various permutations of men and boys, including the Bullock brothers, visiting cousins or uncles, and 'an adopted cousin from Keighley who worked down the pit'.[1445]

Bullock would eventually swap his allegiance to Bowers Row for a long career – first as pony boy and eventually as manager of Fryston pit. During his tenure as manager, Bullock would have a remarkably galvanising effect on the village and its mine; the socialisation he underwent at Bowers (in which the example shown by his parents was paramount) would earn him the accolade from Joe Hall, president of the Yorkshire Miners' Association (YMA), of the 'only bloody socialist colliery manager' in the country.[1446] As a local newspaper once said:

> No one would ever claim that this end-of-the-road mining village is a source of inspiration but, every so often, it bursts into inspirational fireworks. And the man with the match is usually Jimmy Bullock. It may be a fund for invalid chairs for miners; or a concert party; or a boxing match; or a village pantomime, with a flying ballet of miners, to which he directs his abundant energies. Whatever it is, the former pit lad, whose career started with the Bowers Pit at the age of 13, will be there to see it.[1447]

In 1952 alone, Fryston miners under Bullock's management would build their own miners' welfare club and institute and a massive sports stadium from scratch. The village would also achieve national prominence when a local pit deputy carried out the daring rescue of a colleague. Bullock's credo reflected the fact that he was also Britain's 'only communist pit manager'.[1448] In Volume Two , we shall reconsider the shaping effect of Bullock's parents' experience at Altofts and Bowers Row on his outlook.

It is fortunate, indeed, that the twentieth-century history of Fryston village and its pit has been so well-documented, primarily in the photographs of Jack Hulme[1449] and the autobiography of Jim Bullock,[1450] but also in the memoirs of a local doctor[1451] and a Member of Parliament who was also a member of the mine management,[1452] and, of course, in the life stories of 'ordinary' residents.[1453] From these testimonies, it is possible to trace the personalised experiences of Fryston's 'pit-folk' via such major national and international events as two World Wars, the General Strike, the nationalisation of the mines, and the 1984-5 miners' strike.

These stories will unfold in Volume Two alongside an account of the idiosyncratic and often trail-blazing activities, culture and lifestyle that turned this tiny 'mining Shangri-la' into one of the most remarkable – and *remarked upon* – pit villages of the twentieth century and beyond.

Acknowledgements

I would not have been able to write this book had it not been for the constant encouragement and support of my senior colleague at Sheffield Hallam University, Professor Wayne Cranton. It was Wayne who, in his role of Dean of Research, not only arranged an essential period of study leave on my behalf, but also helped fund the vital research and administrative assistance provided by Helen Grantham, Kerry McSeveny, Andrea Moran-Healy and Taraneh Motamedi. I will be eternally grateful for Wayne's support and that of these other friends and colleagues.

I am similarly indebted to Ian Daley and Isabel Galán of Route, not least for allowing me to continue the highly satisfying publishing relationship we first established during the production of my earlier historical study, *Coal, Goals and Ashes: Fryston Colliery's Pursuit of the West Riding County FA Challenge Cup*. Evidence of Ian and Isabel's wise counsel and refinement of my text is discernible throughout the pages of this book. The same could be said of the patience and expertise provided by Ben Summers-McKay, who did such an excellent job as copy-editor. I am proud, as ever, to be associated with such a principled and pioneering publisher as Route.

Since I first started to research and write up this project, I have witnessed the passing of both of my dear parents, Mary and Peter Waddington, and of my beloved wife, Joanna. I know that they were acutely aware of the project's emotional significance for me, and were just as excited as I was at the prospect of seeing it in print. It is therefore with great pride that I dedicate this book in loving memory of all three of these special people in my life. I further dedicate the book to my mother's only surviving sister, Fryston-born Auntie Dora ('Our Dor'), who has always been like a second mother to me.

Notes

1 Waddington (2013, p. 27)
2 Waddington (1988)
3 Bullock (1972, p. 123)
4 *Yorkshire Evening Post*, 17 March 1986
5 McClarence (1990, p. viii)
6 BBC1, 11 September to 2 October 1975
7 *Yorkshire Evening Post*, 17 March 1986
8 Waddington (1988)
9 Bullock (1972)
10 Hodder (2012)
11 ibid., pp. 29-30
12 Hodder (2010, 2011, 2012, 2013, 2014, 2015)
13 Hodder (2010)
14 ibid., no page
15 ibid., p. 43
16 ibid., p. 50
17 Hodder (2011, pp. 265-66)
18 Hodder (2013, pp. 86-87)
19 ibid., p. 87
20 ibid.
21 ibid., p. 105
22 ibid., p. 172
23 Hodder (2015, p. 179)
24 ibid.
25 Waddington (1975, p. 61; 1981, p. 39)
26 Walker (1921, p. 334)
27 Pope-Hennessy (1949, p. 3)
28 Boucher (1935, p. 68)
29 ibid., p. 67
30 ibid.
31 Waddington (1981, p. 39)
32 Waddington (1975, p. 62)
33 Russell (1889/2009, p. 27)
34 Reid (2010, p. 88)
35 Pope-Hennessy (1951, pp. 132-33)
36 Walker (1921, p. 355)
37 Dennis (1877, p. 343)
38 Waddington (1975, p. 62)
39 Pope-Hennessy (1955, p. 5)
40 Tóibín (2004, p. 23)
41 Crewe (1955, p. x)
42 Jacobson (1999)
43 ibid., p. 142
44 Hardy and Pinion (1972)
45 Bailey (2008)
46 ibid., p. 93
47 Williamson (1982)
48 ibid., p. 1
49 ibid., p. 2
50 ibid., p. 5
51 ibid., p. 10
52 Houghton (1873, p. iii)
53 Wemyss Reid (1890a and b)
54 Pope-Hennessy (1949, 1951)
55 Hardy and Pinion (1972); Pope-Hennessy (1955)
56 Bullock (1972; 1976)
57 Lawson (1941)
58 Waddington (1988)
59 BBC North (1969)
60 BBC North (1975)
61 Emery (2019); Stephenson and Wray (2005)
62 Walker (1921, p. 291)
63 Crewe (1929, p. 1)
64 Hunter (1848); Wilson (1971)
65 Daniels (1980)
66 ibid., pp. 102-103
67 ibid., pp. 104
68 Wilson (1971, p. 163)
69 ibid.
70 Daniels (1980, p. 103)
71 Seed (1985, pp. 310 and 312)
72 ibid., p. 312
73 ibid., p. 314
74 ibid., p. 308
75 McCahill (1976, p. 94)
76 ibid.
77 ibid., p. 94
78 Wemyss Reid (1890a, p. 7)
79 Daniels (1980, p. 104)
80 Wemyss Reid (1890a, p. 7)
81 Padgett (1904)
82 Castleford Lending Library (no date)
83 Padgett (1904, p. 242)
84 Wemyss Reid (1890a, p. 7)
85 Forrest (1871, p. 78)
86 Padgett (1904, p. 238)
87 Pope-Hennessy (1949, p. 85)
88 Wemyss Reid (1890a, p. 7)
89 Daniels (1980, p. 104)
90 Wilson (1971, p. 164)
91 Wemyss Reid (1890a, p. 37)
92 ibid., p. 10
93 ibid.
94 ibid., pp. 30-31
95 ibid., pp. 11-12
96 Pope-Hennessy (1949, p. 8)
97 Wemyss Reid (1890a, p. 16)
98 ibid., p. 19
99 Stokes and Thorne (1986, no page)
100 Pope-Hennessy (1949, p. 6)
101 ibid.
102 Crewe (1929)
103 Peacock (1891, p. 27)

104 Russell (1898/2009, p. 25)
105 Pope-Hennessy (1949, p. 6)
106 ibid., p. 10
107 ibid., p. 9
108 ibid.
109 Pope-Hennessy (1949)
110 ibid., p. 11
111 ibid., p. 12
112 Allen (1978, p. 43)
113 ibid.
114 ibid., p. 42
115 ibid., p. 43
116 ibid., p. 45
117 Blocksidge (2011, p. 96)
118 Martin (1980, p. 87)
119 ibid.
120 Lubenow (1998, p. 21)
121 Allen (1978, p. 23)
122 ibid., pp. 24-25
123 Lubenow (1998, p. 30)
124 ibid., p. 125
125 Allen (1978, p. 49)
126 Blocksidge (2011, p. 96)
127 Allen (1978, p. 50)
128 quoted in ibid., p. 51
129 quoted in Blocksidge (2011, p. 80)
130 quoted in ibid., p. 96
131 quoted in Allen (1978, pp. 141-142)
132 quoted in ibid.
133 ibid.
134 Dellamora (1990)
135 Blocksidge (2011, p. 258)
136 quoted in Allen (1978, p. 140)
137 ibid.
138 quoted in Blocksidge (2011, p. 105)
139 ibid., p. 111
140 ibid., p. 124
141 ibid., p. 127
142 Dellamora (1990)
143 ibid., p. 21
144 ibid., p. 22
145 Kolb (2000, p. 385)
146 quoted in ibid.
147 ibid.
148 quoted in Dellamora (1990, p. 26)
149 Kolb (2000, p. 385)
150 Pope-Hennessy (1949)
151 Kolb (2000, p. 386)
152 quoted in ibid., p. 386
153 Martin (1980, p. 89)
154 ibid.
155 Chainey (1995, p. 152)
156 Allen (1978, p. 133)
157 Deacon (1985)
158 Blocksidge (2011, p. 111)
159 quoted in Blocksidge (2011, p. 83)
160 Allen (1978, p. 53)
161 ibid., p. 237, n.5
162 Pope-Hennessy (1949)
163 ibid., p. 32
164 Wemyss Reid (1890a), quoted in Peacock (1891, p. 28)
165 Bullen (2004)
166 Monckton Milnes (1834)
167 Tennyson (1897a, p. 132)
168 ibid.
169 quoted in Blocksidge (2011, p. 223)
170 ibid., p. 224
171 ibid.
172 Pope-Hennessy (1949, p. 79)
173 ibid., p. 79
174 ibid.
175 Pope-Hennessy (1949)
176 Wemyss Reid (1890a, pp. 164-65)
177 Pope-Hennessy (1949, p. 10)
178 ibid., p. 10
179 Russell (1898/2009, p. 25)
180 ibid., pp. 26-27
181 ibid., p. 27
182 Pope-Hennessy (1949, p. 80)
183 ibid., p. 81
184 ibid., p. 84
185 ibid., p. 89
186 ibid.
187 ibid.
188 Wemyss Reid (1890a, p. 170)
189 Ellmann (1950)
190 quoted in Tennyson (1897a, p. 157)
191 quoted in ibid., p. 158
192 quoted in ibid., p. 159
193 ibid., p. 160
194 Rader (1962, p. 266)
195 Batchelor (2014, p. 106)
196 Pope-Hennessy (1949, p. 96)
197 Wemyss Reid (1890a, p. 198)
198 Richardson (1995, p. 181)
199 ibid., pp. 184-86
200 ibid.
201 quoted in ibid., p. 199
202 Blake (1967, p. 149)
203 ibid.
204 *Hansard* (8 December 1837)
205 quoted in Wemyss Reid (1890a, p. 205)
206 *Hansard* (13 February 1838)
207 Pope-Hennessy (1949, pp. 99-100)
208 quoted in ibid., p. 100
209 Wemyss Reid (1890a, pp. 216-217)
210 ibid., p. 206
211 Monckton Milnes (1838a)
212 Monckton Milnes (1838b)
213 Horne (1844, p. 154)
214 Peacock (1891, p. 34)
215 Monckton Milnes (1834)
216 Crewe (1920, p. 203)
217 Peacock (1891, p. 30)
218 Pope-Hennessy (1949)
219 Horne (1844)
220 from Monckton Milnes (1846, pp. 111-113)
221 Pope-Hennessy (1951)
222 Pope-Hennessy (1949, p. 106)
223 Wemyss Reid (1890a, p. 223)
224 quoted in Ashton (2002, p. 180)
225 Kaplan (1993, p. 254)
226 ibid., p. 251
227 Pope-Hennessy (1949, p. 113)
228 ibid.

229 Kaplan (1993, p. 194)
230 ibid., p. 320
231 Wemyss Reid (1890a, p. 234)
232 Monckton Milnes (1840a)
233 Tilton (1990, p. 25); see also Koch (2012, p. 118)
234 quoted in Carlyle (1893 , p. 263)
235 Harvey (2016, p. 3)
236 quoted in Johnson (2014, p. 266)
237 Sommer (2018, p. 129)
238 Wemyss Reid (1890a, p. 40)
239 Carlyle (1893, p. 276)
240 Wemyss Reid (1890a p. 241)
241 Tilton (1990, p. 25)
242 ibid.
243 Rusk (1949, p. 285)
244 Thomas (2005, pp. 1-2)
245 Pope-Hennessy (1949, p. 128)
246 Thackeray (1840, p. 158)
247 Pope-Hennessy (1949, p. 129)
248 Cooper (1974)
249 quoted in Thomas (2005, p. 2)
250 Thackeray (1840, pp. 150-158)
251 Dickens, C. (1846)
252 Thackeray (1840, p. 158)
253 Cooper (1974, pp. 106-107)
254 Pope-Hennessy (1949, p. 130)
255 ibid., p. 133
256 Boase (1954)
257 ibid., p. 321
258 Bullen (2004, p. 279)
259 ibid.
260 ibid., p. 278
261 Kaplan (1993, p. 267)
262 ibid.
263 Froude (1902a, p. 223)
264 ibid., p. 224
265 Pope-Hennessy (1949, p. 140)
266 Froude (1902a, p. 225)
267 letter dated 17 April, quoted in ibid., p. 228
268 Ashton (2002, p. 222)
269 quoted in Wemyss Reid (1890a, p. 256)
270 Carlyle (1893, pp. 323-324)
271 Pope-Hennessy (1949)
272 ibid.
273 Monckton Milnes (1841)
274 Pope-Hennessy (1951, p. 144)
275 ibid.
276 ibid., p. 148
277 ibid.
278 letter to C.J. MacCarthy, quoted in Wemyss Reid (1890a, p. 264)
279 ibid., p. 268
280 ibid., p. 187
281 Monckton Milnes (1844b)
282 Pope-Hennessy (1949)
283 ibid., p. 164
284 Wemyss Reid (1890a, pp. 294-295)
285 quoted in Pope-Hennessy (1949, p. 231)
286 ibid.
287 Gosse (1905)
288 quoted in Pope-Hennessy (1949, p. 231)
289 Gosse (1897, p. 284)
290 Gosse (1905)
291 Symons (1920)
292 Pope-Hennessy (1949, p. 231)
293 Allingham (no date)
294 Monckton Milnes (1873)
295 Hood (1834)
296 Allingham (no date)
297 ibid.
298 Monckton Milnes (1873, p. xv)
299 Wemyss Reid (1890a, p. 347)
300 ibid., p. 348
301 ibid., p. 359
302 Garrett and Robbins (2006)
303 Pope-Hennessy (1949, p. 230)
304 Wemyss Reid (1890a, pp. 295-96)
305 ibid.
306 Pope-Hennessy (1949, p. 230)
307 *Hansard* (1 July 1845)
308 Thomas (2005, p. 6)
309 Cooper (1974, pp. 168-169)
310 Thomas (2005, p. 6)
311 *Punch* (24 Sept. 1842)
312 *The Irish Sketch Book* (May 1843)
313 Thomas (2005, p. 5)
314 Crewe (1929, pp. 9-10)
315 ibid., p. 10
316 ibid.
317 Roberts (1979, p. 4)
318 ibid., p. 244
319 ibid., p. 249
320 ibid., p. 245
321 ibid., p. 213
322 Pope-Hennessy (1949, p. 187)
323 ibid.
324 Monckton Milnes (1840b)
325 Roberts (1979, p. 213)
326 Crewe (1929); see also Horne (1844)
327 Monckton Milnes (1844a)
328 Walker (1921)
329 Horne (1844, p. 156)
330 Monckton Milnes (1844b)
331 Peacock (1891, p. 30)
332 ibid.
333 Crewe (1920, p. 203)
334 ibid.
335 Weeks Jnr (1989, pp. 394-95)
336 Millar (2006, p. 97)
337 Roberts (1979, p. 251)
338 Weeks Jnr (1989, p. 395)
339 ibid., pp. 395-396
340 Millar (2006, p. 7)
341 ibid., p. 10
342 Pope-Hennessy (1949, p194)
343 quoted in Wemyss Reid (1890a, p. 320)
344 Blake (1967); Stirling (1913)
345 Pope-Hennessy (1949, p. 194)
346 Stirling (1913, p. 194)
347 ibid.
348 ibid., p. 194
349 quoted in ibid., p. 196
350 quoted in Gathorne Hardy (1910, p. 53)
351 Millar (2006, p. 7)
352 ibid.

353 ibid., p. 8
354 ibid., p. 10
355 ibid., pp. 9-10
356 ibid., p. 207
357 ibid., pp. 139-140
358 ibid., p. 208
359 quoted in Wemyss Reid (1890a, pp. 364-65)
360 Blake (1967, p. 205)
361 quoted in Russell (2009, p. 26)
362 Blake (1967, p. 207)
363 Monckton Milnes (1847)
364 Pope-Hennessy (1949, p. 204)
365 Blake (1967, p. 207)
366 ibid.
367 quoted in ibid., pp. 206-7
368 ibid., p. 207
369 ibid., p. 209
370 ibid., p. 208
371 O'Kell (2013, p. 217)
372 Wemyss Reid (1890a, p. 377-8)
373 quoted in ibid., p. 378
374 Pope-Hennessy (1949, p. 251)
375 quoted in ibid., p. 253
376 ibid., p. 254
377 ibid.
378 Wemyss Reid (1890a, p. 388)
379 quoted in ibid., p. 387
380 ibid., p. 396
381 Park (1990, p. 3)
382 ibid., pp. 4-5
383 quoted in Carlyle, 1896, p. 188
384 Koch (2012, p. 118)
385 quoted in Sealts (1973, p. 530)
386 Rusk (1949, p. 342)
387 Thackeray (1848)
388 quoted in Sealts (1973, p. 530)
389 Sommer (2018, p. 491)
390 quoted in Sealts (1973, p. 351)
391 ibid.
392 ibid.
393 Rusk (1949, p. 354)
394 Pope-Hennessy (1949, p. 274)
395 ibid.
396 ibid., p. 287
397 quoted in Wemyss Reid (1890a, p. 416)
398 ibid.
399 ibid., p. 417
400 Millar (2006, p. 12)
401 ibid.
402 ibid., p. 239
403 quoted in Pope-Hennessy (1949, p. 289)
404 ibid.
405 ibid., p. 289
406 ibid., p. 290
407 O'Malley (1934); Woodham-Smith (1951)
408 Gill (2004, p. 221)
409 cf. Bostridge (2009); Small (2017)
410 Monckton Milnes (1848)
411 Marquess (1985, p. 38)
412 Allen (1975)
413 ibid., p. 24
414 ibid., p. 25
415 Selanders (2010, p. 72)
416 Sattin (2011, pp. 48-49)
417 quoted in O'Malley (1934, p. 30)
418 Cromwell (2013, p. 48); O'Malley (1934, p. 123)
419 Sattin (2011, p. 49)
420 ibid.
421 ibid.
422 quoted in Bates (2018, no page)
423 ibid.
424 Woodham-Smith (1951, p. 36)
425 ibid.
426 quoted in ibid., p. 45
427 Sattin (2011, pp. 48-49)
428 ibid., p. 52
429 ibid., p. 56
430 Motion (2003)
431 Wolfson (2015, p. 143)
432 ibid.
433 Strachan (2003, p. 25)
434 quoted in Wolfson (2015, p. 142)
435 ibid., p. 143
436 ibid.
437 Marquess (1985, p. 38)
438 Monckton Milnes (1848 I, xi)
439 Atkinson (2000, p. 189)
440 Wolfson (2015, p. 143)
441 Najarian (2002, p. 21)
442 Marquess (1985, pp. 56-57)
443 Saunders Boos (1976, p. 6)
444 Codell (1995); Plumly (2009); Scott (2003)
445 Saunders Boos (1976)
446 Marquess (1985)
447 Motion (2003)
448 Marquess (1985, p. 51)
449 Cromwell (2013)
450 Bostridge (2009, pp. 125-126)
451 quoted in Sattin (2011, p. 58)
452 ibid.
453 Cromwell (2013, p. 64)
454 Bostridge (2009, p. 126)
455 Sattin (2011, p. 59)
456 Bostridge (2009, p. 126) (underlining in original)
457 ibid.
458 Pope-Hennessy (1949, p. 306)
459 Sattin (2011, p. 152)
460 ibid., p. 243
461 O'Malley (1934, p. 173)
462 ibid.
463 quoted in ibid., p. 174
464 ibid.
465 Bostridge (2009, p. 127)
466 quoted in Kenny (2007, p. 235)
467 ibid.
468 Bostridge (2009)
469 ibid., p. 127
470 Pope-Hennessy (1949, p. 308)
471 ibid., pp. 304-305
472 ibid., p. 310
473 ibid., p. 308
474 Pope-Hennessy (1951, p. 58)
475 Pope-Hennessy (1949, pp. 311-312)
476 ibid., p. 312

477 Pope-Hennessy (1951, p. 2)
478 Pope-Hennessy (1951, pp. 9-10)
479 ibid., pp. 11-12
480 ibid., p. 15
481 ibid., p. 3
482 quoted in ibid., p. 4
483 ibid.
484 ibid., p. 26
485 ibid., p. 27
486 ibid., p. 24
487 ibid., p. 29
488 Glasgow (2005, p. 57)
489 ibid., p. 58
490 Fraser (1988)
491 Barker (2010)
492 ibid., p. 802
493 ibid.
494 Smith (2004, p. 8, n. 2)
495 Barker (2010, p. 815)
496 quoted in Smith (2004, p. 8)
497 Smith (2000)
498 quoted in Smith (2004, p. 273)
499 ibid.
500 Harman (2016, p. 331)
501 quoted in Chapple and Pollard (1997, p. 278)
502 ibid., p. 289
503 Wakely and Carson (2011, p. 25)
504 ibid.
505 ibid.
506 *The Morning Post*, 22 November 1855
507 Bostridge (2009, p. 194)
508 Pope-Hennessy (1951, p. 81)
509 ibid., p. 82
510 ibid.
511 ibid.
512 Wakely and Carson (2011)
513 quoted in Bostridge (2009, p. 128)
514 Pope-Hennessy, 1949, p. 307)
515 quoted in Sattin (2011, p. 60)
516 Pope-Hennessy (1951, p. 87)
517 ibid., p. 87
518 ibid., pp. 87 and 89
519 ibid., p. 91
520 ibid., p. 94
521 ibid.
522 Lyndon Shandley (1982)
523 ibid., p. 362
524 *Hansard* (14 May 1857)
525 ibid.
526 Horowitz et al., (2017)
527 Wemyss Reid (1890b, p. 28)
528 Pope-Hennessy (1951, p. 96)
529 ibid., p. 99
530 Roberts (1985)
531 ibid., p. 610
532 ibid.
533 Searle (1998, p. 225)
534 *Hansard* (12 August, 1857)
535 ibid.
536 ibid.
537 Roberts (1985, pp. 625-66)
538 ibid., p. 626
539 Lipzin (1943, p. 171)
540 McMahon (1989)
541 ibid., pp. 138-40
542 Monckton Milnes (1856)
543 quoted in McMahon (1989, p. 134)
544 Lipzin (1943, p. 170)
545 *The Liverpool Mercury* (17 April 1857)
546 quoted in Stewart (1936, p. 420, fn, 8)
547 Waddington (1975, p. 64)
548 ibid.
549 Waddington (1981, p. 1)
550 ibid., p. 66
551 ibid., p. 68
552 Waddington (1975, pp. 52-53)
553 Waddington (1981, p. 54)
554 Waddington (1975, p. 70)
555 Waddington (1981, p. 65)
556 Waddington (1975, p. 71)
557 Waddington (1981, p. 73)
558 Pope-Hennessy (1951 p. 105)
559 ibid., p. 106
560 ibid.
561 quoted in Wemyss Reid (1890b, p. 34)
562 Pope-Hennessy (1951, p. 111)
563 ibid., p. 107
564 ibid.
565 ibid., p. 92
566 ibid., pp. 93-94
567 ibid., p. 112
568 ibid., p. 114
569 ibid., p. 124
570 Colligan (2003)
571 ibid., p. 2
572 Rice (1991, pp. 220-221)
573 ibid., p. 222
574 ibid., pp. 226-227
575 ibid., p. 227
576 quoted in Rice (1991, p. 227)
577 ibid.
578 ibid., p. 228
579 Lutz (2011, p. 73)
580 Burton (1856)
581 ibid., p. 74
582 Dickey (2017, no page)
583 Rice (1991, p. 418)
584 Pope-Hennessy (1951)
585 Lovell (1999, p. 313)
586 ibid.
587 Kennedy (2005)
588 Rice (1991, pp. 420-421)
589 ibid.
590 Pope-Hennessy (1951, p. 125)
591 Rice (1991)
592 ibid.
593 ibid., p. 426
594 ibid.
595 Burton (1861)
596 Dickey (2017); Rice (1991)
597 Dickey (2017)
598 Rice (1991, pp. 428-429)
599 *The Spectator* (1860)
600 ibid.
601 Burton (1898, p. 225)
602 ibid., p. 348

603 Burton (1877, no page)
604 quoted in Rice (1991, p. 458) (punctuation as in original)
605 Rice (1991, p. 458)
606 ibid.
607 ibid., p. 458
608 Vámbéry (1904, pp. 256-257)
609 Rice (1991, p. 458)
610 quoted in Bell (1874, p. 211)
611 Pope-Hennessy, (1951, p. 220)
612 ibid.
613 Bell (1874)
614 Buchanan (1900)
615 ibid., p. 7
616 ibid., p. 16
617 ibid., p. 21
618 ibid.
619 ibid.
620 Monckton Milnes (1862, pp. vii-viii)
621 quoted in Pope-Hennessy (1951, p. 222)
622 Monckton Milnes (1862, p. viii)
623 ibid.
624 ibid.
625 Pope-Hennessy (1951, p. 223)
626 Buchanan (1900, p. 29)
627 ibid.
628 ibid., p. 30
629 Pope-Hennessy (1951, p. 225)
630 ibid., p, 224
631 ibid., p. 226
632 Monckton Milnes (1862, p. x)
633 Pope-Hennessy (1951, pp. 220 and 226-27)
634 quoted in Bell (1874, p. 212)
635 ibid., p. 210
636 Pope-Hennessy (1951, p. 129)
637 Thomas (1979, pp. 60-61)
638 ibid.
639 ibid., p. 62
640 Lutz (2011, p. 69)
641 ibid.
642 ibid., p. 73
643 quoted in ibid.
644 ibid., p. 70
645 ibid., p. 73
646 Rooksby (2017, p. 68)
647 Hare (1949, p. 64)
648 ibid., p. 63
649 Lafourcade (1932, p. 94)
650 ibid., p. 94
651 Thomas (1979, p. 64)
652 Rooksby (2017, p. 67)
653 quoted in Pope-Hennessy (1951, pp. 132-133)
654 Thomas (1979, p. 66)
655 Mitchell (1965, p. 81)
656 Thomas (1979)
657 quoted, in Rooksby (2017, p. 76)
658 ibid.
659 ibid., p. 77
660 Mitchell (1965, p. 85)
661 Gibson (1992)
662 Mitchell (1965, p. 85)
663 ibid.
664 quoted in Gibson (1992, p. 125)
665 Mitchell (1965, p. 81)
666 ibid.
667 ibid., p. 82
668 Wilson (1971)
669 ibid., p. 240
670 ibid., p. 241
671 ibid.
672 ibid.
673 Pope-Hennessy (1951, p. 143)
674 ibid., p. 129
675 Rooksby (2017, pp. 67-68)
676 Foreman (2010)
677 Adams (1918, p. 116)
678 Putnis (2004)
679 Pope-Hennessy (1951, p. 139)
680 Monaghan (1940, p. 103)
681 ibid.
682 Adams (1918, p. 126)
683 Foreman (2010)
684 Jackson (1997, p. 83)
685 Foreman (2010, p. 94)
686 Shain (1962, p. 406)
687 Pope-Hennessy (1951, p. 168)
688 ibid., p. 165
689 Jackson (1997, p. 84)
690 ibid.
691 Foreman (2010, p. 102)
692 Adams (1900, p. 217)
693 Foreman (2010, p. 170)
694 ibid.
695 Duberman (1960, p. 279)
696 Putnis (2004, p. 94)
697 Cohen (1956)
698 Ellis et al. (1886, p. 151)
699 Foreman (2010, pp. 170-71)
700 Putnis (2004)
701 Jackson (1997, p. 85)
702 ibid.
703 ibid., p. 82
704 Adams (1918, p. 124)
705 ibid., p. 125
706 ibid., p. 126
707 Pope-Hennessy (1951, p. 168)
708 Wemyss Reid (1890b, pp. 85-86)
709 Adams (1918, pp. 137-38)
710 Pope-Hennessy (1951, p. 139)
711 ibid., p. 142
712 Adams (1918, p. 139)
713 ibid., pp. 140-41
714 ibid., p. 141
715 Pope-Hennessy (1951, p. 142)
716 ibid., p. 143
717 Stevenson (1997, p. 69)
718 *The Times* (10 January 1862), quoted in Dusinberre (1977, pp. 165-65)
719 Monaghan (1940, p. 319)
720 Adams (1992, p. 60)
721 ibid.
722 Adams (1918, p. 170)
723 Adams (1992, p. 61)
724 Craig (1863); *National Anti-Slavery Standard* (1864)
725 Pope-Hennessy (1951, p. 170)

726 ibid. p. 171
727 no page, fn.1
728 Gosse (1917)
729 ibid., p. 96
730 ibid.
731 ibid.
732 Aplin (2011)
733 quoted in ibid., p. 53 (underlining, punctuation errors and abbreviations in original)
734 ibid., p. 54
735 ibid.
736 Black (2014, p. 172)
737 ibid., pp. 171-172
738 Kennedy (2005, p. 167)
739 Lutz (2011, p. 75)
740 Kennedy (2005, p. 170)
741 Lutz (2011, p. 150)
742 Black (2014, p. 172)
743 Lutz (2011, p. 173)
744 Croft-Cook (1967, p. 35)
745 ibid.
746 Gibson (1992, pp. 240-250)
747 quoted in ibid., p. 242
748 Lutz (2011, p. 215)
749 Dau (2014); Sigel (2005)
750 Sigel (2002); Woollacott (2006); etc.
751 Sigel (2002. p. 51)
752 ibid., p. 52
753 Lutz (2011, pp. 13-14)
754 Gibson (1992, p. 257)
755 ibid.
756 Lutz (2011, p. 114)
757 Knickerbocker (1947, p. 343)
758 ibid.
759 ibid.
760 quoted in ibid., pp. 240-41
761 Rooksby (2017, p. 123)
762 Pope-Hennessy (1951, p. 137)
763 Thomas (1979, p. 95)
764 quoted in ibid.
765 Meyers (1988, p. 196)
766 Pease (2000, p. 37)
767 Hare (1949, pp. 118-19)
768 Meyers (1988, p. 201)
769 Thomas (1979, p. 97)
770 Pope-Hennessy (1951, pp. 137-8)
771 Thomas (1979, p. 97)
772 quoted in Pope-Hennessy (1951, p. 124) (abbreviation in original)
773 Devereux (2017, p. 752)
774 quoted in ibid., p. 755
775 ibid., p. 756
776 Rochford (2016)
777 quoted in ibid., p. 61
778 ibid., p. 62
779 ibid.
780 ibid.
781 Peters (2014)
782 Baker and Clarke (2016, p. 186)
783 Peters (2014, p. 294)
784 Clarke (2004, p. 111)
785 Lycett (2014, p. 277)
786 Collins (2019, p. xii)
787 quoted in Taylor (1946, p. 6)
788 Super (1990, p. 125)
789 ibid., p. 205
790 ibid.
791 Wemyss Reid (1890b, pp. 155-56)
792 ibid., p. 206
793 Kaplan (1993, p. 429)
794 quoted in ibid.
795 quoted in Wemyss Reid (1890b, p. 146)
796 Tyndall (1892, pp. 260-61)
797 ibid., p. 261
798 Symons (2001)
799 ibid., p. 8
800 Froude (1902b, p. 350)
801 ibid.
802 Buchanan (1900)
803 ibid., (no page number)
804 ibid.
805 quoted in Pope-Hennessy (1951, p. 133, fn.3)
806 quoted in Ley (1919, p. 243)
807 ibid., p. 244
808 ibid., p. 245
809 Wemyss Reid (1890b, p. 80)
810 ibid., p. 227
811 West (1995)
812 Ley (1919, p. 245)
813 Tomalin (2011)
814 Ward (1915, p. 66)
815 Tomalin (2011, p. 391)
816 Storey (1971, p. 34)
817 West (1995, p. 24)
818 Wemyss Reid (1890b, p. 228)
819 ibid.
820 ibid., p. 229
821 Mitchell (1984, pp. 23-24)
822 ibid., p. 24
823 *Wakefield Express* (18 April 1873)
824 quoted in Waddington (1988, pp. 2-3)
825 *Wakefield Express* (16 April 1873)
826 Machin (1958, p. 40)
827 ibid., p. 152
828 ibid., p. 154
829 ibid., pp. 155-157
830 ibid., p. 166
831 Bullock (1972, p. 50)
832 Machin (1958)
833 ibid., p. 168
834 Bullock (1976, p. 50)
835 ibid.
836 ibid., p. 51
837 Machin (1958, p. 175)
838 Bellamy and Saville (1978, p. 268)
839 Church and Outram (1998, p. 65)
840 ibid., p. 68
841 Page Arnot (1949, p. 103)
842 Bellamy and Saville (1975, p. 348)
843 Lawson (1941, pp. 12-13)
844 ibid., p. 20
845 ibid., p. 33
846 ibid.
847 Bellamy and Saville (1975, p. 348)
848 Bullock (1976, p. 3)
849 Machin, (1958, p. 183)

850 ibid.
851 Anderson (1982, p. 77)
852 *House of Lords Hansard*,13 March 1873
853 Anderson (1982)
854 Pope-Hennessy (1951, p. 235)
855 Wemyss Reid (1890b, p. 289)
856 ibid.
857 Pope-Hennessy (1951, p. 236)
858 ibid.
859 Hare (1949, pp. 167-8)
860 Gohdes (1942)
861 quoted in Pope-Hennessy (1951, p. 240)
862 ibid., p. 239
863 ibid., p. 241
864 quoted in Pope-Hennessy (1955, p. 11)
865 Wemyss Reid (1890b, p. 325)
866 quoted in Grant (2003, p. 327)
867 Wemyss Reid (1890b, p 319)
868 Elderkin (1895, p. 9)
869 ibid.; Whiting (1899, p. 338)
870 Wemyss Reid (1890b, p. 326)
871 *Sheffield Independent* (18 November 1876)
872 Wemyss Reid (1890b, p. 346)
873 ibid.
874 Pope-Hennessy (1951, p. 247)
875 Ewan et al. (2006, p. 33)
876 quoted in Watt (1974, p. 224)
877 Pope-Hennessy (1951, p. 247)
878 Hare (1949)
879 Remlap, (1879)
880 ibid., p. 30
881 ibid., pp. 30-32
882 Langtry (2000, p. 90)
883 Ross (1959, p. 254)
884 Langtry (2000, p. 90)
885 Bogar (2006, p. 135)
886 Langtry (2000, p. 90)
887 ibid., p. 86
888 ibid., p. 87
889 quoted in ibid.
890 ibid.
891 ibid., p. 86
892 ibid., pp. 86-87
893 Wilde (1877)
894 quoted in Hart-Davis (1962, p. 42)
895 quoted in ibid., p. 41
896 Gamble (2008, p. 199) (emphasis added)
897 ibid.
898 ibid.
899 Lubbock (1920, p. 52)
900 ibid.
901 James (1975, p. 110)
902 Gamble (2008)
903 ibid., p. 255
904 Edel (1975, p. 199)
905 ibid., p. 200
906 ibid., p. 208
907 ibid., pp. 208-209
908 Pope-Hennessy (1955, p. 14)
909 ibid., pp. 14-15
910 ibid., p. 17
911 Wemyss Reid (1890b, p. 384)
912 Pope-Hennessy (1955, p. 18)
913 ibid.
914 ibid., pp. 18-19
915 Pope-Hennessy (1951, p. 250)
916 Richards (2007); Terry (1908)
917 Stoker (1906)
918 ibid., p. 355
919 Bingham (1978, p. 151)
920 Gross (1994, p. 151)
921 Bingham (1978, p. 151)
922 ibid., pp. 151-152
923 Brereton (1908, p. 315)
924 Gross (1994, p. 152)
925 Bingham (1978, p. 152)
926 Yarker (1959, p. 203)
927 Lucas (1982)
928 ibid., p. 173 (emphasis in original)
929 ibid., p. 174
930 Mallock (1920, p. 59)
931 ibid.
932 Lucas (1982, pp. 174-5)
933 ibid., p. 175
934 ibid., p. 176
935 Mallock (1920, p. 172)
936 Wemyss Reid (1890b, p. 401)
937 ibid., p. 407
938 ibid., pp. 408
939 Pope-Hennessy (1955, p. 19)
940 Hardy and Pinion (1972)
941 ibid., p. xv
942 quoted in Wemyss Reid (1890b, p. 418)
943 Pope-Hennessy (1955, p. 20)
944 ibid., p. 21
945 ibid., pp. 22-23
946 Wemyss Reid (1890b, p. 429)
947 ibid.
948 ibid., p. 430
949 ibid., pp. 430-31
950 ibid., p. 436
951 quoted in Pope-Hennessy (1955, p. 23)
952 Pope-Hennessy (1955, p. 23)
953 ibid., p. 26
954 ibid., p. 29
955 ibid., p. 32
956 Pope-Hennessy (1955, p. 54)
957 McKinstry (2006)
958 ibid.
959 ibid., p. 67
960 ibid.
961 ibid., p. 69
962 Cowles (1973, p. 145)
963 McKinstry (2006)
964 ibid., p. 70
965 ibid.
966 Bloch (2015, p. 23)
967 quoted in Pope-Hennessy (1955, p. 31)
968 ibid., p. 32
969 ibid., p. 35
970 Hall (1929, p. 4)
971 ibid., pp. 1-2
972 Henniker (1891, 1892 and 1893, respectively)
973 cited in Sylvia (2003, p. 55)
974 Stewart (1971, p. 29)
975 Sylvia (2003, p. 56)

976 ibid., p. 69, n. 25
977 ibid., p. 58
978 ibid., pp. 57-58
979 ibid., p. 59
980 ibid.
981 ibid., p. 60
982 ibid., p. 61
983 ibid., p. 61
984 ibid., p. 62
985 ibid., p. 63
986 ibid., pp. 67-68
987 Nissen (2000); Scharnhorst (2000)
988 Nissen (2000)
989 see, for example, Harte (1951, p. 357)
990 Nissen (2000, p. 230)
991 ibid.
992 McCarthy (1899, p. 61)
993 Hardy and Pinion (1972, p. xvii)
994 Pinion (1990, p. 176); Tennyson (1897a, p. 395)
995 Hardy and Pinion (1972, p. xvi)
996 ibid., xvii
997 Bullock (1976, p. 173)
998 Machin (1958, p. 234)
999 ibid., p. 236
1000 ibid., p. 244
1001 ibid., p. 245
1002 ibid., p. 246
1003 Bullock (1976, p. 170)
1004 Machin (1958, p. 248)
1005 ibid.
1006 ibid., p. 250
1007 *Leeds Mercury* (7 September 1885)
1008 *Leeds Mercury* (26 September 1885)
1009 *Leeds Mercury* (2 February1886)
1010 *Daily Gazette for Middlesbrough* (19 January 1886)
1011 ibid.
1012 *Sheffield and Rotherham Independent* (16 February 1886)
1013 Machin (1958, p. 256)
1014 ibid., p. 488
1015 Page Arnot (1949, p. 92)
1016 ibid., p. 94
1017 ibid., p. 103
1018 Neville (1976 p. 338)
1019 Geary (1985, p. 12)
1020 Neville (1976, p. 346)
1021 *Glasgow Herald* (9 September 1893)
1022 Neville (1976, p. 357)
1023 Lawson (1941, p. 48)
1024 ibid., p. 357
1025 McKinstry (2006, p. 263)
1026 ibid., p. 264
1027 ibid., p. 266
1028 ibid., p. 266
1029 ibid., p. 267
1030 Page Arnot (1949, p. 251)
1031 Fraser (1999, p. 82)
1032 McKinstry (2006, p. 267)
1033 ibid.
1034 Bellamy and Saville (1978. p. 269)
1035 Church and Outram (1998, p. 65)
1036 Brown (1975); Vessey (2013)
1037 Bellamy and Saville (1975)
1038 ibid., p. 348
1039 ibid.
1040 McKinstry (2006, p. 267)
1041 ibid.
1042 Miners' Federation of Great Britain (1894)
1043 Loughlin (2007a, p. 109)
1044 ibid.
1045 ibid., p. 110
1046 ibid., p. 111
1047 ibid., p. 112
1048 ibid., p. 306
1049 Loughlin (2007b, p. 237)
1050 ibid.
1051 ibid.
1052 Pope-Hennessy (1955, p. 44)
1053 O'Mahony (1912, p. 306)
1054 ibid.
1055 Pope-Hennessy (1955, p. 38)
1056 ibid.
1057 O'Mahony (1912, p. 308)
1058 Pope-Hennessy (1955, p. 43)
1059 Pinion (1990, p. 131)
1060 Millgate (2004)
1061 Pinion (1990, p. 132)
1062 ibid.
1063 ibid.
1064 Millgate (2004, p. 309)
1065 ibid., p. 308
1066 Pite (2006, p. 329)
1067 Millgate (2004, p. 308)
1068 Tóibín (2009)
1069 ibid., p. 217
1070 ibid., p. 218
1071 Edel (1974, p. 6)
1072 ibid., pp. 8-9
1073 ibid., p. 8
1074 Tóibín (2009)
1075 McKinstry (2006)
1076 ibid.
1077 Bloch (2015, pp. 36-37)
1078 ibid.
1079 cf. Bloch (2015); McKinstry (2006); Parris (1997)
1080 McKinstry (2006)
1081 O'Mahony (1912, p. 309)
1082 quoted in Pope-Hennessy (1955, p. 55)
1083 ibid., p. 47
1084 O'Mahony (1912, pp. 308-309)
1085 Pope-Hennessy (1955, p. 46)
1086 Crewe (1895, pp. 377-378)
1087 Hardy (1962)
1088 Pinion (1990, p. 132)
1089 Pite (2006, p. 330)
1090 ibid., p. 334
1091 Millgate (2004, p. 310)
1092 ibid.
1093 Pinion (1990, p. 132)
1094 ibid., p. 133
1095 Pite (2006, p. 331)
1096 Millgate (2004, p. 310)
1097 ibid. p. 311
1098 quoted in ibid.

1099 ibid., p. 312
1100 ibid.
1101 Pite (2006, p. 336)
1102 Millgate (2004, p. 314)
1103 Pite (2006, p. 336)
1104 Stewart (1971, p. 30)
1105 Pinion (1990, p. 142)
1106 Gibson (1996, p. 127)
1107 Pinion (1990, p. 142)
1108 Dalziel (1992, p. 261)
1109 Dutta (2010, p. 139)
1110 Millgate (2004)
1111 Purdy (1944, p. 123)
1112 Dalziel (1992, p. 261)
1113 ibid., p. 263
1114 Dalziel (1992, p. 271)
1115 ibid., p. 268
1116 Dutta (2010)
1117 Henniker (1896)
1118 Purdy (1944, p. 126)
1119 ibid.
1120 Harvey (2003, p. 38)
1121 ibid.
1122 Pinion (1990)
1123 Stewart (1971)
1124 quoted in ibid., p. 30
1125 Millgate (2004, p. 313)
1126 quoted in Gibson (1996, p. 128)
1127 ibid.
1128 Millgate (2004, p. 312)
1129 quoted in ibid.
1130 ibid., p. 352
1131 Ireland (2008, p. 61)
1132 ibid.
1133 ibid., pp. 61-62
1134 e.g. Ireland (2008); Pite (2006); Ray (1977)
1135 Pite (2006, p. 338)
1136 ibid.
1137 ibid.
1138 Gibson (1996, p. 129)
1139 Page (1986)
1140 ibid., p. 152
1141 Pettit (2016, p. 201)
1142 Bullen (2013)
1143 Pite (2006, p. 352)
1144 Moore (1990, p. 34)
1145 ibid., pp. 251-252
1146 Pite (2006, p. 339)
1147 ibid., p. 340
1148 ibid.
1149 ibid.
1150 ibid., p. 341
1151 Hardy and Pinion (1972, xvii)
1152 Sylvia (2011, p. 144)
1153 ibid., p. 146
1154 see Lyons (1968) for further biographical information.
1155 McCarthy (1899, p. 323)
1156 ibid,. p. 325
1157 Lyons (1968)
1158 ibid.
1159 McCarthy (1899, p. 323)
1160 ibid., p. 326
1161 Lyons (1968, p. 246)
1162 ibid. p. 247
1163 Sylvia (2011, p. 147)
1164 ibid., p. 153
1165 Lyons (1968, p. 247)
1166 quoted in ibid. pp. 247-248
1167 Sylvia (2011, p. 148)
1168 ibid., p. 147
1169 ibid.
1170 ibid., p. 149
1171 quoted in ibid.
1172 ibid., p. 155
1173 ibid., p. 150
1174 ibid.
1175 ibid., p. 156
1176 Pope-Hennessy (1955, p. 51)
1177 Rosebery (1955, p. 179)
1178 Thwaite (1991, p. 165)
1179 Blunt, quoted in Waller (2008, p. 248)
1180 Thwaite (1991, p. 165)
1181 Blunt, quoted in Waller (2008, p. 248)
1182 Waller (2008, p. 248)
1183 Thwaite (1991, p. 165)
1184 Nissen (2000)
1185 Harte (1951, p. 418)
1186 quoted in Thwaite (1991, p. 165)
1187 Harte (1951, pp. 418-19)
1188 Thwaite (1991, p. 165)
1189 ibid.
1190 ibid.
1191 quoted in ibid., p. 166
1192 ibid., p. 167
1193 Murray (2006)
1194 ibid., p. 165
1195 ibid.
1196 Mortimer and Willett (1969)
1197 ibid., pp. 53-54
1198 ibid., p. 54
1199 *Leeds Mercury* (4 September 1896)
1200 *Express* (12 September 1896)
1201 quoted in Pope-Hennessy (1955, p. 54)
1202 *Otago Witness* (29 October 1896)
1203 *Yorkshire Gazette* (19 September 1896)
1204 *Yorkshire Evening Post* (18 September, 1896)
1205 Pope-Hennessy (1955, p. 51)
1206 *Yorkshire Evening Post* (18 September 1896)
1207 *Daily Telegraph* (14 February, 2013)
1208 Friends of Queen's Park (no date)
1209 ibid.
1210 Page Arnot (1949, p. 302)
1211 Rubinstein (1978, p. 105)
1212 ibid., p. 106
1213 ibid., p. 121
1214 ibid., p. 123
1215 ibid.
1216 ibid., p. 127
1217 ibid.
1218 ibid.
1219 ibid., pp. 129-30
1220 Lawson (1941, p. 75)
1221 ibid., p. 76
1222 *The Times* (25 October 1957)
1223 ibid.

1224 Greaves (1938, p. 69)
1225 ibid., p. 70
1226 Baylies (1993, pp. 176-177)
1227 ibid., p. 177
1228 *Yorkshire Evening Post* (24 March 1898)
1229 ibid.
1230 ibid.
1231 Baylies (1993, p. 205)
1232 ibid.
1233 YMA Ordinary Council Meeting Minutes, 14 November 1898
1234 Pickles (2010, p. 379)
1235 ibid.
1236 *Yorkshire Herald* (9 February 1899)
1237 *Sheffield and Rotherham Independent* (4 March 1898)
1238 Greaves (1938, p. 72)
1239 ibid.
1240 ibid., p. 76
1241 Baldry (1899)
1242 Pope-Hennessy (1955, p. 56)
1243 Crewe (1955, p. xiii)
1244 ibid., p. xiv
1245 McKinstry (2006, p. 414)
1246 Pope-Hennessy (1955, p. 57)
1247 ibid.
1248 ibid.
1249 Truth (1899, p. 1085)
1250 ibid.
1251 ibid.
1252 ibid.
1253 ibid.
1254 *The Times* (4 September 1899)
1255 Tablet (1900)
1256 *Hansard*, 10 January 1894
1257 Craig (1989); Tablet (1900)
1258 Pope-Hennessy (1955, p. 58)
1259 Crewe (1955, p. xiv)
1260 Ebbatson (1993, p. 104)
1261 ibid.
1262 Badsey (2007, p. 79)
1263 Swart (2010, p. 350)
1264 Ebbatson (1993)
1265 Badsey (2007, p. 79)
1266 Swart (2010, p. 350)
1267 Ebbatson (1993)
1268 Hall (1929, p. 21)
1269 ibid., pp. 38-39
1270 ibid., p. 61
1271 ibid., p. 74
1272 ibid., p. 77
1273 ibid., p. 106
1274 ibid., p. 163
1275 ibid., p. 227
1276 ibid., p. 230
1277 ibid., p. 231
1278 Miller (2019); Minnaar (1987)
1279 Miller (2019, p. 2)
1280 ibid.
1281 Amery (1909)
1282 Hall (1929, p. 238)
1283 ibid., p. 239
1284 ibid., p. 241
1285 ibid., p. 241
1286 ibid., p. 259
1287 ibid., p. 262
1288 ibid., pp. 262-63
1289 ibid., p. 264
1290 ibid.
1291 Creswicke (1902, p. 78)
1292 Hall (1929, p. 264)
1293 Minnaar (1987, p. 11)
1294 Judd and Surridge (2012)
1295 Farwell (1976, p. 330)
1296 Shearing (2005)
1297 Graaff-Reinet Museum (no date)
1298 South African History Online (2012)
1299 Creswicke (1902, p. 146)
1300 ibid., pp. 146-147
1301 Farwell (1976, p. 333)
1302 Allan (no date, p. 9)
1303 ibid.
1304 Farwell (1976, p. 344)
1305 Hall (1929, pp, 296-97)
1306 Judd and Surridge (2012, p. 236)
1307 Morgan (2002); Surridge (1993)
1308 quoted in South African History Online (2012)
1309 ibid.
1310 Swart (2010, p. 349)
1311 West (2017)
1312 Swart (2010, p. 351)
1313 ibid.
1314 ibid., p. 352
1315 ibid., pp. 353-354
1316 Badsey (2007, p. 88)
1317 ibid.
1318 ibid., p. 91
1319 ibid., p. 92
1320 Swart (2010, p. 354)
1321 Franco (2013)
1322 Sylvia (2011)
1323 ibid.
1324 Hardy and Pinion (1972, p. 85); Sylvia (2011, p. 55)
1325 quoted in Sylvia (2011, p. 51)
1326 Sylvia (2011, p. 64)
1327 Major Cecil Pereira, DSO, Coldstream Guards, quoted in Henniker (1912, p. 82)
1328 Sylvia (2011, p. 65)
1329 King and Morgan (1979)
1330 ibid., p. 67
1331 Hardy and Pinion (1972, p. 84)
1332 ibid., p. 85
1333 ibid.
1334 Millgate (2004, p. 370)
1335 ibid.
1336 quoted in King and Morgan (1979, p. 73)
1337 King and Morgan (1979)
1338 Kendall, 2006, p. 18)
1339 ibid., p. 16
1340 ibid., p. 5
1341 ibid., p. 7
1342 quoted in Hardy and Pinion (1972, p. 87)
1343 letter dated 26 January 1900, quoted in ibid., p. 90
1344 Hardy and Pinion (1972, p. 92)

1345 quoted in ibid., p. 92
1346 quoted in ibid., pp. 96-97
1347 letter dated 9 November 1899, quoted in ibid., pp. 86-87
1348 letter dated 25 September, quoted in ibid., p. 106
1349 quoted in ibid., p. 107
1350 Baylies (1993, p. 331)
1351 Page Arnot (1949, p. 311)
1352 ibid.
1353 Taylor (1992)
1354 ibid., p. 250
1355 Baylies (1993, p. 262)
1356 Howell (1983, p. 21)
1357 Baylies (1993, p. 331)
1358 ibid.
1359 Baylies (1993)
1360 *Yorkshire Evening Post* (15 July 1902)
1361 Baylies (1993, p. 231)
1362 MacFarlane (1987, p. 1)
1363 Neville (1976, pp. 152-3)
1364 Gregory (1968, pp. 22)
1365 Baylies (1993, p. 313)
1366 MacFarlane (1987, p. 55)
1367 Baylies (1993, p. 306)
1368 ibid., p. 187
1369 *Express* (2 September 1902)
1370 Baylies (1993, p. 187)
1371 *Express* (18 October 1902)
1372 ibid.
1373 Berthoud (2003, p. 1)
1374 ibid., p. 4
1375 ibid., p. 5
1376 ibid., p. 6
1377 ibid.
1378 Moore and Hedgecoe (1986, p. 11)
1379 Berthoud (2003, p. 6)
1380 *Express* (15 June 1903)
1381 ibid.
1382 ibid.
1383 ibid.
1384 *Yorkshire Evening Post* (11 June 1903)
1385 *Express* (15 June 1903)
1386 *Express* (27 June 1903)
1387 *Yorkshire Evening Post* (9 September 1903)
1388 ibid.
1389 *Sheffield Daily Telegraph* (29 September 1903)
1390 ibid.
1391 ibid.
1392 *Leeds Mercury* (19 October 1903)
1393 ibid.
1394 Baylies (1993, p. 188)
1395 ibid., p. 187
1396 Yorkshire Miners' Association (1903)
1397 Joint Committee (1903)
1398 *Express* (9 January 1904)
1399 ibid.
1400 ibid.
1401 *Express* (30 January 1904)
1402 ibid.
1403 Bellamy and Saville (1978, p. 269)
1404 ibid., p. 268
1405 Pope-Hennessy (1949; 1951)
1406 Boucher (1935, p. 76)
1407 Pope-Hennessy (1951, p. 133)
1408 Boucher (1935, p. 77) (emphasis in original)
1409 ibid., p. 78
1410 Crewe (1955, p. x)
1411 ibid.
1412 Pope-Hennessy (1955, p. 58)
1413 Crewe (1955. p. x)
1414 Soames (2002, p. 35)
1415 Gilbert (1991); Soames (2002)
1416 Soames (2002, p. 36)
1417 Gilbert (1991, p. 169)
1418 Pope-Hennessy (1955, p, 60)
1419 ibid., p. 62
1420 ibid., p. 72
1421 ibid., p. 65
1422 ibid., p. 66
1423 quoted in Crewe (1955, xi/xii)
1424 Gregory (1968)
1425 Taylor (1992, p. 239)
1426 Gregory (1968, p. 22)
1427 Baylies (1993, p. 264)
1428 Gregory (1968, p. 25)
1429 Pelling (1967)
1430 Miners' Federation of Great Britain (1905, p. 64)
1431 Howell (1983, p. 109)
1432 Taylor (1992)
1433 Bellamy and Saville (1975)
1434 Taylor (1992, pp. 248-9)
1435 ibid., p. 249
1436 Howell (1983, p. 51)
1437 McIlroy and Campbell (2004, pp. 56-57) (emphasis added)
1438 *The Times* (17 June 1938)
1439 quoted in Waddington (2013, p. 33)
1440 ibid.
1441 ibid.
1442 Hulme (1986, p. 4)
1443 ex-Fryston woman, quoted in Waddington (2013, p. 33)
1444 Bullock (1976, p. 9)
1445 ibid., p. 9
1446 ibid., p. 150
1447 *Express* (6 October 1950)
1448 Bullock (1972)
1449 Hulme (1986); Van Riel et al. (1990)
1450 Bullock (1972)
1451 Sloan (2012)
1452 Lofthouse (1986)
1453 Waddington (1988)

References

Adams, C.F. (1900) *Charles Francis Adams: By His Son*. Boston and New York: Houghton, Mifflin Company.

Adams, H. (1918) *The Education of Henry Adams: An Autobiography*. Boston and New York: Houghton Mifflin Company.

Adams, H. (1992) *Selected Letters*. Harvard Connecticut: Harvard University Press.

Allan, I. V. (no date) 'Ivie H. Allan – the man who took the historical photographs about the execution', Undated Newsletter, Graaff-Reinet Museum.
https://www.graaffreinetmuseums.co.za/images/News08_02.doc

Allen, D.R. (1975) 'Florence Nightingale: toward a psychohistorical interpretation', *The Journal of Interdisciplinary History*, 4(1): 23-45.

Allen, P. (1978) *The Cambridge Apostles: The Early Years*. Cambridge: Cambridge University Press.

Allingham, P.H. (no date) 'Thomas Hood (1799-1845): A Brief Biography', The Victorian Web. http://www.victorianweb.org/authors/hood/bio.html

Amery, L.S. (ed.) (1909) *The Times History of the War in South Africa, 1899-1902*. London: Sampson, Low, Marston and Co.

Anderson, N.F. (1982) 'The "Marriage with a Wife's Sister Bill" controversy: incest anxiety and the defence of family purity in Victorian England', *Journal of British Studies*, 21(2): 67-86.

Aplin, J. (2011) *Memory and Legacy: A Thackeray Family Biography, 1876-1999*. London: The Lutterworth Press.

Ashton, R. (2002) *Thomas & Jane Carlyle: Portrait of a Marriage*. London: Random House.

Atkinson, J. (2010) *Victorian Biography Reconsidered: A Study of Nineteenth-Century 'Hidden' Lives*. Oxford: Oxford University Press.

Badsey, S. (2007) 'The Boer War (1899-1902) and British cavalry doctrine: a re-evaluation', *The Journal of Military History*, 71: 75-97.

Bailey, C. (2008) *Black Diamonds: The Rise and Fall of an English Dynasty*. Harmondsworth: Penguin.

Baker, C. (1946) 'The road to Concord: another milestone in the Whitman-Emerson friendship', *The Princeton University Library Chronicle*, 7(3): 100-117.

Baker, W. and Clarke, W. (eds) (2016) *The Letters of Wilkie Collins, Volume 1: 1838-1865*. London: Springer.

Baldry, A.L. (1899) *Sir John Everett Millais: His Art and Influence*. London: Bell.

Barker, J.R.V. (2010) *The Brontës*. London: Abacus.

Barker, J.R.V. (2016) 'Subdued expectations: Charlotte Brontë's marriage settlement', *Brontë Studies*. 41(2): 175-178.

Barnard, R. and Barnard, L. (eds) (2013) *A Brontë Encyclopeadia*. London: John Wiley.

Batchelor, J. (2006) 'Alfred Tennyson: problems of biography', *The Yearbook of English Studies*, 36(2): 78-95.

Batchelor, J. (2014) *Tennyson: To Strive, to Seek, to Find*. London: Vintage Books.

Bates, R. (2018) 'The suitor and the sister', University of Nottingham Blog Post, 25 October 2018. Online.

Baylies, C. (1993) *The History of the Yorkshire Miners, 1881-1918*. London: Routledge.

Bell, H.G. (ed.) (1874) *The Poetical Works of David Gray: A New and Enlarged Edition*. London: Macmillan and Co.

Bellamy, J.M. and Saville, J. (1975) *Dictionary of Labour Biography*, Volume II. London: The Macmillan Press. 2nd Edition.

Bellamy, J.M. and Saville, J. (1978) *Dictionary of Labour Biography*, Volume I. London: The Macmillan Press. 2nd. Edition.

Benson, J. (1993) *The Miners of Staffordshire, 1840-1914*. Keele: Centre for Local History, Keele University.

Berthoud, R. (2003) *The Life of Henry Moore*. London: Giles de la Mare.

Bingham, M. (1978) *Henry Irving and the Victorian Theatre*. London: Routledge.

Black, B. (2014) *A Room of His Own: A Literary-Cultural Study of Victorian Clubland*. Athens, Ohio: Ohio University Press.

Blake, R. (1967) *Disraeli*. New York: St. Martin's Press.

Bloch, M. (2015) *Closet Queens: Some 20th Century British Politicians*. London: Little, Brown.

Blocksidge, M. (2011) *'A Life Lived Quickly': Tennyson's Friend Arthur Hallam and His Legend*. Brighton: Sussex Academic Press.

Boase, T.S.R. (1954) 'The decoration of the new Palace of Westminster', *Journal of the Warburg and Courtauld Institutes*, 17(3/4): 319-58.

Bogar, T.A. (2006) *American Presidents Attend the Theatre*. London: MacFarland.

Bostridge, M. (2009) *Florence Nightingale*. Penguin: Harmondsworth.

Boucher, M.P. (1935) 'Richard Monckton Milnes: Friend of genius and patron of letters', *Thought: Fordham University Quarterly*, 10(1): 67-80.

Braun, T. (1981) *Disraeli the Novelist*. London: George Allen & Unwin.

Brereton, A. (1908) *The Life of Henry Irving, Volume 1*. London: Longmans, Green and Co.

Brown, J. (1975) 'Attercliffe 1894: how one local Liberal party failed to meet the challenge of Labour', *Journal of British Studies*, 14(2): 48-77.

Buchanan, R.W. (1900) *The Story of David Gray*. Portland, Maine: Thomas B. Mosher.

Bullen, J.B. (2004) 'Browning's "Pictor Ignotus" and nineteenth-century "Christian" art', *Nineteenth-Century Contexts*, 26(3): 273-88.

Bullen, J.B. (2013) *Thomas Hardy: The World of His Novels*. Frances Lincoln.

Bullock, J. (1972) *Them and Us*. London: Souvenir Press.

Bullock, J. (1976) *Bowers Row: Recollections of a Mining Village*. Wakefield: EP Publishing.

Burnett, V. (1927) *The Romantick* [sic] *Lady (Frances Hodgson Burnett): The Life Story of an Imagination*. New York: C. Scribner's Sons.

Burton, I. (1877) 'Lord Houghton at Fryston Hall', *The World*, 20 June 1877.

Burton, I. (1898) *The Life of Captain Sir Richard F. Burton, Volume 1*. London: Duckworth.

Burton, R.F. (1861) *The City of the Saints, and Across the Rocky Mountains to California*. London: Longmans and Co.

Calé, L., Di Bello, P.D., Di Bello, P. (2009) *Illustrations, Optics and Objects in Nineteenth Century Literary and Visual Cultures*. London: Springer.

Castleford Public Libraries (no date) *The Fryston Estate*. Unpublished Factsheet. Castleford: Castleford Public Libraries.

Campbell, I. (1985a) 'Conversations with Carlyle: the Monckton Milnes diaries', *Prose Studies*, 8(1): 58-57.

Campbell, I. (1985b) 'More conversations with Carlyle: the Monckton Milnes diaries, part 2', *Prose Studies*, 9(1): 22-29.

Carlyle, T. (1893) *The Correspondence of Thomas Carlyle and Ralph Waldo Emerson, 1838-1872, Volume 1*. London: J.R. Osgood.

Carlyle, T. (1896) *The Correspondence of Thomas Carlyle and Ralph Waldo Emerson, 1838-1872, Volume 2*. London: Houghton, Mifflin and Company.

Chainey, G. (1995) *A Literary History of Cambridge*. Cambridge: Cambridge University Press.

Chapman, M. W. (ed.) (1877) *Harriet Martineau's Autobiography, Volume 1*. Boston, Mass.: James R. Osgood and Company.

Chapple, J.A.V. and Pollard, A. (eds) (1997) *The Letters of Mrs Gaskell*. Manchester: Manchester University Press.

Childs, L. (2001) *Battleground South Africa: Kimberly*. Barnsley: Leo Cooper.

Church, R. and Outram, Q. (1998) *Strikes and Solidarity: Coalfield Conflict in Britain, 1889-1966*. Cambridge: Cambridge University Press.

Clark, N. (2015) 'Stranger Than Fiction: The Life of Edgar Wallace, the Man Who Created King Kong', *The Guardian*, 30 July 2015.

Clarke, W.M. (2004) *The Secret Life of Wilkie Collins*. New York: Ivan R. Dee.

Codell, J.F. (1995) 'Painting Keats: Pre-Raphaelite artists between transgressions and painterly conventions', *Victorian Poetry*, 33(3): 341-370.

Cohen, V.H. (1956) 'Charles Sumner and the Trent Affair', *The Journal of Southern History*, 22(2): 205-219.

Coleman, H.T.J. (1920) ''Henry Adams: a study in multiplicity', *Queen's Quarterly*, 28(1): 1- 14.

Colligan, C. (2003) '"A race of born pederasts": Sir Richard Burton, homosexuality and the Arabs', *Nineteenth-Century Contexts*, 25(1): pp. 1-20.

Collins, W. (2019) *The Moonstone*. Oxford: Oxford University Press.

Constantine, R.J. (1993) *The Guerrilla War in the Cape Colony During the South African War of 1899-1902: A Case Study of the Republican and Rebel Commando Movement*. Unpublished Masters Thesis, University of Cape Town, South Africa.

Cook, E. (1913) *The Life of Florence Nightingale, Volume 1*. London: Macmillan and Co.

Cooper, D.D. (1974) *The Lesson of the Scaffold: The Public Execution Controversy in Victorian England*. Athens, Ohio: Ohio University Press.

Cowles, V. (1973) *The Rothschilds: A Family of Fortune*. London: Weidenfeld & Nicolson.

Craig, F.W.S. (1989) *British Parliamentary Election Results, 1885-1918. Chichester: Parliamentary Research Services*. 2nd Edition.

Craig, I. (1863) *Poems: An Offering to Lancashire*. London: Emily Faithfull.

Creswicke, L. (1902) *South Africa and Transvaal War, Volume 7*. Manchester: Kenneth Maclennan.

Crewe, Earl of (1895) 'The outlook for Ireland', *The North American Review*, 161(466): 366-378.

Crewe, M. [Margaret] (1955) 'Preface', in J. Pope-Hennessy (1955) *Lord Crewe: The Likeness of a Liberal*. London: Constable & Co. Limited.

Crewe, Marquess of (1920) 'Lord Houghton', in T.H. Ward (ed.) *The English Poets: Selections with Critical Introductions*. New York: The Macmillan Company.

Crewe, Marquess of (1929) 'Lord Houghton and his circle', in H. Granville-Barker (ed.) *The Eighteen-Seventies: Essays by Fellows of the Royal Society of Literature*. Cambridge: Cambridge University Press.

Croft-Cook, R. (1967) *Feasting With Panthers: A New Consideration of Some Late Victorian Writers*. London: W.H. Allen.

Cromwell, J.L. (2013) *Florence Nightingale: Feminist*. London: McFarland.

Dalberg, J.E.E. (1907) 'The life of Lord Houghton', in J.N. Figgis and R.V. Laurence (eds) *Historical Essays and Studies*. London: Macmillan.

Dalziel, P. (ed.) (1992) *Thomas Hardy: The Excluded and Collaborative Stories*. Oxford: Clarendon Press.

Daniels, S.J. (1980) *Moral Order and the Industrial Environment in the Woollen Textile Districts of West Yorkshire, 1780-1880*. Unpublished PhD Thesis, University of London.

Dau, D. (2014) 'The governess, her body, and thresholds in the *Romance of Lust*', *Victorian Literature and Culture*, 42: 281-302.

Deacon, R. (1985) *The Cambridge Apostles: A History of Cambridge University's Elite Intellectual Secret Society*. London: Robert Royce Limited.

Dellamora, R. (1990) *Masculine Desire: The Sexual Politics of Victorian Aestheticism*. Chapel Hill and London: University of North Carolina Press.

Dennis, J. (1891) 'The friendships of Lord Houghton', *The Leisure Hour*, March 1891, 341-343.

De Tocqueville, A. (1970) *Recollections.* London: MacDonald.

Devereux, J. (2017) 'The evolution of Victorian women's art education, 1858-1900: access and legitimacy in women's periodicals', *Victorian Periodicals Review*, 50(4): 752-768.

Dickens, C. (1846) A letter to *The Daily News*, 28 February 1846.

Dickey, C. (2017) 'How a British spy drank his way across the Americas – and missed the Civil War', *The Beast,* 25 October 2017. https://www.thedailybeast.com/

Duberman, M.B. (1960) *Charles Francis Adams 1807-1886.* Boston: Houghton Mifflin Company.

Dusinberre, W. (1977) 'Henry Adams in England', *American Studies*, 11(2): 163-186.

Dutta, S. (2010) *Ambivalence in Hardy: A Study of his Attitude to Women.* London: Anthem Press.

Ebbatson, R. (1993) *Hardy: The Margin of the Unexpressed.* Sheffield: Sheffield Academic Press.

Edel, L. (ed.) (1974) *Henry James Letters, Volume 4.* Cambridge Massachusetts: Harvard University Press.

Edel, L. (ed.) (1975) *Henry James Letters. 1875-1883, Volume 2.* Cambridge Massachusetts: Harvard University Press.

Eisner, E. (2016) 'A friend by return of the author: John Keats (1795-1821)', in G. Franssen and R. Honings (eds) *Celebrity Authorship and Afterlives in English and American Literature.* London: Palgrave Macmillan.

Elderkin, J. (1895) *A Brief History of the Lotos Club.* New York: Club House.

Ellis, G.E., Rockwood Hoar, E., Lowell, J.R., Parkman, F., Everett, W., Torrey, H.W., Bangs, E, and Peabody, A.P. (1886-1887) 'Tribute to Charles Francis Adams', *Proceedings of Massachusetts Historical Society*, 3: 144-177.

Ellmann, M.J. (1950) 'Tennyson: Unpublished Letters,1833-36', *Modern Language Notes,* 65(4): 222-238.

Emery, J, (2019) '"That once romantic now utterly disheartening (former) colliery town": The affective politics of heritage, memory, place and regeneration in Mansfield, UK', *Journal of Urban Cultural Studies*, 6(2/3): 219-240.

Ewan, E.L., Innes, S., Reynolds, S. and Pipes, R. (2006) *The Biographical Dictionary of Scottish Women.* Edinburgh: Edinburgh University Press.

Fairweather, H.R. (1975) *The Development and Growth of Castleford as a Coal Mining Town.* Leeds: James Graham College.

Farwell, B. (1976) *The Great Boer War.* Barnsley: Pen & Sword.

Fitzgerald, P. (1895) *Memoirs of an Author Volume 1.* London: Richard Bentley and Sons.

Flavin, M. (2005) *Benjamin Disraeli: The Novel as Political Discourse.* Brighton: Sussex Academic Press.

Flynn, J. (2016) *Sense and Sentimentality: The Soldier-Horse Relationship in the Great War.* Unpublished PhD Thesis, University of Derby.

Foreman, A. (2010) *A World on Fire: An Epic History of Two Nations Divided.* London: Allen Lane.

Forrest, C. (1871) *The History and Antiquities of Knottingley in the Parish of Pontefract.* London: H. Williams.

Forsyte, C. (2001) 'Dickens and the Forty Thieves', *The Dickensian*, 97: 146-153.

Franco, N.H. (2013) 'Animal experiments in biomedical research: a historical perspective', *Animals*, 3: 238-73.

Fransenn and R. Honings (eds) *Celebrity Authorship and Afterlives in English and American Literature.* London: Palgrave Macmillan.

Fraser, R. (1988) *Charlotte Brontë.* London: Methuen.

Fraser, W.H. (1999) *A History of British Trade Unionism, 1700-1988.* London: Macmillan.

Friends of Queen's Park (no date) 'Queen's Park Historical Record'. http://www.queenspark.btck.co.uk/ParkHistory

Froude, J.A. (1902a) *Thomas Carlyle: A History of His Life in London, 1834-1881, Volume 1.* London: Longmans, Green and Co.

Froude, J.A. (1902b) *Thomas Carlyle: A History of His Life in London, 1834-1881, Volume 2.* London: Longmans, Green and Co.

Gamble, C. (2008) *John Ruskin, Henry James and the Shropshire Lads.* London: New European Publications Limited.

Garrett, P. and Robbins, H. (eds) (2006) *The Works of William Wells Brown: Using His Strong, Manly Voice.* Oxford: Oxford University Press.

Gathorne Hardy, A.E. (1910) *Gathorne Hardy, First Earl of Cranbrook: A Memoir, Volume 1.* London: Longmans, Green and Co.

Gatrell, V.A.C. (1994) *The Hanging Tree: Execution and the English People, 1770-1868.* Oxford: Oxford University Press.

Geary, R. (1985) *Policing Industrial Disputes: 1893 to 1985.* Cambridge: Cambridge University Press.

Gibson, I. (1992) *The English Vice: Beating, Sex and Shame in Victorian England and After.* London: Duckworth.

Gibson, J. (1996) *Thomas Hardy: A Literary Life.* London: Macmillan Press Ltd.

Gilbert, M. (1991) *Churchill: A Life.* London: Random House.

Gill, G. (2004) *Nightingales: The Story of Florence Nightingale and Her Remarkable Family.* London: Hodder & Stoughton.

Gittings, R. (1978) *Young Thomas Hardy.* Penguin: Harmondsworth. 2nd edition.

Glasgow, E. (2005) 'Manchester and Liverpool: (1) The Manchester Free Library, and (2) George Chandler, librarian', *Library History*, 21: 57-63.

Gohdes, C. (1942) 'Some letters of Joaquin Miller to Lord Houghton', *Modern Language Quarterly*, 3(2): 297-306.

Gohlke, M.S. (1980) 'Re-reading the Secret Garden', *College English*, 41(8): 894-902.

Gosse, E. (1897) 'The history of a poem', *The North American Review*, 164(484): 283-93.

Gosse, E. (1905) *Coventry Patmore.* London: Hodder and Stoughton.

Gosse, E. (1917) *The Life of Algernon Charles Swinburne.* New York: The Macmillan Company.

Grant, Capt. M.H. (1910) *History of the War in South Africa, 1899-1902, Volume 4.* London: Hurst and Blackett.

Grant, U.S. (2003) *The Papers of Ulysses S. Grant: 1875.* Carbondale, Illinois: SIU Press.

Greaves, P.C. (1938) *Black Diamonds: Gleanings of Fifty Years in the West Yorkshire Coalfield.* Published by the author.

Greenberg, R.A. (1971) 'Gosse's "Swinburne," "The Triumph Of Time" and the context of "Les Noyades"', *Victorian Poetry*, 9(1/2): 95-110.

Gregory, R. (1968) *The Miners and British Politics, 1906-1914.* Oxford: Oxford University Press.

Griffiths, S.E. (2011) 'Branwell Brontë, Agnes and Mary Riley', *Brontë Studies*, 36(4): 158-162.

Gross, J. (1994) *Shylock: A Legend and Its Legacy.* New York: Simon and Shuster.

Hall, J.R. (1929) *The Coldstream Guards, 1885-1914.* Oxford: Clarendon Press.

Hannigan, D.F. (1891) 'Lord Houghton', *Westminster Review*, 135(1): 147-157.

Hardy, E. and Pinion, F.B. (eds) (1972) *One Rare Fair Woman: Thomas Hardy's Letters to Florence Henniker, 1893-1922.* London: Macmillan.

Hardy, F.E. (1962) *The Life of Thomas Hardy, 1840-1928.* London: Macmillan Press Ltd.

Hardy, T. and Henniker, F.E.H. (1894) *The Spectre of the Real.* London: Wyman and Sons.

Hare, H. (1949) *Swinburne: A Biographical Approach.* London: H.F. & G. Witherby Ltd.

Harman, C. (2016) *Charlotte Brontë: A Life.* Harmondsworth: Penguin.

Hart-Davis, R. (ed.) (1962) *The Letters of Oscar Wilde.* Bombay: Macmillan and Co.

Harte, G.B. (1951) *The Letters of Bret Harte.* London: Hodder and Stoughton.

Harvey, G. (2003) *Thomas Hardy.* London: Routledge.

Harvey, S.C. (2016) *Transatlantic Transcendentalism: Coleridge, Emerson and Nature.* Edinburgh: Edinburgh University Press.

Henniker, F.E.H. (1891) *Sir George.* London: Richard Bentley and Son.

Henniker, F.E.H. (1892) *Bid Me Good-bye.* London: Richard Bentley and Son.

Henniker, F.E.H. (1893) *Foiled.* London: Hurst and Blackett.

Henniker, F.E.H. (1894) *Outlines.* London: Hutchinson.

Henniker, F.E.H. (1896) *In Scarlet and Grey: Stories of Soldiers and Others.* London: John Lane.

Henniker, F.E.H. (1898) *Sowing the Sand.* London: Harper and Brothers.

Henniker, F.E.H. (1912) *Arthur Henniker: A Little Book for His Friends.* London: A.L. Humphreys.

Hodder, M. (2010) *The Strange Affair of Spring Heeled Jack.* London: Del Rey.

Hodder, M. (2011) *The Curious Case of the Clockwork Man.* London: Del Rey.

Hodder, M. (2012) *The Expedition to the Mountains of the Moon.* London: Del Rey.

Hodder, M. (2013) *The Secret of Abdu El Yezdi.* London: Del Rey.

Hodder, M. (2014) *The Return of the Discontinued Man.* London: Del Rey.

Hodder, M. (2015) *The Rise of the Automated Aristocrats.* London: Del Rey.

Horne, R.H. (1844) *A New Spirit of the Age.* New York: J.C. Riker.

Horowitz Murray, J. and Stark, M. (2017) *The Englishwoman's Review of Social and Industrial Questions: 1873.* London: Routledge.

Houghton, Lord (1873) *Monographs: Personal and Social.* New York: Holt & Williams.

Howell, D. (1983) *British Workers and the Independent Labour Party, 1888-1906.* Manchester: Manchester University Press.

Hulme, J. (1986) *A Photographic Memory.* Pontefract: Yorkshire Art Circus.

Hunter, J. (1848) *Antiquarian Notices of Lupset, the Heath and Sharlston in the County of York.* Wakefield: Published Privately.

Ireland, K. (2008) ''Trewe love at Solentsea? Stylistics vs. narratology in Thomas Hardy', in. G. Watson (ed.) *The State of Stylistics.* Amsterdam: Rodopi.

Jacobson, H. (1999) *Peeping Tom.* London: Vintage.

Jackson, P. (1997) *Education Act Forster: A Political Biography of W.E. Forster (1818-1886).* Vancouver, British Columbia: Fairleigh Dickinson University Press.

James, H. (1975) *Henry James Letters: 1875-1883.* Harvard Connecticut: Harvard University Press.

James, S.E. (2000/2001) '*Wuthering Heights* for children: Frances Hodgson Burnett's *The Secret Garden*', *Connotations,* 10(3): 59-76.

Johnson, G.M. (2014) 'Critics: 1836-1948', in T.W. Mott (ed.) *Ralph Waldo Emerson in Context.* New York: Cambridge University Press.

Joint Committee (1903) Minutes of Joint Committee Meeting [Yorkshire Miners' Association and West Yorkshire Coal Owners' Association], Great Northern Station Hotel, Leeds, 15 September 1903.

Jones, G. (1998) 'The paradise of aesthetics: Sylvester Judd's *Margaret* and antebellum American literature', *The New England Quarterly,* 71(3): 449-472.

Judd, D. and Surridge, K. (2012) *The Boer War: A History.* London: I.B. Taurus.

Jump, J. (ed.) (2013) *Lord Alfred Tennyson: The Critical Heritage.* London: Routledge.

Kaplan, F. (1993) *Thomas Carlyle: A Biography.* London: University of California Press.

Kendall, T. (2006) *Modern English War Poetry.* Oxford: Oxford University Press.

Kennedy, D. (2005) *The Highly Civilized Man: Richard Burton and the Victorian World.* Cambridge, Massachusetts: Harvard University Press.

Kenny, A. (2007) *Arthur Hugh Clough: A Poet's Life.* London: A. and C. Black.

King, L. (2013) *Touchstone.* London: Allen & Busby Limited.

King, K.R. and Morgan, W.W. (1979) 'Hardy and the Boer War: the public poet in spite of himself', *Victorian Poetry,* 17(1/2): 66-83.

Knickerbocker, K.L. (1947) 'Browning and Swinburne: an episode', *Modern Language Notes*, 62(4): 240-244.

Koch, D. (2012) *Ralph Waldo Emerson in Europe: Class, Race and Revolution in the Making of an American Thinker.* London: I.B. Taurus.

Kolb, J. (2000) 'Hallam, Tennyson, homosexuality and the critics', *Philological Quarterly*, 79(3): 365-395.

Lafourcade, G. (1932) *Swinburne: A Literary Biography.* London: G. Bell and Sons.

Lang, C. (1950) 'ALS: Swinburne to William Michael Rossetti', *The Journal of the Rutgers University Library*, 14(1): 1-9.

Langtry, L. (2000) *The Days I Knew.* London: Panoply Press.

Lawson, J. (1941) *The Man in the Cap: The Life of Herbert Smith.* London: Methuen and Co.

Lentz, John W. (2003) 'The *Fox* expedition in search of Franklin: a documentary trail', *Arctic*, 56(2): 175-184.

Ley, J.W.T. (1919) *The Dickens Circle: A Narrative of the Novelist's Friendships.* New York: E.P. Dutton and Company.

Lipzin, S. (1943) 'Heinrich Heine, "Blackguard" and "Apostate": a study of the earliest English attitude towards him', *Proceedings of the Modern Language Association*, 58(1): 170-180.

Lipzin, S. (1944) 'Heine, the Bard of Democracy: a contemporary English Legend', *The German Quarterly*, 17(2): 55-66.

Lofthouse, G. (1986) *A Very Miner MP.* Pontefract: Yorkshire Art Circus.

Loughlin, J. (2007a) *The British Monarchy and Ireland: 1800 to the Present.* Cambridge: Cambridge University Press.

Loughlin, J. (2007b) 'Crown spectacle and identity: the British monarchy and Ireland under the Union, 1800-1922', in A. Olochnowicz (ed.) *The Monarchy and the British Nation, 1780 to the Present.* Cambridge: Cambridge University Press.

Lovell, M.S. (1999) *A Rage to Live: A Biography of Richard and Isabel Burton.* London: Abacus.

Lubbock, P. (ed.) (1920) *The Letters of Henry James, Volume 1.* New York: Charles Scribner's Sons.

Lubenow, W.C. (1998) *The Cambridge Apostles, 1820-1914: Liberalism, Imagination and Friendship in British Intellectual and Professional Life.* Cambridge: Cambridge University Press.

Lucas, J. (1982) *Romantic to Modern Literature: Essays and Ideas of Culture. 1750-1900.* Sussex: The Harvester Press.

Lutz, D. (2011) *Pleasure Bound: Victorian Sex Rebels and the New Eroticism.* London: W.W. Norton & Co.

Lycett, A. (2014) *Wilkie Collins: A Life of Sensation.* London: Random House.

Lyndon Shanley, M. (1982) '"One must ride behind": married women's rights and the Divorce Act of 1857', *Victorian Studies*, 25(3): 355-76.

Lyons, F.S.L. (1968) *John Dillon: A Biography.* London: Routledge and Kegan Paul.

MacFarlane, J.E. (1987) *The Bag Muck Strike, Denaby Main, 1903-1903.* Doncaster: Doncaster Library Service.

Machin, F. (1958) *The Yorkshire Miners: A History, Volume 1.* Barnsley: National Union of Mineworkers.

Mallock, W.H. (1920) *Memoirs of Life and Literature.* London: Clapham and Hall.

Marquess, W.H. (1985) *Lives of the Poet: The First Century of Keats Biography.* London: The Pennsylvania State University Press.

Martin, R.B. (1980) *Tennyson: The Unquiet Heart – A Biography.* Oxford: Faber.

McCahill, M.W. (1976) 'Peers, patronage and the Industrial Revolution, 1760-1800', *Journal of British Studies*, 16(1): 84-107).

McCarthy, J. (1897) *A History of Our Own Times: From 1880 to the Diamond Jubilee.* New York: Harper and Brothers.

McCarthy, J. (1899) *Reminiscences, Volume 2.* London and New York: Harper and Brothers.

McClarence, S. (1990) 'Introduction' in R. Van Riel, O. Fowler and H. Malkin (eds) *World Famous Round Here: The Photographs of Jack Hulme.* Pontefract: Yorkshire Art Circus.

McKinstry, L. (2006) *Rosebery: Statesman in Turmoil.* London: John Murray.

McMahon, A.M. (1989) *Heine and the Victorians*. Unpublished PhD Thesis, University of Oxford.

Meyers, T.L. (1988) 'Swinburne's speech to the Royal Literary Fund, May 2, 1866', *Modern Philology*, 86(2): 195-201.

Millar, M. (2006) *Disraeli's Disciple: The Scandalous Life of George Smythe*. London: University of Toronto Press.

Miller, L. (2002) *The Brontë Myth*. London: Vintage.

Miller, S.M. (2019) 'Edgar Wallace's war: reporting and making the news in South Africa, 1898-1902', *South African Historical Journal*. Online publication.

Millgate, M. (ed.) (1984) *The Life and Work of Thomas Hardy by Thomas Hardy*. London: Macmillan Press Ltd.

Millgate, M. (2004) *Thomas Hardy: A Biography Revisited*. Oxford: Oxford University Press.

Milnes, R.O.A. (2nd Lord Houghton) (1891) *Stray Verses, 1889-1890*. London: John Murray.

Miners' Federation of Great Britain (1894) President's Address, MFGB Annual Conference, 17 January 1894. http://num.org.uk/

Miners' Federation of Great Britain (1905) President's Address, MFGB Annual Conference, Thursday, 5 October 1905. http://num.org.uk/

Minnaar, A. de V. (1987) 'Graaff-Reinet and the second Anglo-Boer War (1899-1902)', *Military History Journal*, 7(3) (online). http://samilitaryhistory.org/vol073vm.html

Mitchell. B.R. (1984) *Economic Development in the British Coal Industry, 1800-1914*. Cambridge: Cambridge University Press.

Mitchell, J. (1965) 'Swinburne – the disappointed protagonist', *Yale French Studies*, 35: 81-88.

Monaghan, J. (1940) *Abraham Lincoln Deals with Foreign Affairs: A Diplomat in Carpet Slippers*. Lincoln Nebraska: University of Nebraska Press.

Monckton Milnes, R. (1834) *Memorials of a Tour in Some Parts of Greece: Chiefly Poetical*. London: E. Moxon.

Monckton Milnes, R. (1838a) *Memorials of a Residence on the Continent*. London: E. Moxon.

Monckton Milnes, R. (1838b) *Poems of Many Years*. London: E. Moxon.

Monckton Milnes, R. (1840a) 'American philosophy – Emerson's works', *London and Westminster Review*, 33: 345-372.

Monckton Milnes, R. (1840b) *Poetry for the People and Other Poems*. London: E. Moxon.

Monckton Milnes, R. (1841) *One Tract More, Or, the System*. London: J.G.F. and R. Rivington.

Monckton Milnes, R. (1844a) *Poems, Legendary and Historical*. London: E. Moxon.

Monckton Milnes, R. (1844b) *Palm Leaves*. London: E. Moxon.

Monckton Milnes, R. (1846) *Poems of Many Years*. London: William D, Ticknor and Company.

Monckton Milnes, R. (1847) 'Mr D'Israeli's *Tancred* – The Emancipation of the Jews', *Edinburgh Review*, 86, July 1847: 142.

Monckton Milnes, R. (1848) *Life, Letters and Literary Remains of John Keats. In Two Volumes*. London: E. Moxon.

Monckton Milnes, R. (1856) 'Heinrich Heine', *Edinburgh Review*, July, 192-209.

Monckton Milnes, R. (1862) 'Introductory notice', in D. Gray, *The Luggie and Other Poems*. Cambridge: Macmillan and Co.

Monckton Milnes, R. (1864) 'England and America – 1863', *National Anti-Slavery Standard*, 24(49), Saturday, 16 April 1864.

Monckton Milnes, R. (1873) 'Memoir of the author', in T. Hood (1873) *The Poetical Works of Thomas Hood*. New York: James Miller Publishers.

Moore, H. and Hedgecoe, J. (1986) *Henry Moore: My Ideas, Inspiration and Life as an Artist*. London: Ebury Press.

Moore, K.Z. (1990) *The Descent of the Imagination: Postromantic Culture in the Later Novels of Thomas Hardy*. New York: NYU Press.

Morgan, O. (2002) 'The Boer War and the Media (1899-1902)', *Twentieth Century British History*, 13(1): 1-16.

Mortimer, R. and Willett, P. (1969) *Great Racehorses of the World*. London: Michael Joseph.

Motion, A. (2003) *Keats*. London: Faber and Faber.

Murray, A. (2006) *All the King's Horses: Royalty and Their Equestrian Passions from 1066 to the Present Day*. London: Robson Books.

National Anti-Slavery Standard (1864) 'England and America - 1863', *National Anti-Slavery Standard*, 24 (49), 16 April 1864.

Najarian, J. (2002) *Victorian Keats: Manliness, Sexuality and Desire*. London: Springer.

Neville, R.G. (1976) 'The Yorkshire miners and the 1893 lockout: the Featherstone "Massacre"', *International Review of Social History*, 21(3): 337-357.

Neville, R. G. (1976) 'In the wake of Taff Vale: the Denaby and Cadeby miners' strike and conspiracy case, 1903-06', in J. Benson and R.G. Neville (eds) *Studies in the Yorkshire Coal Industry*. Manchester: Manchester University Press.

Nissen, A. (2000) *Bret Harte: Prince and Pauper*. Oxford, Mississippi: University of Mississippi Press.

O'Kell, R. (2013) *Disraeli: The Romance of Politics*. London: University of Toronto Press.

O'Mahony, C. (1912) *The Viceroys of Ireland*. London: John Long.

O'Malley, I.B. (1934) *Florence Nightingale, 1820-1856: A Study of Her Life Down to the End of the Crimean War*. London: Thornton Butterworth.

O'Toole, P. (2006) *The Five Hearts: An Intimate Portrait of Henry Adams and His Friends, 1880-1918*. New York: Simon and Schuster.

Padgett, L. (1904) *Castleford and District in the Olden Time*. London: Simpkin, Marshall. Kent and Co.

Page, N. (1986) *Thomas Hardy Annual, No. 4*. London: Springer.

Page Arnot, R. (1949) *The Miners: A History of the Miners' Federation of Great Britain, 1889-1910*. London: George Allen and Unwin.

Page Arnot, R. (1953) *The Miners: Years of Struggle – A History of the Miners' Federation of Great Britain (from 1910 onwards)*. London: George Allen and Unwin.

Park, P.T. (1990) 'Thomas Carlyle and the Jews', *Journal of European Studies*, 20: 1-21.

Parris, M. (1997) *Great Parliamentary Scandals: Four Centuries of Calumny, Smear & Innuendo*. London: Robson Books Limited.

Peacock, E. (1891) 'Art II. Richard Monckton Milnes, Lord Houghton', *The Dublin Review*, 25(1): 22-35.

Pease, A. (2000) *Modernism, Mass Culture, and the Aesthetics of Obscenity*. Cambridge: Cambridge University Press.

Pelling, H. (1967) *Social Geography of British Elections, 1885-1910*. London: Springer.

Peters, C. (2014) *The King of Inventors: A Life of Wilkie Collins*. Princeton, New Jersey: Princeton University Press.

Pettitt, C. (2012) 'Time lag and Elizabeth Gaskell's Transatlantic Imagination', *Victorian Studies*, 54(4): 599-623.

Pettit, C. (2016) *Reading Thomas Hardy*. London: Springer.

Pickles, E.N. (2010) 'Newton Wallis: the evolution of a landscape', *Yorkshire Archaeological Journal*, 82(1): 373-382.

Pinion, F.B. (1990) *Hardy the Writer*. London: Palgrave Macmillan.

Pite, R, (2006) *Thomas Hardy: The Guarded Life*. London: Picador.

Plumly, S. (2009) *Posthumous Keats: A Personal Biography*. London: W.W. Norton and Company.

Pope-Hennessy, J. (1949) *Monckton-Milnes: The Years of Promise: 1809-1851*. London: Constable.

Pope-Hennessy, J. (1951) *Monckton Milnes: The Flight of Youth, 1851-1885*. London: Constable.

Pope-Hennessy, J. (1955) *Lord Crewe: The Likeness of a Liberal*. London: Constable & Co. Limited.

Purdy, R.L. (1944) 'Thomas Hardy and Florence Henniker: the writing of "The Spectre of the Real"', *Colby Quarterly*, 1(8): 122-126.

Putnis, P. (2004) '"War with America": The Trent Affair and the experience of news in colonial Australia', *Australian Studies*, 28(81): 93-106.

Quinton, A. (2011) 'Richard Monckton Milnes', in A. Kenny (ed.) *Of Men & Manners*. Oxford: Oxford University Press.

Rader, R.W. (1962) 'The composition of Tennyson's "Maud"', *Modern Philology*, 59(4): 265-269.

Ray, M. (1997) *Thomas Hardy: A Textual Study of the Short Stories*. Aldershot: Ashgate.

Reid, S.J. (ed.) (2010) *Memoirs of Sir Wemyss Reid, 1842-1855*. London: Aeterna Press.

Remlap, L.T. (1879) *General U.S. Grant's Tour Around the World*. Hartford, Connecticut: James Betts & Co.

Rice, E. (1991) *Captain Sir Richard Francis Burton. New York: The Secret Agent Who Made the Pilgrimage to Mecca, Discovered the Kama Sutra, and Brought the Arabian Nights to the West*: New York: HarperPerennial.

Richards, J. (2007) *Sir Henry Irving: A Victorian Actor and His World*. London: Hambledon and London.

Richardson, S. (1995) *Independence and Deference: A Study of the West Riding Electorate, 1832-1841*. Unpublished Ph D Thesis, University of Leeds.

Roberts, D. (1979) *Paternalism in Early Victorian England*. London: Croom Helm.

Roberts, M.J.D. (1985) 'Morals, art and the law: the passing of the Obscene Publications Act, 1857', *Victorian Studies*, 28(4): 609-29.

Robinson, K. (1952) *Wilkie Collins: A Biography*. New York: Macmillan.

Rochford, M.J. (2016) *Wakefield Then and Now: Extraordinary Tales from the Merry City*. Barnsley: Pen & Sword.

Rooksby, R. (2017) *A.C. Swinburne: A Poet's Life*. London: Scolar Press.

Rosebery, Earl of (1955) 'Lord Crewe's interest in racing: a note by the Earl of Rosebery', Appendix 1 in J. Pope-Hennessy (1955) *Lord Crewe: The Likeness of a Liberal*. London: Constable & Co. Limited.

Ross, I. (1959) *The General's Wife: The Life of Mrs, Ulysses S, Grant*. New York: Dodd, Mead & Co.

Rubinstein, D. (1978) 'The Independent Labour Party and the Yorkshire miners: the Barnsley by-election of 1897', *International Review of Social History*, 23(1): 102-34.

Rusk, R.L. (1949) *The Life of Ralph Waldo Emerson*. New York: Charles Scribner's Sons.

Russell, G.W.E. (1889/2009) *Collections and Recollections*. London: General Books.

Sanders, C.R. (1961) 'Carlyle and Tennyson', *Proceedings of the Modern Language Association*, 76(1): 82-97.

Sattin, A. (2011) *A Winter on the Nile: Florence Nightingale, Gustave Flaubert and the Temptations of Egypt*. London: Windmill Books.

Saunders Boos, F. (1976) *The Poetry of Dante G. Rossetti: A Critical Reading and Source Story*. The Hague: Mouton.

Scharnhorst, G. (2000) *Bret Harte: Opening the American Literary West*. University of Oklahoma Press.

Schiller, A. (1955) 'Thoreau and Whitman: The record of a pilgrimage', *The New England Quarterly*, 28(2): 186-197.

Scott, G.F. (2003) 'Writing Keats's last days: Severn, Sharp, and romance biography', *Studies in Romanticism*, 42(1): 3-26.

Sealts, M.M. Jnr. (ed.) (1973) *The Journals and Miscellaneous Notebooks of Ralph Waldo Emerson, Volume 10, 1847-1848*. Cambridge, Massachusetts: Harvard University Press.

Searle, G.R. (1998) *Morality and the Market in Victorian Britain*. Oxford: Clarendon Press.

Seed, J. (1985) 'Gentleman dissenters: the social and political meanings of rational dissent in the 1770s and 1780s', *The Historical Journal*, 28(2): 299-325.

Selanders, L.C. (2010) 'Florence Nightingale: the evolution and social impact of feminist vales in nursing', *Journal of Holistic Nursing*, 28(1): 70-78.

Shain, C.E. (1962) 'The English novelists and the American Civil War', *American Quarterly*, 14(3): 399-421.

Shearing H.A. (2004) *The Cape Rebel of the South African War, 1899-1902*. Unpublished PhD Thesis, University of Stellenbosch, South Africa.

Sichel, W. (1904) *Disraeli: A Study in Personality and Ideas.* London: Methuen and Co.

Sigel, L.Z. (2002) *Governing Pleasures: Pornography and Social Change in England, 1815-1914.* London: Rutgers University Press.

Sigel, L.Z. (2005) 'The rise of the overly affectionate family: incestuous pornography and displaced desire among the Edwardian Middle Class', in L.Z. Sigel (ed.) *International Exposure: Perspectives on Modern European Pornography, 1800-2000.* London: Rutgers University Press.

Simmons, J.S.G. (1966) 'Turgenev and Oxford', *Oxoniensia*, 31: 146-151.

Sloan, R. (2012) *The English Doctor: A Medical Journey.* Bloomington, Indiana: Xlibris.

Small, H. (2017) *A Brief History of Florence Nightingale: And Her Real Legacy, A Revolution in Public Health.* London: Hachette, UK.

Smith, J. (2015) *Churchill's Secret.* London: Abacus.

Smith, M. (ed.) (2000) *The Letters of Charlotte Brontë, with a Selection of Letters by Family and Friends: Volume 2, 1848-1851.* Oxford: Oxford University Press.

Smith, M. (ed.) (2004) *The Letters of Charlotte Brontë, Volume 3,1852-1855.* Oxford: Clarendon Press.

Smith, R.W. (2014) Bishop McIlvaine, Slavery, Britain and the Civil War. London: Xlibris.

Soames, M. (2002) *Clementine Churchill.* London: Doubleday.

Sommer, T. (2018) 'Shakespearean negotiations: Carlyle, Emerson and the ambiguities of transatlantic influence', in P.E.Kerry, A.D. Pionke and M. Dent (eds) *Thomas Carlyle and the Idea of Influence.* Vancouver: Fairleigh Dickinson University Press.

South African History Online (2012) 'Scheepers' trial and execution'. Posted on 13 January 2012. https://www.sahistory.org.za/

Stephenson, C. and Wray, D. (2005) 'Emotional regeneration through community action in post-industrial mining communities: The New Herrington Miners' Banner Partnership', *Capital and Class*, 25(3): 175-199.

Stevenson, E. (1997) *Henry Adams: A Biography.* Piscataway, New Jersey: Transaction Publishers.

Stewart, J.L.M. (1971) *Thomas Hardy.* London: Longman.

Stewart, R. (1936) 'Hawthorne's speeches at public banquets', *American Literature*, 7(4): 415-423.

Stirling, A.M.W. (1913) *The Letter-Bag of Lady Elizabeth Spencer-Stanhope, Volume 2.* London: John Lane, the Bodley Head.

Stoker, B. (1906) *Personal Reminiscences of Henry Irving, Volume 1.* Cambridge: Cambridge University Press.

Stokes, W. and Thorne, R.G. (1986) 'Milnes, Robert Pemberton (1784-1858), of Fryston Hall, Yorks', in R.G. Thorne (ed.) *The History of Parliament: The House of Commons 1790-1820.* https://www.historyofparliamentonline.org/

Storey, G. (1971) *Dickens and Daughter.* London: Haskell House Publishers.

Strachan, J. (2003) *A Routledge Literary Sourcebook on the Poems of John Keats.* London: Routledge.

Super, R.H. (1990) *The Chronicler of Barsetshire: A Life of Anthony Trollope.* Detroit: University of Michigan Press.

Surridge, K. (1993), '"All You Soldiers Are What We Call Pro-Boer": The Military of the South African War, 1899-1902', *History*, 82(268): 582-599.

Swart, S. (2010) 'Horses in the South African War, c. 1899-1902', *Society and Animals*, 18: 348-366.

Sylvia, R. (2003) 'Rereading Florence Henniker: society, romance and homosocial desire in *Sir George* and *Foiled*', *English Literature in Transition, 1880-1920*, 46(1): 55-70.

Sylvia, R. (2011) 'Florence Henniker, Hardy and the Anglo-Boer War Horses', *Hardy Society Journal*, 51-60.

Sylvia, R. (2011) 'The Henniker/Dillon/Hardy Affair: Florence Henniker's letters to John Dillon, 1894-1896', *The Hardy Review*: XIII (2), 144-57.

Sykes, A. (2014) *The Rise and Fall of British Liberalism, 1776-1988.* London: Routledge.

Symons, A. (1920) 'Coventry Patmore', *The North American Review*, 211 (771): pp: 266-272.

Symons, J. (2001) *Thomas Carlyle: The Life and Ideas of a Prophet.* London: House of Stratus.

Tablet, The (1900) 'The position of Sir John Austin', *The Tablet*, 29 September 1900.

Taylor, A.J. (1992) '"Trailed on the tail of a comet": the Yorkshire miners and the ILP, 1885-1908', in D. James, T. Jowitt and K. Laybourn (eds) *The Centennial History of the Independent Labour Party.* Krumlin, Halifax: Ryburn Academic Publishing.

Taylor, R.H. (1946) 'Letters to Trollope', *Trollopian*, 1(3): 5-9.

Tennyson, H. (1897a) *Alfred Lord Tennyson: A Memoir By His Son, Volume 1.* London: Macmillan and Co. Ltd.

Tennyson, H. (1897b) *Alfred Lord Tennyson: A Memoir By His Son, Volume 2.* London: Macmillan and Co. Ltd.

Terry E, (1908) *The Story of My Life.* New York: Doubleday, Page and Co.

Thackeray, W.M. (1840) 'Going to see a man hanged', *Fraser's Magazine*, 22 (Jul-Dec): 150-158.

Thackeray, W.M. (1848) 'A Dream of the Future', Punch, XIV (349), (Jan-June, 1848).

Thomas, D. (1979) *Swinburne: The Poet in His World.* New York: Oxford University Press.

Thomas, D.A. (2005) 'Thackeray, capital punishment, and the demise of Jos Sedley', *Victorian Literature and Culture*, 33: 1-20.

Thwaite, A. (1991) *Waiting for the Party: The Life of Frances Hodgson Burnett.* Boston, Massachusetts: Godine.

Tilton, E.M. (ed.) (1990) *The Letters of Ralph Waldo Emerson, Volume 7, 1807-1844.* New York: Columbia Press.

Tóibín, C. (2004) *The Master.* London: Picador.

Tóibin, C. (2009) ' Henry James in Ireland: a footnote', *The Henry James Review*, 30: 211-222.

Tomalin, C. (2011) *Charles Dickens: A Life.* Penguin: Harmondsworth.

Truth (1899) 'Girls' Gossip', *Truth*, April 27 1899: 1085-1086.

Tyndall, J. (1892) *New Fragments.* New York: D. Appleton and Co.

Vámbéry, A. (1904) *The Story of My Struggles: The Memoirs of Árminius Vámbéry, Volume II.* New York: E.P. Dutton and Company.

Van Riel, R., Fowler, O. and Malkin. H. (eds) (1990) *World Famous Round Here: The Photographs of Jack Hulme.* Pontefract: Yorkshire Art Circus.

Venables, G.S. (1888) 'With a notice in memoriam by', in R. Monckton Milnes, *Some Writings and Speeches of Richard Monckton Milnes, Lord Houghton: In the Last Year of His Life.* London: Chiswick Press.

Vessey, D. (2013) 'Attercliffe, Sheffield: the rise of Labour examined in two by-elections', *Yorkshire Archaeological Journal*, 85(1): 194-211.

Waddington, D.P. (1988) *One Road In, One Road Out: A People's History of Fryston.* Sheffield: PAVIC Publications.

Waddington, D.P. (2013) *Coal, Goals and Ashes: Fryston Colliery's Pursuit of the West Riding County FA Challenge Cup.* Pontefract: Route.

Waddington, P. (1975) 'Some letters from A.L., I.S. and N.I. Turgenev to Richard Monckton Milnes (Lord Houghton)', *New Zealand Slavonic Journal*, 2: 61-83.

Waddington, P. (1981) *Turgenev and England.* New York: New York University Press.

Walker, H. (1921) *The Literature of the Victorian Era.* Cambridge: Cambridge University Press.

Wakely, E. and Carson, J. (2011) 'Historical recovery heroes – Florence Nightingale', *Mental Health and Social Inclusion*, 15(1): 24-28.

Wallace, E. (1901) *Unofficial Dispatches of the Anglo-Boer War.* London: Hutchinson and Co.

Wallace, E. (1926) *Edgar Wallace: A Short Autobiography.* London: Hodder and Stoughton.

Waller, P. (2008) *Writers, Readers and Reputations: Literary Life in Britain, 1870-1918*. Oxford: Oxford University Press.

Ward, L. (1915) *Forty Years of 'Spy'*. London: Chatto & Windus.

Watt, Rev. L.M. (1974) *Burns*. New York: Haskell House.

Weeks, R.G. Jnr. (1989) 'Disraeli as political egoist: a literary and historical investigation', *Journal of British Studies*, 28(4): 387-410.

Wemyss Reid, T. (1888) *Life of the Right Honourable William Edward Forster, Volume 1*. London: Chapman and Hall Limited.

Wemyss Reid, T. (1890a) *Life, Letters and Friendships of Richard Monckton Milnes, First Lord Houghton, Volume 1*. London: Cassell & Company Limited.

Wemyss Reid, T. (1890b) *Life, Letters and Friendships of Richard Monckton Milnes, First Lord Houghton, Volume 2* London: Cassell & Company Limited.

West, A. (2017) *Thomas Hardy and Animals*. Cambridge: Cambridge University Press.

West, G. (1995) 'Family connections: the influence of the Crewe family on *Bleak House*', *The Dickensian*, 91(1): pp. 5-31.

Whiting, L. (1899) *Kate Field: A Record*. London: Sampson, Low, Marston and Co.

Whitten, M. (2011) *Nipping Crime in the Bud: How the Philanthropic Quest Was Put Into Law*. London: Waterside Press.

Wiener, M.J. (1994) *Reconstructing the Criminal: Culture, Policy, and Law in England, 1830-1914*. Cambridge: Cambridge University Press.

Wilde, O. (1877) 'The Tomb of Keats', *Irish Monthly: Fifth Yearly Volume*. Dublin: M.H. Gill & Son.

Williamson, B. (1982) *Class, Culture and Community: A Biographical Study of Social Change in Mining*. London: Routledge & Kegan Paul.

Wilson, F.A.C. (1971) 'Fabrication and fact in Swinburne's *The Sisters*', *Victorian Poetry*, 9(1): 237-248.

Wilson, R.G. (1971) 'The Denisons and the Milneses: eighteenth-century merchant landowners', in J.T. Ward and R.G. Wilson (eds) *Land and Industry: The Landed Estate and the Industrial Revolution*. Newton Abbot: David & Charles.

Wise, J.M. (2009) 'From Langham Place to Lancashire: Poetry, Community, and the Victorian Press's *Offering* to Lancashire', *Victorian Poetry*, 47(3): 517-33.

Wolfson, S.J. (2015) *Reading John Keats*. Cambridge: Cambridge University Press.

Woodham-Smith, C. (1951) *Florence Nightingale: 1820-1910*. London: McGraw-Hill.

Yarker, P.M. (1959) 'W,H. Mallock's other novels', *Nineteenth Century Fiction*, 14(3): 189-205.

Yorkshire Miners' Association (1903) Report of YMA Wheldale and Frystone Deputation, held at the Great Northern Station Hotel, Leeds, 20 October 20 1903.

Zekulin, N.G. (1976) 'Turgenev in Scotland', *Slavonic and East European Review*, 54(3): 355-370.

David P. Waddington is Professor of Communications at Sheffield Hallam University, where he has been employed since 1983. Fryston-born David has written extensively on the sociology of mining communities, industrial relations in the British coal industry, the regeneration of former coal-mining areas, and the policing of political and industrial protest. One of his previous books, *Coal, Goals and Ashes: Fryston Colliery's Pursuit of the West Riding County FA Challenge Cup*, was published by Route in 2013.